The Theater of
Terrence McNally

ALSO BY PETER WOLFE

Simon Gray Unbound: The Journey of a Dramatist
(McFarland, 2011)

The Theater of Terrence McNally

A Critical Study

PETER WOLFE

McFarland & Company, Inc., Publishers
Jefferson, North Carolina, and London

LIBRARY OF CONGRESS CATALOGUING-IN-PUBLICATION DATA

Wolfe, Peter, 1933–
    The theater of Terrence McNally : a critical study / Peter Wolfe.
        p.   cm.
    Includes bibliographical references and index.

    ISBN 978-0-7864-7495-0
    softcover : acid free paper ∞

    1. McNally, Terrence—Criticism and interpretation. I. Title.
    PS3563.A323Z885 2014
    812'.54—dc23   2013034470

BRITISH LIBRARY CATALOGUING DATA ARE AVAILABLE

© 2014 Peter Wolfe. All rights reserved

No part of this book may be reproduced or transmitted in any form or by any means, electronic or mechanical, including photocopying or recording, or by any information storage and retrieval system, without permission in writing from the publisher.

On the cover: Terrence McNally (photograph by Joseph Bachman); theater interior (iStockphoto/Thinkstock)

Manufactured in the United States of America

*McFarland & Company, Inc., Publishers
   Box 611, Jefferson, North Carolina 28640
      www.mcfarlandpub.com*

With love
to my beautiful wife Retta,
an H.V.M. who doubled her fun
in Dunedin, Moscow and Cologne

Acknowledgments

I would like to thank those friends whose time and energies went into the preparation of this book: Blythe Denham Kieffer and Diana Bell, who chased down important scriptural details; Joseph Bachman, who kindly allowed me to use one of his photographs for the book's cover; Laura Wellen and Richard Workman, who searched out important materials from the Harry Ransom Center, the University of Texas-Austin; J. Kimball King for indispensable bibliographical help; Raymond-Jean Frontain, the Dean of McNally Studies, for giving me copies of his brilliant studies of Mr. McNally's work; Tom Kirdahy, for providing important, helpful details of Mr. McNally's life and career; the great Indian scholar, C. R. Yaravintelimath, for explaining how Indian themes penetrate McNally's 1993 play, *A Perfect Ganesh*; and Kurt Schreyer, for sharing with me so generously his remarkable Shakespearean expertise. The combined help of the following people amounts to a major contribution: Jack Cardwell Hartmann, Jerry Horowitz, Harold Kapsinow, Jane L. Williamson. Wally Waite, Mary Fran Pasek, Karen Bartoni, Todd Brown, Mark Bernsen, and Eloise McClelland.

Table of Contents

Acknowledgments   vi
Abbreviations   ix
Preface   1

One. Tradition and Tumult   5
Two. Alchemizing the Brew   34
Three. Confusions of the Heart   55
Four. Cauldrons of Deceit   76
Five. Sore, Spent and Sage   92
Six. New York States of Mind   143
Seven. The Madness of Art   173

Conclusion   234
Bibliography   251
Index   257

Abbreviations

Bringing It	*Bringing It All Back Home*
Bump	*And Things That Go Bump in the Night*
CC	*Corpus Christi*
"Cleopatterer"	"The Wibbly, Wobbly, Wiggly Dance That Cleopatterer Did"
D	*Dedication Or the Stuff of Dreams*
Door	*This Side of the Door*
F&J	*Frankie and Johnny in the Clair de Lune*
FM	*The Full Monty*
GA	*Golden Age*
IOAP	*It's Only a Play*
LT	*The Lisbon Traviata*
LTTA	*Lips Together, Teeth Apart*
LVC	*Love! Valour! Compassion!*
MC	*Master Class*
MNI	*A Man of No Importance*
Nudity	*Full Frontal Nudity*
PG	*A Perfect Ganesh*
PL	*Prelude & Liebestod*
RC	*The Roller Coaster*
Ritz	*The Ritz*
SM	*Some Men*
SS	*The Stendhal Syndrome*
TB	*Teachers' Break*
TF	*Where Has Tommy Flowers Gone?*

Preface

Special gifts bring special rewards to the theater, like plays both dramatically and psychologically astute. This happy blend has made Terrence McNally one of today's very few dramatists who can raise the emotional stakes of a play-script with a clear head. He does it by matching the scale of his brush strokes with the size and shape of the action developing on stage. What makes this presence of mind noteworthy is his ontology — largely because he'd probably deny having one. Life to him is brutal, full of horror and violence. We're all oddballs, and we inhabit a perilous, unpredictable place. But this place also contains spots of goodness. Nor do these declare or impose themselves passively. As is seen in his striking diversity of tone and style, life happens in his work as if all boundaries had been washed away. Unfazed, he welcomes the task of treating this muddle honestly. The skill with which he invests dramatic warmth and cutting insight into scenarios both unframed and without edges supports Raymond-Jean Frontain's belief that he's "one of the most celebrated playwrights of his generation" ("A Preliminary Calendar" 101). What's more, he has dealt with this task over the past four decades. This Florida-born (in 1938) and Texas-reared dramatist has won, together with four Tonys, awards from the Drama Desk, the Outer Critics Circle, and the New York Drama Critics Circle. And that's only a partial list (see *SS* 168).

Worth citing here is the range of his wit. No one-note writer, he writes plays that can differ from each other in both atmosphere and emotional valence. He often reacts to this variety by enriching it. Unfolding at a tennis match, *Deuce* (2007) includes details of tennis history, strategy, and rule changes. Diligent research touched in with the same tact distinguishes *Golden Age*, a work that features vastly different speech rhythms and habits of perception. This 2010 (New York 2012) play, set in Paris's Théâtre Italien, describes the European opera world of 1835 without breaking a sweat, as does *Botticelli* (1968) depict a combat zone in a Vietnamese jungle, *A Perfect Ganesh* (1993) Bombay, Jaipur, and Varanasi in India, and *A Man of No Importance* (2002) different sites in Dublin. More of God's plenty? On the domestic front, McNally writes mostly about different neighborhoods in New York City, usually favoring that cluster of streets west of Fifth Avenue and south of Fourteenth Street often called the West Village.

This venue makes itself felt in unexpected ways. "The Sunday Times" (2009), with its cast of Manhattan Islanders, takes place in a "well-appointed country house" (*The Sunday Times*, Mark Armstrong and Sarah Brisman, eds., *24 by 24: The 24 Hour Play Anthology*, 129). *Unusual Acts of Devotion* (2008) unfolds on the roof of a West Village tenement. *Frankie and Johnny in the Clair de Lune* (1987) varies the pattern again. Instead of using a handful of characters, it's a two-hander set in a Clinton, or Hell's Kitchen apartment, three miles uptown. A Dutchess County estate, north of Westchester County, sites *Love! Valour! Compassion!* (1994). *Dedication* (2004) unfolds in the small city where a Gotham couple have moved. Not so *Some Men*, which spans 80 years in different Manhattan settings, including Harlem and the Waldorf Astoria Hotel. These settings promote still another aspect of McNally's art — its ability to astonish. His 2007 play includes dialogue between an adult father and son, both of whom are gay. But he keeps going. He'll also portray with the same easy grace the distaff side. Mothers and daughters spend extended time together on stage in both *The Rink* (1985) and *Dedication*, while much of *Deuce* records the talk of two older women. An on-stage murder occurs in *The Lisbon Traviata* (1989).

Though shocked by the murder, we also accept its suitability; McNally has the smarts to put whatever he wants on stage and get away with it. He's more than a playwright, his immersion in theater covering a wide sweep of years and experiences. Besides interviewing Neil Simon, Edward Albee, and Frank Rich, he has also joined or led panel discussions of plays like *West Side Story*, *Gypsy* and *Tea and Sympathy* (see Otis Guernsey's valuable *Broadway Song and Story* [1985]). His words here about the drama carry weight, as they should. He has taught playwriting at New York University and Juilliard, where he also helped found a department of playwriting, and he gave master classes at San Francisco's New Conservatory Theater Center. A member of the Dramatists Guild since 1970, he served as its vice president from 1981 to 1999.

Formal preparations for these labors began in 1961, a year after graduating from Columbia University as an English major, when he took the job of stage manager of New York's Playwright's Union. The grounding in the mechanics of stage production that followed served him well. He still helps cast and rehearse his plays. Branching further out, he adapted for the screen his 1975 play *The Ritz*, as well as *Frankie and Johnny* (1987) and *Love! Valour! Compassion!* (1994). Nor must the work he's adapting be his own. He wrote the book for the musical versions of Manuel Puig's *Kiss of the Spider Woman* (1992), E. L. Doctorow's *Ragtime* (1997), *The Full Monty* (2000), and Mark Shaiman and Scott Wittman's *Catch Him If You Can* (2011). Eager to test himself, he also scripted the book for the musicals *The Rink* and *A Man of No Importance* as well as the more daunting libretto of the 1989 opera version of *Dead Man Walking*.

Through it all, he has remained himself. Rather than scuttling his Texas background, he uses it in his plays. His Texas roots are deep. *Whiskey* (1973) unfolds in Houston, and much of *Corpus Christi* (2002) in the Gulf Coast town where he grew up, which also sites the action of his second play, *The Other Side of the Door* (1962). To infer from these settings that he has remained partly a hick discredits him. He has never tried to pass himself off as something other than what he is. He's not alone. Neither St. Paul's Scott Fitzgerald's nor Dulwich, England's Raymond Chandler grew up in the great cities their work illuminated. Both writers understood the cultural distance between the places where they were raised and the ones they wrote about. Both took in what they saw and heard without being duped by the Angelinos or New Yorkers peopling *The Great Gatsby* (1925) or *The Big Sleep* (1939). Like them, McNally, taking nothing for granted, keeps things fresh and honest.

The ability to use his past creatively has given him the confidence to put it into his plays. A young man in *Dedication* attributes his love of Shakespeare to his high school English teacher, Mrs. McElroy (*D* 31) — whose name, like that of McNally, evokes James Joyce's Irishry. The attribution also prompts the kind of delightful name tracing associated with Joyce. *Some Men* has in its cast a Columbia University English graduate who remembers "a fantastic high school English teacher" (*Two Plays* 2007, 14) he had in Texas. Signs of the influence of Maurine Davenport McElroy had already sharpened. A bit player in *The Ritz* called Maurine (no last name) speaks the words that resolve the plot of this 1975 play. A Mrs. McElroy who teaches high-school level Shakespeare has a speaking part in *Corpus Christi* (e.g., 25). Finally, McNally dedicated both his 1968 collection of one-acters, "Apple Pie" (2) and *Frankie and Johnny*, to Maurine McElroy (*Three Plays* 90). A lovely sidebar to this tribute: His spouse, Tom Kirdahy, said in an email of September 8, 2010, that Mrs. Mac was flown to New York for the premiere of *Frankie and Johnny*, where she was "the hit of the evening." (Mrs. McElroy's career after she finished teaching at Corpus Christi's W. B. Ray High School is discussed in Raymond-Jean Frontain, "Trafficking in Mere Humanity," 111–12, n. 2.)

McNally enjoys sliding himself into these Joycean goings-on. A man in *The Full Monty* (2000) who says, "They laughed at the Wright Brothers" (87) is citing Gershwin's "They All Laughed." Gershwin stays to the fore. In a self-referential whim, he had said in "How About You?" "I like a Gershwin tune." Thus McNally's easily overlooked statement, "I liked *The Rink*," from *It's Only a Play* (1985) (*Three Plays* 165), rings at least three bells. The reference to his own play honoring George Gershwin displays his readiness to fuel his art with his own back-story, and, finally, hints at that semi-outsider's stance that has fueled his sensibility. In still another Joycean fillip, his penchant for antics has boosted his ability to make us care about the people in his all-too-real theatrical world. Rather than existing in a shrill present tense, his people come before us accompanied by the echoes and shadows of their pasts. McNally's prestige as a major playwright tallies the benefits of this alchemy. Hugging his roots has given him insights into his characters that might have otherwise escaped him. One might say of it all, "'S Wonderful."

CHAPTER ONE

Tradition and Tumult

The American flags being waved by the play's four cast members near the end of McNally's *Lips Together, Teeth Apart* (1992) helps make his theater a hybrid tale of America embedded in our country's transmogrifying soil. American morality plays, they are billed as comedies. They're very funny, often shaking our sides with laughter during some of their most serious moments. These find McNally coming just short of embracing Oscar Wilde's belief that serious matters are too vital *not* to be framed trivially. Laughter to him signals comprehension, a function of aesthetic distance; we have to stand back from something to see it clearly. Yet the background dynamics of the plays rule out laughter. Because, for instance, many of his people have prospered and thus made sacrifices (*Love! Valour! Compassion!* has in its cast a lawyer, an accountant, and a world-class choreographer), the Calvinist virtues of rational thought, discipline, and a capacity for hard work drive them in a way consistent with Max Weber's treatise, *The Protestant Ethic and the Spirit of Capitalism.* Weber defined the can-do American work ethic in 1905. According to him, the Protestants who embraced an ascetic moral code based on abstention and individual self-improvement gained an edge in their pursuit of capital.

Work forms a steady, if jittery, undertone in McNally, perhaps even grazing what Weber saw in America's Calvinist roots, viz., confidence in one's own salvation. Humor in the plays, while plentiful, can be edged in black. The theater people — actors, a critic, a playwright, a producer — in *It's Only a Play* find work both a joy and a bane. Work even haunts those members of the presumably safe, substantial managerial class. Sam Truman, owner of a construction firm in *Lips Together, Teeth Apart*, sweats so much over meeting payroll that he sometimes forgets how to knot his necktie. Others in both *LTTA* and elsewhere sweat with him — and not only because of the threat of bankruptcy — original sin in their capitalist society. The kindest, warmest people in *Love! Valour! Compassion!* (Gregory and James, Bobby and Buzz) also suffer the most. Is McNally suggesting, Calvin-like, that man's depravity runs so deep that it overrides good works?

The question pervades his art. The Calvinist tradition of raising children as soldiers of a vengeful God who see life as a constant struggle against sin has failed. McNally's growing Fellini-like preoccupation with the affluent and the successful, for instance Maria Callas of *Master Class* (1995) and the fictitious millionaire rock star Ida Head of *Dedication*, has led him to the comedy of manners, a genre usually linked to the rich and rising middle class. Mostly, the genre shows how customs and conventions shape behavior. Recognizing the importance of social milieu, it will also rate verbal over physical humor, which prevails in a farce like *The Ritz*, the hero of which, a middle-aged heterosexual who runs a garbage collection firm, finds himself surrounded by gays. More typically, the garbage in *Dedication* and *Master Class* is internal. Their public triumphs haven't eased the inner pain dogging both Maria and Ida, and McNally uses the tension between their private distress and the lightheartedness commonly linked with the comedy of manners to highlight the distress of the women.

Tension also stems from McNally's Texas boyhood. This cradle Catholic grew up in a stronghold of Protestant fundamentalism. The singing of Maria and Ida, like the warmth and kindness exhibited in *LVC*, rooted in original sin, offends rather than pleases the scowling Calvinist God whose fury leaped out at McNally from faith-based radio and television stations all along the Gulf coastline. A truck driver in *Corpus Christi* tells Joshua, or Jesus, "Turn on the radio.... 'Course all You're gonna get this time of night is religious fanatics" (*CC* 36). This fanaticism, boosted by a masculinity based on manual work, drinking, and hometown loyalty, stayed with McNally. His calling his thirteen-year-old self Edmund in his autobiographical play, *This Side of the Door*, written at age 20, describes a fledgling dramatist plagued by both vice and sickness; Edmund is the name of both the tubercular alcoholic younger Tyrone brother in Eugene O'Neill's *Long Day's Journey Into Night* (1956) and an outstanding figure of vice in Shakespeare's *Lear*. In a 1960 term paper written at Columbia College ("Spiritual Movement in *King Lear*"), McNally called him "the most fascinating villain in the play"; he had also ranked Edmund the year before ("The Family as a Dramatic Theme in *King Lear* and *The Winter's Tale*") alongside Goneril and Regan as "one of the three most vicious children in literature" (6). The acts performed by McNally's Edmund tally with this dark legacy. After destroying his father's prized record collection (a child had destroyed her dad's record collection in Clifford Odets's *Awake and Sing* [1935]), he pretends to have killed his baby sister. If the threat of a fundamentalist hell isn't still troubling McNally, it *has* lodged in his psyche. He named another stand-in for him, Clarence, in *Bump*, after a villain in *Richard III*, whose crimes, though less vile than Edmund's in *Lear*, sufficed to get him drowned in a butt of malmsey.

McNally's lifetime practice of using the British spelling for the word, theater, i.e., theatre (e.g., Preface, *15 Short Plays*, v), no old-world affectation, slots a cultural shield between him and the radio messages he heard as a boy of depravity and infant damnation (and, with them, the rawness of Corpus Christi's barrio) that shaped his portrayals of both his badgered, infuriating Edmund and his tormented Clarence. No stonewall of elegance and tradition, though, could have protected him from the turmoil wringing him from within. In the end, his greatest strength lies in his refusal to find easy answers to the problems of damaged people. There are no right and wrong choices they can lean on when it comes to facing the road ahead. It's simply about finding ways to put one foot in front of the other.

This said, it follows that McNally has always rated the dynamics of his people's interior worlds over those of plot; he called his work, in a 1996 conversation with Steven Drukman, "very minimalist when it comes to plot" (335). Assuming that he had a choice, he chose well. His characters feel more like unique souls than object lessons. He has overcome the paradox, so fatal to many artists, that all creative work is both a mask and an unveiling. His plays put forth a human landscape that hardly any other modern writer has attempted on such a scale. For instance, we recognize the deranged grief in *The Lisbon Traviata* when Stephen discovers at age 40 that his younger live-in lover Mike is dumping him for a still younger man. What to do next? Irony, the sound of limitation, has become our culture's default position. Because it comments on life without nourishing it, McNally, wanting to build tragic drive, omits it from the scene that shows Mike gathering his effects in Stephen's presence prior to going to Paul's apartment.

Heartache explodes quickly here and elsewhere in the McNally canon. The people rarely analyze themselves. Their psychology shows in their behavior. A wise choice on McNally's part; by acting out their feelings like figures in a western movie or a hard-boiled detective story, they're giving the audience the fun of connecting the dots. This fun is best accessed in the proper mindset. Alluding to the idea that the grotesque deforms life to get at the life behind it, McNally often gives his people a psychological impairment or burden to make them more familiar; they're vulnerable, like us. His lifetime attraction to the deep, the dark, and the lethal helps form this circuit. He can be trusted. Following other important playwrights from Shakespeare to Harold Pinter, he has always believed that the unconscious level of the mind, that area beyond the range of conscious control, dictates most of our actions; instinct and intuition make us tick, not reason.

His avoidance of a liberal sociological approach to gay life frees him to describe the dailiness of gay society without rushing to dramatic climaxes. He has judged well. He has always wanted to write good plays rather than interesting ones. Instead of shaping his characters to a consistent plot, he places them in events that occur as they would in real life. The characters aren't objects of debate or good conduct, vying for our scorn or sympathy. The everydayness that grips them stays taut, keeping the texture dramatic. Credit him for creating scenes that his straight suburban audiences had never witnessed on stage before.

Depending on the intensity of a scene, the action will tune itself to an agonizing verisimilitude because, with McNally's savage comedy leavening the brew, we're meant to be both entrapped and persuaded that our entrapment is abnormally normal. Impeccable timing, for instance, in *Some Men* stirs weird undercurrents, as in the work of Michelangelo Antonioni, whose film *Eclipse* McNally reviewed in 1963. Like Antonioni, he'll decoy us into feeling superior to his people. But then he'll find charm in the charmless and points of light in the most lost of souls. He keeps the pressure high, no sweetness of tone sugaring the mixture or smoothing the hard edge. We've been whipped out of our comfort zones. He has shown straights as well as gays the truth of something that may be far from their lives but that somehow they understand, intimately, all too well. Nothing is lost; he can respect his people without whitewashing their flaws. He thereby transcends the rewards of providing a good evening at the theater. A work like *The Lisbon Traviata* or *Master Class* stays in our hearts after final curtain because he cares so deeply about his people that they inhabit *our* worlds, too.

I

Art provokes discoveries in *Bringing It All Back Home* (1969), *Bad Habits* (1974), and *A Man of No Importance* (2002). The attempts of people in these plays to reach out for *more* usually leave them holding *less*. What *do* they reach for? "Sex is very important in my work" (135), McNally told Daniel Savran in 1999. But he has the savvy to join sex to other things. The prominence of jobs and careers in his plays shows him agreeing with Freud that work and love define most people's lives. Called "a young man in search of something to believe in" (1–2), the Younger Brother in *Ragtime*, his ardor boosted by the young beauty he has been sleeping with, will join a cause, racial equality, so dangerous in 1902 that it nearly kills him, as it does several of his hapless mates. The closeted bus conductor, Alfie Byrne, faces other dangers in *A Man of No Importance*, a work, as its title suggests, that questions established hierarchies of judgment. Who gets to decide what's important? The plays Alfie cheerfully directs in the social hall of a seedy Dublin church anger the sodality. As a result, not only is his production of Wilde's *Salomé* banned after one staging; Alfie must also find a new home for his amateur theatricals, too — hard work now that his recent outing has put his day job at risk.

Alfie, like most of McNally's other people, sets great store by his job. The "tawdry song and dance queen" (Helen T. Buttel, "McNally's Films of His Broadway Plays," Zinman, ed., *Casebook* 73) Googie Gomez speaks for these others when she says in Act One of *The Ritz*, "My career is no joke. Nobody's career is never no joke" (14). To the laid-off factory hands in *The Full Monty*, work provides the necessities of self-validation, belonging, and even identity. Though they couldn't know Malcolm Gladwell's claim that genius in any field of work calls for 10,000 hours of practice, they value the impulse driving it. A male stripper tells one of them how he became Chippendale sexy: "The same way you get to Carnegie Hall: practice, lots of practice" (*ibid.*, 31). Shortcuts and quick fixes make for dead ends. The out-of-work laborer who wants to organize a striptease act with his mates will have to discover for himself, through hours of toil, how to make women cheer and shriek like bobbysoxers.

It follows that McNally called his 2004 play about two veteran stage troupers who moved their routine to upper New York State *Dedication*; these urbanites forfeit the excitement of the city for the chance to stage children's plays. Another display of the Calvinist work ethic without the religious shell is *LVC*. This 1994 play confirms the force of self-discipline by pairing it with sex. This economy of means shows McNally working at top form. Having discovered that his lover Bobby has deceived him with the young dancer Ramon, their weekend host Gregory threatens to slice off Ramon's fingers. Yet minutes later, like a person in Gorky who sits down to dinner with someone he had just been feuding with, Gregory offers Ramon coffee. A moment later, in an act that tops forgiveness, he asks Ramon to take a cup of coffee upstairs to Bobby.

What could have been on his mind? The subtext of this odd scenario explains its fitness. Having danced professionally long enough to judge other dancers, Ramon will later say of Gregory, "He is good. He is so fucking good. I'd give my left nut to work with him" (*Love! Valour! Compassion!* and *A Perfect Ganesh, Two Plays* 126; hereinafter cited as *Two Plays*). Forgiveness, always a major trope in McNally, has done its healing work. Gregory just finished choreographing a scene beyond the reach of his tired, aching legs. He also honors the professionalism of Ramon. The love of dance the two men share has smoothed the friction between them. Too, it has opened between them a channel of honesty and moral clarity heretofore absent from McNally's work. Gregory says, "You're good, Ramon.... You're better than I was at your age [some 20 years earlier], but that's not good enough, you should be better."

Ramon's answer to this compliment-rebuke, all the more telling for its brevity and spontaneity, tallies the sacrifice he's willing to make to meet Gregory's standard of excellence: "Don't you think I know that?" (*ibid.*, 128) He has buried his ego, as Gregory sees — and silently commends. Professional integrity binds the two men. Moved by Ramon's humility, Gregory offers him the solo dance piece they have been discussing; Ramon will open as a soloist in New York in three months time, with Gregory in the audience cheering him on, again silently. He'll be ready to deliver. Though rehearsals begin in about six weeks, he'll start working up his routine in a month, without being paid for his efforts. The pursuit of artistic pre-eminence has trumped the exhilaration of forbidden sex. Bobby will later speak from the best part of himself when he tells Gregory, "You did the right thing" (*ibid.*, 129).

The humility of Ramon, the artist who must remain rigidly self-critical despite whatever gaudy honors he wins, springs to mind in *Golden Age* (2010). When asked if the aria from his opera *I Puritani* he just heard pleased him, Vincenzo Bellini says with dawning puzzlement, "As pleased as a composer can [afford to] be" (18). He knows that complacency will blunt his creative edge. Like all serious artists, Bellini is a battlefield. What should have been a moment of triumph is rankling him. He's nearly ashamed of the music he has been hearing. So aware is he of flaws in *I Puritani* that nobody else will notice that he resolves to begin work on another opera that will surpass it.

His regret that he could have improved *I Puritani* shouldn't surprise us. All artists must depersonalize themselves at every phase of the creative process. When Tony Candolini, the tenor who takes a master class with Maria Callas, says, "I know I have a voice, and I know it's not enough" (*MC* 42), he's glimpsing a future of sacrifice and denial — without any guaranteed payoffs. Maria's childhood ordeals in Nazi-occupied Greece toughened her for the rigors of a singing career. But did they toughen her too much? Instead of helping her enjoy the rewards of that career, they tuned her mind to the trials her career would keep imposing on her.

If this brutality never ends, it does invite the comforts of perspective. A young man in McNally's first Broadway play, *And Things That Go Bump in the Night*, says something that will resound throughout the whole canon. Opposing the idea of man's perfectibility as stated most famously by Plato and Hegel, Clarence says, "It's his imperfectability that counts" (*Collected Plays: Volume II* 36; hereinafter cited as *TM II*). McNally sees the pursuit of the best hamstringing the good. A goal beyond our mortal powers, perfection should be ignored; at best, it's a distraction. Nobody performing an act for the first time, whether playing a tune on a piano or diving into a swimming pool, will do it well. Nothing has been lost. Keep trying, and fail better the next time. Forget too that others are outperforming you. McNally doesn't ask too much from people, a truth seen in his attitude toward his characters, nearly all of whom he likes. Even go-by-the-book sticklers like Margaret Civil in *Ganesh* or Professor Hector Charlotte in *Full Frontal Nudity* (2004) will win our hearts.

McNally always rates the human over the mechanical. A perfectionist nurse in the *Dunelawn* section of the 1974 two-hander, *Bad Habits*, says, "No faults, no feelings, no fantasy. It's a beautiful goal" (*15 Short Plays* 251; hereinafter cited as *15 Plays*). She's looking down a blind alley. Her colleague and protégée will bolt the mental home where they both work because the home's director, though saintly, gives her "the creeps" (*ibid.*, 267). She's right to ditch him. To kill a person's devils is to bushwhack her angels, as well. As in Hawthorne, the quest for perfection in McNally leads to the sin of pride. Those on the rampage to improve others wind up faulting everybody, including themselves, a process that leaves them with nothing.

Belonging beats loneliness. Raymond-Jean Frontain claims that as early as *Bump* McNally was urging community as life's most vital source of comfort and warmth ("There Is Someone Out There" 14–5). The partners and kinfolk who sometimes vex us also provide psychological ballast. Now McNally isn't advising us to find someone who accepts us as we are. Love can grow stale over time, as it does with Stephen and Mike of *The Lisbon Traviata*. He's promoting connection and bonding. Life can zap us in a heartbeat (*LTTA* 108). All we have is each other to cushion us from these random shocks.

But the shocks will ultimately be suffered alone, leaving the self both the source and judge of its actions. We must follow our hearts and minds in our attempts to fail better. Adopting an air of Emersonian self-reliance, McNally told Toby Silverman Zinman in 1994, "I keep saying to myself, write what you want to write" (Zinman, "Interview," Zinman, ed., *Casebook* 11). Our dark gods must be appeased; otherwise, we'll make the mistake of pretending to be somebody we're not. Ex-tennis champ Leona Mullen of *Deuce* cost herself and her doubles partner Midge Barker a Grand Slam when a fugitive impulse invoked Midge's complaint that she never threw the ball high enough on her serve. The lapse of self-confidence that duped her into throwing the ball too high came on her second serve in what proved to be match point in the last set, advantage out. The Barker-Mullen partnership ended there. Though a guilt-racked Leona wanted to keep playing doubles tennis, Midge retired on the spot. She chose wisely. She and Leona, already past 40, had won many prizes and honors, like meeting Queen Elizabeth II after a Wimbledon victory, short of the Grand Slam. Their legacy is solid. Most notably, the majors they won dragged women's tennis out of the fog belt where it had been languishing. Offsetting their big setback in Australia was the timing of the end of their alliance. That neither woman yielded to the temptations of singles tennis after becoming partners confirmed the integrity of the women's doubles game they shored up.

As Frontain reasoned in 2004 ("There Is Someone Out There" 24), McNally always encouraged partnering. Rephrasing W. H. Auden's imperative from "September 1, 1939," Johnny of *Frankie and Johnny* says, "We gotta connect. We just have to. Or we die" (*3 Plays* 136). These words hark to the epigraph of E. M. Forster's *Howards End* (1910), "Only connect" (cf., McNally, *Some Men and Deuce: Two Plays* 29; hereinafter cited as *Two Plays* 2007). The need to bond takes different forms in the plays, as is seen in a retort from his 2009 one-acter, "The Sunday Times": "We need one another or we die" (Armstrong and Bisman, eds. 135). *Dedication* also cites the passage from *Lear* (55) that *LTTA* had referenced thirteen years earlier (100). The appearance of these citations in the closing moments of the two plays clinches their importance: "As flies to wanton boys, are we to the gods/ They kill us for their sport" (4. 1. 156–57). A world that could randomly swat us into oblivion shouldn't be braved alone.

A close look at this imperative reveals bracing complexities. The Platonic ideal of muzzling the passions with reason always bored McNally. Instead, his plays capture both the compulsiveness and the frailty of those passions. Why does Frankie send Johnny home after sex? She wants to watch television and eat ice cream by herself, reminding us that most of the time we opt for that pinchbeck form of intimacy, love on our terms. McNally knows about this deep-seated flaw. He prints a parody of our rage for both space and intimacy on a "great" T-shirt given a rent boy by his girlfriend: "I want you to: Fuck me, beat me, shit on me. Tell me you love me and then get the hell out of here" (*15 Plays* 359). This credo is humbug. That the words comprising it ran together and became illegible in a washing machine depicts the rout of clarity by life's basics, muddle and chaos.

This bedlam evokes the mosaic of our scattered, multitasking lives. It also hints at the toil it takes to sustain erotic love. Infidelity has stressed the fourteen-year bond of one of the most anchored couples in the canon, a lawyer and an accountant in *LVC*. Arthur, the accountant, who, having stepped out on his lawyer-mate, tells Bobby, a recent two-timer, that his treachery, though since forgiven, derailed his sex life with Perry. Had he known when he deceived Perry what he knows now, he'd have remained true. The established union, or marriage, counts foremost. No intrigue is hot enough to risk a solid, enduring bond.

This common sense befits a partner in a long-standing tie. It also foregrounds the shifting valences of sex. A love bond, McNally knows, offers the rewards of both thrills and harmony — but rarely at the same time. The prudent have found a solution to this impasse: Savor harmony's enfolding warmth if it flows from someone who once thrilled you. Count yourself lucky, too; the continuities shaped by your contentment will both nourish and stabilize you.

Say what? Unfortunately, this scenario is often as fragile as it is sounds.

Jeopardizing it is the jungle lure of passion. Men being more promiscuous than women, the threat to long-term bonding rises in the gay community, where, in addition, there are rarely any children whose welfare enters the mix. Voicing a sentiment repeated elsewhere in the canon, a young lady in *Dedication* says of men, "They go where their dicks take them" (45; cf. *Two Plays* 2007, 35). Her argument carries forward. If the men are gay, as they often are in McNally, their waywardness can wreck the stability of one-on-one bonding. As Frontain, the world's leading expert on McNally, has put it, "[M]onogamy is not the norm in the gay community" ("I Don't Believe This Whole Night" 87).

There are other obstacles to love in the canon. McNally's people find love hard to identify, let alone implement and sustain. When Katharine hears Margaret, her travel buddy in India, tell her, "I adore you, Kitty," she replies, "No you don't. I don't think we are best friends. I don't think we know each other at all" (*Two Plays* 186). McNally is riffing on D. H. Lawrence's claim that love is the mystery between people, not the identity. He's speaking in his own troubled voice. He'll do it again. Addressing her former tennis partner inwardly, Midge Barker says in *Deuce*, "I have never felt so close to anyone than I do to you, right now, Lee, but I have never felt more shut out from anyone as well" (*Two Plays* 2007, 157). The opacity of the other emits points of light. After two minutes time, Katharine feels closer to an AIDS victim she has met by chance in Mumbai than she does to Margaret. This spontaneous kinship stems from shared loss, Katharine's gay son having been pounded to death by some street thugs.

Heartache can divide as well as join. A Dubliner who says in *A Man of No Importance*, "Love, Lord that word causes more trouble than it's worth" (87), speaks home. Ironically, the man she's addressing, Alfie, the bus conductor, long a victim of unrequited love, has already felt the force of her words. But not the full force; that will come later the same evening when he's decoyed into an alley where a mob of toughs beat and rob him. Frankie and Johnny had also known the meeting point of love and pain. McNally has two reasons for having Frankie ask Johnny to make her a sandwich. The first is that, if music be the food of love, so is food, a conceit he reminds us of by quoting the opening line of Shakespeare's *Twelfth Night* (*Three Plays* 138) and, earlier, having Frankie tell Johnny to "ravish me with your cooking" (*Ibid.* 131). To call forth the conceit again, he shows Johnny at the cutting board. The repetition is vital; together with sex, food sustains life. Those who feed others are valuable parts of society, any society.

McNally takes his conceit to a level where lesser playwrights would have dropped it. What could be more apt for his purposes than to have the short-order cook Johnny feed Frankie after fucking her? Both parties have been blitzed by love. Later in the play, Frankie displays the scars gouged into her neck by an angry ex-lover. Johnny has scars, too. His hands show the marks of the many cuts, scrapes, and scratches scored into his hands at the cutting board. Then he burns himself on the hot skillet where he's frying eggs. And like Frankie, he's also scarred inside. His ex-wife has made a better marriage than she'd have had staying with him (a trope that will recur in *Full Monty*). He tells how a visit to his three kids at the home of Sheila and her new husband sent him into gales of tears.

He also tells why he looked away from Frankie while recounting this vexed tale; some truths are too desperate for direct speech. Edward Albee had said in *The Zoo Story* that in matters of the heart, the shortest distance between two points is *not* a straight line: "[S]ometimes it's necessary to go a long distance out of the way to come back a short distance correctly" (*The American Dream and The Zoo Story: Two Plays by Edward Albee* [New York: Signet 1963], 30; hereinafter cited as Albee). Another remark Jerry addresses to Peter in Albee's 1959 play also bears on the action of *Frankie and Johnny*; again invoking the uses of indirection, Jerry calls the fusion of kindness and cruelty "the teaching emotion" (*ibid.*, 36).

McNally bends this policy of intermittent reinforcement to his own purposes. One closeted gay in *Some Men* rebukes another over lunch for falling in love with the paid escorts he has sex with (*Two Plays* 2007, 35). Sleeping with her seventeen-year-old student costs a high-school English teacher in *Unusual Acts of Devotion* her job. Sex remains a sore spot. The pain caused Maria of *Master Class* by being dropped by her lover Onassis after she had aborted at his bidding the fetus they conceived keeps racking her. The Greek roots she shares with Onassis also summon up the most strangely prophetic poem of the last century, "Leda and the Swan," which links sex to apocalypse. Orgasm, in the poem Yeats describes, is cosmic destruction: the broken wall, burning roof and tower of Troy, and "Agamemnon dead." McNally knows such devastation. The job of scripting Manuel Puig's *Kiss of the Spider Woman* might have appealed to him because the eponymous kiss brings death. Like Raymond Chandler and Ernest Hemingway, he finds beautiful women lethal. The more beautiful they are, the greater the risk of closing with them. The death by AIDS of two of his dearest friends, James Coco and Robert Drivas, frames a gay version of this scenario; the promise of love, thrills, and self-renewal kills, as it does the leads of Puig's novel (Frontain, James Coco, AIDS 3, 8: n. 2).

Death wears different garb in McNally, all of them dismal and disheartening. Dead sons crush their survivors' hearts in *Bringing It All Back Home*, "Andre's Mother" (1988), *Nudity* (2004), and *Dedication*. In *Ganesh*, not only do the two affluent main figures, one of whose husbands will die during the play's present-tense action, have dead sons; the goddess Pavarti also has, in the play's eponym, a damaged one. The damage resounds. Outpourings of grief blister hearts throughout the canon. Sally Truman, still mourning the death of her AIDS-stricken brother, goes wild with anguish when she finds out that the gay youth she saw dive into the sea hours earlier has turned up both drowned and, wrenching her anew, disfigured. She may be counting lucky the children she conceived with Sam who died in her womb; they were spared such horrors.

McNally takes different looks at the idea that love's most powerful impact comes in its loss. Angel Antonelli, the Liza Minnelli role, returns home in *The Rink* after an absence of ten years, the same span of time, incidentally, that Leona and Midge spent away from each other before reuniting in *Deuce*. McNally is grazing the idea, foremost in the work of James Ellroy, the son of a murdered mother, that loving a dead person interferes with loving a live one, a major accent in *LT*. But even though the idea falls within his imaginative scope, the earlier McNally, shaken by the AIDS-inflicted deaths of two close friends, has turned instead to the soul-bracing virtue of forgiveness. *The Rink* he calls "a story of forgiveness" (8), and, according to Frontain, forgiveness also quickens the redemptive heartbeat of *The Ritz* ("I don't believe this whole night" 100, 104).

Another, more frequently used, emblem of health and harmony is the dance. McNally said on the subject:

> Dance is very important to me. I think dance is the best way of depicting love, physical sensual love between people.... Love is expressed fabulously in dance — I think sexual passion is expressed better in dance than in words [Zinman, "Interview," Zinman, ed., *Casebook* 12–3].

It follows that the cast of *LVC* contains two professional dancers, one of whom says, "I love myself when I'm dancing" and "When I dance I become all the best things I can be" (*Two Plays* 55). McNally keeps it going. In line with his interest in fugue, counterpoint, and crescendo, characters in his work can dance alone, in pairs, or in larger groups; all four actors in *A Perfect Ganesh* dance late in Act Two, scene one. In all cases, their footwork both smoothes friction and affirms the joys of affinity and accord; Margaret's telling the elephant god Ganesha that he's "a wonderful dancer" posits good dancing as a divine attribute.

Frontain has described, in this vein, the dance that marks the finale of *LVC*: "In the [play's] penultimate scene ... six gay men, preposterously clad in tulle skirts and feathered headdresses, rehearse for an AIDS benefit at which they will dance the 'Pas des Cygnes' ('Dance of the Little Swans') from Tchaikovsky's *Swan Lake* ballet ... with surprising grace and dignity" ("TM and the Dance of Death" 25). They're raising money to fight AIDS, the scourge that's already devouring two members of their group. Their efforts go beyond money-raising. "In effect," Frontain adds, "the dancers form a community graced by the love, valor, and compassion of McNally's title" (*ibid.*). The grace they attain, after several botched attempts, bespeaks this devotion. Only two members of the group have danced professionally. The tutus and feathered boas they and the others are wearing in their effort to make cause against the disease that has been killing so many of their kind make them look ridiculous, as Frontain says. But so what? In McNally, as in the work of Robertson Davies, acts of high moral import often come from that which looks ridiculous.

It happens again in *The Full Monty*, a play whose dancers are all straight, blue-collar, and thus shackled by the code of American macho imperviousness; no artistes or Williams College graduates here (*LVC* 53). Having shallow pockets has brought out the worst in these laid-off workers from Buffalo, New York. They laze around the house, drink too much, and resent their wives, some of whom still have jobs, including one who has defected to another (employed) man. It makes sense that they feel defeated. The employed fit into a structure, which helps them stave off anxiety and gloom. By contrast, these very woes have flooded the souls of Jerry Lukowski and his circle. Having lost his pride and self-validation, Jerry won't even fault Pam for moving in with another man.

He's not totally demoralized. When it comes to spending time with his twelve-year-old son, he stands tall. The scenes that show this part-time dad together with Nathan make it clear that McNally's stage version of *The Full Monty* did more than just transpose material from Simon Beaufoy's 1996 movie. An example of McNally's creative engagement with Beaufoy's script comes in his treatment of the poignant subject matter of a part-time jobless dad's love for his son. Jerry risks forfeiting his legal right to see Nathan because he's behind on his child-support payments. McNally's impeccable timing brings his worries to life. Watching the Chippendales perform locally inspires Jerry to make money by mounting a Chippendale-inspired dance routine with his sagging beer-gutted middle-aged mates. These slouches look even sillier on the dance floor than their shapelier, more protein-conscious foils in *LVC*. But the stage direction placed at the end of their big act, "The six men are transformed into something Chippendales would be proud of" (145), shows them energizing each other to reach heights beyond those dictated by the profit motive. The heights they achieve aren't unusual; McNally's people perform feats with others they could never manage on their own.

A man in *Some Men* will tell his lover, "I'm a different man when I'm with you. I could dance right now. Dance like I didn't have a care in the world. Dance in the moonlight like a crazy pagan" (*Two Plays* 2007, 22). The same daily cares that David has forgotten stay submerged for a longer spell in *The Full Monty*. But there's a difference: the laid-off factory hands dance together while David only talks about it. Their team effort both lifts the men's self-esteem and helps them win back the families they were on the brink of losing. And so it goes. Dancing partners in McNally hark to Emerson's belief that every material fact symbolizes a spiritual one. The dancers' everyday concerns have slid into the orbit of art. Nor need this transformation evoke the Judy Garland-Mickey Rooney figures in movies like *Babes in Arms* (1939) who mount their own shows after being thwarted by the adult establishment (McNally used the phrase "Judy and Mickey saving the day" in conversation with Jackson R. Bryer [184]).

So magical is the transforming power of dance that the dancers needn't be lovers. Two ex-army buddies from *The Ritz* both look and feel ridiculous improvising a song-and-dance routine in drag. Before long, though, the spirit of the routine energizes them, drowning their self-consciousness. The men soon perform so well that they win a prize in the talent contest they had reluctantly entered. Then McNally says of a "smouldering pas de deux" danced by a woman while partnered with an old family friend in *The Rink*, "He is terrific and so is ANNA" (38). McNally will also call the slow-dancing in *LTTA* of Sam Truman and his sister Chloe "very, very good" (42). The model for this grace, poise, and elegance comes at the end of W. B. Yeats's "Among School Children":

> O body swayed to music, O brightening glance,
> How can we tell the dancer from the dance? [63–64].

The following stage directions, from *The Rink*, given when Anna and her prodigal daughter see that their need for each other outweighs the anger dividing them, hints at the magical powers of dancing in McNally's work: "She [Angela] is sobbing uncontrollably. So is ANNA. It is impossible to say who moves first but they are in each others' arms" (91). The spontaneity of their embrace (underscored by the absence of a comma between the independent clauses in the compound sentence describing it) invokes the rapture that McNally ascribed to dancing during a talk with Toby Silverman Zinman in 1994: "There's a freedom in dance that I'm trying to find in my writing, the transition between comedy and the serious ... that's how I see life" ("Interview," Zinman, ed., *Casebook* 13).

Performed in the right spirit, dancing is organic, an ideal state that melts all irreconcilables to wrap the dancers in a blend of movement and sound. Yeats saw life as a cosmic drama that subsumes all human faculties. Everything becomes necessary and purposive in dancing. The dancers merge with the dance in the same noiseless way that the final synthesis in Hegel's dialectic folds the creator into his creation, God merging with the Holy Commonwealth.

McNally tempers this metaphysic. He knows that no human impulse or act is strong or pure enough to pierce the mystery of unity. But he hasn't dumped us back in the sludge of brute matter. His mindfulness of Yeats's "brightening glance" discloses divinity in scraps, echoes, and shadows, when, like the sea or Yeats's "great rooted blossomer" of "Among School Children," his dancers are rocking, heaving, and darting together — retracing the pulse of creation. John Clum rightly calls the "Dance of the Little Swans" in *LVC* "an absurd, defiant protest against mortality, but ... also an image of family" ("Where We Are Now," Zinman, ed., *Casebook* 110).

II

Has McNally made himself detractor proof? Few straight reviewers would tell a gay man what to say about his own set. Few fellow gays would feel right faulting another member of their oft-misunderstood and persecuted brotherhood. Homosexuality remains a knotty, unresolved issue of American life. Even a late-middle-aged gay couple in *Some Men* quarrel about their quality of life before the pre–Stonewall riots (on 25 June 1969, the gay patrons at Stonewall, a Greenwich Village bar, fought off a squad of raiding cops). The brawls step up; *It's Only a Play* shows gays tearing at each other. McNally won't back down to his mostly straight audiences by feeding them lazy stereotypes. Instead of peddling flimsy melodrama, he gives them something more startling and impressive. His gays are people, not signposts. Few of them act prissy, queerness being just one part of their characters.

McNally is well grounded. A gay who writes about gays, he shows homosexuality both illuminating and nourishing life. He does this by focusing on people in everyday social settings. Except for *LVC*, where his people work in AIDS clinics and do pro bono legal work for AIDS victims, he says little about causes. The plays don't apologize or fantasize about being gay, either. There's something real and deep to them. Nor do they feel studied or derived. The opposite is often true; his gays will describe themselves and each other, sometimes in uglier terms than straights use when they're safely out of gay hearing range: in an angry moment a man calls his lover in *The Lisbon Traviata* "a miserable fucked-up faggot" (*Three Plays* 67). Honesty has won out again. The impromptu fluency of his dialogue involves us in his peoples' lives.

This fluency can sidetrack the happy ending his straight audiences might have been hoping for. A commercial play, driven by the idea that love conquers all, often ends with a man and a woman in each other's arms. Such embraces in McNally don't happen at final curtain; in works like *Some Men* and "The Wibbly, Wobbly, Wiggly Dance That Cleopatterer Did" (1993), they include male prostitutes. Gay sex is linked to betrayal in *LVC*, *A Man of No Importance*, and *Corpus Christi*. The sad catalog runs on. Andre of *Andre's Mother* and a soldier named Tommy in *SM* both died in combat before curtain rise. A man kills his lover in *LT*. One ties up another in *Witness* (1988), *LVC*, and *Some Men*. (In *Sweet Eros*, the bound victim is a girl.) This havoc has cultural roots. It scarcely needs saying that most gays have straight parents, a truth that distances them immediately from those closest to them. It's loneliness as much as desire that prods a man in "Cleopatterer" to bring a hustler home with him. Loneliness plagues Alfie Byrne in *A Man of No Importance*, too. This closeted busman feels at odds with both the sister he lives with and their many neighbors. But the easy informality of nearest things makes him feel safe. Even this comfort, alas, is taken from him in time. Being outed cuts him off from what was once familiar and supportive. Cut off he'll stay. The daily threat of intimidation and insult has dimmed forever his twinkling Irish eyes and glad-to-see-ya Irish charm.

McNally's contribution to such mash-ups provides undertones of terror. Born in 1938, he came to consciousness during World War II; his adolescence coincided with the McCarthy era, a time when Americans were hunted, found out, and then punished; he came of age during the Vietnam War, which explains the combat deaths in plays spreading 40 years in time — the early *Botticelli* and *Bringing It All Back Home* and, more eerily, the later *Some Men*.

The Window Washer in *Witness* stands for the straight American male who's wrapped up in ego-gratification, masculinity enhancement, and self-promotion. The danger that once threatened him as a GI remains in place. He does the risky work of cleaning the windows of a 40-storey building. He should have found a safer job. Years earlier in World War II he got seriously wounded defending values that built America's greatness. Now he feels sucker-punched; his country's leaders have betrayed these same values. He's losing hope. The tycoons of modern industry have also made him feel betrayed. Though the speed limit on most highways is 60 mph, many of today's cars that can go as high as 85, like the one the Window Washer's uncle was driving when one of its tires blew out and killed him along with six other people.

The Window Washer also bemoans his regimen of living under a government that acquiesces while he continues to smoke three fatal packs of cigarettes a day. This tough talker who prefers being in groups over being alone wants to be led, making *Witness* another chapter in the book of American infantilism. Insolence, swagger, and brutality masquerading as courage in the Window Washer can't hide the futility within. Lacking the willpower to stop smoking, he suffers from an excess of freedom. He talks about wanting to "[s]mash some guy's face open for him, knock out some teeth" (*15 Plays* 120). This won't happen. Instead, he has directed his frustration to blacks. New laws enacted to expand minority rights in the workplace he reads as a conspiracy against him. Yet when he calls himself "the man on the street and proud of it" (*ibid.*), he's not setting himself up to be mocked. He has a steady job and a wife and son he loves. It's the Young Man, not he, who tells a woman visitor, "I ... want to fuck you. That's all, just fuck you" (*ibid.*, 137); this, during a conversation of several minutes duration the Window Washer stays out of.

A more memorable example of McNally's ordinary salt-of-the-earth American male is Sam Truman of *LTTA*. This owner of a construction firm can barely hold himself together. More fully developed than the Window Washer, Sam carries forward the self-doubt that has been troubling stalwarts like him who are valued by many of us as pillars of our market economy. When he hears that a gay swimmer walked naked through a crowd of women and children on the beach, he offers to show him his "real whopper" (*LTTA* 15) of a dick when he returns from his swim. Yet his saying the word, fecund, in the same speech (*ibid.*) infers a secret guilt that being well endowed hasn't masked. He blames himself for his wife's failure to carry her pregnancies to full term. Worse, he suspects that this defect has led his wife, Sally, into an affair.

This employer of labor who also enjoys fiddling with tools fears that his life is lurching out of control. He can't tie his necktie *or* his shoelaces, and he recently spit out a piece of steak he feared might otherwise choke him (*ibid.*, 30). His fixation? It's not blacks, like the Window Washer, but, rather, gays. Which is unlucky for him; the play he's in unfolds in that gay enclave of Long Island, Fire Island, and gay vacationers have filled the houses on either side of the one where he's weekending on this 4th of July. And if that weren't enough to wreck his peace, this house belonged to the gay brother of his wife before AIDS took him down. Sam has suddenly found himself in the minority for the only time he can remember, and he's shaken.

But he shouldn't fret. Distress in McNally is a state of mind, or nerves, conducive to growth. Up to now, Sam had been basing his views of gays on anecdote, not empirical evidence. The turmoil suddenly gripping this true man (Truman) sheds important light on gay-bashing in a supposedly enlightened, humane liberal society. The persistence of this subtext lifts McNally's work above the geniality and safety of popular commercial drama. It calls for a treatment darker, deeper, and more thrilling than the conventional theater provides. As is shown in middle-class mainstays like Sam, the Father in *Bringing It All Back Home*, and the Window Washer, so solid and hearty from a distance, so splintered within, McNally chronicles the wounded heart, not the winded one.

Most of these hearts belong to gays. Often the wounds cut deep, giving the impression that, like Tennessee Williams, McNally is putting down homosexuality as a weakness and an affliction. A rich gay in *Some Men* hates the oppression and furtiveness that keep goading him. "Gay is not good," Will says. "Gay is loneliness and secrecy and a lifetime of shame. Gay sucks but they don't tell you that" (*Two Plays* 2007, 38). Haunted by the fallout that his being exposed will rain upon his wife, parents, and kids, he's always tense. The most he can hope for is the continuance of a hollow marriage as he bleeds from within.

He and his lunch partner at the New York Athletic Club are both married. And so were two of the four gay men who comprise the cast of *The Lisbon Traviata*, both of whom, unlike Will and Bernie, divorced before the onset of middle age. Neither complains about being hassled by the straight world. A scene in *Some Men* that occurs 27 years after Will and Bernie's lunch shows a fifty-something gay discussing pre–Stonewall New York: "[W]e did okay for ourselves" (*ibid.*, 71), says Aaron, who's still doing okay as a successful doctor. He also acts surprised when his young gay interviewer, a gender studies major at Vassar, cites Aaron's oppression "by the straight male white patriarchy" (*ibid.*, 73). He has begged the question. Instead of grousing, like Will, over the penalties of being gay, Aaron and his partner enjoyed life together. Limited as it was, the fun they had took their minds off of "any obstacles" (*ibid.*) imposed by the patriarchy. Other goals were reached, too. Besides Aaron's career as a successful doctor, a member of their group got his Ph.D. and wrote a book about John Milton.

Admittedly, these two occupied a different place on the urban landscape than Bernie and Will. Their having met and bonded as college-age singles set their passage through adult life apart from those of their badgered closeted married foils. McNally does something more important than judge this crucial difference. In still another variation of the theme of gays-in-the-patriarchy, Aaron's Vassar interviewer grumbles that his own generation of gays has known fewer joys. He has a point. The "obstacles" Aaron speaks of (*ibid.*) created a singing tension with his instincts that scored him a quiet but important victory over the status quo.

But what if the obstacles are internal? Yes, gays are bashed by presumably straight homophobes in *Witness*, *Tommy Flowers*, and, fatally, in *Ganesh*. But a fellow gay instigates the beating of Alfie Byrne in *AMNI*; Judas of *Corpus Christi* plots the crucifixion of his ex-lover, Joshua. The ante keeps rising. The AIDS that McNally called "a subtext in *Frankie and Johnny*" (Drukman 340) takes on thematic surge in *LVC* and *LTTA*, the latter work describing with riveting precision both the emotional chaos and moral exhaustion caused by AIDS. For starters, people haven't learned how to discuss the disease. When the topic of Sally's brother David's AIDS-driven death comes up in conversation, it meets a stymied response of approach and retreat by his straight survivors.

This deeply layered complication resonates more than the casualness of the brutality featured in McNally's early plays. Short stripped-down works from this period like "Tour" (1967), "¡Cuba Si!" (1968), and "Last Gasps" (1970) look like mischievous, cold-blooded lab experiments in which lightly sketched characters inhabit a small, intrigue-ridden space where they await some nasty fate to zap them. The subject matter of these works can vary. National institutions, customs, and emblems come under fire in "Next, Witness" (1968), *Tommy Flowers* (1971), and *Whiskey* (1973). "Noon" registers the preoccupation with sex developed more fully in works like *Frankie and Johnny*, *The Lisbon Traviata*, and *LTTA*. This 1969 one-acter depicts the lengths people will go in search of erotic excitement regardless of how they define — or deny — it. The wife of a man wearing "black leather underwear and high leather boots" tells him, "Punish them, Cecil, punish them," i.e., the other cast members who answered the same ad for sex (*15 Plays* 41). Sex enjoys a higher priority with all of them than they'd admit. A woman has come to the lower Manhattan walk-up from Flushing; Cecil and his wife drove down from Westchester County; another hopeful is risking his job ("I don't know if I'll still have a job when I get back" [*ibid.*, 45]).

The four flights of stairs the seekers trek fluster them even before they heave into view. And if we're not flustered with them, we'll soon be. For a while, the dialogue moves in tired circles as the people talk to fill the time before Dale's arrival. A volley of "loud tolling sounds" (*ibid.*, 25) makes Kerry, the first character we meet, do what we want to do ourselves. He covers his ears. The lure of sex has brought together strangers from different walks of life and different sexual preferences. Though shaken, they stay fixed on their common goal of getting laid. When the phone rings, they all rush to answer it. They're not disappointed. On the other end is Dale, who had lured them to the downtown walkup. His new proposal shows how little they've learned. Except for Kerry, they all agree to schlep to Paramus, New Jersey, through heavy traffic.

What happens to them there we never discover. We needn't. The cycle has renewed, the anticipation of sex having reduced them to sheep. So potent is this lure that we can assume that Dale has scheduled another session of hopefuls who'll re-enact his script of letdown and misguided hope carried out by the noon group.

"Noon" has put a dark spin on the truth that comedy affirms the central values of the writer's dominant culture. A voice speaking "from afar" that says "Dale" (*ibid.*, 50) could belong to someone from this later group whose craving for sex brought him to the walk-up. McNally sees this craving as universal. Both men and women go by he name, Dale. The straight woman who answered the ringing phone and called Dale "he" (*ibid.*, 47) might have been fulfilling a wish. There are other possibilities. Perhaps the person Beryl spoke to was Asher, a tall, thin youth who entered the set carrying several books. McNally had left him alone with Kerry for the first third of the play both to develop his character and show that he had caught Dale's intent. This man in his early twenties is using his armful of books to hide his edginess. When he says to Kerry "You could have fooled me" (*ibid.*, 46) after Kerry admits to being gay, he's lying. He wants to save face. He has been yielding all along to Kerry's blandishments. He looks away when Kerry starts to inflate an air mattress, and the gestures of token resistance he mounts to keep Kerry at bay grow progressively weaker.

He's still lying as he makes ready to go to Paramus. The orgy Dale hinted at he views with feigned detachment. He's not prodded by lust, only curiosity: "I never been to an orgy.... To be frank, I could use the experience" (*ibid.*, 49). Maybe he's lying to himself. He had lied earlier when he called himself a Columbia Ph.D. (*ibid.*, 48). But as his armful of books implies, he may be a Columbia undergrad, as was McNally at his age. He could also be a writer like the ex-parochial student (*ibid.*, 106) who abducts a girl in *Eros* (1968). The hunt for parallels keeps enticing us. The name, Asher, invokes the dusty dead end to which the name's bearer is heading. He's drifting toward a gay sexual relationship he hasn't fully bought into. His statement that he has no roommate (*ibid.*, 25) means that he either doesn't want one or isn't ready for one — *if* he's telling the truth. His counterpart, Kerry, whose name rhymes with Terry, a nickname McNally knew, represents a later, franker phase of the process.

To build a seductive mood, the well-prepared Kerry starts playing some romantic music on his portable phonograph. His actions evoke the "trademark use of music as a motivating life-force" that Helen T. Buttel ("McNally's Films of His Broadway Plays," Zinman, ed., *Casebook* 81) sees galvanizing the plays. Nor is she the only critic whose words shed light on *Eros*. Ben Brantley's insight into a world-class orchestra conductor with sexual hang-ups in *Prelude and Liebestod* (1989) chimes with Buttel's remark: "This paradoxical coupling of mortal limitations and immortal music is a favorite subject of Mr. McNally's" (1). Brantley chose his words well; any paradox defies reason. But if that search for meaning called absurdity stems from the clash between the reasonableness of our minds and the unreasonableness of the world, then music, though meaning-free, heightens the clash.

Music makes revelations by probing our deep, unconscious selves along with the mind. By targeting the inner planes of human response, it confirms its mystery. The upshot of music's deep probe defies both access and logic. The opening speech of a tour guide in *Full Frontal Nudity* who's talking about Michelangelo's *David*, "Words would only diminish the experience" (SS 35), applies just as strictly to music, if not more so. (*Ganesh* applies the tour guide's words to the exhilaration of viewing the Taj Mahal [*Two Plays* 253]).

Magnificent music leaves its listeners speechless, too. Hearing a late passage in Bellini's *I Puritani* moves one of them to say, "This is the greatest finale he's ever written, hands down." What follows deflates the speaker's joy. Bewildered rather than pleased by the words he has just heard, Bellini answers, "I don't know where it comes from" (*GA* 85). He's right. He knows that trying to describe the series of technical maneuvers he used to achieve his great finale would fall short — or wide — of the truth. But he couldn't have described it, anyway. Katharine and Margaret were on the right track in *Ganesh* when they agreed to keep silent about what seeing the Taj Mahal meant to them. McNally said, too, of Maria Callas's preordained failure as a teacher of master classes at Juilliard, "She's ... terrible ... in trying to communicate what makes her great. It's her secret and she can't give it away because she doesn't know what it is" (Savran 134).

Bellini had accepted more good-naturedly than Maria the confusion and bewilderment that go with artistic creation. But he also knows the cruel demands posed by his creativity; he'd die at 33 a year after *I Puritani*'s debut. What broke him down wasn't accidental, either. The artist, McNally said in 1989, must be willing to sacrifice everything to his art (*ibid.*, 130).

Bellini's early death intrigues us because, just as Maria burned out her voice in her 40s by overtaxing it, two of McNally's favorite singers, Billie Holiday (1915–59) and Edith Piaf (1915–63), also died young. Judy Garland (1922–69), it should be added, died at the same age as Piaf, 47. But McNally's favorite singers (Crutchfield, 5) have something in common that needs pointing out. Piaf, Billie, Judy, and Callas all let us live vicariously in a world of emotional extremes few of us could otherwise endure.

These four vocal goddesses or freaks knew something vital, i.e., that greatness in singing demands more than technical perfection. Maria tells a student that the great soprano roles like Lady Macbeth and Norma require a gift that "can't be taught or passed on or copied or even talked about" (*MC* 61). Since music expresses the whole self, the great ones sing not only from the heart but also from their guts and bowels, which gives the music a wider, deeper range. More vital than correctness is expressive *élan*. Though mysterious, this internal fire *can* be both accessed and communicated. It can also leap to the fore anywhere. Act One of *The Ritz* ends moments after the no-hoper Googie Gomez's nightclub act. McNally adds a longish stage direction here to note that the spirit, or *Mut* (*MC* 54), the German word for courage, Googie invested in her act redeemed in part her lack of talent (28).

Googie's *Mut* takes on a savagery in *Golden Age*, where a soprano probes areas in her psyche so deep and mysterious that they're usually out of reach, even to her. Contrast her confrontational singing with that of her accomplished golden-voiced rival, a fan favorite who risks less. Mendy of *The Lisbon Traviata* had such a soprano in mind when, hearing Stephen say of her, "She has a beautiful voice," answered him by saying, "It's not enough" (*Three Plays* 9). Maria Malibran calls her voice an anarchic beast with urgencies of its own that can choose tragic defeat as readily as sublime beauty. Hers is an honesty so desperate that it threatens to burst the boundaries of any score she's singing from. She's not alone. In *Master Class*, Maria tries to instill in a student the rage, passion, and "juice" (16) that made McNally prize her as "a great expressive artist' (Zinman, "Interview on Master Class," Zinman, ed., *Casebook* 147).

And the root of this expressiveness? Stephen, an opera buff in *LT*, rejects the heart and soul in favor of "some more intimate place" (*Three Plays* 147). He's right. *Master Class* keeps insisting that a singer must immerse herself in the irrational — even risk destroying herself— to make sublime music. Hilton Als spoke of this rough expressive power in his review of the 2011 Tyne Daly Broadway revival of *Master Class*:

> Callas resembled another singer who changed the rules, Billy Holiday. Like Holiday, Callas used music as a way of expressing her indomitable wounded self.... And, again like Holiday, she was drawn to the wrong men, to men she considered more dangerous and powerful than herself; greatness is isolating [72].

The sounds produced by a Malibran, a Piaf, or a Callas come from a deep, mysterious inner space. They're as dangerous as they are thrilling. The erotic edge Stephen finds in the most inspired singing makes it fitting that that "Liebestod" is sung during McNally's *Prelude and Liebestod*. Wagner's tragic aria sends at least three characters into their primitive selves. They have no choice. This stirring music captures the heady joy (or *Freude* in the German sense) of forbidden erotic ecstasy, a force so deep driving that it razes all definitions and categories. The lovers' ungovernable lyric surrender mandates their deaths; the point where self-discovery and self-attainment meet also houses destruction. The lovers' unstoppable rogue love has crushed them.

They'd welcome the agony of being crushed again. And as rogue as they are, they're not alone. Conducting the performance of "Liebestod" has hurled the orchestra's leader into a Wagnerian ecstasy. As he conducts, he relives the time when, as a twenty-two-year-old *Wunderkind* ("I was the toast of Europe" [*SS* 61]), he blundered into a sea-swell of erotic fervor more exciting than any he had known or *has* known since. In the apartment of a retired Florence optometrist, he joined a local journalist and his sister, uncannily "a mirror image of him." These two, "both nude and more beautiful than anyone I have ever seen" (*ibid.*, 63), stripped, blindfolded, and tied him to a bed. Talk about razing guidelines; vision came to him while blindfolded in an optometrist's apartment. What the beautiful sibs do next rocks him so hard that it scrambles his mind ("I don't know what tense I'm in — what tense I want to be in" [*ibid.*, 62]). Were it not so powerfully physical, he might call it an out-of-body experience. McNally's witty allusion to Poe's "Fall of the House of Usher" joins this "perfect moment" (*ibid.*, 64) to death. And deathly is the intensity of the orgasm the Usher-like pair gives him.

This flame-tip of passion goes beyond blame. He was tied up when it happened (bondage is a leading trope in McNally's *Witness*, "Sweet Eros," and *LVC*, and a man in *SM* needs to be bound and gagged to reach orgasm [*Two Plays* 2007, 96]). But he also consented to it. The imponderables pile up. He can't even identify either the person or the orifice that took his seed. Nor is he sure that the sibs who ushered him into his rapture existed. One oddity, though, of his dying into life has stuck with him. Everything that happened to him in the Florence apartment happened in view of a Renaissance painting of a Madonna, to him a figure of forgiveness. His sin, if it is sin to defy human limits, has been forgiven. That's why he never again saw the painting, the apartment where it hung, or the strange brother and sister. He needn't. An act of grace or divine punishment, his manifestation never belonged to our world. But it *has* lodged in his heart, like one of Wordsworth's spots of time or Keats's nightingale moment. He can draw otherworldly inspiration from it or suffer its wrath. As his memory of it revisits him some twenty-odd years later, it gives him a new command and an authority so vital that others feel it. "This is more like it. I gotta hand it to him, when he's at his best, there's no one like him" (*SS* 60), says the Concertmaster, swept into the surge that's flooding the Conductor.

That special quality of genius that can't be named, let alone analyzed, fuels other kinds of self-transcendence. An admirer at Forest Hills in *Deuce* ascribes the excellence of the two former women's doubles partners about to be honored to "the unexplainable, the inexplicable genius of how they did what they had chosen to do with their lives (*Two Plays*, 2007 131–32). This afflatus even visits amateurs. A dramatic peak comes in *The Full Monty* when Pam offers her estranged husband Jerry a packing job in the factory where she works. Knowing that he needs the $9.50-an-hour job to pay his child support, we expect him to take her offer. We'd be wrong. He rejects it because he must, even though he can't say why (97). He has already failed both Pam and himself by having settled for so little as a blue-collar drudge. But he'll protect those scraps of manhood he hasn't thrown away. Without them, his time with his son lacks meaning.

The rich and better educated can suffer with him. By any natural measure and relative to the hopes of most people, McNally's people in the plays after *Frankie and Johnny* (1987) rank in the top 10 percent of New York's wage earners. Stephen's love of opera has taken him to Epidauras, and he and his physician-lover Mike ski every year in Aspen. What helps bankroll such outings are special skills on Stephen's part that can turn good books into great ones for Knopf, the high-status publisher where he works. But neither these skills nor his expertise in opera stops Mike from leaving him. One reason why he and Mike haven't been connecting is Mike's indifference to opera. This apathy touches at least one more relationship in the canon. Opera once again forms the impasse. The real-life Aristotle Onassis cares little about it despite being the lover of the world's most famous opera singer. "Ha dato tutto a te" (*MC* 60), that singer tells an Ari she has conjured up. She's also voicing the central proposition of *Master Class*. She lost the same man for whom she gave up both her career and, with heartbreaking regret, the baby she conceived with him. As she recounts her grief, we too share her alarm over the same effects of time Frontain might have had in mind when he said, "McNally's theater is increasingly directed toward examining the causes and consequences of suffering" ("TM and the Dance of Death," 33). These momentous causes and consequences need time's passage to release their meaning.

McNally has been pondering from the start of his playwriting career the wrongness of life and the pain it causes. A character in his first play, *Bump*, dwells on "the unbearable difference between the way things are ... and the way they should be" (II 54). Things are also skewed for Ruby, the person being spoken to. So dreadful has life become to her that she only endures it by luring innocents into her basement room and then murdering them. This regimen has been beating her down. She's clever enough to know that the death of each of her victims in her "court of last resort" (*ibid.*, 43) is also killing *her* piecemeal (in another link between music and death posed by Wagner's "Liebestod" aria, Maria will also call her students victims [4, 33]).

III

Even though we'll never fully understand such terrible stories of loss, we can still vent and discuss our feelings about them. And these feelings will always trump John Jeckyll's nihilistic "Anyway" (*Two Plays* 142), the final word of *LVC*. McNally voices *his* feelings without moralizing or sounding formulaic. Key here is his knack of revealing the philosophical in the mundane by facing head-on the gap between the two realms. An example of this strategy comes in the 4th of July visit by two married couples to a house previously owned by an AIDS fatality in a gay enclave of Long Island. That the fatality was also the brother of one of the straight visitors gives *LTTA* some of the drive of *Oedipus Rex*; Sophocles and McNally both dramatize the fallout resulting from calamities in homemaking. Besides moving the barrier between gay and straight, David's death has redefined both his family's history and collective psyche. It's like the corpse in T. S. Eliot's *The Waste Land* that's planted rather than buried. His survivors can't lay it to rest. It now permeates the family's tradition, and any discussion of it returns despairingly to the family's point of origin. David's survivors face a big struggle. Trapped by the past, guilty and at the same time innocent, understanding while not understanding at all, they want to forgive but find themselves doomed to remember.

Signs of this doom can surface at any time. McNally's plays give the sense of both taking place now and circling today like a beam searching for answers to some of life's knottiest problems. His rejections of easy resolutions send us deep into his art—and ourselves, where the shock waves echo. Life for him is galvanized doubt. Shaping his work is an ambivalence that reels between uncertainties and intimations in a landscape without footholds. His plays are a composite state of mind he inhabits. Like his hero, Shakespeare, he rejects playing the role of tour guide and interpreter. *The Lisbon Traviata*, for instance, respects the right of Mike and Stephen to opacity. The two men's attempts to make sense of the disarray of their love bond leaves them confused and hurt. But these attempts have meaning. The pain that both divides and joins Mike and Stephen conveys McNally's belief in the importance of their stories:

> STEPHEN: I was a good lover, Michael.
> MIKE: It's not just about the sex.
> STEPHEN: Yes it is. Right now it is. Most of the time it is.... What happened?
> MIKE: I don't know.
> STEPHEN: So why are we doing this?
> MIKE: I don't know [*Three Plays* 80].

When Tom is asked what he needs to be happy in love in "Cleopatterer" he answers, "I don't know" (*15 Plays* 358). McNally's people, when faced by their deepest needs, act as if they're wrestling opponents without limbs. They needn't be gay, either. When Anna, Angela's mother in *The Rink*, tells her husband Dino that she'll die if he leaves her, he says, "I'll die if I stay here" (37)—before pulling away from her and going out the door. People in McNally do as they must. They're acting out, with some of the same urgency, D. H. Lawrence's belief in the life-giving power of mystery. Lawrence always saw love as the mystery, not the identity, between people. McNally amplifies this view. In his plays, the unknown and the unknowable drive both love and work. This truth has left McNally's characters reeling. Maria offers her students little that's vital about herself or her art, and Tom in "Cleopatterer" has been wearing himself out sifting imponderables.

Nothing really gets sorted out. It can't. The impression forms that only a single thread divides Tom and Maria from the truth — if not the whole bolt of cloth. In either event, it becomes clear that, as time moves ahead, memory and desire snarl the truth, its strands increasingly frayed by those unraveling them, even though unravel they must. Part of being human to McNally means taking charge of one's life despite the near-certainty that the effort will fail. Two dead sons and a dead husband play big roles in *Ganesh*, as do dead sons in *Bringing It*, "Andre's Mother," *Nudity*, and *Dedication*. Death keeps having its innings. Besides being dazed by her brother's death, Sally Truman of *LTTA* can't give birth to the children she conceives with Sam. It's no shock that the drowning death of a swimmer she saw dive into the sea upsets her more than it does the play's other three characters. Even the great sea mother delivers death. The motif of the unborn returns in *Master Class*, crushing Maria. She has been condemned to loneliness. It even drives her closing words in the play. First truths have to be lived; she can experience great singing but not narrate it. What's left is boilerplate. Auguring the emptiness of a dentist's advice that Sam sleep with his lips together and teeth apart, Maria's farewell sounds too safely conventional and warmed over to help her students. All of it could be found in a beginner's handbook:

> Do not think that singing is an easy career. It is a lifetime's work; it does not stop here. Whether I continue singing or not doesn't matter. Besides, it's all there in the recordings. What matters is that you use whatever you have learned wisely. Think of the expression of the words, of good diction, and of you own deep feelings. The only thing I ask is that you sing properly and honestly. If you do this, I will feel repaid [62].

This said, McNally may still be more about continuity than change. Because discernible first causes, flaming quicks, and animating cores elude us, we try to decipher appearances. Which leaves us feeling dazed and adrift: "How hard it is really to describe anything" (37), says Katharine in *Ganesh*; Sally of *LTTA* finds truth "just too formless to grasp" (22).

Perhaps we're best served by ignoring it, as Sally's sister-in-law Chloe advises: "Fuck the truth. It's more trouble than it's worth" (*LTTA* 66). Judas of *Corpus Christi* (1998) agrees, calling truth "brutal," before adding, "It scalds, it stings" (15). McNally would agree with Kierkegaard that truth belongs to God alone and that what's left for us is it, pursuit. His command of the problem that's vexing his people is uncanny, probably because he's not a bottomliner. Like Ibsen's Peer Gynt, he can enjoy eating an onion knowing that, center-less, it consists only of outer folds. But those folds are tasty. The insides of the quartet of visitors to Fire Island in *LTTA* are frazzled. These visitors are starved of faith, a reality made notable by its absence in their lives. And finding God at the bottom of a column of numbers or at the center of an onion isn't faith. It's certainty. Belief is irrational. God isn't proven or provable; God is felt.

The belief that God cares about us and that our lives are part of a cosmic plan *has* a place in the *oeuvre*. To downgrade this place is to forget that faith always has to fight the rational proofs and material evidence constantly hammering away at it. Only by joining the fight does it merit the name, faith. McNally's own belief fits no orthodox system. But its existence can be teased out, first, by his having attended Catholic school as a boy (Zinman, "Interview," Zinman, ed., *Casebook* 3) and, next, by his characters' talk about becoming priests. It happens in his first produced play, *This Side of the Door* (1962, iii, 12), in *Witness* (1968, *15 Plays* 127) and then in *LT* (*Three Plays* 62), where two men discuss their boyhood priestly ambitions. A believer in the force of early influences might add that the speaker in *Door*, Edmund, is thirteen years old (3) and that a major thrust of the play he's in is forgiveness (iii, 16). Nor is this the sole reference to that Christian virtue in the canon. Forgiveness has preoccupied McNally his whole writing career. He called *The Rink* "a play about forgiveness," and his Bellini claims that forgiveness drives his opera, *I Puritani* (*GA* 87).

The redemptive balm of forgiveness always beckoned McNally. Even before his homosexuality put him out of the mainstream of Corpus Christi society, the Catholicism of his childhood had a strong alienating effect. Again, the divisiveness was social. Because Catholicism was also the faith of the have-not Latinos in Corpus Christi's barrio, the McNally family leagued socially with the town's Anglo-Protestants.

Now McNally knows that forgiveness doesn't belong exclusively to Catholics, in Corpus Christi or anywhere else despite the wrathful contentions of Gulf Coast fundamentalists. Far be it from him to steal that virtue for sectarian purposes. But it's also so lofty, tender, and vital (a character in *LVC* says, "We all need it from time to time" [67]) that its implementation grazes the divine. McNally uses it to evoke the influence of unseen forces over everyday events. While pursuing our daily rounds, we're also acting *sub specie aeternitatas*. Forget that we're doing it unconsciously, or even against our wills. God's manifestations, though elusive, remain all important. McNally said in 1999, "I do believe there is a divinity in all of us, and [that] we're all perfect in a way" (Drukman 341). Perhaps he meant in our own ways. While Joshua, the Jesus figure in *Corpus Christi*, says he's the son of God (38), he adds, "He [God] is in each of us" (40), explaining, "We're each special. We're each ordinary. We're each divine" (41).

In another of those Emersonian riffs that brighten the canon, God dwells in the everyday for McNally, both quickening and stabilizing us all. The sordid and the ugly share this blessing. In a motel room next to the one in which Joshua was born, a woman is heard shouting to her lover, "Fuck me, fuck me, fuck me" (*CC* 13). Get in line and call it blasphemy if you like. But be advised, too, that McNally is reminding us that *all* of creation is sacred or none of it is. The divine makes no exclusions; He'd not be divine if He did. The fornicating couple may be creating another child for God to love. All of us, however unlikely, can serve the divine purpose. Great or small, we can become God's instruments. If this idea sounds like Emerson and Whitman, it also brings to mind *E. M. Forster* by Columbia University professor Lionel Trilling, whose Forster book came out in 1943 (New Directions), 13 years before McNally enrolled in Columbia. Whether McNally studied Forster's *A Passage to India* on his own or learned about it from friends and classmates (he told me in conversation, October 2011 that he never had a course with Trilling), the schooling stuck. But this lover of low humor (Guernsey 371) reshaped it to his needs. Both the action and the diction of *Corpus Christi* reach down as well as up, folding the rowdy and the profane inside the numinous.

This makes it relevant that a room clerk in Josh's birthplace call him "little Tiger" (*CC* 19). Much of the ambience of the play — and most of McNally's other plays, too — leans on this reference to "Christ the Tiger" in T. S. Eliot's "Gerontian." Like Eliot, McNally believes that God comes to us in terror, not in fact. He has also bought the corollary of this proposition, i.e., that religious hope springs from religious fear. If Judas was correct to call the truth scalding, stinging, and brutal (*ibid.*, 15), then divine truth can destroy us in a heartbeat; Graham Greene, who was popular among academics during McNally's college days, believed that God's grace often looks and feels like punishment. In a paradox that might explain Greene's maverick belief, the same God that grounds our being can't be faced, or sometimes even named directly. No human impulse is pure, or strong, enough to face up to the living god.

This paradox, which meshes with belief systems as different as those of the ancient Greek matriarchies, Judaism, and today's Mormon Church thrives in McNally's work. Bobby, his most angelic figure (his lover Gregory calls him an angel [*Two Plays* 39]), says in *LVC*, "We love but not unconditionally. Only God is unconditional love, and we don't even love him back" (*ibid.*, 87). Bobby is right. He has offset his blindness with the acquisition of spiritual vision. Would that we followed his lead. Mash-ups of drives and appetites that bewilder us, we have forgotten that indwelling first cause that explains all.

We have also worsened this problem; the greed and vanity governing our exchanges with one another divide us from God. Joshua says in this regard,

"When we don't love another, we don't love God" (*CC* 40). Mrs. Patrick, a mother of three in *A Man of No Importance* who has been cheating on her husband, disagrees. Harking to Chloe's refusal of the truth in *LTTA*, she claims that love "causes more trouble than it's worth" (88). But need it? McNally qualifies Greene's belief that, as imperfect creatures, we're bound to love both each other and God imperfectly. An AIDS victim in *LVC* kisses the lesion of another (*Two Plays* 75). Normal, everyday standards have reversed. The mutual incapacity of the two AIDS casualties for sex has refined their ability to love. Removing sex from the equation helps us see one another more clearly; it frees us to appreciate the other's existence as a whole.

What's the big deal? This showing-forth of Buzz's and James's innate goodness, though stirring, bypasses what most of us know, do, and want. It stands too far from the sexual love that both rivets and roils Mrs. Patrick and her kind, including us. Problems caused by sex have always abounded, McNally knows. He also knows that only a few of us would trade these problems for the refined asexual love shared by Buzz and James. He discussed one major cause of these problems with David Kaufman in 1987; requited love can be as troubling as the unrequited kind: "We all walk around saying we want someone to love us unconditionally, and then when someone does, we make up new conditions" (3).

Seeking love, finding it, and then rejecting it, though wrongheaded and self-defeating, is all too human. Frankie's shoving Johnny away after having sex with him in favor of ice cream and TV signals an imperative driving up from her psyche. Savaged by sex in the past, she has shared as much intimacy with Johnny as she can take. Any more would both glut her and wreck all chances for a future they might share. She keeps referring to "a second date" (e.g., *Three Plays* 119) because she likes him and wants to see him again. But that again can't be now.

* * *

The change of heart that lets Johnny spend the night suggests in McNally a sliding-scale attitude toward sex. His psychology is spot on. The ending of *Frankie and Johnny* shows how any close bond will waver between possible outcomes—even extreme ones, like a break-up. As McNally knows, the euphoria given off by Johnny's unconditional love for Frankie will wane. It has to. As Robert Browning said in "Two in The Campagna," absolute or unconditional love stands beyond the range of human contingency.

McNally's 1963 review of Antonion's *Eclipse* tackled this truth: "Indeed," he asked, "is sexuality sufficient to hold people together, if only for a little while? And after that, what else is there?" (3) *Frankie and Johnny*'s wonderful concluding image, the eponymous couple brushing their teeth (*3 Plays* 156), may only be framing a truce. Having already had sex three times, they both see the folly of a fourth go. They might even feel relieved that the sunlight flooding the room has dampened the ardor that's supposed to be gripping them. But do they feel something beside relief? Freud might have an answer. The two might have imagined farewelling each other during the hottest moments of their three earlier love bouts. The tooth-brushing scene that ends the play foreshadows one in *LVC* that shows two lovers clipping hairs from each other's ears (*Two Plays* 100). But these men have been together for fourteen years; to celebrate their next anniversary, one asks the other, not for a champagne cruise, but for towels (*ibid.*). They're basking in the contentment they share. They've earned this contentment. A full adult bond, they know, rarely includes thrills and coziness at the same time, even though theirs could be a happy exception (*ibid.*, 19). But even if it weren't a rarity, basking in the anchoring warmth and security of domestic peace with someone you lusted for in the past is very special. It deserves special care, too. When Bobby betrays his lover Gregory, he's told of his partner in sin, "He's not that hot, Bobby. No one is" (*ibid.*, 10). No lover is electrifying enough to risk a solid, ongoing relationship for.

Have you caught a whiff of sour grapes and irrelevancy about all this common sense? Except for Scoop and Aaron and Bernie and Carl of *Some Men*, Arthur and Perry are the only gay couple in the canon who've spent as long as fourteen years together. Frankie and Johnny frame an image of contentment because, having already made love three times in the previous hours, they're too bonked out to crawl back into bed. As McNally said in his Antonioni review, sex burns brightly but briefly, an insight that takes on added gravitas for having foregrounded works as different as Tolstoy's *Kreutzer Sonata*, Dreiser's *American Tragedy*, and Hammett's *Maltese Falcon*. Not to fret, though; McNally, using life's disorder as his theater of operations, always respects the concrete and the creaturely. If his faith in the fecundity of disorder has kept him from clarifying it, he also knows that clarity is too heavy a price to pay for the loss of spontaneity and *élan*.

Slack, forgetful characters like Katharine of *Ganesh* and Mike of *The Lisbon Traviata* enjoy life more than their more compulsive, detail-driven counterparts. They're also better company, and they bounce back faster from adversity, as when Katharine quickly forgets having lost the flight bag containing her CD player at the airport. Yet McNally twice calls her and her edgy traveling companion Margaret "two little, insignificant, magnificent lives" (*Two Plays* 160–61). Both women are needed to flesh out his portrayal of the human comedy. Both play important roles in the circles they inhabit. Both help build his vernacular sublime.

CHAPTER TWO

Alchemizing the Brew

McNally's plays have come rapidly and found wide favor. One of his partisans, David Savran, calls him "probably the most successful dramatist to have come of age during the 1960s" (120). No quarrels. McNally's work is warm, true, and thrillingly strange, his versatility steering the inventiveness. The versatility merits discussion. *The Ritz* features manic pacing, seat-of-the-pants plotting, and rapid scene shifts, its characters shooting in and out of doors at a speed reminiscent of Georges Feydeau's *A Flea in His Ear*. Unexpected rewards will follow when the fun slows down. In *The Ritz* and elsewhere, McNally has always displayed in his work a beguiling mix of the introvert and the extrovert. Stagecraft (he has called himself "a great believer in technique" [Zinman, "Interview," Zinman, ed., *Casebook* 7]) fires it all up. His craftsmanship produces angles, ricochets, and resonances out of reach to lesser playwrights.

This reach is all the more formidable because of the fun he has staging it. If he seems to write without straining himself, he also writes like a woman — if that means rating character, feeling, and motive over physical comedy. Kathy Bates and Zoe Caldwell, Marian Seldes and Angela Lansbury, have all acted in his plays because he has always written wonderful roles for women; the female characters of major works like *LTTA PG*, and *MC* are more vivid than the men. Like melodies in a string quartet, conversations and narrative passages in *LVC* sheer off from each other, face different ways, and run in tandem before dovetailing. Stabbing or subtle one-liners alternate, too, with passages of internal monologue evocative of Eugene O'Neill's *Strange Interlude* (1928). Be mindful of this music. Such fugue and counterpoint, no mere decoration, build the ground rhythm for McNally's portrayal of lives complex and strange, but also disconcertingly familiar and recognizable.

The plays featuring these lives aren't simple and reassuring. Those in the audience with preconceived ideas about theater will find their psyches stretched by events startling and often wildly, deliriously funny. They may also feel under attack. "Terrence never plays it safe," said Nathan Lane (Collins

C19). To do so would be to play his muse false. Playwrights more heedful of following their own light than pleasing audiences are more likely to break new ground. McNally's "dangerous" theater (Savran 121) has set him apart. It includes scenes fresh and new. Like *Frankie and Johnny* before it, "Cleopatterer" opens where most plays and movies end — or lead to; the people before us are either having sex or have just finished. A wise move by McNally; having dispensed with the romantic finale, he can work on the human angles. The originality of some of these angles creates different effects. In *Some Men*, a gay man appears on stage with his adult gay son. A thief in *Ganesh* takes his plunder off the stage and down the center aisle. A character in *Dedication* speaks some of his lines from the top of the balcony.

Taking the resources of drama in a different direction, Bobby falls off and then climbs back onto the stage in *LVC*, which also sites McNally's boldest transformation to date. While John Jeckyll is playing the piano in a different room, his twin brother James addresses us. Then he pauses, and this stage direction leaps from the page: "He closes his eyes. The piano music stops. He stands up and looks down at the chair. He is JOHN" (*Two Plays* 124). No slice-of-life realist, McNally revels in such brazenness. Nor can we predict the form it will take. The finale of Act One of *PG* reminds us without using any dialogue that we're in a theater watching characters on a stage: "GANESHA claps his hands together. Once and all sounds stop. Twice and the OTHERS all freeze. The third time and all the lights snap off" (*ibid.*, 204). This magic confirms McNally's genius in bringing down a curtain — an art that also helps put audience members back in their seats after intermission. A dying old hag in *Dedication* offers to give an actor her magnificent old theater on two conditions. Asked to name the first one (which turns out to be identical to the second), she says, "Fuck me" (*D* 39).

Is this the low humor McNally says he loves (Guernsey 371)? Is it black humor? Or the theater of incongruity? As it was when a middle-aged heterosexual turned up in a gay bath in *The Ritz,* the incongruous has again urged an issue. The actor Mrs. Willard has just shocked wants to use her theater to stage children's plays. Though unique in the canon, their confrontation is also familiar, motifs often working at multiple levels.

The shock Mrs. Willard delivers distracts us from McNally's masterful stage economy. Another example of low humor inviting large questions comes in *LTTA*. In a stroke of stunning audacity, Chloe asks to see her brother Sam's dick, and, when he shows it to her, McNally's creativity capitalizing on the moment, calls it "very nice" (*LTTA* 64). Bold enough on its own, this incident reminds us that early in the first act, Sam told Chloe, "If you weren't my sister I'd jump all over you" (*ibid.*, 5). The reminder matters. The play's back-story has put its four characters near the edge. We wonder if we've missed something that told us how close to the edge. Both Chloe and Sam know that their spouses have recently slept together, an anxiety that caused Sam to rehearse Chloe's charms in John's presence. He'll later start a fistfight with John. The more we think about a McNally play, the more significance emerges. In the process, our stake in the action rises regardless of how often we wince. We feel the pressure the foursome in *LTTA* are living with. They're ourselves writ large, faced by agonies of hypnotic force that could cant us over the edge in an instant.

I

This hyper-realism is deliberate. McNally said in his Introduction to *A Man of No Importance*, "The theater is not a place to hide from the world but instead the very place where we may fully discover our true selves" (n.p.). It's also "a place of magic" (Guernsey, ed. xi) whose splendor transcends *verismo* theatrical techniques. An expression of "our humanity" (*ibid.*, vii), it kindles ambiguities and complexities that might crush us were they to invade our lives. The needs and drives of our private unshared selves compel McNally. Credit him for looking hard and steadily at the shadow figure, the occult side of the personality that Jung saw as the sum of all those unpleasant qualities we like to hide. It takes both courage and originality to face a part of ourselves that stirs dread and anxiety. Joan Littlewood's *Sparrows Can't Sing* scores high with him because of the confidence with which it sites vulgarity, earthiness, and knockabout in the human: "[T]he appeal of such art is as direct as life itself" (23), he said in his *Seventh Art* review of the 1964 movie. "The beauty of the film's humor [he adds] is that it is utterly indigenous to both the characters and their milieu [London's Stepney Green], a place where they cry, shout, laugh, drink, and have babies, and in general carry on like recognizable human beings" (22).

McNally's people can express some of this same candor without living in a working-class slum. The affluent, cultivated Mendy of *The Lisbon Traviata* talks about hearing Beverly Sills sing in Athens and Salzburg (*Three Plays* 16, 26). But he talks even more about the pain of being lonely. Closer to home than Athens and Salzburg, degree holders from Dartmouth and Columbia frequent the posh N.Y.A.C. and the Waldorf in *Some Men* (*Two Plays* 2007, 34, 102–6). John's degree in *LTTA* comes from Williams (*LTTA* 7), the same college where Perry of *LVC* studied before going to law school (*Two Plays* 53). The Terrence McNally who parades these academic pedigrees also knows their limits. Thus it's no shock that one of Perry's fellow vacationers in Dutchess County says of the conversational hot air buzzing around him, "This is getting too artsy-fartsy/idealistic/intellectual for me" (*ibid.*, 29).

For all the high-toned buzz, McNally's people also curse a lot, the profanity coming from women as well as men. Virginia Noyes, a famous actress in *It's Only a Play*, walks on stage saying, "Is there a can in here? That fucking Shirley MacLaine's had me in a corner telling me who she was in her previous lives until I thought I would burst" (*Three Plays* 165). Even McNally's more proper, finer-hewn women will curse. After scolding her ex-tennis partner for saying the word, Midge of *Deuce* agrees with Leona that the woman who stole her husband was "a cunt" (*Two Plays* 2007, 168). Some of the randy talk in the plays is hilarious. Asked if Julie Andrews is gay, Buzz, the Broadway musical comedy queen in *LVC* says, "I don't know. She never fucked me" (*Two Plays* 49).

Why such explicitness? Maria says in *Master Class* that the audience is any stage performer's enemy (*MC* 37). McNally agrees in principle with her. He wants his audiences to relax and have fun while taking in his illusion of life. The profanity which has made him both famous and notorious is a tactic he uses to win them over. It's meant to build a winking partnership, even a form of flattery; since we're not prudes, we can take his F-bombs in stride. A close look at the bombs also establishes for the undaunted their artistic relevance. If they fly too often for some playgoers, they're always in character; they fit both the mood and tempo of a scene; they juice a plot. There's nothing a playwright enjoys more than making a crowd laugh, either. In this vein, some of McNally's best laugh lines—and he's one of today's most savagely funny stage writers—turn on profanity.

The laughter bursts from his ability to massage his audiences; few dramatists have been as aware as he of the sensibilities of the people in the seats facing the stage. Playing to our self-images as cool cosmopolites who know all the angles, he'll have a character in *The Lisbon Traviata* say, "Callas sings Mussorgsky. Callas sings the Beatles. Callas sings I'm Bad" (*Three Plays* 15). He has credited us with a worldliness that includes both catching his references and savoring their incongruity. A more exotic one, i.e., referencing Elliott Carter in *LVC* (*Two Plays* 37), camps it up by focusing our attention differently. We want to preserve our implicit partnership with him. And he never forgets it. His mention of blue-eyed soul singer George Michael (*Three Plays* 11) at the start of the second act of *The Lisbon Traviata* serves two ends. Because good storytelling is immersive, McNally has learned how to thicken and thus enrich his dialogue with details. This enrichment has also made us want to know what happens next. But coming after all the high-flown references in Act One of *Lisbon Traviata*, the naming of George Michael early in Act Two shifts the play's mood to a middle-class register. A friendly chord with those younger fans of soul music in the audience who might have been feeling lost or neglected has also been struck. These fans can rest easy that the stage action they're watching concerns *them*, which McNally wants. His play is meant to touch all of us. He's on our database, if he ever left it. But he has also scored a more vital point. Having witnessed his mastery of both pop and high culture, we've also been primed to trust him on more serious matters.

These can surface at any time in the plays; McNally told John DiGaetani in 1991 that, rather than being bouncy and exuberant "in real life," he was "rather cold" (224). This alleged coldness belies the mischievousness he has always enjoyed staging. Like Erik Satie, Marcel Duchamp, and John Cage, he loves pranks. When he joins this tendency to a Beckett-like aggressiveness toward the audience, he can be outrageous. A performer in *Prelude and Liebestod* takes so long to arrive on stage that he makes us "wonder if anything has gone wrong" (*SS* 44). McNally is doing more than bucking the moral authority of the white conservative elite who fill most of the seats on Broadway (Drukman 333). The description by a character in McNally's 1988 play, "Street Talk," of the erstwhile theater of confrontation voices the same defiance: "When actors roam the aisles, you went to the theater at your own peril. A play could be about Vietnam and they'd throw blood at you" (*15 Plays* 366).

The blindsiding continues. Deafening music or garish lights can blast us at any time in his plays, an audacity he took to from the start. His first play, an undergraduate effort called *The Roller Coaster* (1960), opens in a deserted amusement park. Cacophonies and clashes fill the house as a distant calliope plays "louder, discordant" music while "the deafening roar of a roller coaster" bombards us from the flies. Following this racket is "a long silence" (*RC* 42). The extremes of quiet and noise and of light and dark suggest the iconoclastic TV comic and pro wrestling fan, Andy Kaufman (1949–84) and his attempt to find new ways to stretch the minds and hearts of his audiences. Like him, McNally keeps ratcheting up our discomfort level. The "stark and modern" fittings in the basement room where *Bump* begins deny us the comfort of "shadows and semi-tones." Will comfort ever come? McNally's next stage direction calls for a soundtrack of grunts and groans, "amplified to an almost unendurable level" (II 2).

The screws stay tight. "Enormously loud trilling noises" batter us after the first few lines of dialogue in "Noon" (*15 Plays* 25). Trying to say the title of the 1990 teleplay, "Last Gasps," with its double-stressed monosyllables, makes *us* gasp. We keep being shown who's boss. Before putting a character on stage, *Gasps* hammers us with a "deafening, urgent, terrifying" siren ("¡Cuba Sí!," *Bringing It All Back Home, Last Gasps* [New York: Dramatists Play Service: 1970], 47). The characters who *do* appear choke to death within moments. Another work just as defiant of liberal-humanist theater opens with a "mightily amplified clunking sound of a phonograph needle banging across the edge of a record. *Clunk, Clunk, Clunk* (II 80). And just as the ability of an actor at the start of "Gasps" to hold his breath longer than 45 seconds improves "*the play's full effect*" ("¡Cuba Si!," et al. 47), so should the opening racket in *Tommy Flowers* take "five minutes for all I care ... the longer the better" (II 80).

That the actor who shuffles to the clunking phonograph is black, and thus makes McNally guilty of stereotyping, costs him more friends. This is the art of assault, if it's art at all. Is he trying to drive theatergoers from their seats or rewarding them for staying put? The question matters because most of his audience-bashing comes at curtain rise, a time when we're least likely to bolt from our chairs. This, McNally knows. Actors only appear on stage in "Dusk" (1996) after "we feel that nothing is going to happen, nothing at all, ever" (McNally, *Dusk*; Joe Pintauro, Lanford Wilson, and Terrence McNally, *By the Sea, By the Sea, By the Beautiful Sea* [New York: Dramatists Play Service, c. 1997], 51). The ending of a McNally play can frazzle us too. After all the lines in *LTTA* have been spoken, both stage and house are caught in a glare while music is blasting from all over the house: "The opening music, the trio from Mozart's *Così fan tutti*, is heard again, only this time from all over the theatre.... The stage and the theatre are blazing. Audience and actors are in the same bright light. The music reaches a climax. All the lights snap off" (*LTTA* 101).

The short declarative sentences that end McNally's stage direction add to the moment's pizzazz. We've been implicated in the problems of the characters. (Somebody in *Frankie and Johnny* had complained about "harsh, blinding light" [*Three Plays* 100].) *Their* story is *our* story, as it is in *Dedication*, where the players march up and down the aisles both to and from the stage. McNally is chipping away at the barrier between stage and house. Our being blinded by blazing light mimes the pressures squeezing his on-stage people.

The enticement of this theater isn't mental or intellectual as in that of Bertolt Brecht; McNally shirks politics. Instead of using alienation techniques that discourage emotional responses to a staged event, he sees theater as "very visceral.... To me you can feel it and taste it.... I want the theatre to shock me, startle me. But I don't want it to tell me what I should be thinking" (Savran 124). His two-minute, twelve-character virtuoso piece, "Hidden Agendas," enacts this credo. It comes from a character called the Last Subscriber, who's speaking at a performing arts center to both the center's chiefs and his fellow season ticket holders. Cutting to the chase, he calls any playwright's stock-in-trade "things that connect us and make us human. The hope for that connection! That's why we fill your theatres" (*15 Plays* 373). His words end the play because nobody responds to them. Perhaps nobody's listening. This disconnect wouldn't be unique. Some of the most heartfelt insights in Chekhov, one of McNally's favorite playwrights, also go ignored. The sweeping of the Last Subscriber's words into a void suggests the uphill fight to stage plays vital to the humanity of their audiences. In a rare Brechtian stroke, McNally has appealed to those watching "Hidden Agendas" to leave the theater debating both the value and the meaning of what they just watched.

This goal can be met; attention can be paid. McNally sabotages familiar modes of response to expand the theater's freedom. Both his extended torrents of sound and patches of glare challenge stage conventions. The same tumult that makes us wince, though, will put us in his hands. He's unfazed. He has accepted the responsibility. He also understands it. A line from *Whiskey* (1973), "Clothes are symbols, that's all they are" (*15 Plays* 176), reveals in him an ongoing, if indirect, awareness of Emersonian self-reliance. This allusion isn't unique. Emersonian emanations from the Oversoul drive Joshua's belief in *Corpus Christi* that Judas, no less than himself, qualifies as a Son of God (*CC* 51). Concord, Mass., visits Buffalo, New York, in *The Full Monty* when one of the men rehearsing a Chippendale-style dance routine is told to forget John Travolta and step it his own way (*FM* 22-3). This advice is sound. As Googie Gomez showed in *The Ritz*, any hoofer whose routine is lit from within deserves an audience. Keep it personal. Googie's creator learned his art and honed his craft by listening to himself. That creator affirmed to Toby Silverman Zinman, "I keep saying to myself, write what you want to write" (Zinman, "Interview," Zinman, *Casebook* 11).

What he wants to write is plays. He said in 1991, "I think playwriting is the most exciting way to write, to explain what it means to be alive and human" (DiGaetani 227). The theater's uniqueness, he would add in 2003, stems from its distinctiveness as an art form: "The glory of the theater is also its bane: you have to be there to experience it," he said while introducing *A Man of No Importance* (n.p.). Any stage performance is lost for good after final curtain. The grandeur of that loss is its magic, and also, as McNally said, its poignancy. His Introduction to *Man* goes on to call the theater "transitory, unpredictable, and, finally, quite wonderful" (*ibid.*). A tourist in *Full Frontal Nudity* (2004) might be thinking of this evanescence when he says, "Everything is hanging by a thread when you get down to it. Everything" (*SS* 35). *Dedication* applies these words to the drama. Though the play's Lou Nuncle sees theater as therapeutic and redemptive, he's always aware of its evanescence: "It's so wonderful.... And always the curtain will fall, the story will have ended, and we actors will take our bows. Houselights up! It's over. We can all go home now."

But, he adds, "something has changed.... You will go back to your real world and it will still be raw and painful, but maybe a little less so because of what you have seen here today. Harmony and happiness were possible" (*D* 20). The premium McNally puts on drama's ability to create community includes the audience. The "fellow humans" (*ibid.*) who witness a successful stage production help concoct the enchantment unique to live theater. This energy transference makes the theater superior to the movies. Live theater to McNally is "an enormous and seemingly never-ending collaborative process." ("A Few Words of Introduction," *Three Plays*, vii). This is how he wants it. A good thing for him, too; neither he nor any other playwright can change it. Plays need actors, producers, directors, and stage designers to impart "color and movement and life" (Preface, *15 Short Plays* 4). Without their combined efforts, a play-script is a mere gathering of pages, flat paper membranes that haven't started to breathe. But once they do breathe, they can also take on thrilling, memorable life. When Maria Malibran of *The Golden Age* returns backstage after singing the mad song from Bellini's *I Puritani*, she hears from the composer, "It wasn't great music when you sang it. It was something deeper" (*GA* 55). We're back in the realm of creative collaboration, if we ever left it. Besides forcing a composer or a playwright to work at top form, a good stage performer can alchemize the score or script she was given to work with.

Such alchemy delights McNally. Joining his energies with those of theater artists of different skills, training, and backgrounds provides him a chance to improve plays he spent many lonely hours scripting. Improve, not re-script; his plays, he believes, give his actors all they need to create compelling drama. They needn't improvise. An actress should reveal the "inner truth" of Blanche DuBois (Zinman, "Interview," Zinman, ed., *Casebook* 7), not her own. But she's not chained to a script; if she finds nuances and shadings in Blanche's personality consistent with Williams's script, her findings could become stage-worthy.

McNally welcomes such inventiveness during rehearsals. This bonhomie shows again that he chose the right line of work for himself. Every step in the long slog from roughing out a script to seeing its premiere delights him: "I have never felt more alive than when I'm in rehearsal, and I am happy to be working with some great colleagues" (Raymond 68), he said in 2005. Delight elevates all work. The playgoer who recovers from the noise and glare that pelt him at opening curtain will rejoice in McNally's treatment of matters irreparable and inescapable. Folding bawdiness into grief, for instance, doesn't improve things, but the refreshing new light it sheds on life's sludge makes it easier for us to plod through it. The trick lies in re-booting dismay to a pitch of healthy fun, as in the finales of *The Ritz* and *It's Only a Play*, where McNally's trademark blend of wit and intelligence shakes the rafters with laughs. What's more, the laughs are earned. His lifelong passion for opera, Shakespeare, and pop culture has leagued with the mechanics of stagecraft. The juncture is handled tactfully. Even though some people would disagree, this adversarial writer tempers his most visceral effects.

Another unlooked for bonus in the plays: a weakness for his people that warms and softens his work without letting it curdle into a sentimental fug. Nor does he collect oddballs and grotesques for comic relief; no caricaturist or quick-sketch artist, he. The bad guys in his work don't come from the power-hungry middle class, and the good aren't pushed to the margins, as can happen in Chekhov and William Inge. All have enough life in them to come before us without fanfare. McNally's model here is Shakespeare. What he prizes most in Shakespeare he calls "the non-judgmental quality.... Shakespeare just writes the people" (Zinman, "Interview," Zinman, ed., *Casebook* 14). He's democratic enough to have Macbeth mourn his wife's death and Othello confess to the murder of *his*. And it all happens naturally, as it would in real life.

This same freedom McNally extends to his *own* people, letting them be themselves; Zinman speaks of "the democracy of his plays" (*ibid.*). These people are ambiguous, unpredictable, and unafraid of contradicting themselves. The same Window Washer in *Witness* who says that "people stink" (*15 Plays* 120) goes tearful reading a letter his soldier-son mailed from Vietnam — McNally's broad-based humanity giving the letter emotional truth: "I'm so scared. But I'm defending the American way of life. Tell Mom I miss her and am coming home" (*ibid.*, 130). McNally has made us withhold judgment on the soldier's father, a WWII veteran with a leg full of shrapnel that wrecks his sleep. His ability to function has earned our respect along with his rage ("They took my Joey!" [*ibid.*]).

Such naked outbursts of pain are normal. McNally's representative stage character wages a daily fight with demons worse than those evoked by Thoreau's quiet desperation or Freud's common unhappiness. The Window Washer, for instance, tries to blame the growing loss of self-command that has been fraying his nerves on the government. McNally's Everyman *or* Everywoman figure (Maria Callas, was "as fucked up as anybody who ever lived" [Drukman 134]); Sam Truman of *LTTA* strikes macho poses to hide an inner beast that could spring to the surface at any moment:

> No one wants to listen to who we really are. Know you leave shit stains on your underwear and pick your nose.... Or how much you want to fuck the teenage daughter of the couple that lives three doors down [30].

Sam's sister Chloe keeps bringing food on and off stage, clad in different garb nearly every time; her own private trauma is keeping her on the go, lest she stay put and watch it chew her up.

McNally's awareness of devouring crises like hers and Sam's has led him to avoid gloating, lampooning, or sending his people into frenzies of violence. On this score, he stands closer to Chekhov than to Tennessee Williams. While Williams uses violence to swell or purge the anxieties seething inside his people, McNally, holding his strength in check, usually avoids such outbursts. In fact, as in Chekhov, this restraint is shown in his avoidance of melodrama.

Also like Chekhov, he goes light on his people. He extends kindness, even charity, to them by not asking too much from them. They often bear their burdens without needing his approval, too. Despite his wife Cora's complaints, Wilson of "Tour" quietly endures the heat, stench, and bugs swarming the Italian backwater they left the metropolis to tour (*Apple Pie* 6–13). The steadiness with which the twice-divorced Marion Cheever of "Next" (1967) fulfills his duties tempers the character flaws of this poster boy figure of Freud's *Civilizations and its Discontents*: "I visit my kids, I bring them presents; I visit my father, I bring him presents. I visit my sisters, their kids get presents, too. I pay my rent; I pay my alimony; I meet my car payments.... I do everything I'm supposed to do.... I'm never late for work (*15 Plays* 70).

If an army physical exam routs this overweight smoker of 48, it leaves McNally's respect for him intact. This generosity isn't uncommon. Respect, good will, and the suspension of judgment permeate the plays. It gets better. Even characters at odds with each other cool down quickly. Showing admirable moral balance, Stephen of *Lisbon Traviata* sees merit immediately in Paul, his presumptive rival for the love of Mike, Stephen's live-in boyfriend of eight years. He has judged well. There's plenty to respect, even esteem, in Paul, who spent two years in the Peace Corps working in the Congo and now waits tables while attending Columbia, intriguingly Stephen's alma mater, a coincidence that might have brought the best out of the two men. The love rivals even go so far as to joke with each other:

> STEPHEN: You're very sweet when you smile like that. I can see what Michael sees in you....
> PAUL: I can see what you saw in Mike....
> STEPHEN: What did I see in him?
> PAUL: I shouldn't have to tell you. He's a wonderful man. He's warm. He's generous. He's funny.
> STEPHEN: He's not that funny.
> PAUL: You're right [*Three Plays* 63].

Though Paul discreetly cuts off this discussion of Mike's virtues and failings, he does tell Stephen that Mike called him a "very good" editor (*ibid.*, 64). The two rivals won't defame each other. Mike joins them on this high ground. He and Paul have agreed to move in together. But rather than running down the odd-man-out Stephen, they set store by his words. When Mike says of him, "He's really a nice man," Paul tells him, "He spoke highly of you, too" (*ibid.*, 65). For all the chatter about McNally's anti-humanism, he likes people so much that he enjoys showing them liking each other.

Sex continues to forge bonds in the plays, even after its heat wanes. Perhaps like the Lawrence of *Sons and Lovers* (1913), McNally sees a magnetism binding men who have had sex with the same person. This magnetism also unites divorced couples. Mendy calls his ex-wife in *Lisbon Traviata* "one of my best friends" (*ibid.*, 32). Bernie of *Some Men* has been deceiving his Susan for the past three years, but he still winces when asked by a fellow gay, "Has it really been that much of an ordeal to fuck your wife these last ten years?" (*Two Plays* 2007, 37).

"Caterpillarer" changes the dynamic. This 1993 one-acter opens right after two people have just had sex. As in *Frankie and Johnny*, the people are in bed after (during, in *Frankie and Johnny*) their first go at sex together. But the stage lights reveal two men rather than a man and a woman. The sex, a one-night stand, was paid for. The bisexual rent boy Tim had agreed to come home with Tom for $100. The men's names have caught the eye, as did those of Frankie and Johnny, perhaps to infer a kinship between straight and gay sex — but perhaps also for a reason equally important to McNally. The names, Tim and Tom, have the same flat straightforwardness as David Foster Wallace's x and y in "Octet #6." These deadpan monosyllables might have been used to prod us to suspend disbelief prior to making an imaginative leap. Like any other creative writer, McNally both leaves his footprints behind him and tries, occasionally, to erase them.

Could the partly smudged, partly erased footprints in "Caterpillarer" belong to *both* the financially pinched college student Terrence McNally and his later incarnation as a successful playwright? In this play, as in *Some Men*, the hustler flubs his trick's name (*15 Plays* 356; *Two Plays* 2007, 11). Trick and hustler in *Some Men* both majored in English, the hustler, like McNally at his age, a Texan at Columbia who had "a fantastic high school English teacher" (*ibid.*, 12).

The autobiographical source of these patterns accounts for the deep slice they cut into "Caterpillarer." Frankie and Johnny will probably make love again, though McNally wisely keeps silent on the subject. The *Doppelgängers* Tom and Tim have had a one-night stand, and that's all. Just before the men part company, Tim says, "I don't have repeats. There are no repeats in this business" (*15 Plays* 360). His words define his recent transaction with Tom as a commercial one; money was paid for a service rendered. Tim even counts the money Tom gave him before leaving. It's clear why the men won't see each other again. After having agreed to stay the night, Tim announces his departure. He had already lied about having repeat customers, too. Needy and feeling bilked, Tom sounds off, as does Tim in a brief volley of accusations that are immediately regretted:

TIM: I think we all fail one another a lot lately. Male, female, straight, gay.
TOM: A pretentious hustler, just my luck.
TIM: A lonely faggot, so what else is new?
TOM: I'm sorry. I didn't mean that.
TIM: Neither do I [*ibid.*, 361].

Tom has no brief here. Tim gave him good service. Not only did he make sure that Tom had an orgasm; he also asked him if he wants help with another (*ibid.*, 356). He even advises him on his love life. But he shakes Tom's hand in parting rather than kissing him. He's right to do so. He and Tom aren't romantically linked. They also have qualms about having slept together. Tim is right when he says they won't see each other again; each has made the other feel cheap. Yet Tom feels hurt; some part of him expected more for his $100. It still does. The play's final event, his ripping Tim's business card into "a million little pieces" (*ibid.*) says hyperbolically that sex always has different meanings to its participants, both during and after its occurrence.

Tom has thrived. The building he lives in has a doorman. Besides being older than Tim, he also has more cash. Yet other differences between the two men suggest those between McNally himself as a college student and as a successful playwright. No pathetic hangdog queer, Tom. He finds women more emotionally available than men. Nor is he looking at them from a distance. His best friend is a woman. He has also enjoyed having sex, if not with her, then with at least another woman. The rarely performed five-minute playlet in which he appears bespeaks McNally's genius for building scenes of great difficulty with unforced precision. Beyond its flowing dialogue lies a genius for pushing scenes further than we had imagined possible.

Back-story and juxtaposition show him rejecting a simple, continuous, empirically describable stage reality. Like most artists, he's both radical and traditional — a traditionalist with radical ambitions. *The Full Monty*, for instance, finds him engaging with the poignant subject of a part-time father's love for his son. The out-of-work dad, having fallen behind in his child support payments, may lose his visitation rights with Nathan. Meanwhile, his estranged wife, though reluctant to stop the visits, is living with another, employed, man.

McNally has created several fascinating plot points. This 2000 adaptation of a 1996 film script does more than transpose words from the idiom and physical setting of England's industrial midlands to upstate New York. Besides hewing to realistic local rhythms, his Buffalo also fires his fascination with the macabre. A sickly woman dies when she learns that her over-protected bachelor son has joined a striptease act. How would she have reacted if she knew that, after her death, that same son paired off with another man? Now

McNally has always enjoyed black humor, sometimes of a very raw kind. Good storytelling, he has always known, animates a play. It can also take different forms. By steps, the line between victim and tormentor blurs in "Next"; part of the play's merit stems from both the ambiguity of McNally's attitude toward his people and his ironical treatment of them. It's not clear whose side he wants us to be on in this clean-lined, crisp-figured work. Sgt. Thech is off the scene during the play's ending—a monologue by Marion Cheever that exposes the failure of two vital sectors of American life to connect.

At 48, Marion shouldn't have been called to the recruiting office, to begin with, as Sgt. Thech knew at first glance. To his relief, the physical exam ends quickly. Wearing the sergeant's white examination coat, he speaks the play's last word, which is also its title, "NEXT" (*15 Plays* 81). A man with a name that could belong to a woman, he switches places with a butch woman who's doing work usually done by men. What is McNally aiming at? If Marion is only one person in a series to her, so is she to him, at least when he arrogates her power to himself. We can see why he made the switch. His life is so full of setbacks that his borrowed potency half-convinces him that he can banish them. The eventual bursting of this illusion will still leave intact a difference between him and Sgt. Thech that favors him. He can leave the recruiting office where *she* has to stay, examining the rafts of men the selective service, or draft board, mistakenly sent her. His taxes support a demeaning system that's both wasting her time and souring her nature.

"Next" (1967) marks the emergence of a major playwright. As it shows, McNally learned early in his game to avoid rushing to climaxes. Patience continued to benefit his work. The title character of *Whiskey*, the star of a popular television series, is just a scrawny nag, a truth withheld until five minutes before the play ends. *It's Only a Play* also steers Chekhov's device of the gun hanging on the wall to the animal world. Torch, allegedly a dog so ferocious that he's kept locked in the bathroom during the 1985 play, shows himself at final curtain as "an adorable beagle" (*Three Plays* 241). Such reversals can also color the beginning of a McNally play. After her off-stage delivery of her sonorous, menacing Message to the World in *Bump*, Ruby represents a "spectacular disappointment" (*TM II* 13) when she displays her aging humdrum face, her bitten nails, and her dirty feet. These defects have a purpose. The difference between her tacky looks and her thrilling words draw us into the action—and perhaps remind us, too, that the paranoid Stalin stood less than five-four and that he might have murdered his wife. If McNally is looking at Alfred Adler's doctrine of masculine protest, he'd be giving this established cultural and literary fixture an intriguing twist by applying it to Ruby.

Ending a play is another of his strengths; he knows how to temper a play's tempo and drive. *Master Class* conveys his ability to use a scrap of everyday minutiae to slow what looks like a big finish-in-the-making. Just before her student begins singing the stirring "Letter Scene" from Verdi's *Macbetto*, minutes before the play's ending, Maria has, apropos of nothing happening on stage, an amusing loss of focus — unless she has always been sidetracked from the master class she has been giving: "Does anyone know what time it is? I have a beauty parlor appointment after this. I can't get a good wash and set in this city" (*MC* 55). McNally's eye for the perfectly illustrative yet totally surprising detail can leap forth at any time. Joshua is asked in *Corpus Christi* by a fisherman how he hopes to live without money. His answer, "I don't know. The kindness of strangers?" (39), should send the house into gales of laughter, not least because the author of the great phrase, like Josh, was gay. Why stop here? Early in Act One of *Tommy Flowers* (1971), the play's eponym recites a long list of pop-culture figures including "Roy Rogers and Dale Evans, Johnny Weissmuller; Johnny Sheffield; Esther Williams; Joe DiMaggio; Pee Wee Reese; Jackie Robinson; Ralph Bunche; Trygve Lie" (II 82). The catalogs of colorful details in McNally's mature work show more inventiveness. Cameos of comic ingenuity, the following details from *Deuce* (2007) knit satisfyingly in a weft of complex plotting and self-begetting ironies:

> LEONA: All these names! Margaret Osborne. We liked her. Margaret Court. Maureen Connolly. Midge, here's Little Mo's autograph.
> AUTOGRAPH SEEKER: She wrote "Maureen Connolly a.k.a. Killer Connolly." Was she a killer?
> MIDGE: "Killer" was the press's name for her. When she got really serious about her game, they turned on her. They liked her more when she was "Little Mo" — all girlish tears and teenage giggles. In her day, it was unfeminine to win so consecutively [*Two Plays* 2007, 137].

Most of McNally's poetic effects, like irony, spring from the sidewalks of his hometown. His Manhattan resembles Woody Allen's. It's a place of heartache and fear, hopes and joys, energized by Gershwin's *Concerto in F* and *Rhapsody in Blue*. His cosmopolitan swagger combines intellectual rigor with a painstaking observation of his physical surroundings. *The Ritz* and *It's Only a Play* convey the sparkle and pungency of city life along with its arrogance and greed. Thanks to his keen ear for urban pretense, self-promotion, and the sexually touristic life style often affected by the theater crowd, these early works remind us that there's no provincialism as barefaced as that of the urbanite who lacks urbanity.

The sharpness and immediacy of McNally's details create some of the canon's most accomplished, emotional, and hair-raising spells, such as when John Haddock, in a passage of dramatic monologue in *LTTA*, lets on that he has cancer (17). The careful placement of the monologue early in the first act sheds light on his recent — and, as Sally's lover, past — behavior. It also sets it forth in a voice different from the conversational one that moves the rest of the play.

Though different in mood, Maria Callas's monologues convey this same careful word choice and prose rhythms. Her staccato sentences display her confidence in the integrity, power, and beauty of her métier, operatic singing. Those longer, moodier passages devoted to her inner life, which are laced by reminiscences, regrets, and humor, unfurl in long, cartwheeling sentences. In both cases, the language reaches beyond itself. McNally said in 1985, "Plays are about what people *do*, not what they say" (Guernsey, ed. 288). His belief in the centricity of this idea to stage art has stayed with him. He insisted eleven years later: "It's the hardest thing to get through our heads: *playwriting is recording behavior, not dialogue*" (Drukman 337). His people both attack and protect each other. Sometimes, as in Harold Pinter, their words are ruses or stratagems put in place to cover their nakedness. Nearly everything Sam says in *LTTA* refers to the firestorm caused by his belief that his wife and brother-in-law are having sex.

II

McNally said of himself, while leading a panel discussion of Arthur Laurents's *Gypsy*, that he was "terribly conscious of style and tone and consistency" (Guernsey, ed. 73). His discovery of the dynamism welding style, tone, and theme came slowly to him. His first plays included, for instance, superlatives he would later get rid of. The roller rink that sites the action of *The Rink* is "*the most magical, romantic place imaginable*" (10). Then a young skater in this 1985 play lifts a girl above his head in "*the most graceful adagio imaginable*" (12). Even Swiftian catalogs like the following one from *Bump* would vanish from the work: "those magic names: Paris, Rome Vienna, London, Bayreuth, Peiping, Manila, Camden, New Jersey" (II 46). Is this last, bizarre reference to Walt Whitman's home town McNally's cue to us that his catalog is Whitmanesque as well as Swiftian, which would make its impetus both American *and* homosexual? The gays and straights of *LTTA* will celebrate the 4th of July from adjoining houses, the revels of the gays more enthusiastic and spontaneous. These revels spark a conundrum. The reticence of the Trumans and the Haddocks makes them both *less* and, because of its link with the discipline marking Protestant America's work ethic, *more* American than their neighbors.

Characters play word games in *Bump*, McNally's 1964 Broadway debut, chasing around words like vapors, vespers, and vipers (*ibid.*, 14–5). The games would be more accomplished in *Prelude and Liebestod* (1989), when the Conductor, referring to his unfaithful wife, gives the same word three different meanings in four rapid-fire sentences: "She's right up there in a box. She's always right up there in a box. I'd like to see her in a box. It's her box I'm sick of" (*SS* 47). Nathan Lane had it right when he said of McNally,"[H]e likes words" (Zinman, "Interview with Nathan Lane," Zinman, ed. *Casebook* 90). Now we know why the efforts of the two men have chimed so well. In his own interview with Toby Silverman Zinman, McNally said, "I respond to an actor like Nathan — he relishes each word — so many actors don't delight in language" (*ibid.*, 9).

McNally's people show the same admirable sensitivity to words — their rise and fall, their texture, their meaning. Language counts with them. They believe that people should be aware of what they say and how they say it. Ex-tennis star Midge Barker speaks for them in *Deuce* when she says, "Words matter" (*Two Plays* 2007, 161). *Frankie and Johnny*, which was produced 20 years earlier, contained a lot of talk about talk. Johnny complains, "It's getting to the point where you can count on one hand the number of people who speak English in this city," adding, after admitting that he's a chatterbox himself, "I'm locking up my mouth and throwing away the key" (*Three Plays* 100–101). Frankie, who unlike Johnny, hasn't read Shakespeare, notes of his frequent practice of saying, "Pardon my French": "The first time you said it tonight I practically told you I had a headache and had to go home" (*ibid.*, 116).

Later, Johnny parries this dig with one of his own, which targets the idea that people should be responsible for their language: "I never thought I could be in love with a woman who said, 'barking up the wrong tree'" (*ibid.*, 181). And so it goes. A man in *Unusual Acts of Devotion* (2008) tells his wife of five years, "I can't believe I married a woman who says, 'Oh fudge'" (McNally typescript 8 May 2009, 15). But McNally also knows that love, once declared, precludes such judgments. Johnny's repeating of Frankie's phrase, which he knows falls short of the best-spoken English, "in that department" (*Three Plays* 133–4), confirms his joy in being close to her.

The Lisbon Traviata uses spoken gaffes thematically. Stephen, is called by Mendy, "an editor with a lot of influence in a major publishing house" (*Three Plays* 14). Later, he voices the shakiness of his future with Mike, with the phrase, "With Mike and I." In case we missed the flub, Mendy snaps back, "Mike and me. I can't believe you edit for a living" (*ibid.*, 23). His comeback tallies with the play's subtext. Following the example of Ben Butley in Simon Gray's 1971 play, Stephen's fears over losing Mike have led him to misspeak. Mike's later telling Stephen, "I haven't been your lover for a long time" (*ibid.*, 77), harks to Ben's withholding of sex from *both* his former lover and his wife — a lapse that sparks the defection of both to other men. Stephen's having turned 40 might have also derailed his sex drive. And if Ben's neglect of his students, colleagues, and department head is threatening his job security, Stephen, though no alcoholic, stands just as close to getting fired. Not only does his grammatical slip with Mendy signal a loss of concentration on the job. He's also very late revising a manuscript for a client (*ibid.*, 52), and, with the same fecklessness, he's planning to miss work for the third time in a month (*ibid.*, 75).

The Lisbon Traviata was written with McNally's routine readable flow, a virtue that, ironically, can distract from the excellence of his prose. The straightforward deployment of his sentences can hide both their unfussy elegance and their wit. It all looks so deceptively easy. His fluent, intelligent dialogue builds scenes that don't call attention to themselves. His well-judged restraint almost makes his Albee-like concentrated energy invisibly elegant. The artistry passes unnoticed, as it does with the best artists. Only slightly more visible is the ability of his prose to register function and meaning, rhythm and design, all at once. This know-how brings more rewards. His audiences will smile inwardly or sigh in recognition at certain lines. These lines deliver laughs, not merely because they're funny, but, because we identify with them. They hold a shared secret. The fusion of hurt and hostility that's clawing Sam Truman's nerves in *LTTA* feels familiar to many of us.

By being plainspoken enough not to smudge a play's total effect, McNally's precise, carefully weighed prose makes for an ideal dramatic style. His urbanity captures the rhythms and inflections of cultivated American English, an unadorned quality that's more than stylistic. It's the psychological truth of flatness. He has put to good use the skills he has been honing over the years — having his characters speak in a conversational style neither pseudo-quaint nor jarringly contemporary.

It's vital that he has resisted the lure to foist on his people conspicuously modern sensibilities. He writes so well and with such economy that he can call up the poet's precise match. His dialogue is fresh and clean, the length of the sentences stretched or tightened at just the right time. What all this points to is his mastery of the elliptical bank shot of information delivery. The sharp focus of his shorter passages of dialogue accounts for prose that's exacting, buoyant, and snappy. These passages he varies with longer ones that have a force, color, and music of their own. Repetitions, pauses, hesitations, and changes of direction in the longer sentences add depth, light, or shade. As in O'Neill's *Strange Interlude*, this eloquence often comes in internal monologues not intended for other characters to hear. It works beautifully. So sure is McNally's hand that the ongoing stage action will mingle noiselessly polyphony with plainsong.

Vital here is his ability to deflect emotion with laughs. The start of Act Two of *It's Only a Play* shows a group of people fighting each other over a copy of the *New York Times*, a commonplace item produced in the hundreds of thousands — every one of which contain a review of the play the people have a stake in. McNally can also pack a lot of feeling in a throwaway line, as in Act Two of *The Lisbon Traviata*, where Stephen has barged in on Mike's rendezvous with Paul. All three men are in shock. Under the snap and sizzle of their conversation lies a shared remorse. Mood is key. Energizing the careful scene-shifting and verbal jousting in the transition from Act One is McNally's trademark knack for pushing matters further than we'd have thought possible.

Every time Mike stops the CD player to make himself heard, Stephen doesn't just turn it back on; he also raises the volume. A dazed Paul has watched the physician Mike hit Stephen twice, the second time knocking him down and drawing blood. A dismayed and remorseful Mike wants to help Stephen recover from the battering. But, torn in another direction, having just had sex with Paul, he wants to go home with him, too. It's here that Stephen, seeking refuge from pain, says out of a bleeding face, "If this is your idea of safe sex, I don't like it" (*Three Plays* 67). Nothing more on the subject need be said, partly because McNally has judged correctly, like the three men on stage, that we, too, need a break from the passions being staged.

His ability to sense how much an audience can take keeps scoring him points. An irreverent one-liner that shocks us by being so unexpected, unapologetic, and direct smartens the action of *Some Men* during a conversation between two men who have just made love on a beachfront:

PADRIAC: You think all Irishmen are queer? It's against our religion.
DAVID: It's against all religions.
PADRIAC: Feck all they know about it. The first man who put his hand on my cock was a priest.
DAVID: What did you do?
PADRIAC: Nothing, I loved it [*Two Plays* 2007, 21].

Again in the battleground of sex, a woman in *The Rink*, having been abandoned by her husband and daughter, consults a priest for guidance. McNally's word choice and ear are both so sharp that they suggest with a few remarks the futility of a life:

ANNA: Bless me, Father. I have sinned... You gotta help me. I'm having trouble being alone, Father. Alone as a woman, you know?
PRIEST: It's His will, Mrs. Antonelli.
ANNA: I'm not talking about His will. I'm talking about my feelings.

> PRIEST: For your penance, say a Rosary and ask Him for guidance.
> (*He disappears*.)
> ANNA: You say a Rosary. And tell Him I don't like His rules [69–70].

Brief though it is, the passage shows that McNally's people have depths, his scenes, drama, and his sentences, rhythm and precision. He can also hold forth convincingly on any number of subjects, both topical and offbeat, like the subculture of New York's gay baths in *The Ritz* and *Some Men*, the history of tennis in *Deuce*, and the opera in *The Lisbon Traviata* (1989), *Master Class* (1997), and *The Golden Age* (2010) without sounding campy, cryptic, or over-the-top. His 1968 playlet, "Botticelli," joins the snazzy pop-anthropology of Tom Wolfe to an enduring concern about the importance of people connecting. The action unfolds in Vietnam, which is also where the sons of characters in *Witness* and *Tour* are deployed and where GIs in *Bringing It All Back Home* and *Andre's Mother* die in combat.

Two American soldiers are playing a highbrow version of Botticelli, citing Proust, Pushkin, and Dumas *père* on the play's first page (*15 Plays* 53). The men are passing the time in the jungle awaiting the appearance, from his hiding place, of a Viet Cong soldier whom they've cornered and have orders to shoot. Shoot and kill their frightened, emaciated quarry they do — with "a seemingly endless volley of gunfire" (*ibid.*, 59). Neither the learning nor the powerful memories that helped them play Botticelli at such a grand level (other citations in their game include the playwrights Sir Arthur Wing Pinero and Luigi Pirandello [*ibid.*, 55]) have staunched their blood lust. And neither has it, in Eugène Ionesco's telling phrase, taught them how to avoid being victims of duty.

Another of McNally's gifts that improve the plays is the delayed exposition, or the piecemeal revelation of character, i.e., holding back information about a character rather than disgorging it in one lump. *Unusual Acts of Devotion*, a middle- or lower-middle class apartment drama, generates the same big-city poignancy, tension, and fun as two earlier New York City plays, Elmer Rice's *Street Scene* (1929) and Clifford Odets's *Awake and Sing* (1935). It's only on page 69, and pages 72 and 73, that we learn that one of the people in the 93-page typescript is a former English teacher who got fired for sleeping with her seventeen-year-old student. On page 80, a straight, married father-to-be who once slept with his ex-teacher-neighbor announces that he has also gone to bed with four men. The benefits of withholding this data? McNally first commits us to his people to stop us from judging them too one-sidedly; he maintains the evenness of both the pace and the texture of his play; he avoids arbitrariness and artificiality, since in few places outside of Victorian novels is everything revealed about people at first meeting.

Though McNally may have learned the benefits of delayed exposition from the Tennessee Williams of *Streetcar* (1947), a clearer influence on him, as Howard Stein ("The Early Plays of Terence McNally," Zinman, ed. *Casebook* 22) and others have shown, is Edward Albee. This influence has persisted. As in Albee's early work, people in McNally's fledgling *Roller Coaster* (46) and *Bump* (*TM II* 37) will speak in capital letters when they shout. The stock figure of the castrating female from Albee's *Sandbox* (1959), *American Dream* (1960), and *Who's Afraid of Virginia Woolf* (1962) also shows up often. She's only thirteen in *Roller Coaster*, a play, like *Zoo Story*, about two strangers from different walks of life who meet by chance in a public place. And just as young Gertie's pea-shooter hits the middle-aged Rudolph in the eye (55) after she gooses him with it (48), so will the toy dart of Lakme, from *Bump*, who's also thirteen, pelt her grandfather, who reprises the wise, but helpless, Grandma in *Sandbox* and *American Dream*. Albee's fingerprints appear often in McNally's early work. The two-person format of *Zoo Story* (1959) returns in "Sweet Eros," "Botticelli," and "Next."

Albee's influence even extends to the late *Dedication*, where a woman, like Jerry of *Zoo Story*, talks about poisoning a neighbor's dog (*D* 29). Also in this 2004 gem, the truth is described as a difficult, dangerous thing that must be approached indirectly as in *Zoo Story*, where Jerry says famously, "[S]ometimes it's necessary to go a long distance out of the way in order to come back a short distance correctly" (Albee 30).

This echo, though worth noting, also looks like an anomaly or a private joke. As the years have made Albee more of an absorbed than an applied influence, McNally writes more confidently from within himself. He has found his own voice or song. His belief that his scripts give actors all they need sounds like Maria's advice to a student who's getting ready to sing an aria from *Macbetto*: "It's all in the music.... It's always in the music, Sharon. Don't look at me for help. Listen to Verdi. Listen to Shakespeare" (*MC* 53). McNally has written plays for Kathy Bates, F. Murray Abraham, and Nathan Lane because he knew that these actors could carry out his imaginative intent. That intent always came first. Lane said about teaming up with McNally, "Part of what he values in your work is your perfect adherence to his lines," adding, "It's very demanding ... but also very challenging, very exciting" (Toby Silverman Zinman, "Interview with Nathan Lane," Zinman, ed. *Casebook* 91–2)

This means that perhaps McNally's theater is truly collaborative; his dramatic ideal consists of setting up a creative tension with his actors that will elevate his road map or blueprint of a play into art; "Good actors force me to write as honestly as I can," he said in 1994 (Preface, *15 Plays* 4). He crafts a matrix in which the actors can vent their creativity. He introduces his characters in *Whiskey*, for instance, in terms redolent of George Bernard Shaw, interpreting their conduct while describing them physically, but avoiding Shaw's philosophical treatises and jokes: "SOUTHERN COMFORT: Early twenties, red hair and built. She's wild and sexy and arrogant and flaunts her sexuality and drinks a lot and gets like a cat in heat and just generally behaves like a bundle of dynamite" (*15 Plays* 140). Such introductions pilot actors without shackling them. McNally avoids dogmatizing elsewhere, too, as is seen in a stage direction in *It's Only a Play*, where he makes a recommendation to the director while also relying on his discretion: "*Perhaps a wild howl escapes from him* [a character] *at this point, perhaps not*" (*Three Plays* 211).

The director may be aiming at his own effects, and McNally is suggesting ways to achieve them without wrenching the text. He'll also create opportunities by supervising technical matters like lighting, costume and set design, and blocking. And, as is seen in the Property List and Sound Effects that appears at the end of *Dedication* (*D* 64–65), which includes items like a wind machine, a kit kat bar, and a mop (a comparable inventory in *The Rink* runs thirteen pages [93–105]), he'll skimp no detail to give a play its best chance to succeed.

Much has been said by him and others about the importance of dance and opera in his work. Without disputing these words, let us add that he has also, over the decades, lightened or darkened his palette in order to channel his emotions. His genius for matching brushstroke to surface doesn't only enrich his plays. It also shows that mastery of color, line, and composition counts as much on a stage as it does in painting.

Chapter Three

Confusions of the Heart

McNally's early work features many recurring elements: the Vietnamese war of "Botticelli" (1968), "Witness" (1968), and *Bringing It All Back Home* (1969); in *Some Men* (2007), it's updated as the Iraqi war. And even though many of the fledgling plays differ from each other in setting, atmosphere, and tone, most of them reflect the same sardonic, anti-bourgeois mindset that favors disassociation over harmony, coherence, and the other standbys of liberal humanism.

This incivility invokes the political theatrics and angry individualism of Beat Generation writers like Jack Kerouac (1922–69) and Alan Ginsberg (1925–97), English majors at Columbia University before McNally. But in a surprise you might not have been ready for, the fiery rhetoric of Kerouac, Ginsberg, and early McNally conjures up the right-wing Tea Party movement from 2010. Protest groups both, the Tea Partiers and the Beats, equally at odds with the liberals of their times, denounced governmental authority, specifically its power to shape and direct lives. But whereas the Tea Partiers want to supplant government with religion, the Beats found inspiration in hallucinogens and Zen meditation.

The dazed protagonists of McNally's early work, though, stand outside the world they live in. What's more, they lack options. Attacks upon America's military-industrial complex that might comfort them cause regret and even panic instead. The roller coaster standing in "a deserted amusement park" (42) in *Roller Coaster* (1960) attracts grotesques, made all the more chilling by their youth, who prey on the odd adult passer-by. The rink in *The Rink* (1985), a place of fun that has fallen into decay, awaits the wrecking ball. A more vital American institution that comes under threat in McNally's early work is the family. The threat takes on stunning force in the early anti-war play, *Bringing It All Back Home*. Though the play's title refers to the corpse of a GI named Jimmy, it also targets all those forces that brought Jimmy down. These come under scrutiny right away. That the dead soldier is the only member of his family who's named in the play's cast of characters implies the tragic waste of Jimmy's death.

But death doesn't have the last word in the play. Though dead, Jimmy lives more vibrantly than all his survivors. This oddity harks to the unrealistic theater of Albee's *Sandbox* and *American Dream*, in which characters named Mommy and Daddy depict what's wrong with the American family. And like the pushy social worker, Mrs. Barker, of *American Dream*, a television announcer called Miss Horne who visits Jimmy's family in *Bringing It* lacks a first name. She doesn't need one. Even a half-person can expose the tatters and shreds the American family had fallen into. Miss Horne doesn't horn in on the family's grief because there's no grief to horn in on. When she asks, "It seems then that your life has been relatively unaffected by Jimmy's death?" Jimmy's mother replies, "Jimmy was as American as apple pie" (*15 Plays* 18). She's so unmoved that she can only answer with a cliché.

Her amorality refers to the play's title; all of the falsehoods that combined to kill Jimmy began at home. Each of his family members has a different explanation for his death, none of which refers to him personally or suggests tears. That of the Daughter, his sister, has a disturbing Kafkaesque ring: "Don't you study civics? If people like Jimmy don't die for the American way of life, there won't *be* an American way of life" (*ibid.*, 19). His mother, after getting warmed up, prizes his death as proof of his patriotism; to her being American means being dead: "My son died an American! Mothers of the World, may you live to see the day when your sons die American!" (*ibid.*) (Obviously, she missed the similarity between her words, "Mothers of the World," and Marx's "Workers of the World," Jimmy having died fighting, in North Vietnam, America's Marxist enemy.) The Son uses his brother's death as a self-promoting media event. Neither he nor his sister can wait to flaunt their new prominence before their friends.

Neither they nor their parents have learned anything, either. But what *could* they have learned? So little did they care about Jimmy when he was alive that none of them remembers his height or his hair or eye color. They care only about themselves. Both parents accuse Miss Horne of lying when she says that Jimmy suffered horribly for an hour before passing out with pain; they don't want their pride jarred by anything as problematic as suffering. Nor has it occurred to either of them that he died without leaving any progeny. This is a national tragedy. As in Arthur Miller's *All My Sons* (1944), what takes place in American homes and factories tally with deaths that occur in theaters of war thousands of miles away.

The Father is the worst offender. The manhood he preens himself on, he defines collectively, afraid to look at his inner blankness. Its embodiment is his bowling team, "a bunch of ... real men, regular guys, drinking beer, horsing around" (*ibid.*, 10). Yet this cigar-chomping sneak engages in phone sex behind his wife's back and keeps calling his daughter "peaches" (*ibid.*, 11), after one of the most succulent of table fruits. His practice of patting her rump (e.g., *ibid.*) reflects his awareness of this likeness and his implication in it. His fixation on Suzy and her rump has deflected his attention from his other kids. In a riff that works on at least two thematic levels, the Father misnames Jimmy (*ibid.*, 13), an insult that invokes once again the difficulty of distinguishing between the living and the dead in America. To clinch this point, the speech Jimmy gives after rising from his coffin has more spark and vim than anything mouthed by his survivors.

The timing of this speech is important. Jimmy rises from his coffin or crate to speak right after hearing some words from his self-proclaimed "virility nut" (*ibid.*, 19) of a father. That father's peers in works like *Witness* and *LTTA* escape the harpooning he gets here. The Father shrugs off Jimmy's death. But despite telling Miss Horne, "Well, you know, life continues" (*ibid.*, 18), he *has* been deeply rocked. No sooner do his doubts about his masculinity surface than they begin pounding him. It's almost as if he had been viewing his son as both a threat and a rival he's glad to see out of the way: "Thank God for the army," he says, adding, "It really straightens these boys out" (*ibid.*, 19).

In Jimmy's case, he's right. The army stiffened his son into a corpse. The Pentagon has dreamt up a zero-sum game. Despite lacking the manliness of the combat soldier, the Father still lives, but barely. He's one of the reasons Jimmy left home to join the army. In addition to his other failings, he drinks too much, just as his shopping-addicted wife pops pills. Their joint failure to set boundaries for Jimmy's sibs (the 15-year-old daughter has already had an abortion; her brother of 13 smokes pot) bodes ill in the manner of Albee's Mommy and Daddy. These dregs of Tom Brokaw's "Greatest Generation" have stumbled. They've failed to pass any values to their kids because they have none worth passing on. In an echo of one of McNally's favorite plays, Ibsen's *Wild Duck* (Zinman, Interview, Zinman, ed. *Casebook* 14), sorrow hasn't joined them, either. Miss Horne, the TV interviewer, leaves them after having discussed with them a loss they never felt. Then they scatter. Nothing keeps them together besides the Father's erotic fixation on the Daughter.

Family dysfunction had also drenched McNally's first Broadway play, *And Things That Go Bump in the Night*. This 1964 work, though, dwells more on politics than did *Bringing It*. Recalling Kafka's *The Trial*, with its vision of a surreal, victimizing bureaucracy, it unfolds in a garrison state that has been undoing the very principles and beliefs most prized by its American subjects. The political background of this deep probe, the strongest part of the play because it's also the most carefully nuanced, invokes the centralization, hierarchy, and secrecy of Leninist politics. In the background, barely hinted at, are broken highways, collapsing bridges, failed schools, bankrupt cities, and unemployment. (The impact of this devastation upon McNally might have prompted him, decades later in 2001 to script a musical version of Friedrich Dürrenmatt's *The Visit* [1956], a play that foregrounds the same urban distress.) Curfews have been imposed. But this constraint falls short of the ones the public has inflicted upon itself. The family members who drive the action have aggravated it, rarely leaving the property they've surrounded with an electrified fence. The one non-householder in the play, who had marched in a protest rally earlier in the day the action unfolds, kills himself by accidentally stumbling into it.

The melancholy and futility pervading *Bump* also organizes the torrent of rhetoric leading to Clarence's death. This tension makes the play's counterintuitiveness all the more abrasive, owing to its context. *Bump* opened the same year as the British musical invasion. Both the Beatles and the Rolling Stones broke big in 1964 America. They also sped great cultural shifts, viz, the growth of a youth culture, the civil rights movement, and some early antiwar protests. *Bump* conveys but little of the hope driving this surge. Nor does the play nurse a class grievance expressive of its day. Its author's imagination is more scenic than it is panoramic. Like Chekhov, McNally finds meaning in the small things, not the big questions. Despite being strange, confused, and overambitious, *Bump* provides a frightening picture of life out of apparently trivial minutiae. Its people don't come before us in open fields, public squares, or meeting halls. Instead, they reveal themselves in small private acts performed in the company of intimates. They concretize and thus expand our experience of life. "I'm not interested in the overview. What I'm interested in is the small moment — I think there's enormous drama in that" (*ibid.*, 14–15), said McNally famously in 1994.

He spoke home. Most of his people are struggling to find equilibrium, an effort that means the most when carried out close to home, as in *The Rink* and *Unusual Acts of Devotion*. McNally follows Chekhov in denying his people religious or political causes they can flee to rather than grounding themselves in nearest things. But their tactile engagement with the details of living and being extends only so far. Chekhov's people rarely collide, and they only face their emptiness briefly and obliquely, if at all. The influence upon McNally of Edward Albee's compacted energy rules out the slow romantic decline of Mme. Ranevsky of *The Cherry Orchard*,

That said, there's a rootless metaphysical barrenness to McNally's people that *feels* Chekhovian. But it's more desperate, urgent, and less recognizably common because it's often conditioned, if not directly caused, by homosexuality. This template explains much of what goes on in *Roller Coaster*, *Door*, *Bump*, and *Tommy Flowers*, all of which McNally wrote between 1960 and 1971. The leading roles in these works share important traits. Despite ranging in age from 13 to 40 or so (in *Bump*), each of them disavows intellect and reason in favor of the call of raw instinct. Wanting to be great, not good, they seek power rather than contentment. Their quests ends, though, with them feeling stumped; life has withheld from them both catharsis and salvation. They live in small cramped spaces. Where they'll stay; their indifference to the goals of economic growth, full employment, and the health of democratic institutions has left them staring at their own anger and impotence.

The twisted logic of the world has further polluted whatever scraps of calm, judicious thought they're able to muster. In their Hobbesian world, a person's well-being often requires the suffering of another. Even in *The Rink*, the work that begins McNally's middle period, a man's survival depends upon his leaving an adoring, needful wife. Society has grown claws. Survival in it means self-protection, and protecting yourself means being ready to sink your wife, parent, or neighbor.

Aggravating this menace in McNally's early plays, as always, is the way his people speak. Given his acute awareness of words (Zinman, "Interview with Nathan Lane," Zinman, ed. 90), his reversals of traditional speech patterns in *Roller Coaster*, *Bump*, and "Tour" can only be deliberate. The linearity of patriarchal speech, it has long been said, trivializes feeling. The aggressive, self-authorizing talk of the Father in *Bringing It* typifies this reductiveness. In McNally, as in life, speech reflects people's values. Whereas men usually base their moral decisions on justice, those of women stress relationships, i.e., organisms built on selflessness, openness, and reciprocity. The accommodating, non-linear, non-assertive female speech that abets good bonding barely exists in McNally's early work. Logically enough, the females in these plays rarely provide warmth or support.

McNally reverses the archetype of woman as comforter as early as *Roller Coaster* (1960). Thirteen-year-old Gerty, one of the play's two characters, outdoes in precocity those other notable tomboys of mid-century American literature, Frankie of Carson McCullers's *Member of the Wedding* (1946) and Scout of Harper Lee's *To Kill a Mockingbird* (1960). Straightaway, she shoots Rudolph Alexander in the eye with her pea-shooter. The Oedipal stakes rise quickly. The polite middle-aged Rudolph's attempt to take the pea-shooter from her ends with her stuffing it provocatively in the crotch of her blue jeans. Rudolph's de-manning speeds ahead. After goosing him with her phallic pea-shooter, she steals his wallet and knocks him down. Then, having ascended the roller coaster, she tricks him into thinking that she has jumped to her death — pointedly, the same way the kings of antiquity would die when they felt the need to surrender their thrones. This child who claps Rudolph's hand to her breasts and threatens to "rip ... [his] balls off" (*RC* 51) has made the annihilation of maleness a necessity of survival. She's in the grip of an adolescent power fantasy.

But where has this urgency left her? Rudolph dies, as will the soft-spoken Clarence of *Bump*. The butch army examiner of "Next" (1967), Sgt. Thech, jabs Marion Cheever with a needle to draw his blood. She keeps the initiative ("the government doesn't make mistakes" [*15 Plays* 63]). Self-confidence marks her speech throughout. When she's not barking out orders ("Lie down" [*ibid.*, 91]; "Drop your shorts" [*ibid.*, 72]), she's humiliating Marion with intimate personal questions, viz., "[A]ny history of bed-wetting?" and "Have you indulged in homosexual activities?" (*ibid.*, 78). Her invasions of his privacy, though sanctioned by the federal government, join her to Gerty and Ruby, the female destroyer of *Bump*. She decides whether the men she examines are fit for military duty and, perforce, deployment in Vietnam, where they could die in combat. She's also a victim. Although the process differs, she's caught in the same deathly cycle as Ruby and Gerty. The more men she approves for active duty, the higher the body count in Vietnam.

I

Hebe, the mother in *This Side of the Door* (1962), *is* deferential and accommodating in her speech; she *can* provide warmth, support, and comfort, too. Most of her time on stage is spent calming her nerve-raked 13-year-old son, Edmund. She has anxieties of her own that need calming. She tries to maneuver her "tall, stocky" (3) husband into bed to distract him from the bottle. Though Henderson Hobart is always drunk when he appears on stage, the play featuring him includes no George-and-Martha-style drunken brawls. Should it? Perhaps a free-for-all would have lightened an atmosphere so thick with foreboding. As in *Roller Coaster*, the oppressiveness starts building immediately. Before anyone speaks, a phonograph is playing the music of Billie Holiday, whose 1941 rendition of the song "Gloomy Sunday" had been banned from the airways; it follows Edwin Arlington Robinson's poem "Luke Havergal" by beckoning a mourner to the grave of a loved one. Billie's version of the song had led a disturbing number of listeners, not all of them mourners, to kill themselves.

The love-death interplay infusing her singing had lodged in McNally's psyche; his play *LTTA*, produced 29 years after the premiere of *Door*, contains the stage direction, "Music begins from the house on stage right, Billie Holiday singing the 'You've Changed' cut from her *Lady in Satin* album" (28). This lyric infiltrates *Door*, most obviously because, late in the action, Edmund smashes all his father's prized shellac discs. (A man in *Unusual Acts*, which premiered 17 years after *LTTA*, owns a copy of *Lady in Satin*, stretching the references to the sorrow voiced in the canon by Billie to 48 years.)

This act of violence was carefully foreshadowed. There's something skewed and off-kilter about the Hobarts that music, a force for wholeness in works like Mozart's *Magic Flute* and Albee's *Death of Bessie Smith* (1960), might have set right. The youngest occupant, Edmund's baby sister, is sick. Though his boozing has sapped his vim, Henderson looks young for 37. In another reversal, the ordeal of living with him has aged Hebe; despite being younger than Henderson, she looks older. Any helpful effects of her having been named after the goddess of youth have bypassed her to descend on her pale, undersized son. But this descent, which might have pleased *her*, has been rankling Edmund, whose slowness to develop physically has set him off from most of his classmates. In McNally's words, "There is nothing about him to suggest even the slightest intimation of approaching puberty" (3).

The wrongness that begets wrongness in *Door* shows McNally's gift for variety. The breakdown or collapse that shapes the play's unifying conceit takes different forms. "[D]riving winds and rains" (i 2) have run together the colors on Edmund's Halloween costume, after which the drunken Henderson, upset that his son had dressed himself to look like Carmen Miranda, shreds the costume. More devastation follows. After the shattering of Henderson's phonograph records, a doll is smashed against the kitchen sink (iii 25). Henderson has already laid waste to the family car along with the pecan tree on the lawn he drove it into. That symbol of loyalty and trust, the family dog, old and mangy, could die any time.

Another shattering has been mooted. Edmund has been coaxing his mother into divorcing Henderson and then taking him and his baby sister Lillian Sue to Florida. McNally wants us to wonder if she'll agree. Henderson's rejection of her sexual overture in the first act has made her a woman scorned. The play's very title posits division, plenty of which has already sliced through the action. Henderson, the failed father and husband, stays off stage until the play's second act, where he's too drunk to perform sexually. Who would buy insurance from such a man? And what's he doing at home on a workday? If the Hebe of antiquity married the mighty Hercules, her contemporary namesake has a drunken lout of a husband whose virility and know-how to support his family have both washed away on seas of booze.

Family worries crest at play's end when Edmund claims to have murdered his sister. Like father, like son? His fatal battering of Lillian Sue would be a grotesque exaggeration of the slow death Henderson has been inflicting on Hebe. The goblins called forth by Halloween have already invaded the Hobart home. But they haven't razed it. The bundle in the blanket Edmund has been smashing against the sink is only a doll. The doll, though, is his (iii 25). Some of the family secrets lodged in *Door* (DiGaetani 225) refer to *him*. Not only do boys of 13 rarely own dolls; Edmund also belongs to a small minority of classmates who still go trick-or-treating in costumes on Halloween (i 3). And no doubt he's the only one who does it dressed like Carmen Miranda. "They all laughed at me, momma" (i 5), he says of his classmates—who'd screech even louder if they knew that he still played with dolls.

Still more screeches might erupt from them were they to hear of his plans to become a priest. An imaginative leap of three decades finds later incarnations of him getting gay-bashed in Alfie Byrne of *A Man of No Importance* and *A Perfect Ganesh*'s Walter Brynne. Edmund's first act in the play saw him "burrowing into [Hebe's] ... bosom" while "nearly naked," his Halloween costume having been split by heavy rains (i 4). It's no wonder he has reverted to infancy. This reversion is but one of his rituals. Later, when he begs his mother to take him to Florida, he gives her the box containing the shards of his father's record collection. The box is a coffin housing his dead father's bones. In his mind, he has already displaced Henderson. Displacement has been on his mind. The hormone shots he talks about taking (iii 11) will make him tall enough to stop looking like Hebe's little boy. Any other benefits he sees coming from the hormone shots he keeps to himself. (the gay-leaning 13-year-old son in *Bringing It* also talks about getting hormone shots [*15 Plays* 7]). But Hebe has caught his drift. His pipe dream ends when she lashes him across the face after his refusal to turn over the bundle that she fears might contain the pulped remains of her baby daughter.

He had just withheld the bundle from his father. Henderson he finds it easy to deny. Edmund resents him. He keeps holding back from his father the love and respect Henderson wants but keeps fending off. Late in Act 3, he barks at Edmund, "Go lay your mother. She'd probably let you" (iii 16). Edmund was given the last name of Hobart, which is also the name of Tasmania's capital city, because of its connection to distance, remoteness, and prisons. And his effeminacy has barely started to show.

Validating these motifs are some of the turns and maneuvers in a play produced 46 years after the debut of *Door*. "Teachers' Break" unspools in the faculty lunch room (*TB* 13) of a New York high school. It's an odd place. The same teachers who address each other as Mr., Mrs., and Ms. curse freely and frequently. One recalls having taught "*rich* little motherfuckers" (3) at an exclusive prep school, while his colleague, Mrs. O'Neill, mentions seeing on a blackboard the words, "Mrs. O'Neill eats pussy for a living" (6). Still another teacher, a Mr. Butler, says in a different vein of his son, "Jerome has just started taking harp lessons, and he wants a dressmaker's model for Christmas so he can practice draping. Marsha [who's presumably Mr. Butler's wife and Jerome's mother] says he gay already" (3). These words may have reawakened what McNally was feeling when he was writing *Door*.

The fifth grader, Jerome, though two years younger than Edmund of

Door, is living in a faster, more advanced environment nearly half a century later. He's also cultivating both the artistic bent and effeminacy that will stir the derision of his classmates. His spirits will soon be crushed. What awaits him is loneliness — the bane of gay men throughout the canon. McNally named him after a saint who became a hermit for the same reason that Edmund's last name, Hobart, rings of exile and obscurity.

This reading of a play that's scarcely more than an anecdote would be reckless and irresponsible if it didn't mesh with some of the major themes of both McNally's life and work. Like *Door*, *Teachers' Break* displays its author's abiding a-historical self, the gay artist. The 2008 play's abundance of profanity coexists with references to both major writers like Chaucer (1), Shakespeare (6, 13), and Milton (5), all of whom are taught to the students. What's more, the off-duty teachers share the trademark concern with language found in *Frankie and Johnny* and *Unusual Acts of Devotion*. And like the musicians in *Golden Age* (2010) who are watching a production of an opera from the wings, they come before us both away from — by sitting in the teachers' lounge — and attached to their workplace.

Language becomes an issue immediately. When Mr. Butler, a recent Fulbright fellow in Oxford (2), refers to potato chips as "crisps," his colleague Mr. Short rubs his nose in cockney slang: "Jesus, *crisps*! They're called potato chips this side of the Atlantic, governor. Six weeks summer program in Oxford reading Chaucer and 'e wants 'is bleedin' crisps. Blimey!" (1) Short isn't only chiding Butler for an affectation that might have tempted McNally himself, given his career-long preference for the British spelling, "theatre," and his putting the word "Valour" in the title of his 1994 hit play. The newest faculty member in the lounge, Short speaks of his "love of the English language" (8). This alleged love hasn't cleansed his speech of flubs, as is seen in his archaism, "Dare we not?" Which Butler, whose name recalls the English institution of butlering, jumps on in retaliation: "Dare we not? What the fuck kind of locution is that?" His barrage continues, Butler deflecting the flunkeyism connected to his name. His earlier reference to "crisps," perpetrated to boost his image, had smudged it. To recover lost ground, he tells Short, "And you spent three semesters in Dublin sucking up to James Joyce's fifth cousin's daughter-in-law. She didn't even know who you were talking about" (12).

This broadside refers to the practice of some gay men in New York and other big cities of indulging in borrowed glory, usually in vain. Short evokes the mama's boy, Edmund, who's short for his age. And though Edmund is probably not gay, his proclivities are steering him towards homosexuality. Edmund was also accused of furtiveness (*Door* ii 3), an attribute of Joyce's Stephen Dedalus (and of closeted gays like Will of *Some Men*). Other likenesses come to mind. Edmund's tendency to "run ... on in those long sentences" (*ibid.*, iii 10) when speaking to his mother tallies with Short's professed love of language. Short's visit to the birthplace of Joyce, the writer who brought English prose to an exciting new level, moreover, suggests literary ambitions of his own.

We don't know if he smashes things, as Edmund did both his father's records and his surrogate sister's head, destructiveness being an attribute of the creative artist in Freud and Joyce (in Mann, the artist directs this venom to himself). But Short laughs convulsively when he hears the word, "farting" (7). Perhaps like many writers before him, he lives in a private world with its own codes; Dickens concocted a London of his own because the real-life one maimed his childhood. Fabrication of this sort undoes both Edmund and Short. Had his stint of teaching the kids of rich fathers worked out for him, he'd not be sitting in the lounge or lunch room of a different school. Accordingly, Edmund's dream of bolting Texas to live in sunny Florida fizzles out (McNally lived in both Florida and Texas as a boy).

McNally hints at Short's homosexuality as he did Edmund's emerging homosexuality. And if Short *is* gay, he has company in the lunch room, his colleague Ms. Agnew announcing that she has a partner called Louise (*ibid.*, 10). He winces when his foil Butler spits out the vulgarity, "Cocksucking Queer Takes It Up The Bung Hole" (*ibid.*, 4). Why, though? A dab hand at cursing himself, he had said earlier, "There's never been a cunt like me" (*ibid.*, 2). And he said it in tandem with his reference to the Nighttown, or Circe, episode of *Ulysses*, during which Joyce's Everyman figure, Leopold Bloom, painfully confronts his female side. Short's mention of his daughter Rachel, a grade-schooler who's appearing in a production of *The King and I*, which like "Teachers' Break," deals with a teacher who has a daughter, proves nothing. Gays with wives or ex-wives had appeared in both *Lisbon Traviata* and *Some Men*.

Yet this Joycean trope suggests that McNally has kept his options open. Even for him, a writer known to strew his plays with profanity, the seas of language rise atypically high in *Teachers' Break*. Talk about anger. The name Rachel, a form of *Rache*, the German word for revenge, darkens matters still more. Even McNally's high school English teacher, Mrs. McElroy, feels his spite. Revered by him for having spurred in him his enduring love of Shakespeare, she speaks the closing words of *Teachers' Break*, which cite Shakespeare (*ibid.*, 13). She also has a different Irish name, Mrs. O'Neill. Speaking of Irish, is McNally playing the Joycean game of fitting several meanings inside of one groove? Spelling and all, Mrs. Mac's new name replicates that of one of McNally's favorite playwrights. There's more to his renaming derby, though. If her fictional name honors Mrs. Mac, her language does *not*. Besides telling her colleagues that one of her students wrote on a blackboard, "Mrs. O'Neill eats pussy for a living" (*ibid.*, 6), she says, "I've been called much worse things than a cunt" (*ibid.*, 4).

The subject matter she had prepared for the day was, pointedly, Shakespeare's sonnets. This swipe at his beloved Mrs. Mac is shocking. But, besides linking up with McNally's lifetime fascination with betrayal, it also suits the tone and action of the play. "Teachers' Break" spares no one, not even McNally. Having taught at Juilliard and NYU, he overheard cattiness and backbiting in teacher's lounges. Like the Simon Gray of *Butley* and *Quartermaine's Terms*, he might also be indicting teaching as a form of slow death. The characters' loss of control displayed in *Teachers' Break* shows that the deathly process can be sped. The setting of his unrealistic play must be some nearby future date when colleges and universities will have not merely stopped hiring new faculty but have even fired many of those already on staff. Academics who want to stay in the profession are now teaching high-schoolers. As their overseas fellowships and heady literary references show, they're overqualified for their jobs. Their fine words about *Ulysses* and *Beowulf* (11) pass over their students' heads, and they know it. They also know that their failure to connect with their students makes firing inevitable, news too desperate to face, let alone discuss. But it's also news hard enough to sweep ambitious academics like them into torrents of invective.

The lines they speak, though, came from McNally. His internal quarrels, personified by the well-traveled colleagues Butler and Short, represent the struggle that besets *all* artists; McNally's time in the classroom stepped up his knowledge that all artists are battlefields. Less eager to cover his tracks than to vent the turmoil that stokes his creativity, he flooded with profanity — not only to yoke himself to his heroes Shakespeare and Joyce, who did the same outspoken thing on a different scale. He's also resigning himself to the sad truth that the important work of teaching literature to America's youth is being done by misfit-pretenders like Short and Butler.

References to other non-commercial writers are in order. At the level of content, *Teachers' Break* depicts McNally at his most brutal. It lays out, with some of the intense self-scrutiny found in Kafka, Kierkegaard, and Dostoevsky, narcissism, compulsiveness, self-deception, and doubt in the possibility of love. And it lays these failings out while rolling its audiences in laughter. We've been won without being pushed, always a satisfying outcome.

II

Doubleness shows in McNally a drive to excel partnered with one, just as strong, a compulsion to fail; failure is what he sometimes feels he deserves.

Rebels and outsiders always contain in themselves that which they want to crush. As an example of this inner turmoil, Dostoevsky feared that his epilepsy and his gambling fever would either drive him mad or kill him. Yet he also knew that these torments fired his imagination. No fiction writer of the nineteenth century enacted more vividly Nietzsche's belief that an artist must not only be sick; he must also work from his sickness. The narrator of *Doctor Faustus* by Nietzsche's fellow German, Thomas Mann, calls the title character's greatest work, an apocalyptic oratorio, a "substantial identity of the most blest with the most accurst" (Thomas Mann, *Dr. Faustus*, 1948, trans. H. T. Lowe-Porter [New York: Knopf, 1963], 486).

The greatness of the great invalid (Rimbaud's term for the artist, which Patrick White quotes in his epigraph to his 1970 novel, *The Vivisector*) stems from his disease, which explains his attraction to what's disgusting and vile. The ritual murders in *Bump*, the disfigured drowned swimmer in *LTTA*, and the generic, steroid-fed tennis players of today in *Deuce* describe the formation of McNally's sensibility as a function of inner conflict, a furtive destructive process both disabling and favorable to regenerating creative acts. Like Dostoevsky before him, McNally writes, not for an audience, but for himself: "I keep saying to myself, write what you want to write" (Zinman, "Interview," Zinman, ed. *Casebook* 11), he told Toby Silverman Zinman. He knew he was in for a fight. The "great Invalid ... great Accursed One — and ... Supreme Knower" of the Rimbaud's epigraph used in *Vivisector* mingles the ugly and the beautiful in shockingly new off-putting ways, as in John's reference in *LTTA* to "the dark beauty ... and malevolence" of the cancer burgeoning "in this feeble bed of malignancy that has somehow become my body" (17).

Dostoevsky can be invoked again. Why shouldn't a man plagued by gambling fever and epilepsy strike out at civilization, democracy, and humanism — as McNally did too in his early work according to Howard Stein (Zinman, ed. *Casebook* 19)? Dostoevsky's recognition of anguish as the source of his genius led him to incongruity and contrast. The main figures of "The Double" (1846), "Notes from Underground" (1864), and "The Gambler" (1867) all sabotage their best chances; Ivan Karamazov's fixation upon child abuse wrecks his mind. All four of these characters would snap to John's lyrical lament on the cancer that's overtaking him in *LTTA*. We should too if we want to grasp McNally's inventive intent; his work discloses a similar craving for the strange and the incompatible. *Roller Coaster* depicts the bullyragging and soul murder of a middle-aged man by a girl of thirteen; the two lifetime achievers being honored at a tennis match talk about miscegenation and adultery, subjects unsuited to the dignity of the ceremony where they're to be fêted. The same can be said in a different register of the misrepresentations of the television announcers at the match, whose words combine an ignorance of tennis history with the wish to keep the program's advertisers happy.

But what *is* that indwelling anarchy that uroboros-like, feeds McNally's muse as it saps it? Its home is his homosexuality. "[P]ale" (*Door* 3) Edmund Hobart ("The Pale Heart" is a chapter heading in Nietzsche's *Zarathustra*) feels blocked at both school and home. He feels trapped in an atmosphere of malaise, a horror of hidden conspiracy that keeps turning up in unlikely forms, like the wet, wind-torn Carmen Miranda costume he's first seen in. His being one of very few of his classmates to go out trick-or-treating on Halloween shows his reluctance to grow up. He's out of step with life, as will be the childish middle-aged protagonist of *Dedication* (2004). His dream of bolting to Florida with his mother runs afoul of an imperative he's too young to understand—Hebe's adult challenge of balancing the claims of motherhood against those of being a wife.

His ensuing frustration takes the only form he knows, destructiveness. His paleness, no casual afterthought on McNally's part, has precedents in American literature in the deathliness associated with both Melville's white whale and the snow that fascinates the narrator of Robert Frost's "Stopping by Woods." Equally germane in this regard is D. H. Lawrence's essential American, an "isolate, [an] almost selfless stoic, [an] enduring man, who lives by death, by killing" (1923; *Studies in Classic American Literature*. New York: Viking, 1964: 63). For another slant on the trope, McNally's self-image calls forth the pithed zombie-like "pale kings" of Keats's "La Belle Dame Sans Merci." This world-renowned playwright who said of himself, "In real life I'm rather cold" (DiGaetainu 224), has internalized the role of the afflicted celebrity in order to keep focused on "the causes and consequences of human suffering" (Frontain, "Terrence McNally and the Dance of Death" 33). Playing it safe would be a form of death to him. In order to write, he needs to open a vein. The "dangerous theater" (Savran 121) he has committed himself to would lose its sharpness were he to turn away from his innermost anarchic self. A man in *Unusual Acts* equates listening to Billie Holiday with having at hand "a packet of single-edge razor blades" (14).

Edmund's destructiveness channels into his emerging homosexuality through his disapproving father. Pointedly, Henderson Hobart spends most of his time on the other side of the door from Edmund and Hebe. Not a bad idea; perhaps he'd be better off remaining a stranger in his own home. When he crosses into the area where his wife and son spend time, he incites chaos. The absence in him of "a certain vitality" (*Door* 3) makes him a poor role model for Edmund, driving his son to Hebe's side, where he unconsciously learns to think and feel like a woman. For one thing, Henderson, no storehouse of energy like Saul Bellow's Rain King, is childish. His looking younger than his years bespeaks a silliness that takes the form of lazing drunkenly at home during normal business hours, crashing the family car, and, most dramatically, failing his wife. As has been seen, Hebe, having to pay for his failures, looks older than Henderson despite being some five years younger (*ibid.*, 3). McNally underscores this important point visually. While Henderson is drinking and listening to music, Hebe stays busy cooking, sewing, and trying to comfort her distraught son.

It follows that Henderson will fail to perform the husbandly role of lover, a pity because his fondness for Billie Holiday, in McNally's scale of values, signals the good taste indicative of other virtues he has been throwing away. Hebe has to ask him for sex, as might be expected. The advances she makes to him, she soon regrets. To undo the numbing effects of alcohol in his system, he tries to fire himself up by inciting love-play that grows "vulgar ... finally obscene" (*ibid.*, ii 3). Now this obscenity takes place out of Edmund's view. McNally, though, might have been unlucky enough to have watched such a scene. He did tell DiGaetani that *Door* told "the secrets of my family" (225). Apart from physical violence, the secrets of the bedroom are the most shocking and indelible in any family.

Once his shock wore off, McNally, who caught the meaning of what he saw, might have resolved on the spot to avoid damaging and degrading any woman he loved. What path to take to block the guilt already churning his psyche? Edmund knows that he ranks only slightly better as a son than Henderson does as a husband and father. He feels both stumped and stymied by the adult world. He thought that smashing his father's phonograph records would please Hebe. Instead, it frightens and upsets her. The box holding the broken pieces of shellac represents, coffin-like, the death of his hopes. This is typical. Whatever he does meets grief, like his naive Galahad-like plan to make off with her to Florida. He even smashes the doll he rated higher than any of the accessories of boyhood, like a baseball glove or a football. It's no wonder he wants to join the priesthood (*ibid.*, iii 12).

The Church keeps looming. "[T]hose long sentences" (*ibid.*, iii 10) his mother says he favors invoke the monk-like dedication of the creative artist made famous by Stephen Dedalus's view of himself in *A Portrait* as a priest of the eternal imagination. Hebe's words also prefigure the sense of mission driving her 23-year-old creator. Like any other imaginative artist, the McNally of *Door* knew that his vocation demanded that he indulge, rather than suppress, his feelings, an imperative that sunk any ambitions he may have had for the cloth. He chose well to follow his creative impulses. He kept reaffirming his need as an artist to be one-to-one with physical reality.

The unedited and the everyday have always piqued in him a childlike wonder that would lead him to write, in *Dedication* (2004), a play about children's theater. His imaginative preference for the textures of daily life gives his work an astonishing immediacy and presence, which, as he knew beforehand, would come with a cost. Like Dostoevsky's, his stewardship of his muse has brought pain. Though brought up to prize the humanist values of pedigree, provenance, and civility, he has often struggled with dissolution, waste, and shame.

Dislocation poisoned his experience of growing up gay in south Texas, a stronghold of revivalist Christianity that not only went against the grain of his Roman Catholic upbringing. More dauntingly to him, it also valorized a mannish preoccupation with firearms, booze, and an inflated sense of male pride. Everywhere were robust philistines with rifles and Bible Belt mentalities. To extend the ethos, introspection was mocked with some of the intensity matching a trademark scorn of effeminacy. Manhood in mid-century Corpus Christi meant acting with speed, strength, and even violence if one's honor was at stake. These virtues, it was understood, bypassed the world of limp-wristed bookworms. What the girlie-men did together when they *weren't* reading didn't bear thinking about. A contempt for effeminacy hallmarked the manly independence of the Texas stud.

The basis for this contempt, though, could prove unexpectedly fragile. The sight of a gay bruiser who looked as if he had walked out of a picture book by Tom of Finland would fluster many Texas studs. Still worse, an effeminate gay man who set a fire going inside the stud's tough hide could become the victim of homophobic panic; to lash out at a gay man is to attack, by proxy, one's own forbidden gay impulses. The gay-straight polarity can shake down in other ways. As Annie Proulx showed in "Brokeback Mountain," from her 1997 story collection, *Wyoming*, weathered prospectors and cattle drivers who work together for weeks on mesas and buttes can also tumble into bed. But no red-blooded outdoorsman wants to be suspected of doing this. To deflect suspicion, macho-looking gays might become avid gay-bashers. McNally knew this cover-up well enough to transplant it to the 1964 Dublin of *A Man of No Importance*, where a fellow gay decoys the play's hero into the alley where he's bushwhacked by a waiting mob.

The 2002 production date of *Man* confirms the impact of this lesson on McNally, who first came to live in New York in 1956. What he found there, if not total freedom for gays to meet and bond, were places where he could feel more accepted than in Corpus Christi. It's safe to say that his lifestyle, starting with his Columbia years (1956–60), resembled what's said about Aaron and Scoop, from *Some Men*, two fiftyish gays who paired off soon after meeting as college students decades earlier. So long as they observed certain guidelines, they and other gays could relax. It helped being in the arts, an area where very few linked manhood to physical strength and violence. As stage manager of Molly Kazan's Actor's Studio, his first job after college, McNally would hear actors like Marilyn Monroe and Laurence Olivier discuss the theater with various stage directors (Drukman 337). Working for Kazan proved a terrific boon. Not only did her studio reduce by light years any problems posed by being gay; McNally's job also exposed him to a wealth of insights and ideas that would bolster his art — a process both sped and deepened by his years (1957–64) with America's hottest living playwright of the day, Edward Albee.

Hindsight explains that his art was always heading, however fitfully, in the right direction. After calling *LTTA* his most operatic play in 1994, he said, "My early plays are all arias" (Zinman, "Interview," Zinman, *Casebook* 4). He meant that rather than engaging internally with his characters in works like *Bump* and *Tommy Flowers*, he substituted stage technique and vocal impersonation. He had not yet learned to see and experience the world as his people did. This failing made his apprentice work stronger in literary intelligence than in heart knowledge. The early plays only graze life's richness and complexity. Post-aria works Like *LTTA* and *Master Class*, on the other hand, link McNally's words to the feelings that lie beneath.

Forget dichotomies and binary codes. Despite appearances, signs of his later mastery appeared as early as *Roller Coaster*. The "well-dressed, middle-aged" Rudolph walks onto the stage wearing "black rubbers over his brown shoes" (42), gear that stamps him a nerd, i.e., the sort of person 13-year-old Gerty can shred at will. The vocal interplay of the work's two characters makes this dismemberment inevitable; everything that happens on stage leads to Rudolph's downfall. Whereas he speaks politely, Gerty is always snappish, cynical, and potty-mouthed. Even before curtain up, McNally had foreshadowed the coming action, much of which he intended to stun the audience. Rudolph will be stunned; the play's first event, which we hear rather than see, is the distant sound of "The Good Old Summertime" (which will later introduce the second act of McNally's *LVC* [*Two Plays* 65]) being sung in harmony. The song grows "louder, discordant," as it fuses with "the relentless, whirring and clinking" (*RC* 42) of a nearby roller coaster. What was pleasant and far off has grown menacing.

Once we recover our wits, we note still another clash. The action is unfolding in early April, not the summertime evoked by the 1902 Evans-Shields song we've been hearing. This divide helps set the play's edgy tone. McNally has made his strident opening the ground rhythm for several carefully pointed contrasts: middle age and puberty, male and female, gentleness and aggression, observing and acting. But Rudolph is no bystander. His entrapment by his guilty past, which brought him to the roller coaster, has made him a seeker of redemption — unless, feeling unworthy, he's indulging his guilt. As a boy, he always resisted boarding the speeding, juddering roller coaster.

He's still scared, as the impulsive, quick-tempered actionist Gerty spots — and despises — immediately. His cowardice has collided with her belief in the proper use of roller coasters. And anyone who opposes her had better watch out. She has failed to see that his complex decades-long fixation on the roller coaster denotes in him a deeper bond than hers. Rather than apologizing for hitting him in the eye with her pea-shooter, she steps up the pressure. She's just getting warmed up. The relentless self-entitlement with which she keeps squeezing him for cigarettes and personal information recalls the smugness and propensity to violence of the archetypal caveman bully from McNally's Texas boyhood. A malignancy his parents can't protect him from, she's an urbanized, feminized version of McNally's worst boyhood nightmare.

Having armed herself with several pea-shooters, she has left nothing to chance. The job this punisher-avenger has come to do ranks foremost with her. She walks away when Rudolph patronizes her ("You're a nice little girl once you start behaving" [*ibid.*, 47]). She interrupts when he reminisces about his boyhood, asking him, "Did you beat off in the bathtub?" (*ibid.*, 53). Such verbal assaults have re-sited the archetype from Corpus Christi to New York City. The city-based family man (Rudolph mentions "my wife and children" [*ibid.*, 52]) gets crushed by his anti-foil, a member of the dispossessed urban proletariat; Gerty has inherited no tradition except that of the macho Texan that haunted McNally's youth.

She has made herself a protector of this actionism. The roller coaster's connection with danger and death — like an out-to-pasture horse, it will never be ridden again — appeals to this rootless brat, a parody of the Lone Ranger figure who rights a wrong and then leaves mysteriously the settlers he had saved. No righter of wrongs, Gerty; the threat she symbolizes to a Texas-drawling university student in New York goes far beyond cadging cigarettes and picking pockets. Reaching into himself helped McNally sharpen his play with a dazzling economy. Along with its frequent references to sex, *The Roller Coaster* also makes Gerty a metaphor for the rough trade that enticed Yukio Mishima, Tennessee Williams, and Joe Orton. Rudolph's earlier domination by his mother (*ibid.*, 53) gives Gerty's resemblance to the young toughs who hustle middle-aged gays a sinister twist. Though McNally wasn't middle-aged when he wrote *RC*, he did belong to an establishment, Columbia University. Nor had this undergraduate learned his way around the city at the time of the play, the defunct gyrating reminder of which he might have clung to as a relic of a stable past that kept beguiling him — except for his suspicion that his past was neither stable nor safe.

Stephen tells Mike in *The Lisbon Traviata* that Columbia University is in Harlem, a place where cars get vandalized (*Three Plays* 56). This danger invokes the "Get Whitey" poems of one time–Columbia student Amiri Baraka's black male-centric *Preface to a Twenty-Volume Suicide Note* (1961). If McNally felt uneasy coming back, as a gay white man, to the 116th Street subway station after a night at the theater a freshman, he had good reason; a major episode of *A Perfect Ganesh* would show a gay white man being clubbed to death in New York City. The unstated black presence in *Roller Coaster* is strong, to the point where the play's setting, Kingston (*ibid.*, 50), could be in Jamaica, capital city of the British West Indies if the play's roller coaster didn't refer to the Airplane Coaster in Playland, Rye, New York, near Port Chester, where the McNally family lived during WWII (McNally email to author, July 10, 2011).

Gender, if not racial, instability recurs in his work. At one point in *Dedication* (2004), the gay Lou Nuncle summons his female business partner Jessie with a line belonging to Shakespeare's Juliet (30). The effeminate city rat Breton Beret of *A Man of No Importance* quotes Juliet to the lonely, closeted gay Alfie Byrne (65) prior to punching him in the face. A supposedly chance reference to Dublin, Alfie's and Breton Beret's home town in *Dedication* (34), could apply to McNally's self-unfolding. The battered Alfie stands as a direction McNally might have taken had he not started living as a junior with Edward Albee in a West Village apartment far from the Columbia campus. The same truth applies to Breton Beret; the outcast often hates the perceived defect or flaw that caused his casting-out. Tellingly, he's the only character in *MNI* referred to in the play's stage directions by his full name; the enemy within always causes the most damage.

The deep structure of *Roller Coaster* springs other revelations. As Gerty often does with Rudolph, Breton Beret asks Alfie for a cigarette (*MNI* 65) soon after materializing before him, Gerty-style, without warning. This episode matters to McNally, who smoked from his late teens through most of his adult life. Breton Beret's parting words to Alfie, "Fecking queer" (*ibid.*, 92), finally, look back to Gerty's comparison of Rudolph to "a fairy [she met and beat up] last summer" (*RC* 45).

Rudolph's last name, Alexander, alludes to McNally's fear of both the street hustlers he met in New York and the homophobes from his Corpus Christi youth. The name is ironic. Alexander the Great, ruler of the ancient world swathing Asia Minor, Egypt, and India, groused at age 31 that he had no more worlds to conquer. McNally's Rudolph Alexander, on the other hand, gets routed quickly by an urchin half his size and a third his age. Nor will she be bought off. She rejects his offer of a dollar to stop shooting pellets at him, and she ignores the paper money wafting down from the roller coaster late in the action. What she wants has no cash value.

Where does all this leave us? The strange frightening rush of events comprising *Roller Coaster* has dumped us in a clammy darkness void of footholds. The play's absent deity, Hank, the sadistic operator of the roller coaster, offers little hope. Perhaps he couldn't if he wanted to, however unlikely *that* prospect is. Hank only runs the roller coaster; its owner is unknown. Besides sharing Ruby's alacrity for human weakness, Gerty has both the same name and the same sexual eagerness as Hamlet's mother. But even though these markers forecast Rudolph's overthrow, so little has he advanced from his south Texas prototype, Edmund Hobart, that he might have fallen anyway in this prequel to *Door*. The two males mirror each other. Shame and ridicule have stung them both. Just as Edmund's teacher sat him with his female classmates, Rudolph's teenaged friends mocked and jeered his refusal to ride the roller coaster. The comparison lengthens. Echoing Hebe's remark about Edmund's "long sentences" (*Door* iii 10) is Gerty's slur to Rudolph, "Ain't you full of big words!" (*RC* 52)

Rudolph is also the name of the youngster Gerty and her friends "beat the shit out of" (*ibid.*, 50) the previous year for cringing from the abandoned roller coaster. She obviously had as little trouble rounding up a gang of thugs to beat up young Rudolph as Breton Beret did in *MNI* when he decided that Alfie needed a pasting. Western society's newly acquired rage for violence spares nobody. Gerty thinks from his photo that the elder Rudolph's son looks fat and effeminate, traits that make *him* ripe for a trouncing. The conflation of the two Rudolphs and Edmund provides insight into McNally. This Phi Beta Kappa graduate with a promising career looming before him is also the ambitious outsider of humble origins who disbelieves in his success. Part of him assumes that both his former social superiors and tormenters are conniving to throw him back into the pit where in his heart he fears he belongs.

Yet some points of light pierce the darkness. Spellbound by the dilapidated roller coaster, Gerty and Rudolph both visit it the same time. Both of them smoke. They hum a tune together (*ibid.*, 46). He was *her* age when he first visited the now-deserted amusement park where the rundown roller coaster droops. There's a kinship here. So close has the roller coaster brought them that they finish each other's sentences (*ibid.*, 56), and the closing words of the play, spoken by her ("Nothing's changed. Nothing's changed at all" [*ibid.*, 60]) copy verbatim the ones he spoke at curtain rise (*ibid.*, 42). So totally different in age, lifestyle and temperament, the play's only characters have agreed on the importance of roller coasters. Perhaps McNally, who would later lament the tearing down of some tradition-rich old Broadway playhouses (*Three Plays* 228), is suggesting that they could have been friends in different circumstances. This theoretical bond would have helped them both. Gerty flouts the civilized guidelines and boundaries she needs to put in place to develop normally. Her evasiveness about her parentage suggests that having a dependable father figure might soothe the rage in her psyche. And Rudolph? Spending time with a firecracker like her might take his mind off the past; at the least, having her nearby would prove to him that roller coaster-riding provides no key to happiness and fulfillment. Look what a mess it made of Gerty.

Such rays of hope, though dim and easily overlooked, do matter if only because they show that the anger and cynicism fueling much of the play didn't smudge its 20-year-old author's ability to see both sides of an issue — if there are two sides; Rudolph might have conjured up Gerty out of his frustration. A shortened form of his last name, Alexander, i.e., Alex or a-lex, meaning against the law in Latin, implies on Rudolph's part regret over having an unlived life. McNally deserves high praise for exploring issues that were themselves smudged and shapeless. *Roller Coaster* conveys his understanding of selfhood as a crabwise process of becoming. This work of contrapuntal consciousness voices alternative histories and epistemologies, each of them consistent in its patterns and conceits. Yes, Rudolph stands for those civilized values Columbia had been teaching McNally to cherish and advance. But there's more at stake. Cardboard thin, Rudolph is such a pushover for Gerty that he's little more than a plotting device. Gerty is the character through which McNally explores himself together with Rudolph's moth-like desire for the flame.

Gerty and McNally are victims of gender confusion. Her slurs against gays resemble those that McNally might have credited on some inner level in light of the hardships that being gay inflicted on him in his teens. And will continue to bring? Those lines that both open and close the play, "Nothing's changed at all" (42, 60), spoken in two voices, signal McNally's acceptance of the heartbreak, voiced by a gay man in *Some Men*, that could darken his every act: "Gay is not good. Gay is loneliness and secrecy and a lifetime of shame" (*Two Plays* 2007, 38).

If *Roller Coaster* finds McNally both bogged down but also poised to take flight, his Janus-like evolution from displacement and dislocation owes a great deal to Gerty's youth. Youth reigns in gay transactions. Both a vehicle of and a force for male beauty, it works like a trump card among gay men. In McNally's case, it represented a boon he could exploit more confidently in New York than in Corpus Christi. He voiced his awareness of this benefit by making Gerty 13, which is also the age of Edmund, the son Johnny in *Bringing It*, and Lakme in *Bump*. The subtext of *Roller Coaster* suggests that he had his first orgasm at 13. This milestone heralded the new freedom of self-expression New York would bless him with. But the doubleness so characteristic of him during his early New York days had *its* say, too. Guilt sapped some of his euphoria; Edmund and Gerty are two of the most nerve-raked characters in the canon.

If their disquiet matches McNally's, the more power to him. Didn't Dostoevsky and Nietzsche match literary creation to anguish, even the most soul-splitting sort? Yes, *Roller Coaster* is more aria-like than operatic, to use the markers McNally chose to divide his early work from the riper ones of his maturity. But, to its credit, the steadiness with which it portrays two cultures in collision merits high praise. It reaffirms the truth that settling into a new environment always revives, rather than buries, the aches of an earlier one. The realignment of values and the reshaping of loyalties take the most dogged self-exploration. If *Roller Coaster* is an aria, it's also a balanced study in bravery and honesty. Little to no self-pity or self-indulgence mars it. Balance is vital here, along with craftsmanship. The ability to synchronize the store of materials that had put McNally on an emotional roller coaster marks a flying start to his playwriting career. This aria hits the right notes.

CHAPTER FOUR

Cauldrons of Deceit

And Things That Go Bump in the Night (1964), McNally's 1965 Broadway debut, deepens issues found in *Roller Coaster*. He had set himself a big test. The play tries to yoke the traumas of family dysfunction to the dying gasps of a long history of urbanization dating from the rise and enfranchisement of those commoners whose forebears fled their rustic roots. Again, characters lurch between the real and the inexplicable. We lurch with them. And we feel just as dizzy and shaken. Humid and dreamlike, the play harks to Kafka's *The Trial*, with its vision of a surrealistic, victimizing bureaucracy. That bureaucracy is all the more sinister for its absence. The play ignores the big-media issues of the mid–1960s like U.S. military power, the ubiquity of the Pentagon's footprint, and its inevitable byproduct, America's global passion for intervention and state-building.

But a curfew has been imposed, and, to discourage burglars in this straitened time, some families have surrounded their homes with electrified fences. Credit McNally for his thrifty treatment of this motif. Using very few details, he has created a sinister world of poverty, distrust, and fear. A strong but inscrutable central government controls everything, having in the process harried its people. Though organized protest rallies and parades occur, protesters can also vanish, never to return. *Bump* shows how such anxieties control families. The politics informing them are more arbitrary and invasive than those found in McNally's later, more commercial plays, *Bringing It All Back Home* (1969) and *Whiskey* (1973).

I

To clear their minds of fear, most of the people in *Bump* try to ignore the political consequences of their acts. This tactic fails them; they replicate in little the cruelty of the state. Recalling Ibsen's *Wild Duck* (1884), Pirandello's *It Is So* (1917), and Albee's *Delicate Balance* (1966), the family at the heart of

Bump is freakish and bizarre. The two adult males in the home are so weak that they go unnamed. Fa, as the family head of smudged paternity is called, spends most of his time in an escapist sleep. He's protecting himself; life in the basement where the family lives, or subsists, is too ugly to face. Perhaps his eyes will open soon. He's slated to leave the basement soon after Grandfa, an elder whose "quick and bright eyes" (II 2) see the vileness the others want to hide, is dumped in an old folks' home. The rest of the zoo? The children, Sigfird and Lakme, bicker often, as do many sibs of 21 and 13. But they're just as likely to enjoy each other's company, as McNally says in some well-chosen words: "They laugh and jostle each other like the best of friends ... which of course they often are" (*II* 9).

Albee's influence in *Bump* is clear. Besides its weak father, the play includes an astute sympathetic elder who's blindsided by his daughter. Grandfa is angry. This former Shakespearean actor winces when Ruby misspeaks. He recoils, not for the sake of linguistic propriety, but because, like his mentor, he has yoked proper usage to civility: "Shakespeare *respected* words! And do you know why? Because Shakespeare respected *people*! ... [H]uman beings ... ! But *you* ... this family!" (*ibid.*, 16) He's writing a chronicle (*ibid.*, 15), or a history, of his time, both to make sense of the moral devastation around him and to give proper English a good workout. From Albee's *Zoo Story* comes the chance meeting, in *Bump*, of strangers in a public place. A character even repeats Jerry's phrase from *Zoo Story* (1959) "the teaching emotion" (Albee, 36; *II* 67).

Bump leans on modern playwrights besides Albee to show what befalls Clarence, the man Jerry's phrase is addressed to. These forebears can be British. *Bump*'s setting harks to the basement apartment where Shelagh Delaney's kitchen-sink *A Taste of Honey* (1958) unfolds. At play's end, Clarence is less than human, as was Stanley Webber in Pinter's *Birthday Party* (1958). From Samuel Beckett's *Godot* (1952) comes *Bump*'s reliance upon absence, a conceit that explains in McNally's play the need of Ruby and her kids to destroy a shy librarian like Clarence (at one point Clarence says, "It's the waiting that is so terrible" (*ibid.*, 53]). What he's waiting for, half-consciously, is a heavy dose of malice. He has come to the right place. Ruby intones after first showing her face,

> If we are without faith, we find our way in the darkness.... If we are without hope, we turn to our despair.... And if we are without charity, we suckle the bitter root of its absence.... Spoken by me this December morning. Unwitnessed, unheard, alone [*ibid.*, 13].

Her moral compass has gone haywire. Her craving to strip, drain, and leach life of decency helps make *Bump* a minimalist play made from maximalist building blocks. Über-geeky Ruby is an infuriating, tantalizing destroyer out of Strindberg and the Puccini of *Turandot* via Albee. Her version of Get the Guest, from Albee's *Who's Afraid of Virginia Woolf* (1962), targets open-mindedness and civility, two virtues that both express and help us fulfill our humanity. Every day she sends her son Sigfrid into the city to lure an innocent stranger into her den. She murders to stay alive. Unless she kills a stranger a day, she believes that she'll die. But will she? She lacks the imagination and self-confidence to find out.

Clarence, the night's sacrificial victim, describes the tragedy she has set in motion. After meeting him at a political rally, Sigfrid brought him home for sex. He was lowering Clarence's guard. Then the ritual starts. As in "Cleopatterer," the aftermath of gay sex brings conflict. Sigfirid, Lakme, and Ruby fire questions at Clarence, demanding to know what he stands for. They want to belittle any transcendent values he prizes before killing him. What they hear whets their craving for the soul murder they're concocting. Clarence, a humanist, wants to improve the quality of life in the repressive police state where the play unfolds. Modestly, though, he sees himself as more of a work in progress than a leader. He finds beauty and goodness in absurdity and imperfection. Sometimes, he finds nothing. But, rather than surrendering to the moral void that has swallowed Ruby, he keeps looking. What eludes him, he can imagine: "I'm ... not strong. But I think things" (*ibid.*, 59). Fueling his thoughts are his healthy instincts. There's virtue in quietly continuing, he believes, taking small steps and accepting the imperfectability of things. And he has learned where to trawl for imperfection in his quest for the miraculous and the life giving.

Reason and logic don't govern his life. He finds happiness in the moment. Blessings come and go, which preserves their freshness; they're gifts, not burdens: "There are too many good things in the world not to want to be alive.... Music, art, literature... Shakespeare alone is a reason to be alive.... [T]here is a city in Italy named Florence.... It makes the rest of the planet tolerable. Florence is why we're alive." But, he continues, in an Emersonian vein, we needn't go to Florence or see a Shakespearean play to feel blessed. Life at its most ordinary is extraordinary: "And the things you can do! The simple things.... Just to take a walk even. It can be wonderful.... Or just to sit in a park ... watching the people. The other people. They're not you, and that's what's so beautiful about them.... Sit and wonder who they are. What they had for breakfast, what paper they're reading" (*ibid.*, 58–9). This isn't theodicy, the moronic belief that everything is ultimately for the best. The salvation he's seeking doesn't make the bad good. Instead, it's the gift of finding a way to keep faith with goodness and love despite knowing that the odds are stacked against you. It's close to what John Stuart Mill called "the inward rush of humanity."

Piqued by Clarence's faith, Ruby tries to probe the flaws in it: "Marching and waving that sign and being committed and all.... No matter how committed you are, you certainly don't pass up a good-looking distraction like Sigfrid" (*ibid.*, 56). (*SM* includes a gay librarian called, not Clarence, but Carl.) She keeps pouring it on. After Clarence has sex with Sigfrid, she makes him watch a sound-tracked slide show of their tumble. She has also hidden his clothes. The only piece of clothing around between him and nakedness is a woman's dress. It's not enough for his tormenters to simply murder him. The brutality of the politics that define them has taught them to twist the knife, as well.

They must shame Clarence to the point where he *wants* to die. To this end, they mock his belief in Shakespeare, the city of Florence, and sitting in a park (*ibid.*, 50–51). They do it while he's wearing a dress. As with Edmund's soggy, tattered Carmen Miranda costume and the drag worn by Gaetano Proclo in *The Ritz* (1975), the McNally hero feels most vulnerable when he looks ridiculous, a time, interestingly, when his inner strength can flare out therapeutically. The householders know this. They must crush Clarence's gentle, wondering side lest it expose their barrenness. Grandfa, who had warned him to bolt the lair, must go too because, content to be on a level with life, he knows that some things are worth doing for their own sake (*ibid.*, 73).

Notable here is the tendency of goal-directed behavior in the canon to go smash; decisive acts in *Tommy Flowers*, *Lisbon Traviata*, and *LVC* end in catastrophe. The play's arch-exemplar of this danger is also the one who talks the most (the talkiest people in *Brothers Karamazov*, the Grand Inquisitor and the Devil, also cause the most damage). The play begins, aptly, with a five-minute speech from Ruby. Frontain calls her "the strongest-willed yet emotionally least secure member of the household" ("There is someone out there," 13). He's right. She could profit mightily from adopting Clarence's goal of living deliberately. She's weary of everything, including her own weariness, which has warped her sense of purpose. So out of control is she that, instead of curbing her destructive urge, ritual serves it. Her long curtain-up speech is at once eerily formal and unhinged. Distortions and self-intoxication sabotage it throughout. Everything in it is real and not quite realistic. Its effect is both incantatory and soporific; you have to pay close attention to work out what, if anything, matters.

One thing, though, becomes clear in the words of "this paragon of evil with a sarcastic malicious tongue" (Stein, "The Early Plays," Zinman, ed. *Casebook* 20), as Howard Stein calls her. Having lost belief in herself, she rates doing over being. She'd rather wear herself out performing activity of any kind than face herself squarely. Fixated on immediate gratification, she knows that demolition provides rewards faster than the slow civilized patient-taxing work of creation or compromise. We're also aware of this sad truth. The bombs that razed Winchester Cathedral in WWII undid the work of centuries. But, unlike Ruby, we don't go around brandishing the wrecking ball. A good thing, too; serving the false gods of demolition has disjointed her from herself. She can't recognize her best chances. Though presumably American, she gave her children German (Sigfrid) and Indian (Lakme) names. Her language suffers from the same ill-judged sprawl. Not only does Grandfa call her out for her faux-cosmopolitan throw-it-all-in speaking style: "It's criminal how you abuse the gift of speech, *criminal*," he says. Lakme sees her straining for verbal effects as a denial of reality: "I'm sorry, Ruby, but we can't *all* of us be opera queens.... Some of us speak *English* when we want something" (*II*, 15). Lakme, who always addresses her mother by her first name, might have remained silent. What can she have expected from someone with Ruby's Nietzschean (indeed, borderline Nazi) contempt for human frailty?

Ruby is a poor show; frailty in people easy to find. It's natural that McNally notes, early in her first appearance on stage, the clash between her soaring rhetoric and her tumbledown, seedy look. She could have been compelling, a contemporary Raskolnikov, i.e., a revolutionary who has fled society and its constraints because she's made for greater things. She could have also become a dark believer who commits terrible crimes for honorable reasons. But she's bogged down in destructiveness. Clarence runs into an electrified fence without shedding any blood. His having thus flubbed his victim's role has reinstated his tormentor's old fears. Her victory is empty. Tomorrow the frustrating ritual will be repeated. She and the other householders are trapped in the same cycle of repetition that Dante, Nietzsche, and Freud all equated with the death wish. Ruby and her kids admired in Clarence a humanity that might have redeemed them, but killed him anyway. As with Nietzsche's eternal recurrence doctrine, the coils of moral darkness in which they've been wheeling have tightened a notch. And that's what happens when people don't believe in themselves. Self-hatred erodes the soul. Experts in it like Ruby will find new ways of self-torture to relish. When the pain grows too harsh, they'll seek relief and comfort by tormenting others.

* * *

Weighing in at 78 closely printed pages, the definitive text of *Bump* that appears in Volume Two of the *Collected Plays* provides fullness, richness, and theatricality. For instance, the precocious monster-in-training Lakme puts on a Green Hornet outfit to meet Clarence. Yet McNally's knowledge of the value of color and visual contrast on the stage takes him only so far. *Bump* never lets anything get in the way of the story it wants to tell. For most of the way, it's sluggish, self-indulgent, repetitive, and thus starved of drama.

Its ideas and conceits drown in gaudy effects, some of which invoke Leni Riefenstahl's *Triumph of the Will* (1934) and its stepchild, Orson Welles's *Citizen Kane* (1941). The play is too long, too noisy, and too corrosive. Its gifted young author didn't know when to back off and, more vitally, when to stop.

By naming one of the play's leading figures Sigfrid, for instance, the eponym of the third installment of Wagner's *Ring* cycle, he overstepped. Sigrid helps give *Bump* has a peculiarly Wagnerian atmosphere of incessant crisis. If *Die Walküre* has a theme, it's tenderness and its savage defeat by hostile forces. These forces are epical in stature. Richard Wagner's (1813–83) harmonic audacities tried to make opera an act of collective mythical hypnosis. Wagner also helped design the theater at Bayreuth that was built uniquely for the staging of his *Musikdramen*. In the light of this immensity, *Bump* looks puny and slipshod; its Wagnerian trope was ill-advised. For one thing, characterization, and not only that of Sigfrid, defeats McNally. The people talk to each other as if they're addressing a town meeting, disfiguring *Bump* with dead spots. Except for Grandfa and Clarence, they all lack inner lives, which robs them of having something worth saying. Another blot: these others are wicked, which needn't hurt the play, but it does. Though Iago is evil, his flaws have a riveting grandeur. McNally's villains stir in us little fear, grudging respect, or troubled envy. They bore us. McNally has boxed himself in. Because he didn't engage with his characters, neither do we.

The blunders don't end here. In his favor it can be said that he clothes his people with enough high consequence to provoke revelations that would certainly count tremendously if they happened. But they don't happen. The plot's discontinuity cuts off their oxygen. Another first full-length play by a contemporary of his, Alan Bennett's *Forty Years On*, requires too many props and scene changes to be staged by most producers. But Bennett's 1963 play, which also premiered in its author's 20s, depends less on noisy self-conscious effects. Less self-insistent, too, it gives us breathing room. *Bump*, which is always up in our faces, feels too full, too calculated, and too much.

Though we rarely feel any page-turning anxiety and suspense as we clump through the play, we can imagine the relief McNally felt finishing it. *Bump* is more puzzling than compelling. Yes, it sometimes reminds us that an ambitious failure can trump a lightweight success. McNally sought in *Bump* something deep and elemental; Ruby's opening speech refers to death several times. We soon see why. Both her fear of being alone and the imposition of a curfew give the sense of time running out. The electricity that later sizzles Clarence reminds us of Chekhov's gun hanging from the wall. Thematic too is the tie-in between homosexuality, betrayal, and death implicit elsewhere in McNally that sets off the electrified fence. But these gems lie buried in gunk. McNally's failure to link politics, family dysfunction, and high culture have blocked outlets of growth. Despite all the risks *Bump* takes, its slow, tangled effects make it a static work whose mingy people rarely touch our hearts.

II

Like *Bump* before it, *Where Has Tommy Flowers Gone?* is a mega-play that keeps knocking us off balance, as when, apropos of nothing taking place on stage, it throws in a reference to the little-known American lawyer, politician, and abolitionist, Wendell Phillips (1811–84) (*ibid.*, 120). And that's not all. Later in the play, a sunglassed woman recounts in her sole on-stage appearance, her meeting with Elvis Presley in a rural Oklahoma nightclub. Her soliloquy, which comes from nowhere and leads nowhere, lasts three times as long as Lucky's in *Godot*. McNally designed his 1971 play on lines sharply different from those of *Bump*. Its lead figure is a bachelor in his mid–20s, not a middle-aged mother of two. He's a man on the go, suggesting that other wanderer of the urban maze, Leopold Bloom, of Joyce's *Ulysses*, who writes letters under the name Henry Flower. Rather than breaking in one place, the action moves freely around Manhattan Island, touching down, for instance, in Lincoln Center, Bloomingdale's (another allusion to Joyce's Everyman figure?), and the Women's House of Detention in Greenwich Village (where the play ends). This variety helps make it refreshingly brighter than *Bump*. There's more. The play's eponym disguises himself as an Italian musician, a cockney ballerina, and, again wearing drag, a German diva.

In a postmodern stroke rare in McNally, Tommy will address the audience (*ibid.*, 96). This frolic shows a self-composed McNally flaunting the artifice of his creation; he tells rather than shows because he's reminding us that his play is made up (*ibid.*, cf. 143). The artifice keeps its swagger. It divides the play into scenes with names like TOMMY'S MOTHER OR I AM THE WALRUS (*ibid.*, 94) and CALIFORNIA DREAMIN' (*ibid.*, 139), after tunes by the then-popular rock groups The Beatles and The Mamas and The Papas. McNally is assuring his audience; they won't have to brace themselves for profundities or Wisdom. They will also enjoy the physical comedy the play revels in. Whether or not McNally was pleased with *Bump*, he wanted his next full-length play to be more fun to watch. A shoplifter, for example, leaves a ladies' room in Bloomie's carrying a cello case from which she removes, Harpo Marx-like, a clock, a sweater, and some shoes (but no oil can). Later, the frozen turkey she had stuffed inside her coat after stealing it from the A&P starts leaking all over the stage. Still another sight gag in this part of the play shows Tommy dressed like a nun (*ibid.*, 115).

His later on-stage appearance draped in the American flag (*ibid.*, 143) adds a touch of carnival aimed at the dark underside of America's grandiosity. He's showing off to Bunny Brown, a young California beauty whose propensity to violence has made her more American than she knows. Bunny says, in a disturbing echo from "Next," *Bringing It*, and *Bump*, "I think that people who don't like America should be electrocuted" (*ibid.*, 142). Incongruity drives much of the action. Recalling *Roller Coaster*, violence keeps company with a medley of old national favorites like "America the Beautiful," during which, in another legacy from *Bump*, pictures of the Empire State Building and Grant's Tomb show these national landmarks exploding.

The assaultive had swept to the fore soon after curtain rise, where it became clear that Tommy likes to blow things up. He came to Lincoln Center for the Performing Arts in order to bomb it. But, in an original, if macabre, touch, "America's cultural center" (*ibid.*, 8) deserves to be bombed. Not only would it merely speed an ongoing breakdown; it would even represent a public service. Time is wearing down this badly maintained monument. Its poor lighting puts at risk visitors who might stumble on the broken glass littering the place. Water from the fountain adorning its courtyard has leaked into the underground parking garage. The handrails on one of the stairways are loose.

If Lincoln Center has put the able-bodied at risk, it gives the handicapped little chance of moving about on their own. A nasty moment of black humor shows a floral bouquet blowing up in the face of a mentally challenged blind girl. But Rachel Gonzalez, the "'Fight for Sight' poster girl of the year" (*ibid.*, 126) is played, once again in drag, by Tommy Flowers. A sequence of events that recalls the biter-bit device of Renaissance drama ends with Tommy, who's usually in charge, taking several hard falls. Are we meant to laugh? Or are we witnessing justice? After allowing his girlfriend to go to jail for a crime *he* performed, his dog is stolen and his best friend dies.

A triumph of narrative self-indulgence over theatrical expertise, *Tommy Flowers* strives for effects at any cost. Its dazzle out-blazes its drama. As a result, its effects are too calculated to check out. It's also jerry-built. Some slimming down and stripping away would have both trimmed fat and offset the impression that the play works by accretion rather than interior development. (McNally said he conceived the work "as some kind of an epic" [Guernsey 289].) As it stands, it has much action but no core, which is why Tommy, a version of Turgenev's Superfluous Man or Dostoevsky's Underground Man, keeps casting around for a fitting opponent or cause. This problem accounts for McNally's unawareness of his characters' potential for growth. None of the characters are becoming because none of them *become* in any meaningful way.

The failings of *Tommy Flowers* are serious, making the play, on balance, more of a disappointment than a waste of time. Yet time is precious. If there's a play of McNally's you can miss, make it this one.

III

The Ritz puts us on firmer artistic ground. McNally's command of stagecraft in his 1975 frolic represents the advance he had in mind when he called his mature plays operas in contrast to the aria-like ambience of their predecessors. Harking to Joyce's dramatic ideal in *A Portrait*, the "dizzy absurdity" (Frontain, "I Don't Believe This Whole Night" 92) governing *The Ritz* has a professionalism missing from the earlier work. McNally's suppression of himself has brought some important gains, including some screamingly funny lines. His putting himself out of action clears the stage for fun stemming from the mistaken identities, the screwball comedy (*ibid.*, 89), and the "Keystone Kops-like chase scenes" (*ibid.*, 80) that sometimes reverse, the pursued becoming the pursuer.

The laughs pile up in this comedy of marital confusion and mismatched purposes, often because of McNally's skill in weaving into its fabric many influences. Seamless in its embroidery, *Ritz* includes in its heritage, alongside the Rabalaisian tropes and conventions noted by Frontain (*ibid.*, passim), the classic Victorian standbys of contrivance, implausibility, and sentimentality. Its plot also unwinds steadily while following the insane logic of French farce. The insanity is pleasingly tempered by a cadence of chance and inevitability in which lives cross and re-cross.

This rhythm draws us in. Comic misunderstandings and coincidences abound in *The Ritz*, together with visual double entendres that both aid and thwart the people's aims. These aims, both unconscious and deliberate, gain urgency from the play's setting. a men's bathhouse, where society's laws and guidelines are "rendered ... maddingly uncertain" (*ibid.*, 97). McNally's control of his materials makes this uncertainty a force for fun. In the play's climax, not only does the hero "assert his masculinity after being reduced to wearing a dress" (*ibid.*, 88); his wife must also cross-dress to save his life.

This happy outcome begins in darkness. To the strains of the funeral march from Verdi's *Nabucco*, old man Vespucci issues the death-bed command that his son-in-law Gaetano Proclo be killed; a contract goes out on Proclo immediately. *The Ritz* is a domestic drama like *Bump* and *Bringing It*. But the parents are all dead, and their children are middle-aged, Proclo and Vivian having been wed for 20 years. Another difference: the play's happy ending. Which, in line with the operatic ideal the play attains, is fragile; as Pinter's comedies of menace showed, violence can walk in tandem with knockabout.

Four. Cauldrons of Deceit

To foil his pursuers, Gaetano Proclo goes to a gay bath, judged by him the last place his brother-in-law Carmine would look for him. What happens to this Everyguy before the play's hilarious climax turns his mistake into an opportunity for growth.

Identified by Frontain as "a straight, warm-hearted and sexually unsophisticated sanitation executive" (*ibid.*, 79), this dazed Clevelander starts reeling immediately. If he was looking for safety and repose, he came to the wrong place. All the men he meets in the baths (male prostitutes and lonelies seeking company) have come there for sex. One denizen, in fact, got himself banned from another New York bathhouse for kicking in the door of a guest who blocked his advances.

Proclo's freedom is running out. Carmine, having just entered the baths, speaks both the words that end the play's first act and, armed with a handgun, a knife, and a pair of brass knuckles, open Act Two. This portent holds despite what follows it. Sight gags and other kinds of physical comedy pack the play's second act. Characters dart in and out of rooms with split-second timing, sometimes to chase characters chasing other characters. Stalkers have to stop stalking. Claud, who fancies Proclo, gets his robe torn off of him by the nightclub entertainer Googie Gomez. The merriment also takes a postmodern turn. After using the ancient device of hiding characters under a bed, McNally jokes about it. A man who hears that a friend of his is hiding under a bed answers, "Why not? Everybody else is" (*Ritz* 35). On the next page, the man and Googie Gomez dive under the bed, too. But not all is for laughs. McNally's theatrical savvy has kept the fun from slipping into excess. Has he also lowered our guard in order to body-slam us? Proclo's crossing himself just after our Blessed Lady is invoked by his pursuer, Carmine (*Ritz* 29, 30) sharpens our attention for what ensues.

How safe will Proclo's faith keep him? Selfhood has been peeling off of him in a process that could end in death. Despite his being the only straight patron at the baths, he's thought to be gay by all the others. Googie, whom he mistakes for a man, mistakes *him* for a theatrical producer who could boost her singing career. Does her error fit a pattern of self-undoing launched by Proclo himself? In what in retrospect looked like an unconscious death wish, Proclo signed into the bathhouse as Carmine Vespucci — who turns out to be one of the bath's owners.

Retribution looms. The importance of family honor and the *Cosa Nostra*'s hallowed code of *omertà* both return from the play's opening scene. The force they've built rises from that scene's ominous mood. First, the gay-straight connection, or split, that has been unifying the action claims more authority than expected. But the authority manifests itself in a surprising way. At the moment of Proclo's entrapment, his captor Carmine's secret is bared by an employee of his: "Thirty-even five hundred on the week. The rain killed us tonight. And next week we got the Jewish holidays coming up. Good night, boss" (*Ritz* 55). This wink at the audience dispels some of the built-up tensions, as McNally might have safely forecast. On any given night, at least half the house at New York's Longacre Theatre, where the play debuted, would be Jewish.

This winking partnership with that house sets the tone for the play's finale. Carmine, mortified by the horror of losing face with the mob, must keep hidden his ownership of the baths; gangsters are supposed to hold no truck with gays. He has become blackmailible. In exchange for his sister Vivian's promise to conceal his tie with the gay world, he agrees under duress to call off the contract his father had put out on Proclo. (McNally's sharp insights into the collision between underworld codes of conduct and the Catholic Church, to which most mobsters belong, have never been spoken of.)

For the first time in a full-length McNally play, everybody in the audience leaves the theater feeling good. The work's carefully made characters, its convincing dramatic trajectory, and its consistent moral attitude have all won the day for an excellent reason. The recognition of the meaning of the play's finale has chimed with its proper expression. Though some of the audience members have seen more homosexuality than they'd have fancied, an Apollonian sensibility restores life to an order they'd both recognize and accept. Add the immaculate timing of this affirmation to the play's many merits. If *Ritz* lacks emotional resonance, these merits and the depths they graze both make it more than a charming bagatelle. We've been made to care about what happens to the people. To invoke Mozart, the play is McNally's *Idomeneo*. Think of *The Magic Flute* and *Master Class*, and the point is made.

IV

It's Only a Play has the same healthy vital signs as *The Ritz*, which came out ten years earlier — crackling, witty prose and engaging characters whose carefully timed movements cause gyrations and dark undertones that keep us alert. The action takes place in the New York City townhouse of Julia Budder. Julia is hosting an opening-night party for a play that premiered earlier the same evening. McNally, who knows his way around opening-night parties, calls his play "an attempt to describe exactly what it was like to work in the Broadway theater in the 1980s" ("A Few Words of Introduction," *Three Plays* x). A year later he called the work a commentary on "the state of the America theater, fame, and money" (DiGaetani 223). Was he too modest? Because nearly every character in *IOAP* survives on his/her charm, brains, and daring, taken together they symbolize the American dream.

Timing helps deliver this significance. The partygoers are all waiting for Frank Rich's *New York Times* review of the new play they all have a stake in. The waiting has been making inroads on them. Tired by the lateness of the hour and sluggish from the free food and drink they've been stuffing themselves with, they're losing patience. In addition, a collective fear of the worst has gripped them. The actors in *IOAP* just don't act; they're fully absorbed in both the acting culture and their place in it. The waiting has become for them a waiting-for.

They're aren't only nervous about what Rich is gong to say. Status anxiety has been gnawing at them. Where professional friendships recently stood, rivalries are sprouting. The intrusion of the improbable has suddenly made this glamorous urban world dangerous. One guest, Ira Drew, a theater critic notorious for his poisonous opening-night takedowns, carries a pistol to protect himself from angry theater people who have blamed him for wrecking their careers. This feared and hated man, whose name means anger in Latin, already knows this wrath. The harshness of his reviews has gotten him banned from the press list of the League of Producers. Unknown to the others, he's bracing for a different kind of blow, one that bullets won't stop. He has been peddling a play he wrote surreptitiously as Carolyn Comstock.

More friction stems from two people closely bound by *The Golden Egg*, the play that debuted several hours earlier. In a surprising twist, both Julia Budder, its producer, and its director, Frank Finger, have been banned from the theater where *Egg* is being performed. This departure from stage protocol has confused and upset the other party guests; anybody could get the boot. The defensive campy humor, cattiness, and name-dropping build. Most of the guests, being actors, feel insecure, to begin with, owing to their large, but fragile, egos. The TV soap-opera star who says, "You could stuff a *moose* with the egos in this room" (*3 Plays* 209), has it nailed.

It would take little to bruise or draw blood from any of these egos. Virginia Noyes, called a "firecracker" in McNally's list of characters (*ibid.*, 160), ranks high on his list of those at risk. Like a firecracker, Miss Noyes is noisy, and she could explode at any time. She's also starring in *The Golden Egg*, mostly by default, her last two Hollywood movies having flopped. Performing at age 37 in what could be her last starring role has shaken her. She resents criticism, even when it's disguised as an attempt to improve one of her scenes. When told, for instance, that she dropped a bottle on stage, she snaps back, "I didn't drop the fucking bottle. It fucking slipped." She reacts to being told that she muffed a line by telling the playwright who tried to correct her, "So bring me up on Equity charges" (*ibid.*, 186).

The young playwright who called her out is named Peter Austin because his creator has a brother named Peter, with whom he was raised in Texas, the capital of which is Austin. He's best friends with James Wicker, whom Southern California has been treating better than it did Virginia Noyes. James radiates self-confidence and cheer. This television star has flown to New York for the premiere of Peter's new play. But the vagaries of their profession have strained their reunion. James starts regretting having turned down Peter's offer of the play's male lead. Then he's rocked hard; he learns that his sitcom has been canceled. He keeps reeling; Rich's hatchet job has shut down *The Golden Egg*. (Ironically, Rich gave *IOAP* an excellent review ["True to Form. The Theater was Full of Surprises" (*New York Times*, 28 Dec 1986): C1].)

McNally's play turns inward here. Looking to justify his rejection of Peter's offer, James had been half-hoping to find poison in Rich's review. He suspects, to his dismay, that his career counts more to him than friendship. Peter, whose reactions toward *The Golden Egg* are simpler, feels crushed, as do the actors who appeared in it. Like them, he resists taking full blame for the flop. His claws come out. Perhaps, exaggerating only slightly, he says in a letter to someone else, but that James reads, things that justify McNally's saying of him in the play's stage directions, "Don't let his good looks fool you" (*ibid.*, 180): "The play never really had a chance without James Wicker in it. Of course, he was a son of a bitch not to have done it and I wish him and his fucking series a sudden and violent death. No hard feelings, Jim, you miserable no-talent fruit, but you will rot in hell for this" (*ibid.*, 177). This malice was foreshadowed — and not only because friendships have a hard time surviving in the charged air of the theater. James had little reason to bridle when he found his name left out of the bio of Peter in the *Playbill* of *Egg*. But perhaps like some of the actors McNally had met, he finds reasons to be offended. His first conversation with Peter displays his gift for slipping in the knife:

PETER: I wanted you up there so bad tonight.
JAMES: Jack's marvelous.
PETER: I know.
JAMES: Not that marvelous.
PETER: They're already talking about Redford for the film.
JAMES: What of? [*ibid.*, 184–85].

Nor can Peter complain about this snub. Asked about Lanford Wilson's new play, he answers, "It's terrific. I hate it" (*ibid.*, 219). A countering note of a different kind comes from the play's director, Frank Finger. Another of McNally's self-haters, this brooding Chicagoan is so puzzled by his success that he fights it; he neither believes it nor wants it. Prodded by guilt, he steals his producer-hostess's pepper shaker. The punishment he's coveting springs from McNally's knowledge, dramatized in *The Roller Coaster*, that achievement of any kind both starts with and ignites further painful self-probing.

McNally's creative spark, though, has survived his description of the theater as a blood sport whose main event pits him against himself. The intractable urge of his stand-in, Peter, to mount a play prompts him to bring together the cast of *Golden Egg*, the very name of which posits renewal. Fighting past the woe caused by Frank Rich's diatribe, he and his cohorts will stage in the same hall where *Golden Egg* flopped a brand of instant theater that, like Chicago's Second City, does without rehearsals, rewrites, and previews (*ibid.*, 227). Humpty-Dumpty's broken shell needn't rejoin. The delighted actors have forgotten their enmities now that they're looking at an egg that can nourish them; in a truth foreshadowed by the playwright/theater critic Ira Drew (*ibid.*, 200), *IOAP* is a looking-glass play.

Those involved in its production can now join ranks because the survival of their play has come under threat; all of them believe that the show must go on. To mount their production, they both need each other and can count on each other's commitment to the stage; McNally has always seen the theater as collaborative; playwriting for him is less of a solitary pursuit than an attempt to connect with others (Zinman, "Interview," *Casebook*, Zinman, ed. 8). The fast, allusive patter heard earlier resumes. Peter and Virginia hug after she stops fuming over his reproof. They both know in the best professional parts of themselves that the common purpose they're serving subsumes ego. Of the surrogate family they belong to, Ira Drew says, "I don't understand you people. One minute you're at each other's throats, the nest you're sticking up for one another like you're in some kind of club" (*Three Plays* 234).

A shared love of the stage has dissolved their differences. This love also drives them to excel, and, like all other driven souls, they pursue their common goal ruthlessly. McNally will probe this ruthlessness in *Master Class* and *Dedication*. *IOAP*, which is more lighthearted and upbeat, only grazes it. But it's always nearby. The words, "It's only a play," spoken first by Peter Austin (*ibid.*, 184), will be voiced several more times as the action builds, each voicing more thought-provoking than its predecessor.

It's intriguing, too, that the words, "It's only an opera," are spoken in *Golden Age* (15), a work that premiered 25 years after *IOAP*. That 2010 work also shows the 19th-century composer Vincenzo Bellini picking at notes on the piano that segue first into Harold Arlen's "Stormy Weather" and then Stephen Sondheim's "Send in the Clowns," songs that will remain unwritten for another 300 years. This head-scratcher has affinities with the Zen koan, "What is the sound of one hand clapping?" It was framed to trick the mind into greater clarity and realization. To examine it, let's take our cue from the longstanding idea that the house of fiction has many rooms. McNally has given the idea a Bergsonian twist to argue that *all* music fits inside one vast, all-encompassing, open-ended organism that defies the constraints of time. From this rich harvest, a musical genius like Bellini can sometimes happen upon a handful of notes that fuse as a song that hasn't been written.

By analogy, McNally views the whole theatrical canon, from Sophocles to Neil LaBute, as a heaving, undulating whole that flouts the strictures of time. Breaching linearity again, a crisis like the sudden closing of a play that many had counted on to pay their bills and further their careers will remind these many of both the inviolability of this mighty whole and their duty to it.

* * *

The motif started taking shape at the end of Act One when Emma, a taxi driver, brought to Julia's penthouse a copy of the *New York Times* containing Rich's review. Emma's arrival perturbs the uneasy guests. Yet her being the only non-theater person on the set helps her quiet the frenzy in Act Two, where, having kick-started the plot, she now tempers it. McNally had called attention to her importance by making her the only character in the play with no last name (*Three Plays* 160). At work here, among other things, are McNally's democratic values. The "no-nonsense" (*ibid.*) working-class sturdiness that clashes with the agitation surrounding her keeps the stage from bursting into wholesale dementia. In line with the idea that *IOAP* is McNally's paean to his love affair with the theater, she plays the role, from classical tragedy, of the messenger. But that's not all she plays. Add to that role a second one — also from the Greek stage — of *deus ex machina*. Contrary to her royal counterparts in Molière's *Tartuffe* and Shakespeare's *Measure for Measure*, she uses working-class pluck to help steer the action to its happy conclusion.

The theatrical culture of her time, the 1980s, had stiffened into hierarchy, intolerance, and ego-gratification. Rich's putdown causes a crisis in McNally's subset, or microcosm, of this culture, shattering professional and personal bonds. If not for Emma, they'd stay shattered. She sees things the egos of the others have blinded them to. But, in line with her being a messenger, she can't join the others in the promised land she has led them to. The words with which she closes the first act, "What's wrong with these people? It's only a play!" (*ibid.*, 204) foretells her job in the second. If her later statement, "I wouldn't be in the theater if you paid me" (*ibid.*, 213), has set her off from the others, it also poses an issue McNally wants us to think about.

There *is* a place for blue-collar people like her in the wide-ranging culture of the Broadway stage. Emma's remark, "New York without a theater district might as well be Newark" (*ibid.*, 228), signals an appreciation of the drama that McNally respects. Though she can't make plays, she can enjoy them. They matter to her, too, as they should. Many have argued, from Aristotle to August Wilson, that in a healthy community the theater has the same familiarity a school or a grocery store. McNally would prefer to write plays for *her* kind than for the rich suburbanites and company heads who've priced Broadway theater tickets beyond Emma's ability to pay.

This democratic view sorts well with the plot of *IOAP*, a very busy one that smoothes out rough spots between its component parts, adds bridges, and sets it all in a coherent dramatic form as it moves ahead. Though sketchy, the people are always individualized, with their special personalities and problems — until the crisis they share mars their defining marks, as tragedy often does. And the threatened end of any artistic career qualifies as tragic for the fretful artist. McNally implicates himself in the mess, too. He says, through the words of Peter, "If I wasn't a playwright, I'd be a very nice person" (*ibid.*, 224). His point is duly noted. The tensions of the evening, some of which he instigated, strain and then snap his friendship with James. In a riff borrowed from Pinter's *The Caretaker*, Emma nearly runs him down with a vacuum cleaner before telling him, "If I had a best friend, I'd cherish him" (*ibid.*, 226).

McNally's willingness to air his faults in public sits well with us; a writer who shares his vulnerabilities, rather than denying them, wins our hearts. In *IOAP* this openness also channels into the play's escalating rhythms, all of which he will resolve. The tidiness of its resolution, moreover, doesn't make *IOAP* shallow or trite. Nearly effortlessly, the play blends sociology with group psychology to the betterment of both. It's more than an art curiosity. It's a searching, formally disciplined work — a triumph of stage syntax — built with rhythm and pace. The spots of theatrical twaddle it uses it then redeems without being stuffy or arch.

Worthy in its own right, *It's Only a Play* also marks a watershed moment in McNally's artistic growth. He couldn't have written it earlier in his career and may not have wanted, or needed, to at a later stage.

Chapter Five

Sore, Spent and Sage

Beginning with the plays of McNally's middle period, a Dickensian sympathy for the put-upon and the disenfranchised began shaping itself as feminism. It takes us by surprise. Spite has been frazzling the recently reunited mother and daughter of *The Rink* (1985). The two women are both ready and reluctant to forgive the hostilities that drove Angie, or Angel, the daughter, from the nest years earlier. A new complication reignites the long-seething rancor. Angel's homecoming is spoiled by the dilapidated roller rink of the play's title. A drain on both her mother's energy and her finances, it has been sold to pay for Anna's long-deferred trip to Rome. But the 30-year-old Angel, who connects the rink to her happiest childhood memories, claims it for herself. A plot has emerged from the play's early going.

As far as any of McNally's plays admit to a resolution, the plot of *The Rink* is later resolved by the presence on stage of Angel's daughter, who was named after Anna despite the antagonism that had been dividing her mother and grandmother. Little Anna's appearance on stage causes an emotional climax; the women embrace each other in a show of spontaneity so swift that we can't know which of them made the first move (*Rink* 91). Evident here is a sympathy with women that will recur in *Frankie and Johnny*, *A Perfect Ganesh*, and *Deuce*. This recurrence is no casual afterthought. McNally knows how hard women work, how undervalued their labors can be, and how much this injustice has cost. But he hasn't overplayed his hand. No beauty, the "attractive but somewhat overweight" Angel resembles "hundreds, no thousands, of young women who have not realized their own specialness because no one ever told them that they were" (*ibid.*, 9). Driving this intensely affecting thought dramatically is the power of the blood tie to survive conflict. This affirmation is perforce nuanced. Though Angel and Anna don't confirm the triumph of goodwill, they're nonetheless inspiring. The rink will stay in the family, a drain on its finances. No, Grandma won't visit Rome, but she *can* face the ordeal of being short-funded alongside loved ones. The same truth will apply to those taken down by the scourge of AIDS in *Love! Valour! Compassion!* (1994).

AIDS also informs *Frankie and Johnny in the Clair de Lune*, another work expressive of McNally's use of close observation to find importance in the banal. The disease isn't mentioned in the play. Referring to it, though, McNally told Steven Drukman, "It was certainly a subtext." More pointedly, he said to John M. Clum that "his most autobiographical" play was inspired by "the loss of dear gay friends [James Coco and Robert Drivas] to AIDS" (Clum, *Acting Gay* 190). But McNally knew that over-explicitness could sink his play. He muted the impact of HIV-AIDS, at the time of his 1987 play commonly judged a gay disease, by viewing it through the prism of a straight couple. Vital here are the ages of Frankie (46) and Johnny (40). McNally, himself 38 when *F&J* premiered, aimed the play at audiences in early middle-age (Zinman, "Interview," Zinman, ed. *Casebook*, 11).

Dating changes at age 40. A shrinking field of eligible partners has dimmed prospects for finding long-term love. Another constraint: it has become tougher in one's 40s to find mentally compatible people who can also rouse one sexually. Though Frankie and Johnny both remember the heady optimism of the 1960s, they've also slogged through the disenchantment and ennui of the two following decades. They haven't trekked this rubble alone. The sexual marketplace of 1987 includes possible deterrents caused by their counterparts' ex-spouse or spouses and kids. And prior lovers? At a time in history when contraceptive devices all but ruled out accidental pregnancies, many straights drifted into casual sex. The chances of becoming HIV-positive rose accordingly. One can see why. Sometimes, temporary relief from loneliness makes casual sex a tolerable risk, even factoring in the remorse and self-questioning that may follow. This post-coital self-probing justifies McNally's calling *F&J* "more of a poem about feelings than a true story" ("A Few Words of Introduction," *Three Plays* xi). These feelings can deep-cut tender places. One of the major issues of the play rises from the clash between the joys of wild, spontaneous sex and its all-too-common offspring, the hurdles we put in place to thwart partnering. Where do these hurdles come from? So terrified are we by change that, when somebody touches our hearts, we create new ones. All premarital sex drifts toward exogamy.

I

Frankie and Johnny aren't the "middle aged losers" ("McNally's Films," Zinman, ed., *Casebook* 86) of Helen T. Buttel's reckoning. Johnny comes much closer to the mark when he says of Frankie and himself, "There's a man and a woman. Not young, not old. No great beauties, either one.... They meet [at work] but they don't connect" (*Three Plays* 125). True, they need their menial dead-end jobs to make rent on their one-room apartments (Frankie has lived in *hers* for 8 years). Yet neither feels defeated. Just as Johnny sites his apartment in Brooklyn Heights to set it off from scruffier digs, Frankie claims that she lives in the Clinton district, not Hell's Kitchen, a sleazier name for the area bounding her flat on Tenth Avenue and Fifth-Third Street.

Their evasions notwithstanding, they're both holding their own. Though neither party is socially ambitious, they don't feel buried in the sludge of daily routine. Frankie, who takes time from her table-waiting to chat with an aging regular customer at the diner where she and Johnny work still wants to teach. Her lack of a high-school diploma has all but blocked this hope. But she might have a better chance developing a talent she has overlooked. Her calling Bach's *Goldberg Variations* "chaste" and "pure" and then saying that they remind her of "grace" (*ibid.*, 94) bespeaks an elevated sensibility. Her mentioning chastity just moments after having wild orgasmic sex with Johnny is not ironic. By linking chastity, purity, and grace, she has dovetailed music and salvation. This blend of the Catholic faith of McNally's childhood and, by implication, dance — to McNally the sublimest form of human interconnection after sex — augurs well for the couple's future.

But, as Hamlet told Horatio, just before his fatal duel with Laertes, augury can be defied (5.2.137); we're not slaves to fate, probability systems, or hunches. Should we protest? The alarming rate with which McNally's people blight their best hopes implies that the "special providence" that dictates a sparrow's fall (*ibid.*) can serve people better than their whims and yens. McNally knows, as all creative writers must, that people want, with equal fervor, not only several things at once; they also crave mismatched or incompatible goals. Frankie knows what she wants — an intimate exclusive bond. And she thinks Johnny could provide it. But this prospect has run afoul of the vigor and urgency of the same animal attraction that provoked it. Too much has happened too quickly. She's too engulfed to take stock of her feelings.

Her first words after having sex show her in retreat: "God, I wish I still smoked. Life used to be much more fun" (*Three Plays* 93). It's as if sex with Johnny has failed her. Which, perhaps, he senses; later, when he proclaims that he and Frankie made "[g]reat love together," she says, "Okay love" (*ibid.*, 120). Feeling blocked, Johnny backs off, too. He needs to protect himself. Asked why he's laughing — a question he can't answer — he says, "[I]t has nothing to do with you" (*ibid.*, 93). This is an odd thing to say to someone you've just slept with for the first time. Yet it squares with his behavior at this early stage of the play, when both parties fear that sex has let them down in some vague way.

The duel with invisible weapons continues. Minutes later, Johnny foolishly talks about how he lost his virginity. Have his inner demons replaced real worries? He had to know that women don't like to hear about their lovers' past bedmates, certainly not right after sex. And his answer to her claim that she's not a prude shows common sense restraining him only at the last split second: "I know that! Any woman who..." (*ibid.*, 95). He nearly said that a woman who has sex on a first date is anything *but* prudish. It all registers with Frankie — both the bitten-back insult and the incongruity of her first-date sex with the self-entitlement she will later voice. She and Johnny are fencing both hard and carefully. She has played false her declared preference for a cooler, drier sexual style. The aftermath of her rut with Johnny is disorienting her, as it has him.

She needs to trust her feelings more. As he did with the cabdriver Emma in *It's Only a Play*, McNally has gifted her with a sensibility and verbal fluency that most social comedians restrict to her social betters. Frankie not only values words for themselves. She also sees language as an expression of character. Responding to Johnny's habit of repeating the phrase, "Pardon my French," she says, "The first time you said it tonight I practically told you I had a headache and had to go home" (*ibid.*, 115).

She has the goods to support the standards she imposes on the men she dates. The acuteness of her response to Bach's *Goldberg Variations* was wholly credible. She used to dance well, always a plus for McNally. She could also sing and act, having played the female lead in a high-school production of *Brigadoon* (*ibid.*, 117), a 1947 Lerner-Loewe Broadway musical that takes place on an enchanted, or bewitched, evening, which, again like *F&J*, features an up-and-down romance. She was well-suited for the role. Like Clarence of *Bump*, she has the openness and cheer to warm herself reflecting upon a remote goal, in her case, a career in teaching.

Her off-sider Johnny follows her by depicting the uncommonness of the commonplace; a close look at the banal again turns up gold. This short-order cook keeps both a dictionary and a volume of Shakespeare's work in his locker. He consults them, too. Besides quoting *Hamlet* (*ibid.*, 118), he cites an act and scene from the lesser-known *Merry Wives of Windsor* (*ibid.*, 122). He's at least as verbal as Frankie, as is shown in his phrase, "not knowing how to segue from one mood to the next" (*ibid.*, 131). He also excels at his job, a point important enough to the play that McNally shows this "*virtuoso*" (*ibid.*, 138) of the cutting board slicing, dicing, and cooking the ingredients of a western. When Frankie says that she has never seen peppercorns cut so fine as his, he says of his fellow cooks, "They're looking for shortcuts" (*ibid.*, 139). He prides himself in his work.

What she likes most about him, though, is his vulnerability, not his expertise. She's impressed when he calls "the afterglow of sex" the "most beautiful part of making love" (*ibid.*, 125). Equally impressive is his gift for winning intimacy from what first looks like ruin. At curtain-up for Act Two he feels intimidated and useless. The "male menopause" (*ibid.*, 133) he has been dreading seems to have kicked in. Insisting that it never happened before, he goes limp inside of Frankie. He's upset. He has failed to see that Frankie means more to him than a casual one-nighter; she has hit him with more psychological data than he can process. He feels overwhelmed and confused. His performance anxiety has addled his mind so much that he underrates the tenderness and fellow-feeling of her response to it: "Just be glad you have someone as sympathetic as me *to share it with you*" (*ibid.*, 133; emphasis added). She hasn't distanced herself from his plight. She shares it with him just as Eve, rather than tricking Adam into sin, shared it with him.

His problem — if it is a problem and not an opportunity — lets her soothe his flustered manhood, an act worthy enough in its own right that takes on added charm by evoking her gentle, loving grandmother, her only relative she remembers fondly. People who help others also help themselves. This connection to a happy past calms and stabilizes her. Other rewards follow. This representative, or prototypical, woman hates trailers or mobile homes (*ibid.*, 99). She has made an important self-disclosure. Like a motel room, a trailer symbolizes the make-shift and the short-lived to searchers for stability and roots. She has already thought about bonding with Johnny. "I'm glad what happened happened. If we both play our cards right, maybe it will happen again" (*ibid.*, 102), she tells him. As women are said to do, she's thinking beyond the revels that just ended. She's on the right track. This woman who had the grip and self-command to stop smoking both tobacco and pot is willing to work hard to connect with Johnny. "I like you a lot" (*ibid.*, 102), she tells him.

Their Saturday night date has invoked the exhilarating ones of her past. It comes forth early in the text that she and Johnny are *both* eyeing the same goal, viz., closeness, and that each of them hopes the other can provide it. But Johnny needs to pursue it more prudently. He denies her breathing room. His practice of staring at her at close range and his nonstop love chatter ("Pretend that we're the only two people in the entire world" [*ibid.*, 120]) is choking off her oxygen. She needs space and air. She keeps saying things like "Maybe next time" (*ibid.*, 114), "I was looking forward to seeing you again" (*ibid.*, 120), and "What happened to a second date?" (*ibid.*, 119) because she needs to sort out in her mind the meaning of the events of this first date — something she can't do in the glare of his devouring intimacy. She resents him going through her purse, putting on her sunglasses, and opening both her refrigerator and her medicine cabinet. Boundaries be damned for him. When she cuts her finger, he sucks the blood from it. Has he become her Dracula? He's leaving her nothing that's entirely her own. How can their intimacy build? she wonders. Someone who has tapped into her bloodstream will shove his mitts into everything she owns.

Perhaps she's not ready for intimacy. She claims that self-loathing drives us into the arms of people we know will hate us (*ibid.*, 146). This orphan whose boyfriend betrayed her with her best friend has little reason to expect happiness from a man. The last one she loved, seven years ago, beat her so badly that he stopped her from having children. He also scarred her in other ways. Her suspicion, gleaned from her sad history with men, that she doesn't deserve a stable ongoing love tie has been duping her into breaking off with her lovers; she doesn't want to get hurt again. McNally might have had this preventive action in mind when he said in 1994 that he identified with Frankie ("A Few Words" xi). Author and character share other affinities. *F&J* recalls works of Joyce Carol Oates and Jonathan Franzen that feature black humor, a sense of detachment from family (Frankie's mother, like Johnny's, bolted the nest when she was small), and a main figure who frustrates the very bonding he/she both craves and needs. The feelings of inadequacy and inferiority found by Clum in *A Perfect Ganesh* and *Lips Together, Teeth Apart* permeate much of the canon, including *F&J*: "McNally believes that self-loathing is an American problem, not a gay one" (Clum, "Where Are We Now," Zinman, ed. *Casebook* 108) — a malady that has been gaining steam from today's economic uncertainties, extreme weather, and the accelerating growth of hate groups.

The decades since *F&J* premiered haven't changed McNally's mind about the sameness of the byproducts wrought by gay and straight sex. What *has* changed is his slant on the stalemate facing Frankie and Johnny. In an email dated 14 August 2011, he said that he now identifies with Johnny, too, a "guy," claims Anita Gates, "with rough edges who has somehow come to know his own worth" (2). Part of this assurance stems from his job. Those who feed others befriend society. Like sexual love, food sustains life, a central point of Patrick White's 1965 novel, *The Solid Mandala* and Mary Troy's *Beauties: A Novel* (2010). Discontent dogs Johnny, anyway. During the two years he spent in jail for forgery, his wife divorced him to marry up, giving herself and the two kids she had with Johnny a smarter home than they could have known with him. Another reason why he talks about having children with Frankie: the erectile dysfunction that seized him at the start of Act Two. This shock awakened in him the insecurity he displayed in Act One when, reaching for borrowed glory, he yattered about how the 1985 movie, *Prizzi's Honor*, was shot in his Brooklyn Heights neighborhood.

His boasting recoiled on him. Even though he doesn't know it, he's most human and lovable when he forgets about his image. He had rebuked Frankie for her frequent apologies early in the play (*Three Plays* 104). Yet as the action grows, the apologies come mostly from *him* (e.g., *ibid.*, 119, 131), a fidget that gives *her* the confidence to speak both intimately and at length. Unmindful of guilt, the once-zipped-up Frankie grows expansive. The air has cleared. Both she and Johnny have gained ground without losing any. Offering protection to Johnny has made her feel protected herself. His dysfunction has made her feel warm and connected.

This matters to her. Mostly it's Johnny who'll queer the pitch even though he has at least as much to gain from bonding as Frankie. Like her, he wants to set down roots. His alcoholic mother left him when he was eight, after which he "bounced all over the place" (*ibid.*, 117), mostly in foster homes in Baltimore, Washington, D.C., and Allentown, Pennsylvania. This instability has made him, says Frankie, "very intense" (*ibid.*, 102). She also tells him, "You're too needy. You want too much" (*ibid.*, 113). He agrees. "I don't let go of old things easy and I grab new things too hard" (*ibid.*, 147), he admits after recounting the story of his devastating visit to the new home of his kids and his ex-wife following his prison release.

Security-starved, he wants things his own way, regardless of others. Soon after curtain rise, he asks Frankie to stop apologizing; he asks that she keep the light on in the room they just made love in; he keeps ignoring *her* demands that he go home. She feels stumped. His impulsive talk of marriage and children has skewed her dating protocol ("Whatever happened to a second date?" [*ibid.*, 119]). He may be right when he tells her, "People are given one moment to connect, not two or three" (*ibid.*, 121). There's a scene in Scott Fitzgerald's "The Rich Boy" (1926) where the title figure and the girlfriend he's walking with on a Florida beach both snap to the truth that if he doesn't propose now, he never will (he doesn't, ending the courtship).

Conversely, McNally has described a couple on their *first* date who believe they can build a future together. They also see this future as fragile. *F&J* describes the large, heartbreaking gap between life as it is and as it ought to be. An erotic tie between two mutually attracted people may die at first blush. The real distinction of *F&J* comes from the counterpoint created by its fast pace and its stubborn, powerful undertow of regret. What attracts us also terrifies us. This sad maxim often plays out to our disadvantage. With his usual wit and acumen, Frontain has shown what makes *F&J* so disturbing and challenging. The play scrapes at us because it shows "how the need for love is tempered by resentment of the compromises that any relationship entails." Frontain continues to describe our self-defeating tendency to drive away what we most need: "McNally's Johnny pleads with Frankie in a play that dramatizes a hunger for connection so powerful that it drives people to create seemingly impregnable defenses lest, they fear, they'll be consumed by it." ("Mutual Admiration: Sondheim and Playwright Terrence McNally" 132).

A further hindrance to connecting boils up from the play's *noir* setting. Whether it's called Clinton or Hell's Kitchen, the neighborhood where Frankie lives forms a moody urban landscape after dark that invites associations with corruption and incontinence (no sooner do Frankie and Johnny enter Frankie's one-room flat than they tumble into bed). This dark, deliberate moral universe denies second chances. Perhaps, left to their own devices, Frankie and Johnny would meet grief as a couple, an outcome foreshadowed by the song of the same title, in which Frankie shoots her two-timing man. Speaking of straight males as well as gays, Ida Head of *Dedication* will say of men, "They go where their dicks take them" (*D* 45).

What joins McNally's Frankie and Johnny much of the way are those grace notes that sound intermittently. They give the impression that the same power or providence that brought the forty-something couple together wants to keep them that way. Both of them come from Allentown. Each had grandmothers who liked meatloaf served with gravy and mashed potatoes (*Three Plays* 106). The mothers of both left home when their kids were seven or eight (*ibid.*, 114). These coincidences impress them. The self-protective Frankie owns up to her age (*ibid.*, 128). And looking back on the events of the past hours, she values the emotional distance she and Johnny have covered together without having bothered to learn each other's last names. An important lesson has been served. In the sphere of love, things needn't be named or spelled out.

Our bedazzled pair gets the crisis it needs to sustain this swell. While preparing Frankie's western, Johnny backs into a hot skillet. Frankie shares his pain the only way she can — by trying to soothe it. She applies to his back butter, ketchup, Noxzema, and even peaches — this after being assured in a brilliant incongruity, "Canned are okay" (*ibid.*, 145). The conversation at this tense time will become more honest and self-probing if also surprisingly funny. The urgency spawned by Johnny's burn has sparked the flow of home truths while also lifting Frankie's veil of self-protection. It's here that Johnny talks about his visit to his ex-wife and kids and Frankie says, "We hate ourselves" (*ibid.*, 146–47).

Both of these self-disclosures come when she's standing behind him, tending to his back. The point isn't lost on Johnny: "It's funny how you can talk to people better sometimes when you're not looking at them" (*ibid.*, 148). This paragon of the over-explicit (whose hernia is totally in character [*ibid.*]) has lit upon a vital truth. He's voicing in a different key Jerry's argument in *The Zoo Story*: "[S]ometimes it's necessary to go a long distance out of the way to come back a short distance correctly" (Albee 30). This schooling seems to have stuck. Moments later, when Frankie grumbles about the disinclination of the disk jockey they've been listening to to name the piece of music she has been enjoying, Johnny answers, "Maybe it doesn't need one" (*Three Plays* 148). As with Keats's doctrine of negative capability, with which McNally has been having an underground relationship, the taking on trust counts more than any heap of facts. Frankie and Johnny are joined by an act of faith. The play's many references to cruelty and pain (the wife-beating that goes on in a nearby apartment, Johnny's hernia and burned back, the hysteria that overtook him on his visit to his former wife, the scar on Frankie's neck that was inflicted in the same beating that stopped her from having children, the upshot of the ill-timed flight of the two mothers) tally the obstacles love must hurdle to survive. Frankie and Johnny are glimpsing the faith and tenacity needed to keep love strong and healthy. The events of the evening have been teaching them how to cope with the trials that time's passage will throw at them, as it does all couples.

Symbolizing the strokes of grace that occur along the way — even those that look like punishment — is the moon. Claude Debussy's *Clair de Lune*, the "most beautiful piece of music" (*ibid.*, 116) Johnny knows, plays at both opening and final curtain. Moonlight either flickers over or drenches Frankie's room for much of the time during this one-set play. Why? Moonlight beguiles, enchants, and deceives, playing tricks with objective reality. Like love, to which it has always been linked, its effects can defy description or decipherment. As confused by its onset as well as it departure, we can't fathom either its powerful hold on the imagination or how it works this magic. Though it emits little light and no heat, its departure from our lives makes us feel dazed and disillusioned, as it did Keats's knight in "La Belle Dame sans Merci." Its enchantment, all the more precious for its impenetrability, segues into the final moments of *F&J*. The lovers are brushing their teeth prior to facing a new day, their first as a couple. Instead of closing the blinds, moments earlier, as he had planned to do, Johnny opens them. He and Frankie no longer belong to the night. Their acceptance of the sunrise (*ibid.*, 153) signals their agreement to move together into the world of fact and deed. Whatever ordeals this daylight world hits them with, they can face better together than alone. This recognition goes against the grain of Greek tragedy, where every change brings a new disaster.

But we're not meant to be buoyed up by it. Imponderables remain together with an animating tension between order and collapse. While brushing their teeth, Frankie and Johnny are connecting without words. Perhaps they're closer than they've been at any time in the play, even though this original, quirky concluding visual image brings no guarantees. Johnny, his mouth full of suds, has to bridle his inner demon of improvement. Whereas Frankie is content to brush her teeth while also enjoying *Clair de Lune*, he breaks the silence by touting "fluoride toothpaste with [a]nti-tartar buildup." But the last word spoken in the play ("Johnny!" [*ibid.*, 156]) comes from her. She's voicing in a different key what she had growled to him near the end of Act One: "I don't want to hear your voice again tonight" (*ibid.*, 120). Having already been accused of squandering providence, viz., the sex that opened the play (*ibid.*), by discussing it in detail, he must still learn that the wellsprings of erotic intimacy, D. H. Lawrence's dark gods, follow rules hidden from both the reason and the will. It's not for nothing that *Clair de Lune* bookends the play. Love belongs to the world of music, dance, and poetry — and perhaps lunacy.

* * *

The work's striking opening, a "portrait in sound of a passionate man and woman making love and reaching climax together" (*ibid.*, 93), puts great demands on audience, actors, and playwright. Where can McNally take matters from here? Romantic comedies sometimes *end*, not *begin*, with the leading players heading for bed, not *in* it and certainly not climaxing together. McNally has lent *F&J* a powerful economy and compression by eliminating the earlier part of the evening, during which the couple had dinner, saw a movie, and then enjoyed ice cream together before spending an undisclosed amount of time in Frankie's one-room walk-up. What's left for McNally to work up are the human angles. These exist in abundance. How are Frankie and Johnny to treat one another in the aftermath of first-date sex? What will they expect from each other as co-workers? Their first challenge looms straightaway; a goal achieved has already lost some of its luster. In their case, it risks losing more. Having rushed into sex, neither party wants to look cheap, bored, or apologetic. The opposite also holds true. Each party has to decide if their revels meant more than a one-night stand. If so, can one distance oneself from the other without either hurting his/her feelings or damaging their workplace connection? Still on the subject of distancing, what's the next step if one of them suspects that he/she is being cast aside? Finally, does a decision to bond or part have to be made immediately? If not, what are Frankie and Johnny supposed to do while they think things through? Their wild, impulsive act has smacked them with a swarm of questions.

All of which help form the play's subtext; hard enough to face on their own, the questions take on added weight by popping up on a first date. The co-workers Frankie and Johnny have no guidelines to help them decide what they want from each other. This void bothers them more than it does McNally. Rather than theorizing, he finds significance in the supposedly prosaic and trifling exchanges of ordinary people. Putting his egalitarianism to work avails him. When Frankie claims that she's not good at small talk, Johnny, who has already invested a great deal in her, disagrees: "This isn't small talk. This is enormous talk" (*ibid.*, 112). Like Chekhov, McNally grounds his play in those easily overlooked moments that light up a character's inner world. If these moments look humdrum, everything about their setting-forth — the pacing, the clarity, the valence between expression and restraint — is elegant. Familiar, too, is the truth that most of what we say to each other is commonplace; sometimes, it wishes itself unsaid. The inner worlds of Frankie and Johnny resemble our own.

Disciplined, propulsive writing has made the play remarkable. Though shredded with loss, it's often darkly, ripplingly funny. Its sinewy textures, earthy rhythms, and open-ended plot lines unwrap a wealth of thematic ground. This spread has carried McNally a big step forward on the path of artistic self-discovery. He, like Chekhov, has taken on the monotony of socializing, showing us that sooner or later it gives us the sinking feeling that life is useless, trivial, and dull, so just get on with it without pretending otherwise. In *F&J*, the quality of the getting-on matters most. Eyes and hearts must open, allowances must be made, and some issues, even if not understood, must be left to the imagination rather than stated directly.

This "most poetic play" (Zinman, "Interview," Zinman, ed. *Casebook* 8) in the canon through 1987 gains from its organic structure. Frankie and Johnny move closer and further apart with all the uncertainty of life. Nothing is overstressed, but nothing is wasted. Pressing forward with a rhapsodic urgency that includes flashes of violence and pungent humor, the richly imaginative *Frankie and Johnny* fuses extremes of romanticism and cynicism. The genius with which it performs this high-wire act makes it a genre-buster. At the personal level, it taught McNally the importance of artistic self-confidence; his best play to date was also the one where he took the greatest artistic risks.

II

The McNally of *F&J* empathized with apparently ordinary mid-lifers in a voice that made verbal economy a function of strength and elegance. These virtues also mark *The Lisbon Traviata*, a much darker play that does *not* rescue love from disruption and chaos. Augmenting the darkness is subject matter close to McNally's everyday self. The four on-stage speaking roles in his 1989 play are all gay men (a woman's voice is heard on an answering machine). This similarity with their author doesn't make the play they're in better than *F&J*. In fact, a lesser gay playwright might have failed to distance himself properly from heartfelt materials like those of *LT*. The same materials that fuel a literary work can also muddle it or turn it into a rant.

Not so with this one, which is melodrama, but melodrama come by honestly. Boy and boy have fallen in love, but one of them falls out, both of them wishing it weren't so. Though this topic is hardly fresh, McNally has crafted it into something of startling directness and might. Much of this power stems from his appreciation of human ambiguity. His people, being human, are complicated and contradictory. As in Shakespeare, the rogues have redeeming traits; the virtuous ones, defects. The primacy of sex in *LT* galvanizes the ambiguity. Mike wants to end an eight-year-long love bond with Steven to ramp up the one he has been enjoying with Paul for the past six months.

The figures in this love triangle, while tossing in the same erotic current, don't only act. They also observe and even judge their actions. Mike's outburst ("Jesus, what are we trying to do to each other?" [*Three Plays* 69]) reflects his complicity in the emotional mess caused by Stephen's intruding upon a love scene between him and Paul. Because sex both clouds and magnifies emotions, the men in *LT*, like Frankie and Johnny, often apologize to each other. Eros keeps knocking them off course. They can't square their behavior with the standards they had set for themselves.

Setting the play's historical and social contexts will focus their plight. Though gay marriage isn't an issue in *LT*, gay bonding *is*. Mendy, at whose West Village apartment the play's first act breaks, has no man to bond with; he has been feeling lonely. Credit Stephen when he accuses the cultured, intelligent, but eccentric (*ibid.*, 4) Mendy of hurting his chances of finding a man by looking too hard for one. He has lit upon a guiding principle in McNally's treatment of sex, even his ontology. Happiness, a byproduct of some activity, like work, usually catches us unaware. Sought directly, it eludes us. McNally had referred to this idea as early as 9 January 1959 when, in a term paper called "Shakespeare's Early Development A Tragedian," he quoted Father Laurence's advice to Romeo: "[L]ove moderately; long love doth so" (2.6.14)— before adding in his own voice, "Frair Laurence has recognized the fatal implications of the lovers' impetuosity" (1). But Mendy's impetuosity includes an under-discussed irritant. Searching for a partner means spending scads of time and cash. It can also sweep a gay man into a cycle of bar-cruising and towel-twitching in bathhouses, like the one in *The Ritz*, neither of which activity promises a healthy, dignified relationship.

Mendy and the play's other three characters all question the monogamous tie they treasure. Monogamy evokes marriage, an institution often scorned by gays as conventional and bourgeois. Mike and Mendy were both married. Having wed partners of the wrong sex has deepened the two men's distrust of marriage as a patriarchal trap. Legal restraints sour this cynicism still more. Gay men in the late 1980s had no rights concerning medical decisions, health insurance, or the burials of their beloveds.

A gay-rights issue that McNally addresses is the HIV-AIDS epidemic.

A friend that Mendy speaks to on the phone fears that he has AIDS (*ibid.*, 30). Later in the first act, Mike mentions a friend having died of AIDS (*ibid.*, 45). Driving Stephen's remark, "I've always wanted someone" (*ibid.*, 36), is the comfort provided by being able to find out if one's partner is STD-free; to their relief, Mike and Paul have been recently tested and pronounced clean (*ibid.*, 69–70). But how relieved can they be? Gay bonds at the time were rarely monogamous. In fact, Stephen and Mike have agreed to sleep out occasionally if either man wants to host an overnight visitor. Has the visitor taken an STD test within the last week? Probably not. But even though the incubation period of HIV-AIDS still remains unclear, luck has favored Paul and Mike. The fear of infection plaguing committed partners stings less than following a routine of bringing home strangers met in bars. Casual sex can't purge loneliness, the bane of gay men in McNally's work. In fact, it sours whatever short-lived comfort or thrill it brings by occurring in the shadow of AIDS. Sam Abel has seen this undercurrent of panic as an organizing force in *LT*: "*The Lisbon Traviata* is in many ways a play about AIDS, and Mike's death evokes the persistent pressure of death hovering over the New York gay community" (47).

All of the play's characters feel trapped in time's relentless forward flow. McNally was thinking of the psychological effects of time when he told John DiGaetani, "the sixties look like a golden age. So I think the characters in *The Lisbon Traviata* are bemoaning the loss of that age. They also mourn for the loss of a relationship.... They all love the wrong person" (221). They're not only vexed that the demon of AIDS has curtailed their bed-hopping. They're also suffering from a sense that the opportunities of the 1960s are gone forever. When Stephen insists that he wants a lover, Mike, his partner and flat-mate of the past eight years, agrees: "So do I" (*Three Plays* 78). Though the men have the same goal, they can no longer achieve it together. Neither of them is guilty; neither has been wronged or betrayed. Something of great value has slipped noiselessly away from them, and it's too late for either of them to retrieve it.

One of the things that we know about human nature is that things can occur — or stop — often on the spot, for no palpable reason. Sadness and helplessness are engulfing both men. We feel stunned, too. Aching with desire to join Paul, Mike asks, "My dear, sweet wonderful Stephen, why can't I stay here with you?" (*ibid.*, 84) Meanwhile, this deeply divided physician knows that he should have left Stephen three years ago. He's more sensitive to the unspoken turns in relationships than Stephen, who maintains that his bond with Mike is strong and healthy despite their not having made love for a long time. He's as shocked to learn that Mike told his brother about their troubles as he is by the news that that same brother accompanied Mike and Paul to a production of *Cats* to celebrate the couple's six months together. Stephen is either too thick to catch Mike's drift or, having caught it, denies its meaning.

A play's main goal is to usher the audience, as if by magic, into an alternative comic universe, and *LT* does. By telling Stephen, "I just want to be away from you" (*ibid.*, 85), seconds after declaring his love, Mike is displaying a face of Eros rarely if ever put on show in fiction or on the stage (*F&J* excepted) since D. H. Lawrence shocked readers with it in works like *The Rainbow* (1915). The play's McGuffin is a recording of *La Traviata* performed in Lisbon in June 1958 with Maria Callas singing the title role. Because of the poor sound quality of this pirated or bootlegged version of Verdi's 1853 opera, only the most loyal, or fanatical, connoisseurs of opera, viz., opera queens, would invest so much emotion into hearing it as Stephen and Mendy do. Only an opera queen would claim, as Mendy does, that people who don't like opera don't like life (*ibid.*, 29).

Stephen's response to opera transcends liking. He's crushed by the news that a local Discophile is sold out of copies of the Lisbon *Traviata*— this, after a crisis nearly erupts in Mendy's apartment over the identity of the singer the two men have been listening to on the phone while the store clerk has them on hold. The prospect of hearing the low-fidelity *Lisbon Traviata* has disoriented the two men. Mendy comes close to the knuckle when he calls getting a copy of it "a matter of life and death" (*ibid.*, 28). He's prepared to taxi through half a mile of dark, rainy streets to the apartment of Stephen and Mike to fetch a copy now that Discophile has none to sell.

Here is where the plot begins, wedding the play's first and second acts and thus silencing those critics who faulted McNally's 1989 work for thematic disunity (e.g., Simon 71; Gussow 1989, 22). *LT* soars above the issue of making mountains out of trifles. Stephen wants to keep Mendy away from the apartment he shares with Mike — who soon hand-delivers a copy of *Traviata* to Mendy and Stephen himself. His reason for taking this trouble surfaces quickly. Waiting for Mike in a cab downstairs is Paul, his overnight guest. Stephen is anxious because Mike had never previously asked for exclusive overnight rights to the apartment (*ibid.*, 32). His anxiety builds. Mike has mistakenly brought the London *Traviata* to Mendy's. Importance will drain quickly from his mistake. The copy of the Lisbon version that Mendy has in his hands soon becomes irrelevant. The volatility of our feelings, an issue raised in Act One, has been confirmed. The mad impulse that sends Stephen home at the start of Act Two after agreeing to stay away creates another thematic bond between the play's two acts.

Much of Stephen's pain is self-inflicted. In this vein, Wayne Kostenbaum finds gays a "dispensable" (135) group dangerously inclined to the self-imposed fate of vanishing into an obsession with opera. Kostenbaum has carried forward Susan Sontag's belief that camp consists of seeing the world as an aesthetic phenomenon, a mindset, she, like he, links to the gay sensibility. "[U]niquely and tragically nostalgic" (*ibid.*, 147), the opera queen, says Kostenbaum, has turned opera into a self-negating toxin. He crawls under the mound of pictures, programs, and operatic recordings he keeps collecting. Furthermore, he prefers, to his detriment, listening to operas at home rather than watching them live. Talk about toxicity: the routine of hearing recorded operas creates a hermetic world that cuts the listener down to a disembodied ear.

It gets worse. Kostenbaum's angry magisterial *The Queen's Throat: Opera, Homosexuality, and the Mystery of Desire* (2001) invokes a danger that suffuses the action of *LT*: "'Queen' is a term of reproach and defamation because it means a willed and hapless effeminacy, and male effeminacy is one of the least accepted behaviors in Western culture" (*ibid.*, 108). Opera has given Stephen and Mendy a template for living a shadow life, a proposition that supports Kostenbaum's belief that "[l]ove of opera seems a sickness that must be controlled" (*ibid.*, 29–30). It follows that, having fled the sexual market place, Mendy can't find a lover, and the prospect of losing Mike is making Stephen panic because he's afraid at age 40 that no one else will want him (*Three Plays* 84).

The indifference to opera of both Mike and his new lover Paul has helped make them more stable, cheerful, and productive than the disconnected Stephen. Mike's grueling regimen as a hospital physician and the two part-time jobs that occupy Paul when he's free from his rigors at Columbia's Master of Social Work program match up well. Conversely, Stephen's hold on his job at Knopf may be slipping (*ibid.*, 52, 75). Also, the well-clad Mendy, who lives comfortably, nearly elegantly, while supporting his 13-year-old son, may be jobless. Though he holds forth on a slew of topics, he says nothing about working. Perhaps he's "excessive" (*ibid.*, 4) because he lacks a job to direct his energies to.

His aestheticizing of life has blocked outlets to being. Character development in *LT* flags amid such dryness, dividing people into categories of actors and onlookers. Things have gone haywire for them. Yes, Mike brings the wrong *Traviata* to Mendy's. But had he brought the right one, it wouldn't have mattered to Stephen, whose heart drops when, minutes later, he sees Mike climb into a cab with Paul inside (cab drivers are also kept waiting by their fares in *The Ritz* and *It's Only a Play*). Matters keep running downhill for Stephen. His tentative date with one Hal — a non-event McNally calls the play's "turning point" (DiGaetani 222) — falls through. Then Stephen rejects Mendy's offer of a night's lodging to go home at early dawn, where he discovers a naked Paul and Mike kissing.

He's astonished. The play's terrifying conclusion will join the different strands of the plot, catching Mike and Stephen in a spasm of violence that invokes this earlier moment. The moment's blinding force clinches it. Pertinent to Stephen (and Mendy) is the warning Kostenbaum serves to opera queens: "Love of opera seems a sickness that needs to be controlled" (29–30). The life signs in Mendy's apartment have dimmed. Stephen alleges to Mendy, "I think you'd rather listen to opera than fuck." Mendy's retort, "Opera doesn't reject me. The real world does" (*Three Plays* 24), hits the nub of his problems. The people in *LT* often communicate by auras, facial expressions, and body language. Mike, who's seated at Paul's table in a restaurant the first time the two men meet, is suffering so obviously from the gay blahs that Paul feels safe asking him to wait for him until his shift ends. (Stephen had no idea Mike was gay at first meeting [*ibid.*, 20].) Immersion in opera dulls, rather than sensitizes, the feelings.

Mendy's opera-queen ambience drives prospective lovers away; one look disqualifies him as a candidate for intimacy. Not wanting to double *his* losses, Stephen had already rejected Mendy as a boyfriend. He should have continued to trust his heart. His proposition, "I can't think of anyone who ends happily in opera" (*ibid.*, 20), has defined opera as a dead end. Like Mendy, he prefers the non-negotiable raptures of opera to the tough work of love. Stripped of immediacy, life for them has grown stale and cold. It makes sense that *LT* unfolds on a cold, rainy night.

Stephen's obsession with opera runs so deep that he questions the date of an operatic performance given on the dust jacket of an LP. McNally was certainly thinking of him when he said that the people in *LT* "all love the wrong person" (DiGaetani 221). Rather than engaging with the failings on his part that have been alienating Mike, Stephen crawls beneath them. Like Mendy, he's bloodless. Mike has been shrinking from him because he won't or can't have sex. It follows that he neither advises nor comforts a distressed Mike the night before Mike was going to meet his ex-wife for the first time since their divorce. He's a stranger to adult feelings. When Mike brings the London version of Maria Callas's *Traviata* to Mendy's apartment in Act One, Stephen scolds him for dressing so lightly on a cold night.

McNally hasn't blurred the play's dramatic focus. Stephen's fussiness is a pinchbeck substitute for love. The "mirthless attention to details" (76) that Mimi Kramer saw governing Stephen, reflected in his alphabetically arranged record collection, has stifled in him the flow of true feeling. His play-ending calamity with Mike shows that he has run out of options. He keeps playing records during this scene, as if *they* could convince Mike to stay with him. Never have the men been further apart. When Mike, at wit's end, frets about his inability to convey anything of value to Stephen, he's told, "Maria does this phrase better than anyone" (*Three Plays* 86). Stephen has been ignoring him. Nor can Mike compete for his attention; opera occupies the center of Stephen's life, and that's that. He's helpless dealing with feelings beyond the range of opera.

This sad truth also describes Mendy; he has buried his heart inside a mound of operatic lore. Like Stephen, he lives through Maria. Though the two men start discussing her soon after curtain up, they withhold naming her until several minutes have passed (*ibid.*, 8). She needs no name. Maria is the dead woman who stands between them and life. Together, they celebrate her birthday every year, and they relish nothing more than digging up obscure facts about her life and career, the more trifling the better. The words of Michael Tanner, from the 21 April 2012 issue of *The Spectator*, explain the love-bereft Mendy and Stephen's fascination with Maria. What appeals most to the gay sensibility, Tanner said, "is the suffering diva, suffering preferably both in life and art," an issue McNally will return to with frightening clarity in *Master Class*. Tanner continues: "Hence the uniquely high—and deserved—ranking of Callas, whose life was wretched and whose repertoire in her great years was almost exclusively nineteenth-century Italian, where there is the largest concentration of mad or dying women [like Amina of Bellini's *La Sonnambula* and Verdi's Lady Macbeth, both of whose arias are sung in *MC*]" (44).

Yet the opera queens Mendy and Stephen differ from each other, as is decreed by the law of dramatic economy. In contrast to Stephen and Mike's tidy, coldly efficient digs, Mendy's are cozy, warm, and ramshackle—a place to invite one's soul. A lovable mess like Sancho Panza, Mendy (no last name given) has traveled the world to attend operas; he also seems to have season's tickets to every one in town. This fanaticism hasn't quieted his roiling psyche any more than his Volvo station wagon. He enjoys the company of his ex-wife and their 13-year-old son (that age again)—mostly because he doesn't live with them. Perhaps he invites Stephen to overnight with him because he knows he'll be leaving the next morning at the latest. He has been drawing air and space around him.

None of the six analysts he hired in the past decade (*Three Plays*, 33) have opened him up. Yet this man who has said no to life is more than Stephen's foil. McNally gave him the play's longest speech (*ibid.*, 34–35), which swells with references to opera and opera criticism. Once warmed up on his favorite subject, he's unstoppable. He'll even buy recordings of operas he dislikes to show off to himself. But his page-long screed isn't all campy self-indulgence. At one point, before calling Maria "the greatest singer who ever lived" (*ibid.*, 35), he says, "This doesn't seem to be such a terrible existence with people like her to illuminate it" (34). He doesn't develop his thought. He probably can't. For him, Maria's singing hasn't illuminated life. It has replaced it.

Stephen's love of opera, though similar, hasn't only turned him away from life; it has also blighted his coping power. In the words of Mel Gussow: "Stephen ... has been trapped within opera. He aspires to heightened emotions, and, inevitably, he's unable to differentiate between the stage and the world of real relationships" (1985, C14). The big difference between him and Mendy comes with his life orientation. As a man with both a full-time job and a live-in lover, he has duties to others, at least one of which Mendy scuttled by getting divorced. Stephen says nothing when Mendy calls him "an aging, immature queen" (*Three Plays* 28). But the shaft has struck home. At 40, Stephen's life is mostly maintenance. Little can be done to improve it. He's unlikely to find a better job, and he believes his best chance for happiness remains alongside Mike.

The two phone messages he plays at the start of Act Two, from his mother and an unhappy client, bespeak his negligence. Like Johnny of *F&J*, he's fretting over male menopause. Age stymies him. His love rival, Paul, who's ten years Mike's junior, is too young for him to consider dating. Mike's outburst, early in Act Two, "What a fucked-up time we picked to live in" (*ibid.*, 53), applies more strictly to Stephen than to both Mike and Paul.

The obsession with identity and image that started overtaking the United States in the late 1980s has been vexing him largely because, like most of McNally's other people, sex (corrupted by the conventions of opera, in his case) ranks foremost with him. His telling Mike, "I was a good lover" (*ibid.*, 86), makes sex the linchpin of their bond; the magnetic sex they once enjoyed proves they should stay together. Mike disagrees, with good reason; whenever Mike starts discussing one of the problems besetting their relationship, Stephen begins fiddling with the record player or talking about opera. He's undermining his own argument; sex can't flourish if other forms of communication in the relationship have failed.

Speaking of Stephen's plight, McNally said, "I don't think we live in a romantic age, but Stephen is a romantic character, and it's romantic characters who are driven to acts of violence" (DiGaetani 221). Romantic characters also feel caught in the gap between fantasy and reality. Badgered by domestic woes, Stephen tells Mendy of Mike and himself, "We're going through a phase. I hate phases. I hate change" (*Three Plays* 37). His denial of both the forward flow of time and time's effects has made him fantasy's fool — a vital point because, just as myth joins people, fantasy divides them. He insists that his life with Mike, being "fine" (*ibid.*, 75), needs no fixing.

This delusion provokes others. This man who hesitated to put on a record in Act One (*ibid.*, 36) keeps raising the volume on the records he plays nonstop in Act Two. Control keeps slipping from him. After Paul and Mike both decline the go-cups of coffee he has brought home for them, he brews more coffee on his coffee-maker. "Not for us" (*ibid.*, 55), "I said not for us" (*ibid.*, 56), and "We're fine" (*ibid.*), Mike says to Stephen's offers of coffee — both regular and decaf. His message is clear: he and Paul are a pair. But if Stephen feels defeated, he's not to be pitied. The pain of being snubbed is becoming familiar to him. When he rebukes Mike for giving Paul a towel from a prized set rather than one from an odd lot, he's answered in a way that describes the freakishness of the regimen he has been imposing on Mike: "Yes, Mother" (*ibid.*, 55).

Matching Stephen's denial of change is his fixation on male beauty. Perhaps seeing Paul, whom he had heard of, scotches any thought he might have had about stealing him from Mike. But, playing the trouble-maker, Stephen tries to spark conflict, instead. As Kerry did with Asher in "Noon" (*15 Plays* 28), he praises the cut of Paul's trousers (*Three Plays* 28). Then he compliments Paul on his beautiful body (*ibid.*, 61). His biggest shock comes when he looks at some pornographic Polaroids snapped of Mike and him eight years earlier. The snaps evoke no tender memories of their bygone bliss. All is surface to him: "The real tragedy," Stephen later groans to Mike, "is neither one of us is ever going to look that good again" (*ibid.*, 71).

His dismay is that of a lonely man upset with himself. He broke a promise by showing the forbidden snaps to Paul after telling Mike he had thrown them away. He had already broken his word by coming home in the middle of the night, having guaranteed Mike the privacy of the place until breakfast time. He's on a rampage. Stripped of reserves to fall back on, he keeps flailing out. "I'm a shit" (*ibid.*, 66) and "I lied" (*ibid.*, 69), he admits but, like a tragic hero, can't alter his self-destructive course of action. Though he knows Paul's name, he calls him "Jim"; he's saying that Paul is just one more of Mike's many overnight visitors (*ibid.*, 59).

Stephen's lie mires him deeper into the quagmire of his loser's identity. Here and later, he understands that Mike is better off with Paul than with him. His flirting with Paul to rile Mike gets him nowhere. Paul rises above the mess he finds himself implicated in. A mess it is. Mike hates himself for bloodying Stephen's face, his first act of violence since the fifth grade. He has made himself Stephen's victim, violence being a form of weakness. Paul, meanwhile, remains spotless — perhaps because of his moral character but perhaps also because the newness of his relationship with Mike has left him the least blameworthy. Sexual love, always a rough ride in McNally, whether gay or straight, challenges the men in *LT*. The words, "I'm sorry," for instance, occur more often in *LT* than in *F&J*; a random count shows the words coming from Paul (e.g., 59, 60). Mike (e.g., 65, 67, 68), and Stephen (e.g., 58 [twice], 73, 75, 78).

It's fitting that Stephen apologizes more often than anybody else in the play. Unable to quiet the hysterics building inside him, he has the most to apologize for. Desperation prodded him to barge in on Mike and Paul to begin with. Othello-like (in one of his evasions of adult responsibility, he quotes Hamlet [*ibid.*, 75]), he craves the defining evidence, or ocular proof, that tells him that he has lost Mike forever. He had been dying inside by stages. Revealed to him piecemeal has been the truth that matters between Mike and him have been worsening more quickly than he had imagined.

It's no wonder that in Act One Stephen tells Mike to take Paul to "the new Almodovar" (*ibid.*, 45), which in 1989 would have been *Women on the Edge of a Nervous Breakdown* (1988). The movie, advisedly, includes a scene pertinent to the action of *LT*; it shows a woman going into hysterics after being dropped by her married lover. Whatever movie Mike took Paul to see, though, wouldn't have mattered. Stephen's homecoming recoils on him. First of all, his entry into the apartment shocks everybody. Then, besides losing Mike, he forfeits both his personal dignity and, with it, that of their eight years together. The mud keeps flying. It comes out that Mike lied to Paul about not having emotional strings on him. Paul, though, holds his poise and integrity. He won't accept Mike's luncheon invitation until he's sure that Mike has doctored the wounds he inflicted on Stephen.

Stephen, on the other hand, has fallen so far in Act Two that, unable to speak for himself, he uses passages of music, usually operatic, to argue his points with Mike. When Mike misses his drift, rather than explaining himself, Stephen turns up the volume on the record player. McNally has gone noisy for a reason. He wants to spell out stylistically the difference between the inner worlds of Stephen and Mike. Mike speaks simply and directly. When Stephen does talk, he lards his words with quotations and campy references. All this has a rankling consistency. Whether he's speaking or playing music ("I can't say it better than this" [*ibid.*, 93], he says of a Villa-Lobos piece), he's hiding. To paraphrase Harold Pinter, all his deeds cohere as a stratagem to cover nakedness.

His dodge fails. The emotion he directs to having heard Maria sing the prelude to *La Traviata* (*ibid.*, 82) is misplaced. He should be investing in the more vital and immediate work of salvaging his bond with Mike. But he can't. Human ties defeat him, revealing his poverty of heart knowledge. His expressions of love for Mike lack the rhapsodic grandeur of his words about Maria. When a distraught Mike tells him to bequeath his estate to a memorial statue of her, he answers, "You know, that's not a bad idea." The timing of this exchange is immaculate. The play needs comic relief at this fraught point. Yet, rather than diverting our attention, the comic relief that McNally supplies sharpens it, as Mike's reply shows: "She's dead. It's the living you have trouble with" (*ibid.*, 82).

The finale of *LT* delivers the inevitability that Joseph Conrad connected with tragedy. Stephen's consuming devotion to the voice of a dead singer validates his stabbing of Mike. After referring to Tosca's knifing Scarpio to death, Stephen had said, "I can't think of anyone who ends happily in opera" (*ibid.*, 19, 20). After stabbing Mike with the same scissors Mike used to destroy the forbidden Polaroids, he adopts the posture of Bizet's Don José upon knifing Carmen, an event he had discussed in Act One (*ibid.*, 20, 24). The last object to enter the bodies of both Mike and Carmen is a lethal weapon. Though nothing in *LT* is predictable, everything that happens in it looks inescapable.

Charles Marowitz has explained in *Theater Week* how Stephen's enslavement by opera has made opera his prison. There's no precedent in opera that tells Stephen to call for help while a dying Mike languishes in his arms. He has razed the difference between art and life to the detriment of both. If opera contains no happy endings, neither should life: "*Lisbon Traviata* makes the wry astute point that life aspires to the condition of art, and that on those few occasions when the goal is reached, it turns to tragedy. We need art to ventilate the clogged-up arteries of our mundane lives, but when we overventilate them, it blows us away" (39).

The bogus act of lyrical surrender that turns Stephen into a murderer comes quickly. A few minutes of chatter in Act One tells us that we'd be hard pressed to find two New Yorkers capable of conversing like Stephen and Mendy. We're being treated to a version of drawing-room comedy in which the witty backchat that distinguishes the genre refers to opera. Stephen and Mendy try to outdo each other in their knowledge of the production dates, venues, cast members, and conductors of Maria's operas. Emerging from their exchange is true satire, satire at its best describing the waste of time and effort. A discussion of Maria's sharping and flatting on different notes (*Three Plays* 25) serves little purpose outside the graduate seminar. What could better represent frittered-away energy than the following exchange?

STEPHEN: It's not that good a performance. The London is better.
MENDY: You just said it was fantastic.
STEPHEN: It is, but not that fantastic [*Three Plays* 9–10].

Such distinctions carry no weight. Their fixation on opera hasn't made Mandy and Stephen happier, more productive, or more fun to be with. Mike and Paul, both of whom feel indifferent toward opera, lead fuller, richer, and busier lives, and it takes more to stress them out. Mendy and Stephen, who argue whether Maria sang a high C or a flatted one during a performance at La Scala years earlier, are half-lifers by comparison. It's fitting that Mendy is disconnected from life and that the equally sexless Stephen feels off track.

McNally foreshadows this derailment ably. The "Characters" page of *LT* calls Stephen "[s]omewhat closed and guarded," and at curtain rise he's "*seated in the end of a chair, not lying back in it*"; the needle of Mendy's record player, having missed its groove, is scratching the edge of an LP in a way that's "loud and painful" (*ibid.*, 6) to hear. As he'll do again in the play's last scene, Stephen sits tight at a time that calls for action. His life, like the scraping needle on the tone arm of Mendy's record player, is a painful discord. Wisely, McNally made him an editor. Stephen has never written a book. The one lurking inside him consists of his infatuation with opera, a subject not even an operatic composer would find worth scoring.

But no composer would gainsay the strong psychological undertow of *LT*. Stephen subverted his love of Mike by having cast himself as the embodiment of a grand undying tragic passion. His enthrallment to a heroic role is more obsessive than erotic. It explains Mike's death. It also tells why he and Mike haven't had sex for a long time. A stroke of genius on McNally's part made him an editor (in an earlier version of the play, he was a doctor). Though Stephen excels at his job at Knopf, he edits material written by others. Because his mind is more editorial than creative, he does secondary work. Rather than imagining something new into life, he pores over what other people say. Though both important and inventive, this work doesn't qualify as creative art. Interestingly, the same verdict applies to the main figure of *Women on the Edge of a Nervous Breakdown*. Not only does Almodovar's Carmen Maura make a living dubbing female voices in American movies, but the main scene of *Johnny Guitar* (1954), one of the movies she dubbed, describes a deadly shootout. That the shooters are women, not men, casts dark, ironic light on both Stephen's telling Mike to see the movie with Paul and the calamities of *LT*'s second act.

"The real tragedy is neither of us is ever going to look that good again" (*ibid.*, 71); Stephen's fixation on the physical beauty of himself and Mike eight years earlier in the Polaroids shows, first, that he brings no urgency to his bond with Mike at the time of the play's present-tense action and, next, that this failure has blinded him to the changes that time has brought to that bond. He wants everything to stay the same. His hatred of change presupposes the denial that life *itself* is change along with its corollary, viz., that the self is constantly in flux, too. It's his rejection of change — particularly the one that has sent Mike into the arms of Paul — that goads him into showing Paul the Polaroids.

This move backfires on him, as do his other attempts to re-enter the past. In an echo of Albee's *Virginia Woolf* (and of Eric Berne's *Games People Play* [1964]), Stephen has violated both a foundation law and a basic decency by showing an outsider photos meant only for his eyes and Mike's. That they were hidden in a bookshelf behind Will and Ariel Durant's *Story of Civilization* creates, along with a striking juxtaposition, another leavening laugh in the high-intensity action; moments of high seriousness have their funny side.

Wittily thematic, too, is Mike's inability to tear the randy Polaroids, themselves a stunning example of the juncture of opportunity and solid preparation. Lewd pictures like the ones of Stephen and Mike in the early prime of their love couldn't have been developed commercially. Self-developing Polaroids bypassed this law — but with an add-on. The developed prints appeared on tough multi-leaved product resistant to tearing. They had to be cut with scissors. Love can make extra demands on us, too. In this mode, the hand that cuts the Polaroids also balks at pushing Stephen away; though Mike had long since resolved to part with Stephen, he's only now getting around to it. He's botching the job, and Stephen is making it still more difficult for him. Both love and its image resist destruction. The love that joined the two men is as stubborn as it is rankling. Mike wore while in bed with Paul an expensive ring given him by Stephen. Nor does he offer to return it to Stephen after having enjoyed with Paul his "best sex ... in three years" (*ibid.*, 70).

Stephen parries this incongruity by invoking the timeless perfection of art. But art, a story that has been told, lacks the throb and surge of cluttered, disordered reality. In his beloved opera, love always walks with death. This law has taken hold of him. As in one of McNally's favorite plays, Ibsen's *Wild Duck*, a weapon in the hands of a child or a childish adult (Mendy had called Stephen an "immature queen" [*ibid.*, 28]) portends calamity. Stephen stabs Mike with the same scissors that Mike used to cut the Polaroids. The version of *LT* that appeared in the 1990 Plume collection, *Three Plays by Terrence McNally* (and that we have been referring to), ends with Stephen relenting on his threat to stab Mike to death. This "terrible, tremendous moment" (*ibid.*, 97) the play had led up to finds the two men in a farewell embrace, the scissors in Stephen's hand while Maria's recorded singing fills the house. The suspense stops our hearts. McNally might have ended the play here, as Pinter did *The Dumb Waiter* (1959) and Sam Shepard did *True West* (1980) — at a moment when all the tensions of the foregoing action are poised to erupt. The finale of *LT* has its own intrigue. Our Plume version shows Mike leaving the apartment and closing the door behind him, his departure accompanied by Maria's aria, "Sempre Libera" from *La Traviata*.

Then McNally changed his mind, even though it couldn't have been easy. The first ending, the one where Mike walks off stage, works well. McNally improved the play, though, by writing the harder-edged ending included in the Dramatists Play Service text. Rejecting easier outcomes, this 1992 re-write marks out unflinchingly the contagion of Stephen's opera fetish. What's more, it anchors this danger to Stephen's destructive self-image in a compelling visual image the creepy power of which builds from a musical accompaniment chosen for both its beauty and it tragic appropriateness.

* * *

LT excels for other reasons. Boldness braced by psychological insight boosts McNally's portrayal of Paul's confrontation with Stephen early in Act Two. So much for John Simon's disclaimer that the play's second act is "unconvincing, glued-on, [and] melodramatic" (71). An audacious self-confidence also fired McNally's decision to let 15 seconds pass before Paul and Stephen walk into the empty room where their confrontation will occur. McNally wouldn't have paused the play's action unless he knew that he'd hold our attention. Which he does; the short wait is no distraction. Though jarred by Stephen's ill-advised entry along with his sexually charged words, Paul holds his poise. As he'll tell Mike, he handles Stephen without sacrificing his dignity. Not so with Mike, the kind of self-questioning self-doubter McNally admires. Mike blames himself for smashing Stephen's face (e.g., *Three Plays* 67, 70). McNally's most upright people aren't boring, as they'd be in the work of lesser playwrights. Clarence of *Bump*, Gregory of *LTTA*, and Lou Nuncle of *Dedication* ask themselves tough questions that wreck their inner peace. Stephen, by contrast, wastes little energy on self-scrutiny. He's shrouded so tightly by operatic conventions that issues of morality have bypassed him.

The 1992 DPS version of *Lisbon Traviata* ends with Mike throwing away the expensive ring Stephen gave him, an act that leads to his death moments later. Rather than calling for help while Mike lies bleeding in his arms, Stephen savors the beauty of Maria's voice. Mendy then speaks on the answering machine. He's inviting Stephen to see Wagner's *Meistersinger* with him that evening. Stephen needn't go. His worship of a masterful singer has just abetted a murder, which, delusional now, he blames on his victim: "[People] die for what you're doing to me" (Terrence McNally, *The Lisbon Traviata* [New York: Dramatists Play Service, 1992: 88]). In another passage missing from the better-known Plume text, Mendy says, "I hope you two are all right" (*Three Plays* 84).

A tiny touch can shore up a play's motivation. Stephen's sentimental, unprovoked references to dogs in both acts of *LT* (*ibid.*, 30, 72) allude in cameo to the contrast between his responses to dead women and living men. Whereas Mike clicks with Paul, Stephen got rebuffed by another waiter, Hal (*ibid.*, 13, 43). Gussow dreamed up the problems of "structure and invention" (1999, 22) marring *LT*, a mistake he could have avoided had he thought harder about the play's imaginative intent. The delight that one of the dogs took in his owners' lovemaking (*Three Plays* 72), Stephen recalls, invokes the attention Johnny's Great Dane paid to Johnny's masturbating in *F&J* (*ibid.*, 127). Our ties to the dog world may be stronger than we realize, an idea perhaps borrowed from Albee's *Zoo Story*. Or perhaps they're not strong enough, dogs setting a standard of loyalty rarely matched in the human world of the plays (the dogs in *This Side of the Door*, *It's Only a Play*, and *Dedication* remind us of the absence of cats in McNally's work). There are other resemblances between the two plays. A customer in the diner where Frankie and Johnny work called Mr. Leon (*ibid.*, 110) returns to *LT* as a *Mrs.* Leon, a grandmother and neighbor of Stephen and Mike (*ibid.*, 68).

Theft is also a recurring trope, as it might well be in a world of misguided attempts to tame the surge of present-tense reality. The acquaintance of Mendy's who stole money from a mutual friend to buy himself an expensive sweater (*ibid.*, 13) perhaps writes novels because, unhappy with the world he lives in, he must create his own. He also harks to a waiter that Frankie saw stealing tips (*ibid.*, 135) — and, before that, to Frank Finger, the director of *The Golden Egg* in *IOAP*. Frank pinches, among other things, his hostess Julie Budder's pepper shaker (*ibid.*, 189). A weekend visitor in *LVC* (1994) will try to steal his host's boyfriend.

These similarities and echoes conjure up others. The PBS presenter whose words end Act One of *LT* (*ibid.*, 48–49) reminds us of Marlon at Midnight, the radio announcer whose talk, again about music, closes the first act of *F&J* (*ibid.*, 129). Finally, in keeping with the idea that the clair de lune describes an emotional combat zone, medicine chests are rifled in both plays (*ibid.*, 108, 70). *F&J* not only exerts more force on *LT* than *Zoo Story* or *Virginia Woolf*, but, rather, more than *all* of Albee's writing to the time of its debut. No worries; starting with the works of McNally's early maturity, repetition becomes less a sign of haste than one of thematic consistency. The great strides he made since *F&J* stem from the traction his art has gained by developing from within. While of a piece with his earlier work, *LT* describes gay New York with more depth and context than heretofore. McNally might have known this. In a rare, uncharacteristic moment of immodesty, he defined himself as as good a judge of his plays as he was a playwright when he called *The Lisbon Traviata* a work "I am especially proud of" (DiGaetani 223).

III

A play can burst out of the gate that's utterly specific and original. The one-act "Tour" (1967) portrayed an American couple that forsook Italy's customary tourist sites to visit the back country. This risk-taking recoiled on them, as will that of the two travelers to India in *A Perfect Ganesh*. "Tour" stands as little more than a warm-up for McNally's 1993 work, with its terrific sense of the uncanny rising from an atmosphere so strange and suggestive that, alienating as it is, it can also become wildly appealing.

The India of *Ganesh* stands closer to the one depicted in the 2008 movie *Slumdog Millionaire* than to that of Gandhi and his spiritual legacy. While omitting all references to Gandhi, it shows signs of rapid industrialization, urbanization, and Western-style consumerism. But, like Forster's *A Passage to India* (1924), the India of McNally's play resists generalizations. Money, for instance, denotes failure rather than power or success. In a crucial scene, a visitor to Bombay, i.e., today's Mumbai, can't fight the revulsion she feels when a "diseased and hideous" leper (*Two Plays* 250) asks for her love.

For a mad moment, she had thought about kissing the leper on the lips to show that she loves him unconditionally, as God does. Instead, she tosses money at him; rupees buy her way out of spiritual growth. But, in line with the stubborn irrationality of things Indian — if not of things everywhere — the event that shames Katharine Brynne buys the leper "the finest meal of his entire, miserable life" (*ibid.*, 251).

Despite the freakish forms they take, family, religion, and the traditional values of simplicity, patience, and frugality rule India's villages and towns, where most of her people live. The incursions of India's indecently rich industrialists barely ruffle this everydayness. The last question put by the husband of one of the travelers before she walks out of the door of her southern Connecticut house ("You sure you have enough money?" [*ibid.*, 152]) suggests the importance Americans devote to money; money can solve all problems. But its possessors, as in works ranging from Sinclair Lewis's *Babbitt* (1922) and Scott Fitzgerald's *Gatsby* (1925) to Jonathan Franzen's *Freedom* (2010), risk moral corruption. This cuts two ways. As McNally's Ganesha says, "Your poverty [in the United States] is angry. Ours is not. In India, poverty is not an emotion. It's a fact" (*ibid.*, 180).

The effects of this outlook both charm and mystify Margaret Civil and Katharine Brynne. They're ready to be charmed and mystified. Bored with their annual routine of vacationing with their husbands in the Caribbean, these two well-heeled matrons from Greenwich opted instead for two weeks together in India. The question of whether their act of daring profits them calls up issues that defy western reason and logic. India means "[t]oo much everything" (*ibid.*, 221) says Katharine. Her New England upbringing skirted the prosaic realities of smells, sounds, and crowds that exist in such profusion in India. It's this head-on clash with tough, intractable reality that gives *Ganesh* much of its strength. Its inscrutability notwithstanding, India's poverty, disease, and dirt can gush forth tsunami-like at any time. A fellow passenger on a train tells Katharine that "being in India is rather a solo project.... It's finally just you and it" (*ibid.*, 222). You can't hide from it, and nobody is immune from its intransigence — which can look like a sick joke. During the train ride, Katharine's husband dies instantly in a car crash over 8,000 miles away. Whether George Brynne would have driven on that patch of black ice that hurled his car into a tree had Katharine been with him remains unclear. Less doubtful is the truth that this woman whom opportunities of inner growth sent to India wound up losing the most vital part of herself, any husband being flesh of his wife's flesh. The urge to live more fully has blitzed another of McNally's sympathetic, intelligent characters.

Katharine's personality and temperament both invited this onslaught. As soon as she's seated on her Air India flight to Bombay, she plays a self-improvement audio tape that touts the primacy of love. She'll learn that fulfillment and authenticity can't be sought directly; they take us unaware or not at all. Schooling she needs, and not only in love. She had lost both her camera and cassette player before boarding her plane. She had packed her bags carelessly. She probably packed the wrong things, too, for her long flight. She walks onto the set weighted down with "an alarming amount of" (*ibid.*, 155) carry-on luggage and two oversized suitcases that don't match. But the first words spoken by this scatterbrain plumb depths: "O for a Muse of fire" (*ibid.*). She's one of McNally's lovable oddballs. This opening line from Shakespeare's *Henry V* will apply to her as much as it did Shakespeare when he saluted London's Globe Theater. Shakespeare is announcing his intent to do justice to the Globe, the recently opened "wooden O" where his play is premiering.

Katharine aims Shakespeare's words to her resolve to savor each moment in India; to her, vibrating keenly rules out being upset by the loss of a camera and a cassette player. Rather than being distracted by material objects, she wants to submit to life, ignoring nothing and relishing everything. "Take my heart and do with it what you will," she says to India in another speech that opens with the words, "O for a Muse of fire" (*ibid.*, 178). This faith invokes Gerard Manley Hopkins's invitation to God, "Batter my heart." Unlike her companion Margaret, she wants to connect with the spirit of India at whatever cost. The oft-repeated mantras she learned from attending self-help meetings ("I choose to be happy. I choose to be loving. I choose to be good" [(e.g., *ibid.*, 171]) drop out as the play advances, as she's priming herself to be on a level with life rather than imposing expectations on it.

Pondering the tricky connection between the sacred and the profane, she sees that we must repudiate experience to commit to reality; being must be appreciated in regard to *it*self, not *one*self. Submitting to India and letting herself be devoured by it can lead to self-discovery: "My dream of India is this: that I am engulfed by it, that I am lost in a vast crowd and become part of it" (*ibid.*, 202). Note that she's not deliberately getting lost so much as putting the reality of others on a par with her own in order to merge with them. Unity with God's creatures has started to supplant her inclination to judge.

Her statement, "Nothing is right, nothing wrong" (*ibid.*, 249), no abdication of accountability, endorses life's oneness. To the Hindus, good and bad represent different sides of God. She craves insight into a divine harmony that precludes moral judgment. She had heard that going to India would shake the walls of her ego. What she discovers is that India will crush her before it refines and renews her. But how much of her will be left to be refined and renewed? No place for the unwary, India can be dangerous. An American tourist that the women meet on a train says that India's poverty and disease shortened his horrified wife's visit. Katharine understands. Sickened by eating papaya even after taking precautions, she knows first hand the penalties of opening herself to a place so excessive and intense: "Too much everything. The colors, the smells, the sounds. My head is whirling, when my stomach isn't heaving" (*ibid.*, 221).

The indigestible papaya symbolizes India for her. It also challenges her. If she can't connect with the place physically, how can her heart or her spirit take hold of it? Where she had sought promise and hope, she has been flattened by diarrhea. Her last name, Brynne, calls forth the fire invoked in her personal call-to-arms, "O for a Muse of fire"—as it does the travel firm that arranged her and Margaret's trip to India, Red Carpet Tours (*ibid.*, 177). Now fire can be of great value. The fire Prometheus gave to mankind ended an era of cold, dark, and ignorance. Fire burns away dross and decay in Dickens's *Little Dorrit* and *Great Expectations* (Dickens is mentioned in the play [*ibid.*, 189]). Yeats's "Byzantium" calls forth God's holy fire to burn off the impurities in him that have been blunting his response to beauty.

But McNally has also been thinking about the physical cost of fire's ability to purify and renew. The same fire that cleanses and revamps also devastates. Its color is that of both Satan and his empire; hell's flames burn red. India might destroy Katharine or at least enough of her to scotch rebirth and renewal. As Ganesha says, Indian wives who rile their mates fare badly; if they're allowed to live, they do so under the heavy thumbs of their mothers-in-law. It gets worse. The ritual of suttee dictates that wives, obedient and disobedient alike, are expected to incinerate themselves on their husband's funeral pyres (*ibid.*, 180).

From the start of the play, Katharine outdoes Margaret as a risk-taker. As soon as their plane takes off, she starts listening to a cassette. The ability of sounds to make deeper impressions on us than visual fields has sprung to mind; Margaret is watching a movie. Nor is this the first contrast drawn between the two travelers. Air India's computer system had lost their business-class reservations on the fully booked plane to Bombay. After listening patiently to Margaret's complaints and condemnations, the reservations clerk offers her and Katharine a first-class upgrade — a stroke of luck that Katharine revels in but that Margaret, ruled by a go-by-the-book rectitude, accepts only grudgingly.

This contrast holds. In place of Margaret's *Realpolitik* and her control freak's resistance to change, the self-questioning Katharine accepts her complicity in error without feeling crushed by it. One of her mantras, "Above all be patient. Allow, accept, be" (e.g., *ibid.*, 168), though sourced in popular self-help manuals, steels her. Speculative and curious, she even ponders, like Oedipus, the vagaries of fate and free will: "[M]aybe we aren't so helpless. Maybe we are responsible. Maybe it is our fault what happens. Maybe, maybe, maybe" (*ibid.*, 166). Such passages discourage lazy reading. The popularizing of life's most valuable lesson doesn't cheapen them. Katharine is ready to stand up to India. Her readiness might be godlike (*Hamlet* 5. 2, 160). Ganesha uses the word, "serenity" just after hearing Katharine say, "serene" (*ibid.*, 170).

McNally wants to connect with our imaginations, not solve literary puzzles — contrary to many of his Columbia College English professors, advocates of the then New Criticism, which found thematic gold by analyzing a text's clever ironies and ambiguities (the gnomic utterances of John Donne and T. S. Eliot suggest themselves as ideal subjects of the New Critics). Katharine came by her gift for spiritual enlightenment the same way that most of us discover love and vocation — by default. Three years before the play's present-tense action she was devastated by the murder of her son. Six black thugs had beaten him to death.

Walter was no ordinary son. Katharine keeps blaming herself for having rejected him as a gay man. In the play's strongest example of the penalties of sensitivity, she equates this rejection with the chains, baseball bat, and golf club that hammered Walter to death. She's stuck at this point. She feels trapped inside the equation, her very being an obstacle to the freedom she's seeking in India.

She was fighting heavy odds from the start. India, she knows, can only be faced bone-to-bone; "It's finally just you and it" (*ibid.*, 200), she remarks inwardly after a visit from Walter's spirit. India, she suspects, is tearing her apart in order to remake her. It also offers second chances to those survivors of its havoc. When Katharine visits the burial ghats at Varanasi, or Benares, the place where the Ganges is the holiest, she says of the corpses floating by, "Everything in and on the river seems inevitable and right" (*ibid.*, 247). No, she hasn't attained the vision or faith that reveals the divine necessity of Walter's death. But give her credit. Her oneness with the voiceless dead of India who had borne the indignations of poverty and hunger does mark a spiritual breakthrough.

Perhaps her first inkling of imminence came during an earlier trip to Amsterdam's Rembrandt Museum, where she saw the painting called *Woman Bathing*. She tells a foreigner she meets by chance in an Indian village what she found so moving in the painting's eponym: "Her isolation. Her independence. Her strength" (*ibid.*, 230). Katharine will invoke these virtues while floating on the Ganges near Varanasi, another body of water. Her freedom to speak out comes in part from the foreigner with whom she shares her thoughts about Rembrandt's painting. As in Act Two of Chekhov's *Three Sisters*, where Andrey Prozorov unburdens himself to a deaf servant, Katharine speaks freely about the "dark power" (*ibid.*, 239) of the bathing woman because her interlocutor doesn't speak English.

Water remains prominent. A scene interposed between a village puppet show and the visit to Varanasi's ghats shows Margaret wading in a river represented by a bolt of blue cloth. Bodies of water, artificial as well as natural, can stir rebirth in McNally. Katharine, holding back at water's edge, plays the scene on dry land. (The major epiphany in Joyce's *A Portrait* takes place on the banks of the Irish Sea.) While she's standing, advisedly on the opposite side of the blue ribbon from Margaret, Ganesha's sudden embrace of her shows her that the sorrow and guilt that have been gouging her will reshape themselves as new forms, or expressions, of the therapy she has been seeking. She immerses herself in her adult primal scream by shouting the same insults aimed at Walter by his attackers while they were killing him: "Fag! Queer! Cocksucker! Dead-from-AIDS queer meat!" (*ibid.*, 242) Then she asks Walter to forgive her. It's unclear whether she has purged the heartbreak that, she now sees, brought her to India. She needs to free herself of the moral equality she shares with he son's killers — a horror she must embrace before purging it. She has served herself well. After her curses, a vision of Walter floats by long enough to blow her a kiss.

This isn't his last manifestation. On an adjoining balcony of her and Margaret's Bombay hotel suite, she meets an AIDS patient. The time of their meeting, "almost morning, not quite dawn" (*ibid.*, 187), like that of her later skiff ride through the ghats with Margaret, puts her at that moment when material things change forms. Such moments are friendliest to the Joycean epiphanic mode — an accretion of everyday facts unexpectedly transfiguring a life. Underscoring this incident is Margaret's appearance on the balcony. Frankie and Johnny brushing their teeth together at daybreak at the end of *F&J* come to mind (Margaret enters the scene stage brushing *her* teeth [*ibid.*, 190]). So does *A Passage to India*. In one of the resemblances between Forster's novel and *Ganesh*, Indians in both works often ignore differences between indoors and outdoors. The sleepers packed in the plaza below the balcony foreshadow the corpses that strike the ladies' skiff, suggesting the continuity between life and death.

The AIDS victim Katharine meets on the balcony, a carrier of death, provides another foreshadowing. Like Walter, he's gay. And besides having recited the prologue to *Henry V* in a college production years earlier, this sick doctor goes by he name, Harry, which is what Henry is called in the part of the prologue he quotes. He's not done quoting. The song he sings, "Blow the Wind Southerly," was Walter's favorite. Fired up by the song, Walter's mother joins the "mob of homeless, dirty, disease-ridden beggars" (*ibid.*, 195) thronging the plaza below. This ugliness is more of a prod than an obstacle to her. In Frontain's words, "McNally insists that we must swim in the pool of our common humanity, whatever the possibility of contamination" ("Allow, Accept, Be" 214), an issue that will recur in *LTTA*.

The dawn breaking over Bombay Harbor boosts Katharine's sense of oneness with her surroundings. She sees that life at its most squalid must not only be accepted but also cherished and honored (earlier in "Allow, Accept, Be," Frontain had referred to "the fullness of the life cycle": *ibid.*, 213). The mystery of unity precludes distinctions; either all of life is sacred or none of it is. It even has room for the insanity of Harry's being a doctor who's dying from a disease that has foiled medical science. Referring to the change caused by the stripping away of Katharine's defenses, Ganesha says, for our benefit as well as hers, "Be careful of India.... If not, you may find yourself here" (*Two Plays* 192). She might not recognize that self. She had objected that the puppet show she watched in Act Two, scene three, included the device of a play within a play that, like its counterpart in *Hamlet*, deviates from its original script. She had reason to object. The puppet playing Shiva, the Hindu god of destruction, beheads — her son Walter.

Hearing that the deviation had upset Katharine, Ganesha replies, "Perhaps she needed upsetting" (*ibid.*, 285). This verdict is hard to quarrel with. Katharine isn't the first character since Job who needed to be shaken and torn before being remade; nearly all of Graham Greene's heroes fit this pattern. Abandoning schedules and timetables abets this process. It's when Katharine and Margaret dump their itinerary, a step encouraged by Katharine's loss of her guidebook (*ibid.*, 201), that the affirmations she and Margaret have been grazing start taking hold.

Katharine responds to them more heartily than Margaret because she holds no truck with the self-assurance and entitlement that go with Margaret's inherited class privilege. In a motif that will return in a later play McNally built around two women, *Deuce*, Katharine lacks her companion's breeding. She only met her future husband by crashing a country club ball. Like Emma Bovary at Vaubyassard, she warmed to this first taste of elegance. Dancing with George Brynne, advisedly like her "a wonderful dancer" (*ibid.*, 211), emboldened her to ask him for his class ring — which slipped out of her soapy hands and fell down a drain within minutes of the time she started wearing it. She knew how to undo her flub. This trespasser in the world of preppiedom and old money quickly maneuvered George into bed.

But all did not follow according to plan. If having sex with George set matters right with *him*, it soured her. At least four times in the play, she refers to herself by her maiden name, Mitchell (*ibid.*, e.g., 158, 178, 185, 203). She still feels unworthy in late midlife (George dies at age 62 [*ibid.*, 231]) of the comforts and conveniences her marriage has brought her. In Act One, she tells Margaret, "You are traveling with a woman whose father was a postal clerk and whose mother did ironing" (*ibid.*, 210). Not born to the manor, she has spent her adult life haunted by her lack of social credentials. She calls herself low-class. Where can she turn? If being hobbled by her blue-collar bloodlines weren't enough, she's thumped by her moral affinity to Walter's murderers. Yet she rebounds from the thumping. Frontain might have been thinking of her when he called "religious humanism" ("Allow, Accept, Be" 238) a theme of McNally's later work. Katharine's survival depends upon her forgiving herself, an act that entails a confession of wrongdoing. As in *Dead Man Walking* (2000), a sin denied can't be redressed. Before her trip to India, she had been running out of moral oxygen. Going through life stained by a sin she couldn't wipe out had made her a half-lifer at best. And now she has polluted this half-life to the point where she questions her right to it; her long-awaited punishment for gate-crashing the ranks of the gentry has finally arrived.

At some level, though, she understands the paradox underlying forgiveness; that certain sins don't *deserve* to be forgiven is the whole point. This truth makes forgiveness liberating and creative. *Dead Man Walking*, which McNally wrote with Jake Hegge, links forgiveness to divine love. This link had already been forged. By forgiving herself, Katharine is imitating God. She has earned the right to visit the Taj Mahal, the wonder of which she takes in directly, unimpeded by guidebook catchphrases.

* * *

Some of her questions remain unanswered ("Maybe, maybe, maybe" [*ibid.*, 166]). She might always recoil from her compulsion to kiss a leper full on the chops. So might have Mother Teresa. She has asked too much of herself. Again, deep, honest self-questioning has brought a lovable McNally character to grief. It all seems unfair. The kindness, simplicity, and reconciliation she has been seeking take gnarled, outlandish forms. Like the Marabar Caves in *A Passage to India* (which is mentioned in the play [*ibid.*, 226]), India translates to raw experience without the cushion or buffer of civilization. As Forster's two earlier visitors to India, Mrs. Moore and Miss Adela Quested, learned, it finds the weak point in one's psychological armor and probes it relentlessly. Making herself receptive to whatever answers God has in store for her nearly undoes Adela; perhaps it killed Mrs. Moore.

Katharine's quest has put her on the right track. The bare, unaccommodated state is most favorable to renewal and redemption. But if enlightenment, or satori, entails suffering, she'd not have achieved it alone. She needs Margaret to share her ordeal. Don't be shocked. Not always the "pain in the ass" Katharine accuses her of being (*ibid.*, 185), Margaret gives her the pep talk she needs to continue their pilgrimage when her anxiety about Walter has shaken her resolve. A reminder of the endings of the two parts of *Godot* occurs in Act Two, Scene Five of *Ganesh* when Margaret is talking about her breast cancer. She and Katharine stay put after agreeing to pack their bags. In their ways, they're as stripped down as Beckett's two bums. But it's the cancer victim Margaret, not the more adventurous, self-governing Katharine, who makes sure that their trip will continue as planned.

McNally has again invoked Albee's success formula from *The Zoo Story*; that people often have to go a long distance out of their way to cover a short distance correctly. For most of the time, grouchy Margaret seems to lack the imagination to complete the two-week trip, let alone join Katharine in converting it to a fresh start. This "aloof and starchy" matron (Montgomery, Zinman, ed. *Casebook* 136) had known exactly what she wanted from the trip and had also prepared beforehand to achieve her goals with minimum effort. She's first seen rolling the pieces in her set of matched luggage to the reservations desk of Air India. Unlike Faust's Gretchen or Margaret, she has taken the proper steps to avoid being left behind. But the other side of her practicality is a tendency to fluster when things go wrong. A computer glitch at Air India that temporarily leaves her without a seat on her Bombay flight makes her panic.

The resourcefulness McNally admires in her has also put her out of step with life. It has certainly routed her patience and reserve. No sooner does she try to comfort Katharine when the subject of Walter's death comes up than she criticizes her for humming. This isn't unusual. She corrects people with such aplomb that it never occurs to her that she might also be offending them. Ironically named Mrs. Civil, she needs to cultivate the art of civility. She needs mellowing, too. Her first words to Katharine, "Will you keep your voice down" (*Two Plays* 155), invoke the conformist's slavery to appearances and the authoritarian's passion for control. The name "Civil" posits a body of laws that must be obeyed, silently and without arguments.

Her need to be in charge takes different forms. When the subject comes up of her and Katharine's husbands having gotten sick the previous year from eating *langoustes*, she insists that they ate crayfish (*ibid.*, 165). Why did she bother to contradict Katharine on such a trifle? The two spiny crustaceans look so much alike that the tiny physical differences between them hardly merit a word. This egoist spent $3,000 to have the liver spots removed from her hands (*ibid.*, 166) to disguise her pushiness. A wise investment; she has to have the upper hand all the time. Nobody is safe around her mitts. Brittle and uptight, she's always looking for something wrong, as when she asks if some chewing gum from the packet Katharine offers her had stuck to her crowns (*ibid.*, 104). She's even afraid that the Taj Mahal will be a bust (*ibid.*, 167).

She had only agreed to go to India because she thought she might find something there that she didn't want to miss. But would this self-seeking mind-set let her understand or appreciate that prize? She likes to have her ducks in a row. She insists on being guaranteed an aisle seat before boarding her plane. Once in the air, she becomes disturbed by some turbulence ("I hate this. I hate it, I hate it" [*ibid.*, 160]). Katharine parries her grumbles that they should have flown TWA by saying, "TWA is for sissies. Anyone can fly TWA. Air India is an adventure. I feel like we're already there" (*ibid.*, 163). For her, the journey has at least as much drama as the arrival. Maybe it has more; she finds reasons to tarry in the airport once their plane lands in Bombay.

Differences between the travelers have been sharply drawn. Katharine wants to relish all that India offers, including the turbulence on the Air India flight. Conversely, Margaret's propensity for worst-case scenarios has distracted her from a central tenet governing all social interaction, viz., the individuality of individuals, let alone their sacredness. When Katharine delights in the turbulence that's rocking their plane, Margaret answers, "You're the type that would" (*ibid.*, 164). She has overlooked her good luck. She has typecast the person her hot-tempered bossiness has made her ideal traveling companion. What's more, her crabbiness is self-imposed. She insults Katharine at the start of their trip, a bad time to cause a rift. In a trope that will return in *Deuce*, her inner demons have replaced honest worries.

But the enjoyment McNally takes thwarting probability judgments, educated guesses, and trends tempers the growing rift between the women. The differences between them, though sharp, can be overcome by goodwill. In spite of herself, know-it-all Margaret does muster the warmth and buoyancy to open herself to India. Richly conceived, she's inwardly contradictory without flouting laws of probability. She rejects Katharine's comforting hand during the bout of turbulence that shakes their plane. Then, after a king-size heave of the plane, Katharine reaches again for her hand, anyway—which leaves Margaret grumbling that her grip is too tight (*ibid.*, 168).

The hand motif carries forward. After the plane begins coasting smoothly,

Katharine apologizes to cover Margaret's overreaction. But later, when thoughts of Walter send Katharine into tears, Margaret takes *her* hand — "soothingly" (*ibid.*, 175). Katharine is moved. Thinking about Walter will fuse homosexuality in her mind with death — either a speedy, violent one that strikes suddenly and violently or a painful, prolonged one. She tells the AIDS-stricken Harry, "We must hold hands and we must never let go of each other" (*ibid.*, 200). Direct physical contact can ease grief. Katharine needs the touch of another hand to help her cope with the truth that early death will take her surrogate son as it did her natural one.

Margaret's ministry is different, not inferior. The slow crabwise steps by which her consciousness is refined should be honored. For example, a humanizing impulse from within agrees to a Coca-Cola in her Bombay hotel room after she had ordered a Diet Pepsi (*ibid.*, 181). Yet she'll backslide. Katharine warns her that getting constantly nagged by Margaret to stop humming is spoiling her trip (*ibid.*, 184). Margaret deserves this rebuke. In view of McNally's love of music, Margaret's rudeness may be depriving her something of great value. Katharine's humming, like her habit of singing to herself, signals an affinity to the celestial harmonies.

What eventually tunes Margaret to music is pain. As is typical of McNally, her vision takes root in suffering. Like Katharine (whom she always affectionately calls Kitty), an exchange with a stranger opens her inner planes of perception. A Japanese woman on an adjoining balcony in Bombay touches her breast when she hears that Margaret has breast cancer. Right after this scene, another, more heartfelt, similarity with her friend Kitty occurs. It comes out late in Act One that they both have dead sons. Margaret's four-year-old Gabriel pulled away as she was wiping chocolate from his face. His momentum carried him into the street, where his head was crushed under the wheels of a passing car — just as a volley of blows delivered by some homophobic thugs who had left *their* car would later brain Walter, also in Greenwich Village. The women don't need to compare notes on these deaths. They resemble each other more than they know. They're joined by an everlasting grief.

But the same grief that led them unconsciously to choose each other as traveling mates can be lightened. Revealingly, it strikes a chord with Christian myth. Christ came to Earth to be crucified. His passion on the Cross brought Him closer to us than at any other time in His life. Pain joined the human to the divine. Because Jesus died to redeem our sins, our pain makes us one with Him on the Cross. Having grown up Catholic before the onset of Vatican II under Pope John XXIII, McNally has bought into this analogue of the Job story that joins human suffering to divine love; whom God loveth, He chasteneth. In our distress, God has privileged us to be one with His Son in Calvary. He has also offered opportunities for self-transcendence, including the warmth and comfort of physical contact. Margaret goes beyond civility by putting her arm around a frazzled Katharine and saying, "I love you very much. Offamof" [a near anagram of Katharine's favorite passage from Shakespeare, "O for a Muse of Fire"] (*ibid.*, 231).

It's here that the trippers devise a new itinerary. Margaret's declaration of love also belongs to the time when she lies to Katharine about never having lost a child (*ibid.*, 229). In a surpassing grace, she won't let her heartbreak rival or intrude upon the dignity of Katharine's. Katharine needs love and understanding, not a competitive claim. At some level, Margaret knows that people show their love of God by loving each other. Another passage of delayed exposition that improves the play reveals that her husband Alan, not the cold fish Katharine believes him to be (*ibid.*, 184, 224), has been keeping a mistress for the past seven years. Talk about losses: the "bossy bitch" (*ibid.*, 196) Margaret has put up a smokescreen to distract others from the heartache caused by Alan's betrayal. The inner strength she musters to dissuade Katharine from cutting short the Indian visit both stems from her grief and tops it.

The differences between *her* path to illumination and Katharine's count less and less. Besides invoking McNally's *F&J*, Ganesha's description of the women, "two little, unimportant, magnificent lives" (*ibid.*, 160–61), confirms the equality, uniqueness, and interdependence of the two women. Margaret and Katharine not only co-exist; as their trip shows, they also need each other to lend the trip meaning. To voice his recognition of Margaret's centricity in this dynamic, McNally gives her one of the play's wittiest lines. To Katharine's jest, "As Rudyard Kipling said, 'Bugger off, Margaret,'" Margaret ripostes, "I'm sure Rudyard Kipling never said, 'Bugger off, Margaret.' Somerset Maugham maybe" (*ibid.*, 232). Later, she bristles when Katharine forgets to reciprocate her declaration of love (*ibid.*, 255). Her moment of indignation doesn't diminish her. The play's unsettling thrills don't lie in its resolution but, rather, in its contradictions and incongruities.

McNally hints at the contrarieties of selfhood, building tensions slowly till they gain a critical mass. Margaret and Katharine reach the point where they can't contain themselves any longer, and a cascade of irritations erupts that the women finally accept as natural, even inevitable. Their mutual acceptance comforts them. Two women living alongside each other for two weeks are bound to quarrel; neither should be upset at a falling-out or two. Margaret says in Act Two, Scene Two, "We love each other. We just don't especially like each other" (*ibid.*, 228). She has reminded us of love's power to trump ill will. Rather than dividing the travelers, their irritations build a climate of sharing. Their sorrows have steered them toward God; India has helped them discover the divine within themselves. Margaret and her friend Kitty are robustly imagined creations with bruised psyches and complex back stories that both describe and honor their status as "two little, insignificant, magnificent women (*ibid.*, 160–1)."

Benilde Montgomery says of Ganesha, the women's observer and spiritual guide, "In appearance, he is a god and an elephant; in outlook he is a child and an adult; in manner he's masculine and feminine" (Zinman, ed. *Casebook* 137). We can add that there's something dangerous about this elephant-headed god of good luck. This believer that nothing is intrinsically right or wrong lives in a way that we mortals could not. Multi-dimensional, he's both a metaphor and a microcosm; he inhabits everything we could possibly be or know: "I am in what you eat and what you evacuate. I am sunlight, moonlight, dawn and dusk. I am stool. I am in your kiss. I am in your cancer.... I am everywhere. I am happy" (*Two Plays* 151). His joy springs from his total acceptance of life. Rather than judging, he revels in whatever confronts him: "Is there a more joyful sound than children?" he asks. "A more lovely sight than their precious smiles? A sweeter smell than their soiled diapers?" (*ibid.*, 153)

This love has qualified him as a guide, a witness, a showman, and a chronicler of Indian legend. He plays these roles to the hilt. He unspools the plot's complexities; his inter-scenic commentary moves the action; the historical details he provides lend it authority. Between times, he'll act the parts of an air passenger, a representative of Red Carpet Tours, a Japanese tourist, even Katharine's Walter. While organizing the action for the playgoer or reader, he's also razing the defenses of Katharine and Margaret. In Varanasi, he splashes Margaret with the same Ganges water in which animal and human corpses are seen floating.

Defying reason, he owes both his birth and his survival to miracles and, boxing the compass, to the kindness of strangers. He first appears eating fruit and vegetables left by some followers. He also expresses his love of dance straightaway (*ibid.*, 151). The play's title, like his take on Katharine and Margaret ("insignificant, magnificent") is an oxymoron. His physical self bespeaks *im*perfection. His broken tusk has ruled out the perfection that Katharine reaches for when she tries to force herself to kiss the diseased lips of a leper. Her motive is clear. Whereas anybody can love a beauty, only the saintly can be close with a leper — even if the gruesome mask he just took off exposes the chubby, joyful face of the god Ganesha. Katharine must stop faulting herself. If she believes she can love the leper unconditionally, as God does, she has set the bar too high.

Each of the Ganeshas she begins to collect has perforce a broken tusk; as soon as Ganesha took physical shape, he forfeited the perfection that belongs only to the gods. He takes it all in stride. Contradicting Katharine, he finds perfections in *all* her elephants. As in the story of the Prodigal Son, the stalemate is broken by charity. He and Katharine are both right. If her search for perfection has thwarted her, it has at least moved her along the road to self-forgiveness.

Ganesha continues to play an essential part. At once communal and all-knowing like a Greek chorus, he has been focusing both the play's themes and, with his freedom to intrude on the action, its organization. The stabs of pain he brings to the stage, he also relieves. After recounting George Brynne's death, for instance (*ibid.*, 231), he indirectly helps Katharine cope with it. Nor are his interventions arbitrary or unnatural. This "quieter of obstacles" (*ibid.*, 151) remains active. A choric figure, he's also a stage manager. He'll clap his hands to change scenes, to quiet noise, to freeze characters, or to snap off the house lights. He's a marvel. Defying augury, he makes the play brazenly theatrical while keeping it as omniform and shocking as India itself.

* * *

The shocks come often, a feat accomplished through exquisitely chosen sensory details, i.e., many internally plausible touches that vibrate with emotional intensity. These take different forms. McNally's knowledge that ugly ideas and images pack more emotional power than benign ones breeds rhetoric that's nightmarish, heartbreaking, and hellish as well as thematically right. This master of scenic immediacy wastes no time stunning us. The stage where the action unfolds is "painted a blinding white" (*ibid.*, 151) at curtain rise. Comfort seems far away. Well aware of the importance of variety in stage production, he'll blast our ears together with our eyes, the "roaring" [of the people waking in the square below the travelers' Bombay hotel room] being "almost unbearable" (*ibid.*, 204) just before first intermission.

Ganesh is a high-wire act that has replaced the wire with an exposed nerve. McNally timed his effects carefully after meticulously selecting them, making us share the physical malaise and confusion of his people. Some demonic words that push us uncomfortably toward the action come from the manager of the Udaipur hotel the travelers have checked into. The passage might be called McNally on McNally, hideously reshaping details bland and easygoing on their own: "The ... sun hits the water. The Moghuls used to tie their prisoners to stakes and sew their eyelids open and make them look at the water until they went blind or mad or both" (*ibid.*, 207).

McNally names the actor speaking these percussive words The Man. A gift to any actor, the role is just one of many in the play that could also be played by a woman. Nothing would be lost. The women we know best in the play, Margaret and Katharine, travel by air, sea, and rail. Even when they're passive, they're busy adjusting to new environments. Act Two, Scene Two shows the train they're riding passing through India's longest tunnel, the Chittamgahr Pass, a distance long enough to darken the stage for several minutes.

The following scene breaks in the "humble village" (*ibid.*, 239) where the puppet show is held. It's nearby that the women find themselves on opposite sides of a river represented by a "bolt of blue cloth ... rolled across the white floor of the stage" (*ibid.*, 239).

This stagecraft is central to the play's strategy — which was not devised to help us relax. Brechtian reminders that we're watching a play rather than a slice of reality, the more naturalistic scenes will oscillate with hyper-realistic ones that reveal the interior lives of the women. We're never on safe ground watching McNally's 1993 gem. Reviewing a 1995 revival of it in Croton Falls in rural Westchester County, Alvin Klein suggested how the play's deft organization keeps sending us ever deeper into its people's lives: "Mr. McNally interweaves time and space in an ingeniously complex trek through the seamless scenes" (1).

Stoking McNally's treatment of the time-space continuum is the prominence of dawn. Katharine's acceptance of her moral complicity in Walter's death in the crowded plaza of her Bombay hotel at early dawn stirs her rebirth. It should. Dawn is the best time for fresh starts and second chances. As was seen in Whitman's *Song of Myself*, life and death are different faces of the same reality; there's no rebirth without death. Contingent on this belief is another. Since life and death take their meanings from each other, neither can be understood without a full, close look at the other. In Act Two, Scene Three, Ganesha, acting on this truth, embraces Katharine at a time she most needs it — when thoughts of Walter are piercing her heart. She had earlier joined the throng of natives stirring to life as the first rays of dawn began outlining the nearby Gate of India. Forming part of the same event, Katharine's agonies regarding Walter resemble those birth pangs that precede the onset of new life. Her rebirth forms part of a larger one. The daybreak drama at Bombay of things becoming other things includes all of local life. The motif will recur at the "eternal city" (*ibid.*, 249) Varanasi's burial ghats, soon after which a postcard arrives from Ben and Harry (*ibid.*, 254), the two AIDS victims the women had met in Bombay.

More counterpoint layers new melodic traces into the mix. The same balcony where Katharine first met the men sites another upsurge of life moments later when Margaret shares the secret of her breast cancer with a Japanese stranger. The fugue-like drama takes a new turn. While wearing the stranger's kimono — against both the cold and the chilly indifference of reality to her plight — she discusses the death of four-year-old Gabriel. Her final words in the scene, "It's not warranted, such kindness" (*ibid.*, 199), said about her new kimono, the giving of which coincided with the dawn, marks a crossroads. She has started to take India on its own terms. This means placing herself in God's care, where spiritual values trump personal ones. She's on the brink of accepting Gabriel's death as a gateway to enlightenment.

A feature of which is merriment; near the end of *A Passage to India*, the celebration of the birth of Krishna contains as much rowdiness and knockabout as it does gravitas. McNally, too, eschewing the piecemeal work of reconstruction, aims in *Ganesh* at an organic wholeness. In contrast to the bleak solemnity of American Protestantism conveyed by Grant Wood's "American Gothic," Hinduism, knowing their uses, welcomes frolic and fun. McNally took on extra work to keep us honest. The phrase, "just a little joke" (*ibid.*, 154, 157, 177), always spoken by Indians to relieve stress, performs a double service. Mood brighteners, these phrases sideswipe dramatic momentum and thus discredit the burgeoning inevitability that promotes lazy thinking. Accordingly, the sexless Ganesh, whose face appears on the postcard from Ben, will collapse into a fit of giggles (*ibid.*, 240) as readily as he'll discuss Hindu legend (*ibid.*, 179).

As Klein said in the *New York Times*, the play's many elements coincide and knit, combine and recombine, masterfully (1995, 1). Both McNally's choice and treatment of them call forth the Hindu mind-set that sees oneness in places where western pragmatism finds only fragments and division. Katharine and Margaret have been detecting faint strains of this harmony. Their two new friends, Ben and Harry, are traveling as a pair, as are they. A new melodic line has risen and resonated. Harry's middle name, Walter, evokes Katharine's Walter, whose swift violent death mirrors the slow, agonizing one consuming Harry, her surrogate son. This kinship begets another. Unlike Gabriel's head, which was crushed under the wheels of a car, Walter's was spared crushing because one of his attackers had the "humanity" (*Two Plays* 174) to redirect the wheels of the car speeding toward him.

This touch of humanity was pointless; Walter died an hour after getting mugged. But in keeping with the play's expansive spirit, it should be noted that Walter and Gabriel both died in Greenwich Village. Perhaps the impulse that led the mugger to steer the car away from Walter's dying body *had* meaning. All faiths allege that no act of kindness is wasted. An early scene in Act One shows a conjured-up Walter dancing with his mother, a reminder that McNally has always prized dancing as one of the most pristine, deeply felt forms of human contact.

Perhaps dancing puts us in God's hands; it certainly prompts epiphanies. Suddenly, during the dance, Walter says, "This is a long tune" (*ibid.*, 213). His remark isn't random. Just moments earlier, Katharine, "a wonderful dancer" in her day, recalls her first dance with George, Walter's father. The tune they stepped, "Begin the Beguine" (*ibid.*, 211), happens to be one of the longest in the American songbook. It might have also been included in the cassette of its composer Cole Porter's music (*ibid.*, 172) that Katharine loses by accident. That is, if there are any accidents in the play or if we believe, along with Freud, that everything happens in life for a reason; the beguine that Katharine dances years apart with her husband and their son draws some of the sting from the deaths of these two most important men in her life. The full meaning of this convergence we lack the information to decipher. But what we do know or can surmise stops us from dismissing it.

Nor are we trapped between two imponderables. Both the family context of the dance and the song *being* danced, with the word "Begin" in its title, along with its thrilling mandate, "let them begin the beguine; make them play," summon up McNally's deep faith in the connection between dance and love; dancing with Katharine led George to give her his class ring, have sex with her, and then marry her. So what if we can't love one another unconditionally. Nobody can. God has seen to it that we're not equipped or programmed to. We mustn't reject flawed love; it's too important. What's left for us to do is to love more selflessly. If no act of kindness is wasted, the same can be said about love, as flawed as it is. Divine intervention might have brought George Brynne together with Katharine Mitchell on the dance floor. The dance plays on in its own way. Later, Ganesha jounces sore places in both Katharine and Margaret to elevate their spirits,

A Perfect Ganesh has cast the bait, and we bite. Fluent, effortlessly entertaining, and fascinating in its implications, it's ample as well as ambitious, as agile and unpredictable as it is viscerally moving.

IV

Ganesh confirmed McNally's commitment to two major cultural issues of the last quarter of the twentieth century — the subordinacy of women and the importance of God in our lives. His artistry is on target on both counts. Once a year, a big festival honoring Ganesha takes place in Mumbai, the Bombay of McNally's 1993 play. The ordeals undergone by Katharine and Margaret illuminate those facing everybody, including other Americans who try to turn their lives over to God.

McNally's muse led him to enact this ordeal with women. Plays like *The Rink*, *F&J*, *Master Class*, and, most recently, *Deuce*, reflect an accelerating moral and imaginative involvement with women, how hard they work and how misprized their labors are. As a singing Ganesha draws down the curtain on *Ganesh*, an unidentified man meant to embody male indifference to women is snoring. It may be past his lifetime before the play's feminism gains public favor. Meanwhile, he remains ignorant of the treasures offered by feminine attitudes and values. The play's final stage direction, placed after the last voice is spoken, runs, "The man is still snoring" (*ibid.*, 256).

McNally isn't one of those men who snore while women toil. Offsetting Maria Callas's world celebrity in *Master Class* is the painful shambles of her everyday self. And despite the on-stage absence of women in *The Lisbon Traviata*, the play extends McNally's phylogeny. Mike dwells on the distressing blow he dealt his former wife Sarah when he told her he was leaving her for Stephen ("I hurt her in a way I was ashamed of" [*Three Plays* 76]). Tellingly, *she* has asked to see the shamefaced Mike during a later visit to New York. She has company on the fringe. Stephen's mother has dwindled to a voice on an answering machine. She needn't show her face. Like Sarah, she feels hurt ("You don't have to call back, if you don't want to" [*ibid.*, 52]). Stephen has apparently been casual about returning his mother's phone calls.

Women who are ignored can't expect much; Stephen's mother doesn't want to risk the mite of attention he extends her. McNally's insights into the material and emotional obstacles suffered by women have sharp edges. If admiration for female stoicism abounds in the canon, it's rarely accompanied by conferrals of overdue rewards to suffering heroines. Katharine's husband in *Ganesh* is dead, and Margaret's keeps a mistress. Even Joshua, the Jesus figure in *Corpus Christi*, rejects *His* mother (*CC* 52), and the sons who might have comforted Katharine and Margaret are both dead. Women in Connecticut and beyond with grown children bleed with them. McNally applies Ganesha's pronouncement, "The outlook for women in India is very, very dismal" (*Two Plays* 180), to North American women in general: "What happens to women?" Margaret asks. "Who are we? What are we supposed to be? Men still have all the marbles. All we have are our children, and sooner or later we lose them" (*ibid.*, 250).

The tennis metaphor that unifies *Deuce* (2007) tallies with this view. During their reign as women's doubles champions, Leona Mullen and Midge Barker had to keep outscoring their opponents to stay in the public eye. The sneaky top-spin drives that won them points on the court dictated what happened off. One can see why McNally based a play on these doubles partners. Like their efforts to overcome obscurity, even as tennis stars, members of another underclass, gay men, must struggle to fend off the *wrong* kind of attention from their own kind in *A Man of No Importance* and *Corpus Christi*. Yet women run afoul of gay men in *LT*. As has been seen, Stephen ignores his mother, and Mike replaces his wife with a boyfriend.

And for what? That boyfriend's later murder of Mike, brutal enough on its own, represents an outer edge of the turmoil facing gays. Ironically, while dining elegantly at the New York Athletic Club, Will and Bernie of *Some Men* discuss the pressure they face every day heading off the obloquy of being outed (*Two Plays* 2007, 34–39). By contrast, a generation of college-age gays in the same 2007 play bemoans missing such dangers and thrills (*ibid.*, 70–80). But rather than taking comfort in the easing of obstacles to gay rights in succeeding decades, we should look again at Mike, the man who left a wife he shouldn't have married in the first place. Or replaced with Stephen? McNally's position on this bond hits home. It concretizes and thus expands our experience of life. Rather than punishing Mike for marrying and then dumping Sarah, he describes the fallout of his actions, which crosses families and generations as well as gender preference. It's Stephen's mother who phones the apartment, not Mike's, who might have turned her back on him after he botched his marriage.

We're all wading in the same moral soup. Much of the excitement generated by *Corpus Christi* comes from the skill with which McNally lays out the world in which his people move. This world swathes Corpus Christi, Texas, where he grew up, and Bethlehem and Golgotha, or Calvary, places where Jesus, either explicitly or tacitly, holds sway. This adroit mirroring, or doubling, effect universalizes the action of McNally's 1998 one-acter. Both closed-in and far-flung, *Corpus Christi* delivers heaps of suspense and complexity. The heights it attains result largely from the bountiful inventiveness of McNally's storytelling. This bounty is rare. Writers who turn to the supernatural as subject matter often flatten and/or dwarf their characters. Characters in Biblical drama and fiction face the threat of losing both dimension and IQ as they get batted about the Holy Land. Not in *Corpus Christi*; McNally is too respectful of his subject and his craft to let this happen. The inhabitants of the play would rivet us even without the myth that joins them to us.

* * *

McNally knew that the story of Christ's life and crucifixion needed no cosmetic makeover. He knew, too, that, when the conclusion of a story is known beforehand by its audiences, details become everything. *Corpus Christi*'s cast members, 13 barefooted men dressed alike in clean white shirts and pressed khaki pants, walk unceremoniously onto a bare raked stage, addressing each other and even members of the audience. The informality holds. Once in place, the men stay put, seated on benches at the rear of the stage when they're not playing a scene. Not playing, but involved; the seated actors keep abreast of what's going on, sometimes reacting to it with words or gestures. The play's bare-bones ambience creates the impression that we're watching a rehearsal of a sketch of a play-script. McNally reinforces this impression. Most of the actors may play several different parts, some of them female.

This rehearsal-studio quality persists. Only after the men sort themselves out on stage and one of them talks to us for about a minute do the houselights dim. The "three knocks from off stage" (16) that herald the onset of the plot, a borrowing from the traditional opening of an act in French opera (e.g., *GA*

64), introduce the play's first formal effect. They suit McNally's intent of getting to the quick of theater. Their resemblance in our minds to church bells announcing the start of Sunday services reminds us that T. S. Eliot designed *Murder in the Cathedral* (1935) to be performed on a church altar. No surprise; seminaries have always provided friendly settings for stage productions. In this regard, the play's epigraph from the first act of Chekhov's *Seagull* pares things down to basics to sharpen its thematic focus. The unfolding of a myth commands this attentiveness: "KOSTYA (*Looking round the stage.*): There's a theatre for you! Just a curtain, two wings, and then open space. Not a bit of scenery. A view straight onto the lake and the far horizon. We'll raise the curtain at half past eight, exactly, when the moon rises" (*ibid.*, 8).

Corpus Christi (1998) isn't just a crackling yarn but also a demonstration of why the Gospels have always captivated readers. Like *Ganesh* before it, it unfolds *sub specie aeternitatas*, or under the aspect of eternity. It also finds McNally on familiar turf. In line with the prologue from *Seagull*, Christian myth exerts so much force in the Western world that it needs little explanation or theatrical heightening. Thus the play's unfinished look; at one point, the Lord's Prayer is recited in full to good effect. Confident in his belief that all of life is holy if any part of it is, McNally will glide or jump from the secular to the profane without warning. An actor who quotes Scripture ("The man was much amazed") is answered with a curse ("Holy shit!" [*ibid.*, 55]). Such linguistic leaps can be more disturbing than funny. A Biblical passage used to accompany Joshua's trudge through Golgotha, weighed down by His Cross, ends, "The crowd grew silent. They stripped Him of His garment, which was of a color purple [not the more demotic "purple color"] to mock His Divinity." The passage keeps its Biblical flavor and gait. The words immediately following, though, "I got dibs on the purple dress" (*ibid.*, 58), yank us back into our own lives.

This most Brechtian of McNally's works sustains its unfinished, makeshift look. Augmenting its casualness, the people will handle some of the stage props. After drawing lots to see which roles they'll play in the coming action, one says, "Much scenery will be chewed at this performance" (*ibid.*, 15). A stroke of black humor will lace solemnity and tears with fun, McNally believing that laughter and irreverence can support vision. Included in an inventory of props, like a "hammer to drive in the nails," a "crown of thorns," and the "spear that pierced His side" is "His mother's Grand Ol' Opry souvenir ash tray" (*ibid.*, 15). McNally's sensitivity to the secular world keeps extending the play's relevance while making us laugh. References to pop culture icons like Marilyn Monroe and Lucille Ball also shorten the gap between Joshua's story and that of theater audiences. Like His all-inclusive forgiveness, His earthly pilgrimage touches us all.

Granted, the practice of following a passage that tunes the action to the somberness of Scripture with one in which a woman shrieks, "Fuck me, fuck me, fuck me" (*ibid.*, 21), can repel audiences. James Nuechterlein, for one, saw *Corpus Christi* as both "boring and offensive" and "a leaden script that veers between sentimentality and juvenile satire" (9). There's something else at stake here that has escaped Nuechterlein and many of he play's other detractors. McNally has forfeited propriety to develop stylistically a vital issue, the difficulty of sustaining one's Christian faith. Told to "[c]herish and love" her baby, Mary replies, "What does it look like I'm doing. You have some kid chewing on your tits and see how you like it." Moments later, she'll remind us again of human frailty while, in the same stroke, criticizing the role she's playing. When Joshua identifies her, i.e., the man playing her, as "The Mother of the Son of God," she carps, "I don't know if I can do this" (*CC* 20).

This touch of humility charts McNally's keen audience awareness. This includes a refusal to let us off easily. We need to be receptive rather than passive to take in the play's meaning, which, appropriately, is couched in a run of vivid sensory impressions. The lightning, thunder, and howling wind that fill the house at Joshua's death gain terrific force from the climactic raising of the Cross minutes earlier, which revealed "[f]or the first time ... how horribly Joshua had been battered." McNally isn't through elevating our awareness of Christ's ministry. The familiarity of Joshua's last words, "Father forgive them: they know not what they do," besides cushioning the insult of His being called "cowboy" (*ibid.*, 59) during His Passion, sharpen our involvement in the action. McNally wrote *Corpus Christi* to revere Christ and Christian ritual, but also to rouse the unawakened Christ in us, an appeal he invested in all aspects of the play. Note, for instance, the amazing thoroughness of his property list, part of which includes

> Fish (THOMAS)
> Vinegar (BARTHOLEMEW)
> Sponge (ANDREW)
> Spear (THADDEUS)
> Chalice (PETER)
> Stuffed dog on wheels (SIMON) [*ibid.*, 61]

Downplaying the diligence behind this preparation, the play's opening words sound apologetic, even self-demeaning. The actor who's addressing us sounds as if the data he's sharing with us is so unpromising that it has to be tugged out of him: "We are going to tell you an old and familiar story.... There's no suspense and fewer surprises. You all know how it turns out" (*ibid.*, 9). He has lost McNally no ground. Vital to him is the truth that *Oedipus Rex* and *Hamlet* both came from old stories familiar to their viewers when first staged. People like rehearing old stories they may have forgotten, particularly when they're told freshly and originally; familiar turf is often friendly turf. McNally's inventiveness, though, can make it unfriendly. When Joshua tells an angry, resentful Judas, "I did love you, you know," He's answered, "Not the way I wanted.... I've got a big dick.... It's important to me" (*ibid.*, 14).

It's exciting to watch the Gospels unfold in new ways. Judas's remark, voiced after his demurrer to Joshua, "No one has told this story right" (*ibid.*), bespeaks a staple of the play. Our imaginations have stirred. We all know enough about the story he's referring to to heed his take on it. This is dramatized rather than argued. Like a Greek chorus or communal *raisonneur*, the actors move in and out of their roles to comment on the progress of the story, supply historical background, and share their feelings about each other. Matthew, for instance, says of Joshua, "I didn't like Him. I'd worked very hard to get this much of a piece of the pie .... My father [like Katharine's in *PG*] delivered mail and here He was saying I had to give it all away" (*ibid.*, 11). This conversational American idiom, though easy to mimic, is hard to create. Create it McNally does, both squaring it with Jesus' unaffected honesty, and, in a fugue-like stroke, contraposing it with the liturgical quality conveyed elsewhere in *CC* by repetitions and periodic cadences evocative of Holy Writ.

Judas brings a different kind of counterweight. At the start, he's sitting apart from the others; like them, he'll be baptized, not by John, like the others, but by Joshua — looking advisedly straight at Him rather than bowing his head. He has fixed on Joshua just as Breton Beret of *MNI* (2007) would do on Alfie Byrne before betraying *him*. Betrayal drives Judas. Later, he'll rescue Josh when, during their high-school prom some rowdy classmates try to stuff His head down a toilet. Some rescue; it soon becomes clear that, rather than acting on friendship, he expects Josh to reward him with sex. This He does, as He will with all His disciples. *CC* reworks the Gospel along gay lines both to extend the range of Jesus's ministry and to add to its jolt. The many times Josh and Judas have made love (*ibid.*, 14) intensify the shock and terror of Judas's rhetorical question: "Who would betray the Son of God and be damned for all eternity?" (*ibid.*, 53)

* * *

Corpus Christi opened the same week that one of America's most ugly hate crimes occurred. In September 1998, a 20-year-old University of Wyoming student, Matthew Shepard, was pistol-whipped and then tied to a fence on the outskirts of Laramie. Matthew was gay. His death five days later had an overlapping double effect on *CC*. The unfriendly publicity it brought to the play also created shock waves felt by non-theatergoers. A greater number of noisy protesters and counter-protesters than the play's subject matter called for thronged the Manhattan Theatre Club, where *CC* was premiering. Patrons had to pass through metal detectors. Bomb threats were aimed not only at MTC's executive board but at McNally, too. Responses to the play stayed polarized. Writing in the *New York Times*, Jason Zinoman called *CC* "an earnest reverent spin on the Jesus story" (1). But he was writing about a 2008 revival. Nearly all who commented on the play's debut production took conflicting moralistic stands.

These commentators overlooked the play's artistry, which is abundant. After His senior prom at Corpus Christi High, Josh drops from view for a number of years. He's preparing Himself for His mission on Earth. He returns well prepared. Like Jesus, He's seen with ordinary people in unlikely places, where He does extraordinary deeds. He heals the sick, raises Lazarus from the dead, and performs the miracles of the loaves and fishes. His deeds at the wedding at Cana, though, tack differently. The wedding partners are two men. Using a phrase, "the other groom" (*ibid.*, 49) that will recur in *Some Men* (*Two Plays* 2007, 7), the episode makes clear Joshua's preference for the spirit of the law over the letter. This preference, spelling out the difference between Old and New Testament moralities, turns on the question of homosexuality. This part of McNally's script features condemnations of gay unions, citing the Biblical passage that damns all partakers of gay sex.

Joshua's response to this stand has the elegant brevity — and conviction — of Christ's conduct with the Grand Inquisitor in *Brothers Karamazov*. Solid on its own, the truth needs no window dressing. Joshua also reminds his audience, "God loves us most when we love each other" (*ibid.*, 48). Then he asks for the wedding ring. He holds center stage. After scolding some of the guests for giggling, He gives a brief homily, blesses the marriage, and says, "Now let's all get very, very drunk" (*ibid.*, 49). In keeping with the play's tenor, He has deflated the solemnity infusing the sacrament of marriage. He has also restored to view the paradox that Jesus was *both* God and man.

An even bolder conversion comes in McNally's treatment of the temptation. A scene like this would look hopelessly shopworn in less capable hands, capsizing the play in the process. Played by James Dean clad in a red windbreaker, Satan offers to swap Joshua the earthly kingdoms for what he calls "[a]lmost nothing." Joshua needs only one sentence to fend off Satan's dazzling persuasive technique: "But I am the Son of God" (*ibid.*, 38). The argument He hears next, that the treasures of the earth trump by eons the Cross offered Him by God, gets the same short shrift. As Ivan Karamazov learned, choosing God only matters if we can also choose the devil.

This choice can be galling to lesser mortals like us, a point made eloquently through the resemblances between young Joshua and that fledgling creation of McNally's, Edmund Hobart of *This Side of the Door* (1962). For some of the way in *CC*, Josh is 13, Edmund's age. Both boys are small for their age, indifferent to sports, and slow to develop sexually. Edmund's plea to his mother, "Maybe I'd get my growth if you let me get them ... hormone shots" (*Door* iii 2), comes back, grammatical flaw included, in *CC* in a priest's jibe to Josh: "They ought to get You some of them hormone shots" (*CC* 23). Now 17, Josh acts as Edmund might have done had *Door* been set four years later than it was. Still looking younger than his age (*ibid.*, 25), He attends play practice and sings a duet from a Broadway musical with the same nun who routed the priest who had bullied Him. Competing in sports is still far from His mind, as it would have been that of Edmund, who keeps a girl's doll instead of a baseball glove or a football. After singing with the nun, Josh supplies a "feminine touch" (*ibid.*, 28) to the adornments draping the gym of Pontius Pilate High School, where the senior prom is to be held.

The prom turns out to be a rite of passage for Him. Though He goes without a date, He dances with a girl who makes Him feel clumsy and wrong-footed. His discomfort notwithstanding, He follows some of McNally's most endearing characters, viz., Frankie of *F&J* and Katharine of *Ganesh*, by apologizing excessively to His dance partner (*ibid.*, 32). Thoughtful and considerate, He wants to do right by her, even though He's not sure what that is. He keeps groping, and gets groped; prom night is when He loses His virginity— to Judas, an outcome that justifies R-J. Frontain's calling *CC* "an alternative gospel" based on the claim that gay sex is a "form of grace" ("All Men Are Divine" 236–37). His lover of the night, Judas becomes the last person He spends time with before His "many years of wandering" (*CC* 84), i.e., those purported lost years designated in the Bible as spanning His 13th and 31st years.

He returns well schooled. The play's next scene finds Him riding in a truck through the desert, a place where prophets acquire wisdom. In a possible dig at the swaggering he-men of his south Texas youth, McNally makes one of Joshua's chief attributes His propensity both to doubt and criticize Himself. No one irks McNally more than people who believe they have an answer to everything; no one, as he shows through Sam Truman of *LTTA* (1992) and Leo Sampson of *Full Frontal Nudity* (2004), gets more pie in his face than when such self-righteousness meets grief. When told that God is pleased with Him, Joshua asks, "How can He be pleased with Me when I am so displeased with Myself?" This meekness might have even survived His knowing that all pronominal references to Him are capitalized. He keeps insisting that He's unworthy to be called The Son of God (*ibid.*, 36).

McNally believes this meekness and the open-mindedness it fosters is the best outlook to bring to both personal relationships—and the creation of art. Ironically, Pontius Pilate will order Joshua crucified for "His damnable pride" (*ibid.*, 56). Snubbing Satan's offer of boundless wealth and property assured Joshua that He *was* indeed God's Son (*ibid.*, 78). But far from being prideful, He grounds His proof in His belief in the divinity of *all* people. He has found something godly in us all. When James confesses that he's not ready to forgive his worst enemy, Joshua answers, "Would that we were all as honest as this man" (*ibid.*, 47). He kisses the feet of Matthew, who had balked at kissing *His* (*ibid.*, 45). He even heals the "disease-ridden, filthy" (*ibid.*, 43) male prostitute Philip while being mocked and cursed by him.

He can rise above insult and mockery because He has chosen God; He follows His divine impulses. He can do this without effort. Whereas secularists prize autonomy and the piling up of earthly goods, religionists favor self-abnegation and submission to God; oneness with God imparts an inner light we can follow for the rest of our lives. Just before having sex with Judas, Joshua says, unloverlike, "You can come no closer to Me than My body. Everything else you will never touch. Everything important is hidden from you" (*ibid.*, 33), a statement He'll also repeat to Simon (*ibid.*, 50). Reality for Him is spirit, which means that He'll survive His mortal death, as will leaders like Gandhi and Martin Luther King; the physical death of the man-god leads to his spiritual rebirth. Joshua's divinity connects with that of His followers. This divinity He insists we all share. McNally underscores the authenticity of this belief by having none other than Judas declare, "We are all the Son of God" (*ibid.*, 51).

Joshua's first act after His 18-year absence from society confirms this belief. He guides a blind, leprous truck driver (*ibid.*, 35) to the place in the desert where He'll stand up to Satan. His resolve here displays the strength He'll later need to counsel Lazarus, just risen from the grave, to pray, not with his head bowed and his eyes shut, but, instead, "standing tall, eyes open, smiling even," adding, "this is how we talk to God" (*ibid.*, 46)—as Whitman does to his "Great Camerado" in Stanza 45 of *Song of Myself* (l. 1999).

The hammering that Joshua hears early in the play and that he keeps dwelling on (e.g., *CC* 32) traces the contour of His life. This man-god whose end was contained in His beginning had a carpenter for a father (*ibid.*, 52). The truth that crosses were made by carpenters in Jesus' day joins His end to His beginning, Joseph's job chiming with the divine intent. The crucifixion, a deed mandated by God, crowns Jesus' life. God and His Son act together here. The stopping of the hammering in *CC* tells Joshua, "The trap is set" (*ibid.*). But instead of avoiding the Cross, as He could have done, He remains in God's hands.

The actor who opened the play with the words, "There's no suspense and fewer surprises. You know how it all turns out" (*ibid.*, 9), was right. The play's ending both explains and justifies its opening. It also strengthens our bond with them. Though *CC* contains no information we didn't already have, it rearranges it as a mythical drama. Joshua's fate is only the dramatic unfolding of what was *meant* to be, a working-out of the inevitable. Nor is Joshua a victim of chance; nothing is wasted in the divine economy. This graduate of Pontius Pilate High School (*ibid.*, 28) has His death sentence pronounced by Pontius Pilate (*ibid.*, 56).

* * *

The question of recrafting the Jesus myth torqued on McNally's attitude toward his audience. His college days, the late 1950s, produced a large middle-class culture with high hopes. Its bourgeois earnestness, moreover, fused democratic (culture for all) with elitist (culture can improve you) positions. McNally's endorsement of this fusion shows in the compatibility of highbrow and lowbrow materials in his work — which includes the raunchiness spewed out by teachers of Chaucer, Shakespeare, and Joyce. Dialogue in McNally bubbles with surprises. In contrast to the language in *Teachers' Break* (2008), shocks can come from a passage's amiability. A character in *CC* will advise us good-naturedly how to best enjoy it. He explains the benefits, while watching any play, of suspending disbelief: "I've seen audiences fight a play for an entire performance. At the end of an evening, they're exhausted. So are we.... Why do that to yourself? Or us? We want to take you to someplace beautiful, someplace thrilling.... At least meet us halfway" (*ibid.*, 25–26).

The tremendous surge of the play he's appearing in will also take on the authority of a Victorian novel bound to give its readers their bearing before moving to the next phase of the action. Peter is speaking: "Joshua had endured His time in the desert. He had embraced His destiny. His time had come. He would live as the Son of God in peace and love with all men" (*ibid.*, 38).

McNally's acute audience awareness has come to the fore again. It lifts *CC* to exhilarating heights. The play's action is so familiar that, to hold our attention, McNally approaches it from different angles. Though demotic, outrageous, and over-the-top, *CC* anchors itself in piety. It quotes the Bible (*ibid.*, 37–38) as well as the Lord's Prayer (*ibid.*, 46), and it all works. The play is an uplifting lesson in human betterment. Its language is one of the means that serves this excellent end. Perhaps its most notable success comes from the ease with which this linguistic range captures the divinity of man without smudging the divine mystery.

In view of this feat, the perspective afforded by time has calmed the row about the play's subject matter. McNally's 2008 statement about his intent in *CC* sounds more than reasonable today: "I was trying to invite gay men and women back to the table of spirituality. We've been made to feel we are sinners and that we have no business in this story" (Blankenship 4). His point needed to be made. Christ's martyrdom would lose meaning if it excluded *any* group of people. If that group is a misunderstood, sometimes demeaned underclass, the inclusiveness of God's love ("All men are divine," *CC* 20), calls for amends. Lawrence said in *The Plumed Serpent* (1926) that Jesus must come to Mexico wearing a serape if He wants to win the worship of Mexicans. His argument is relevant. At any time in history, the gays, lesbians, and transgendered people in the world have outnumbered the Mexicans. But let the final judgment of McNally's all-male-cast play belong to a woman, one from England, no less. Winning this honor for the *Guardian*'s Lyn Gardner is her vision of how love at both the human and the divine level not merely surpasses but, rather, subsumes and refines the energies rippling through *CC*: "There is nothing remotely blasphemous or offensive about this [play]. Indeed, the tenderness of the play and of Joshua and his disciples toward each other is as good an illustration of the Christian idea of God as love as you could get" (19).

She's right. From the very start, McNally began rewriting the rule book. The Gospels are daring, subtle, profound, and psychologically gripping. Tormented expletives and all, *Corpus Christi* doesn't compete with them. Instead, it marks the rare artistic occasion when a mind of extraordinary power takes a text, tosses aside or re-imagines all its conventions, and raises it to a new plane of sophistication and universality.

Chapter Six

New York States of Mind

The superb one-act play *Deuce* takes place during a tennis match at the U.S. Open in Forest Hills, New York. The play taught McNally something important about perspectives and angles of vision. Its action develops from the grandstand, a device McNally will restore in *Golden Age* (2010), which takes place back stage during the premiere of Vincenzo Bellini's final opera, *I Purtani*. A sense of last things also permeates *Deuce*. Two former greats are about to be honored for their pioneering feats in the heretofore neglected or even derided game of women's doubles tennis.

The McNally of *Deuce* has once again called attention to the easily disregarded and ignored; the doubles partners had to invent their own chances and continuities, often before small crowds. Not so the high-profile millionairesses playing on the court below the grandstand seats of Leona Mullen and her ex-cohort, Midge Barker. These youngsters could be earning more for today's match than Leona or Midge did in their whole careers. Another source of interest during the play is the television booth, where two younger tennis veterans, Ryan Becker and Kelly Short, are commenting on the game. Though the players on the court stay out of view, what is said about them from both booth and grandstand infuses McNally's 2007 play with insights into the words and actions of three generations of intimates of the game. The long proud tradition of tennis and the hard, challenging work it entails unify the action. Doubles tennis was chosen because of the added virtues of trust and teamwork it demands. Without a strategy built upon these virtues, the most brilliant groundstrokes can run to waste.

Midge and Lee played together for a long time. And they did so by preference. They weren't frustrated singles players who drifted into the doubles game by default. To become Hall of Famers, they had to master a discipline and precision irrelevant to the singles game. But these masters of the sport that won them world titles had more to do than to coordinate their quick, smart on-court decisions. They also had to move swiftly, stealthily, and, most significantly, in rhythm with each other. Like stage actors or members of a jazz combo, they had to tune themselves instinctively to what their off-sider would do several steps before she would do it.

The record book supports Midge's statement that "together we were the greatest doubles players in the history of women's tennis" (*Two Plays* 2007, 175). Midge and Leona compiled an unprecedented run of 12 championships in the French Open, Wimbledon, and the U.S. Open (*ibid.*, 142, 144). Against odds, this success might have continued. Their last match, the Australian Open in 1974 at Melbourne took place when Midge was 40 (*ibid.*, 118). Her memories of her great giddy days with Leona stand behind her introducing herself to the spectators at the stadium where they're being fêted as "Midge Mullen" (*ibid.*, 177). So totally did she and Leona improve each other's game that they might have fused as a single engine on the court. Such magic will out. Their partnership sped the formation of the Women's Tennis Association by decades.

This outcome was far from anyone's mind when Midge and Lee first teamed up. In fact, women's tennis was such "a genteel pastime for rich white women" (*ibid.*, 126) at the time they began playing together that they had to wear makeup and jewelry on the court. Tennis's aristocratic origins had produced an ethos of amateurism; women in particular didn't want to seem to be trying too hard. Coaching, even practicing, was, well, unsporting. Nobody was ready to accept Midge and Lee as first-rate athletes. Another hurdle: a society that prized individual over collective achievement expected them, if they were as good as their long list of triumphs implied, to disband and begin careers as singles players.

Though arriving late to declare itself, the *Times* coined a term to describe their court ambience, "Brutal Finesse" (*ibid.*, 154). Intriguingly, this oxymoron reflects by chance both the background and upbringing of the women. Whereas Midge, the Park Avenue deb, graduated from Vassar, Leona, whose father worked as a conductor for Pittsburgh Transit, left Penn State after two years to focus on tennis. She chose well. The superior groundstrokes Midge deployed from the base line forced weak returns that Lee could smash for easy points.

Yet, when reminded of her cerebral approach to tennis, Midge tells Leona, "You had your strategies, too" (*ibid.*, 120). She's right. The head-heart split the *Times* spoke of had shadings to it. Lee's power game stemmed from long practice. Only a student of the game could have cultivated her net skills. It's she, not Midge, who faults the backhand of one of the players on the court below: "The French girl's backhand is going to be her downfall. Her racquet is never far enough back and the angle is too high. Down and up, not straight across," says Lee (*ibid.*, 154). Both women also have more layers to their personalities than their public images suggest. They're also more alike than the finicky opera queen Stephen and the humane self-doubting Mike of *LT* or *Ganesh's* socially correct Margaret and her intuitive travel-mate, Katharine. They'd have had to connect at some deep level to thrive so long as a team.

But something else helps explain their success. Like Katharine and the talented California tenor, Tony Candolini of *Master Class*, the blue-collar-bred Leona plays the role of gatecrasher in *Deuce*. That all three characters feel like impostors restores to the canon the undercurrent of authorial self-criticism that runs through the canon. McNally could write with flair about the outsider's urge to climb to the top (Tony's "I want it all" [*MC* 39]). He knew firsthand the internal barriers that he, like the Steel City brat Leona, had to hurdle while learning his art and refining his craft, a hard enough job for an insider. He only had to look at the faces of the New Yorkers who were hearing his south Texas drawl for the first time. That this drawl came from the mouth of a gay man posed other burdens and penalties. Humiliation, both real and imagined, dies hard. One might even argue that, resentful of the image changes McNally had to make on his way up, he punished Leona for her ambition to succeed in a different line of work. A new trespasser at the top table could feel inclined to blow the cover of one already ensconced there.

Leona's line of work has many sides. Pondering the meaning of the title he gave to the 2007 work she's appearing in, McNally has Midge say she loved playing at deuce, the stage in a tennis match "when the score remains tied" (Two Plays 2007, 110) after each side has won three or more points. Deuce exhilarated her; "standing on the brink of utter triumph or complete annihilation" (*ibid.*, 178) freed that jet of adrenalin that boosted her urge to win. Lee's path to victory lacked this harsh clarity. Her working-class truculence clouded her vision of the grace and elegance of tennis. The game never gave her the warmth of family connection as it did Midge (*ibid.*, 178).

Their attitudes toward tennis differed in other ways, too. It was a short step for Midge to see the matches she was playing in as a living organism whose pace and direction she could control by steadily building the pressure on her opponents. Conversely, Lee played each point as a distinct challenge she could often meet with a savage lunge at the net. If Midge saw the game as a continuum, Leona broke it into parts. That's why she loved charging the net; she could smash the ball so hard that it couldn't be returned. Her inferiority complex drove her to seize an opportunity she didn't deserve before it vanished forever.

Yet she wound up getting whacked by life. "I lost everything I loved — first tennis, then Kip" (*ibid.*, 175), she says of the aristocratic husband who died accidentally. But perhaps by design from her standpoint; this lover of horses and expert rider (who went by an unassuming, even silly, name to show that neither his riches nor fine breeding stopped him from being a regular guy) died after being thrown from a horse. This irony echoed Lee's own downfall; the game that made her famous also did her in. "There's hardly a day I don't think of it" (*ibid.*, 142), she says of the Grand Slam she lost by double-faulting at match point. This wasn't any Grand Slam. She and Midge had already won Wimbledon, the French Open, and the American Open in 1974; a victory at Melbourne would have won the 40-year-olds the only Grand Slam of their careers. Lee's continuing to blame herself for throwing away this prize has kept her close to the game; she has a debt to pay. Whereas Midge lives contentedly far from tennis, Lee, in full damage-control mode, runs a tennis clinic in Tucson. Like Rudolph of *The Roller Coaster*, she has a longstanding debt she can never repay, a feeling lively enough in McNally's psyche to steer plays of his written 47 years apart.

But what, specifically, about Leona's having double-faulted at Melbourne has kept gnawing her? Midge has said little to the press about retiring from tennis after Melbourne. How to explain to reporters that a distressed Lee had rejected her forgiveness? Remember, McNally had defined *The Rink* as a play about forgiveness (8). He made good on this definition by reconciling an antagonistic mother and daughter at play's end. No such reconciliation of women crowns *Deuce* (or *Dedication*). Instead, the play's finale shows why the ex-teammates only see each other every ten years or so. Lee spurned Midge's forgiveness because she couldn't forgive herself, a far tougher job in her competitive society, where finger-pointing has become the norm when something goes awry. The acceptance speech she gives after winning her lifetime achievement award at Forest Hills tallies the cost of her having hugged her guilt. "I double-faulted once," she tells the Forest Hills crowd. "It became the story of my life. Don't let it be yours" (*Two Plays* 2007, 178).

This advice she can give but without applying it to herself. She has lived with her guilt for so long that she wears it. She has accepted it as an extended act of justice; it's what she deserves. She was even in its grip while preparing to serve match point, advantage out. Recalling Midge's oft-voiced rebuke that she never threw the ball high enough when she was serving, Lee scuttled the self-confidence that had availed her for decades to take Midge's advice. A photo of her in the Melbourne papers the next day captures her on-the-spot decision to forsake her reliable service strategy for an untested one (*ibid.*, 174). Tellingly, the news photo captures her panicky face together with her act of tossing the ball up — too high to hit comfortably. She might have let the ball bounce at her feet without hitting it. But she couldn't. Her moment of reckoning had come. Her statement, "Things happen because we want [them] to happen" (*ibid.*, 175), shows that she had discovered the precise moment, the Grand Slam within reach, to strike down her upstart's arrogance to gate-crash a sport that belonged to her social betters.

Her willingness to sacrifice Midge to her fixation gauges its force. Preparing for her second serve at base line, she had no reason to charge the net, where she felt most at home. The need to muster poise and self-presence had collided with her red-meat aggressiveness. She relieved the stress she was feeling in her usual way, as quickly as possible. The tension of serving at match point snapped her judgment along with her defenses. In another echo in McNally's work of *Brothers Karamazov*, *Deuce* portrays masochism and its dirty byproducts as a spreading stain. Midge judged well to stop playing with Lee. They'd never win a Grand Slam; one's inner demons are the hardest to tame. Gene Forrester pushed his friend, the admirable Finney, down a flight of stairs after feeling horrified by his shaking him out of a tree in John Knowles's *A Separate Peace* (1959).

The pathological selfishness on Lee's part that resembles at first look an exaggerated form of modesty can poison everything in sight. She probably also believes her marrying up to wed the love of her life and then losing him before his time was what she deserved. The near coincidence of Kip's death with the end of her tennis career (*ibid.*, 153) worsened her ordeal. But it also justified it. She has no charity for herself. Haunted by the idea that she'll take her guilt to the grave, she has asked to be buried alongside, not Kip, but her parents to compensate for having neglected them when they were alive (*ibid.*, 171). But she'll remain in default mode; she'll find something else to blame on herself. As Midge tells her, "I knew my limitations. You invented yours" (*ibid.*, 143).

Lee bridles at this dig. Like Katharine of *Ganesh*, Midge feels closest to another woman when that woman seems most closed and distant (*ibid.*, 156). She sees only the effects of what it cost Lee to become her own worst enemy. Lee offends others with her bossiness (*ibid.*, 151), her insistence on having her own way (*ibid.*, 121), and her profanity — which signals a paucity of reserves rather than a dirty mind. In a laugh line delivered, as is McNally's aim, at a fraught moment in the action, it comes out that her calling a linesman in Berlin an "asshole" (*ibid.*, 157) cost her and Midge DM5000.

A good writer can parlay such small touches. The spot of delayed exposition concerning the match in Berlin tempers our understanding of Lee. This hard-charger had acquired in the presence of luminaries like Cary Grant and the Queen of England more social skills than she credits herself with — and that Kip had valued in her? She'll change the subject of a conversation when she sees it sliding toward a dangerous edge (*ibid.*, 121). She earns style points by calling the loud grunts or screams erupting from some of today's woman players "unladylike" (*ibid.*, 146). (She'd have to watch women's tennis on TV today with the sound off.) A charitable remark Lee made earlier would have sounded more in character coming from the gentle-born Midge. To Midge's glum take on the changes time has wrought in both of them, "How the mighty have fallen," she ripostes, "We haven't fallen. We've aged, gotten older, through no fault of our own" (*ibid.*, 130).

This discord is but one of many in the women's long association. "We didn't agree about many things" (*ibid.*, 112), Lee tells Midge early in the play. But her disputes and fallings-out with Midge haven't blunted her admiration for her old buddy. She doesn't resent the serenity the years have brought to Midge's face any more than she recalls her game as nothing less than first rate ("God she was good" [*ibid.*, 147]). She knows when to hold back from contradicting Midge, too. For instance, she'll only qualify Midge's statement that they both played tennis for love with the common-sense rejoinder, "I loved it even more after we started getting paid" (*ibid.*, 131).

Midge might disagree. She still sees the game's lack of mass appeal as one of its strengths (*ibid.*, 113). Her easy acceptance of the benefits of her Park Avenue breeding has made her less edgy than Lee, whom she would always rile by speaking French and then translating it (*ibid.*, 119). Why should Lee worry about being patronized? Her ferocity at the net improved Midge's unforgiving base line game. Midge was as competitive as Lee. She still can't watch a tennis game with another person without insisting that each of them root for a different player.

She knows, though, the limits of competitiveness. Having formed one half of a star-quality women's doubles team that improved the lot of all future women tennis players has left her happy. Competitive though she may be, she competes within brackets. Taking the large view, she prefers to remember herself and Lee as winners of multiple majors rather than just the losers of one. And even their losing the Australian Open in 1974 she explains as a confluence of many factors, not just one. A deft student of the survivor's art, she knows how to throttle anxiety; any search for defects will succeed — and bushwhack the seeker. She defuses the malaise behind Lee's despairing remark, "Maybe they should take us out behind some barn and kill us," by taking it to the next level: "Good idea. Does your condo have a barn?" (*ibid.*, 169)

She has settled comfortably into knowing that life goes on and that she gave her best to the game she loved. If the game withheld some prizes, it provided still more. Goodwill (*ibid.*, 130), not faith in God, has made her value this windfall. Goodwill has also helped her slide it into the past, where it should stay if her future is to have meaning. That future perforce is unclear. Squeamishly, she covers her eyes when a streaker speeds across the court below. She chides Lee for using profanity. But moments later she says, "fucking what" (*ibid.*, 131), using invective never voiced earlier in our presence by the more earthy-spoken Lee. Revealed later in the play is an affair Midge had, during the 1950s or '60s, with a black man. After the affair became public knowledge, catcalls and boos erupted from audiences whenever Midge and Lee took the court.

The women responded characteristically. The jeers weakened Lee's game; no matter that she never shared a black man's bed. Hearing the same hoots fired up the self-acting Midge; internally strong, she always had the pluck to shrug off burdens. And she still has no regrets about Sam. Nor does he. A couple of years before the play's present-tense action, he and his wife, whose job as an admissions officer at a chic private school presages that of John Haddock in *LTTA*, had lunch with Midge in her home town of Blue Harbor, Maine. The post-lunch goodbye look she shared with Sam confirmed their gratitude for their time together years ago. Perhaps Blue Harbor had boosted her spirits. Energized himself by New York City ("A Few Words of Introduction," *Three Plays* ix), McNally understands the benefits of a fixed residence. Midge opted to keep foraging in Blue Harbor's alien corn after her husband dumped her for another woman. The serenity Lee sees in Midge shows that she chose correctly.

Midge's happiness, though, like that of the happiest of all of us, has fallen short of her hopes. She takes little pleasure in her middle-aged children. This grandmother of six may have no issues with her kids other than asking of them late in the play, "Why were we blessed and our children weren't?" (*Two Plays* 2007, 164). Leona, who likes pinning blame, bemoans the futility of the psychotherapy *her* kids have been undergoing. Without laboring the question of family curses like Hawthorne and O'Neill — even though her regrets about Melbourne may have created one — she also agrees with Midge that very few people are happy. In a different vein, the two disenchanted mothers are seething about the direction women's tennis has taken. Always ready to carp, Lee frets over the "synthetic surface [today's players, male and female,] play on [using] metal racquets the size of snow shoes and neon balls" (*ibid.*, 140). She had already cursed the machines that decide whether a ball landed in or out of bounds. Though accurate, these machines have smudged the game's human face.

Not that there's much humanity left to save. Most of today's tennis stars hail from Florida, Arizona, or California because, as David Foster Wallace noted in *Infinite Jest* (1996), the youngsters with the brightest prospects are now snatched from their schools and homes at an early age and shipped to sunbelt tennis academies to build their games; Victoria Azerenka, the 22-year-old winner of the 2012 Australian Open had left Minsk to train in Scottsdale at age 14 (Wertheim 58).

This training has a disturbing side effect that the academies' chiefs have chosen to ignore. It stunts and flattens the trainees while priming them to get rich endorsing products like "tennis costumes, soft drinks, the kitchen sink"

(*Two Plays* 2007, 112). Greed has replaced the love of the game that drove Midge and Leona to excel. This venality has spread. The jumbotrons in tennis stadia have raised ticket prices, because every seat now provides a clear, close-up view of the action. Missing from the mix, though, are intimacy and warmth. In the smaller stadia of the past, fans sat close enough to the court to witness first-hand the subtleties and psychological shifts of a match. Which is to say that the game's fans are missing the inexplicable intuitive genius of tournament tennis; as Leona says, tennis as "a duel of muscles, wits and nerves" (*ibid.*, 102) is quickly becoming a lost art.

Replacing it is Leona's "freak show" (*ibid.*, 126) and "circus" (*ibid.*, 130). Today's women players grunt and scream every time they hit a ball (perhaps starting with the retired Yugoslavian singles champ of the 1990 French Open and the 1996 Australian Open, Monica Seles [b. 1973]). *Sports Illustrated*'s L. John Wertheim said that the 2012 Australian Open women's champion, Victoria Azarenka, punctuated "each shot [at Melbourne] with a noise resembling a stuck pig in labor" [58]). Other objections? These grunters and screamers wear blouses cut to show their (rouged?) nipples (*Two Plays* 2007, 150). Their names also expose the game's galloping commercialism. Ute-Lynn Sawallich has been pitted against Giselle Lanvin-Grillet in the match at hand. Thanks to sophisticated talent-scouting, a scholarship to a tennis school had taken the 19-year-old Giselle six years earlier from her native Corsica. It's hard to imagine that the school taught her anything besides tennis and English. She now lives, predictably enough, in Orange County, near Disneyland and numerous right-wing fanatics.

Her opponent Ute-Lynne's standing as "the most controversial figure in women's tennis" (*ibid.*, 133) could have been forecast. Brought from Krakow to the United States at age ten, she missed out on the sensuous joys of childhood during her most vulnerable, impressionable years. And what joys she had to give up. She inherited bloodlines enriched by a famous Japanese opera singer for a mother and a father who was a "respected judge" (*ibid.*, 132). This cosmopolitan legacy was scuttled for a tennis career. Still more might have been lost by Ute-Lynne's move to the U.S. The disclosure that her accomplished, urbane parents separated soon after her move implies strife brutal enough on the subject of Ute-Lynne's, or Willy's, future to wreck the marriage.

The French Open and two-time Wimbledon finalist Willy is still reeling from the blowback caused by her parents' split. It explains why she has won so far fewer endorsements than Giselle despite her better court record. During her match against Giselle, an "[a]udible obscenity" (*ibid.*, 139) she utters after losing a point draws an umpire's warning. She has a history of riling courtside officials. She was disqualified at match point at Wimbledon for slapping a 12-

year-old ball girl she accused of distracting her by yawning. The television announcer who attributes such outbursts to Willy's "fierce Polish temperament" (*ibid.*) has it wrong. Willy never learned good manners, kindness, and the anchoring warmth of family life, and she's fuming about it.

We have something to fume about, too. The intractable monster inside Giselle, her hyphenated last name, and even Willy's hyphenated *front* name all point to that splintering of identity that has been mangling tennis's human face. Leona miscued, but not by much, when she put tennis in 2007 on a par with professional wrestling. The women slated to play after Giselle and Willy are known only as The Wonder from Down Under and The Next Great American Hope (*ibid.*, 170). They might as well take to the court wearing masks, so close are they already to the mat game's many masked marvels. Their humanity is irrelevant to the promoters of their match.

But humanity will trump marketing ploys. The Forest Hill audience will see these court foes soon because the match between Giselle and Willy, like that of Midge and Leona at Melbourne, ends with a double fault. The match has thus restored this oddity from the game's proud past. Perhaps the server at the match at Forest Hills lost her nerve at second serve as Leona did an ocean away and more than 30 years earlier; repetition supports both tradition and myth. Chances are it was Willy. Advisedly, McNally doesn't say. His stage direction after the doomed second service reads, "Player who double-faulted screams" (*ibid.*). Both this player and her opponent share some blame for the smirching of women's tennis. Though Leona double-faulted, she never screamed.

* * *

Deuce has two choric figures, The Admirer, later The Autograph Seeker, who remains unseen by Midge and Lee, the luminaries he admires. His aim: to witness the Giselle-Willy match from their informed standpoint so he can savor its beauty. It's clear why he comes close to achieving it. He and his incarnation as The Autograph Seeker provide details about tennis history, strategy, rule changes, and, above all, the game's grand tradition. The book he brings the Grand Masters to sign belonged to his father. He honors this legacy. Proudly, he shows them the autograph of May Sutton, the first American Wimbledon champ of either gender, a feat witnessed in person by The Seeker's grandfather (*ibid.*, 135). Add to this distinction The Seeker's father having seen Midge and Lee twice win the U.S. Open, and a strong case will have been made for the tribute that they, and through them, the Women's Tennis Association, are receiving that day at Forest Hills.

But has rarely gotten, even from those who have cashed in on its heritage; Willy Sawallisch's temper tantrum will swamp any memories of Mae Sutton's heroics for today's fans of Wimbledon tennis. The TV announcers commenting on Willy's match with Giselle Lanvin-Grillet, two high-ranking tennis pros from the past, supply gaudy, easily digestible facts about both the contestants and the two honorees sitting in the grandstand. This pap is aimed at their audience. Accurate enough, it omits both the nuances and the historical background of the day's match. It has to. The program's sponsors and studio chiefs want the audience entertained, not enlightened or challenged. That said, it's also clear that the announcers, Ryan and Kelly, alumni of tennis training centers, waste no effort defying them.

Both Ryan, who won his first major at age 19 (*ibid.*, 124), and Kelly lack the education to do justice to both the game they're commenting on and its place in tennis tradition. While discussing Giselle's Corsican birthplace, Ryan asks if Napoleon, too, came from there. Kelly can only respond lamely, "It doesn't say so in my notes" (*ibid.*, 123). It wouldn't. Those in charge of the telecast want a pop-culture gloss on tennis and its past. Kelly and Ryan have miscued in their willingness to oblige them. They either don't know or don't care that their carefully prepared script has flattened their account of a game whose thrills come from the tension set up by its spontaneity and its rhythmical flow.

McNally holds his ground. Despite them, excitement and joy brighten the afternoon's doings. The play's action will sometimes pause for those internal monologues written in a more meditative prose that records doubts and regrets too desperate for the give-and-take of dialogue (*ibid.*, 143, 147). Less Chekhovian but revelatory in another important way are those close-up shots of the Grand Masters on the TV monitors. McNally has given the lie to commercial sportscasting. Enjoyable on their own, these shots sometimes capture qualities in both the faces and body language of Midge and Lee that belie the stereotypes being mouthed about them.

Then, the conversations being held in the booth and the grandstand can overlap. At one point, Lee, bristling that Willy and Giselle have put their nipples on show, talks about the indignities of age. The action cuts to the booth where Ryan, oblivious to her dismay, turns his attention from the court to that part of the grandstand where the ex-greats are sitting. He says into the microphone, "What fascinates me is how these two women once so active in the sport spend their twilight years." The play's next line, said by Midge, "It's their nipples" (*ibid.*, 150), has an off-key relevance and incongruity that displays McNally's counterpoint at top form. Did moral indignation or envy drive Lee's protest about the cut of the tennis players' blouses?

Don't be shocked. Few playwrights apply the art of the fugue to their craft as well as McNally. While dramatic continuity is being inflected from the booth, it follows that what's being seen and heard from the seats should skew the play's focus. Variety in *Deuce* is so well timed that it's always dramatic. A half hour or so after the streaker incident, another stoppage of play occurs. A spectator has presumably fainted. The resumption of play soon after a doctor treats the fainting victim provides a sweet note. That both victim and doctor, like the players on the court and the former doubles partners watching them, are all female symbolizes both the cohesion and integrity of women's tennis. This conceit, an affirmation of McNally's evenhandedness, matters. Like the gays of *CC* and *LVC*, women are a minority often misunderstood and discounted when they're not being mocked.

The play's title, though, is non-partisan; it doesn't signify a stalemate or an impasse. Though Leona and Midge reacted to deuce game in ways consistent with both their psyches and biographies, their court skills were countersupporting. To rate one of them over the other would be pointless and meaningless. Each player brought out the best qualities in the other; each energized the other. It's also safe to say that neither of them would have reached the heights she did teamed with other partners. No resentment here, either; they knew they took to the court to win games. The recognition that they needed each other equally made them a stronger team. So what if Lee told Midge, "We didn't agree about many things" (*ibid.*, 112)? Their differences and disparities built the same singing tension found in a well-tuned violin string. Only when this tension slackened at Lee's end did the music stop. Deuce or snake-eyes on a pair of dice registers an immediate loss.

Then why do the women only look at each other when the play is more than half finished?

They don't need to. They were so keyed in to each other's court moves and strategies that watching each other would have distracted them from more vital endeavors. During their time together before us, this mindset revives. They're looking at two women playing tennis as they might have looked at two opponents on the other side of the net decades earlier — to spot weaknesses they can probe. But McNally hasn't poured his title's whole meaning into this reading. It can be added that the title, *Deuce*, captures how each woman sees stamped in the other her own mistakes together with the triumphs. These qualities have been defining them so long in tennis circles that they stand on their own. Neither Lee nor Midge needs to be reminded of them with eye contact. That's also why these frenemies are content to let a decade or so pass between meetings. As their conversation proves, they respect and admire each other. But *Deuce* is not precisely a looking-glass play. Their admiration and respect flourished at a different time, one during which they spent so much time together that they're content now to move on without any sense of loss or regret.

The umpire in charge of the match between Giselle and Willy frequently cries "Deuce!" (e.g., *ibid.*, 111, 114, 146, 152, 172, 175) not only to tally the score of a game; she's also proclaiming the equality of Midge and Lee. But the very word implies, if not antagonism, competition and rivalry. This opposition is eternal. Life is a struggle, we keep hearing and discovering. But the repetition of the word generates a more specific meaning. People who spend a lot of time together will get on each other's nerves. From this standpoint, Lee and Midge fared quite well. Their many disagreements never threatened their partnership. They always pulled together on the court to win tennis games.

When Midge says, "You're supposed to contradict me," she's answered, "I can't" (*ibid.*, 128). The conversation of the two women lacks the witty backchat found in Shaw and Coward. Such fizz has no place in *Deuce*. Midge and Lee joined forces on the court to defeat others, not to snipe at each other. As was seen in *IOAP*, *F&J*, and *CC*, McNally had mastered conversational glitter. He underplayed it in *Deuce* because he knew that it clashed with the play's intent. Readers or playgoers who feel puzzled by its near absence from *Deuce* can console themselves with the truth that they've learned something about dramatic technique. Though funny, shocking, and moving, the words that pass between Midge and Lee aren't tipped in mercury — or poison.

They do, though, illuminate tennis tradition. *Geist* has developed in tennis, as in Hegel, as an expression of history and human consciousness. People like Midge and Leona feed into this grand unfolding. In a way it doesn't matter that they're unknown to most of today's tennis stars. The devotion of The Admirer, The Autograph Collector, his father, and his grandfather emit points of light in the extravaganza tennis has slid into. For now, splash and spectacle rule. Giselle's match against Willy was billed as a clash between a Czech against a Frenchwoman. Though this billing was good box-office strategy, no facts supported it. The only thing French about Giselle Lanvin-Grillet is her name. She has been living in the U.S. for the past six years, and she was born in Krakow to a hybrid Italian and a Croatian in northern Corsica. Her part French-Basque father probably hates having his daughter labeled French. Hewing to their own language and tradition, the Basques have long made it clear that they want to split from France — whose language Giselle's father might have forbidden her to speak.

This enigma inflects the action of *Deuce*. McNally's 2007 one-acter reminds us that our lives are shaped at least as much by our mistakes as by our ideals and achievements. As is seen in her acceptance speech at the Grand Master Award ceremony, Lee defines herself by her double fault at Melbourne (*ibid.*, 178). But her self-imposed loss of the Grand Slam of Women's Tennis in 1974 has an upside, were she ever to credit herself for any of her attainments, like having taught decades of trainees that tennis is "a duel of muscles, wit, and nerves" (*ibid.*, 122). The disbanding of her professional bond with Midge has benefited scores of youngsters who weren't even been born when it happened.

McNally clarified this vital point. "I realize it was my decision, Leona" (*ibid.*, 148), says Midge of her earlier resolution to retire from the game and thus strip Lee of another chance for a Grand Slam. Midge only addresses Lee as Leona to underscore the meaning of a statement. Nor has she been shattered by the loss of either the tennis tour or the husband who ditched her and their three kids. She remembers him as "very, very weak" (*ibid.*, 164). Paul's (*ibid.*, 163) weakness has made him forgettable. She has been comforting herself with the dailiness of Blue Harbor. She deserves the comforts of forgetting just as Leona has earned *her* lot by clinging to the great setback of her past.

Lee's statement, "I don't believe in choice. Things happen because we want [them] to happen" (*ibid.*, 175), hews to Tolstoy's and Emerson's denial that life is fate or destiny. No victims of chance or a preordained design, we create the routines that define us. We're *always* creating them. We deserve the faces, marriages, and jobs that go with them because we've spent our lives shaping them. And once they're in place, they shape the lives we've been wanting, no matter how much we deny it.

II

Like Chekhov's *Uncle Vanya*, McNally's *Love! Valour! Compassion!* casts light and shade on a series of interrelated lives, some of them inconveniently miles away from the big city of their roots. This resemblance invites the idea, that like *Vanya*, McNally's *LVC* could also be subtitled, *Scenes from Country Life*. Chekhov's 1899 play is a curiously uplifting tale of boredom and sexual frustration in the depth of a Russian summer. Sexual rivalries also surface and seethe in *LVC*. And though no handgun is fired, a character comes close to losing his fingers to the anger of the love rival who jammed them into a kitchen disposal. Standing in for the talk in Chekhov's play about green politics is an anxiety about AIDS, one so harsh that anybody who's caught mentioning the disease is penalized five dollars (*Two Plays* 24). Money has little importance in the play. The idea, from *Ganesh* and *CC*, about God's ability to cross into the human sphere and heal the sick returns, but with a more secular slant. Playing down miracles, it now features the palliative effects of bonding, both one-on-one and in groups. Meals are prepared and taken, sometimes downed with bottles of booze. Then the diners team up to wash the dishes. Away from the table, they swim and play tennis. But no amount of food and drink, fellowship and fucking, can help them love each other as God does, viz., unconditionally (*ibid.*, 87). *LVC* is a troubling play brightened by moments of hilarity that struggle toward hope and cheer.

Recalling *F&J* and *LT*, the words "I'm sorry" or "Sorry" are spoken many times (e.g., *ibid.*, 17, 18, 33, 34, 41, 61, 89, 104, 105, 123). Nearly every character in the play apologizes. They feel they must. Virtue is so rare, almost unnatural, in fact, that it stumbles over itself, gets misinterpreted, and causes harm. McNally's pre–Vatican II schooling, with its belief in original sin, never sunk its claws more deeply into one of his plays than it did *LVC*, a truth suggested by his having sent at least two of the play's eight characters to Catholic boys' schools (in Kansas City and Ponce, Puerto Rico [*ibid.*, 17, 115]). In what may be a corollary to the schooling of Arthur and Ramon, forgiveness ranks higher than retribution in his 1994 play. Besides infiltrating the action, its importance is voiced by the play's most wicked character — a surefire way to grab any theater audience's attention. John Jeckyll's cold-heartedness has taught him by negation the value of forgiveness. "Forgiveness is good," John says. "We all need it from time to time" (*ibid.*, 61).

We all need it because life, as it's described in *LVC*, seems hostile to human purpose and activity itself. The play's three acts unfold on the long weekends of Memorial Day, July 4th, and Labor Day, times set aside for people to relax and have fun, which many find easier to do away from home. Away from home in *LVC* is a large property in Dutchess County, about a two-hour drive north of Gotham. Manderley, the 1915 domain that focuses the action, fosters relaxation and tranquility, its original furniture and fittings sending out signals of permanence, settled judgments, and, to use William Gaddis's phrase from *Carpenter's Gothic* (1985), that accumulation of years in walls, or lived-in authority, that quiets the urban jitters.

As gay urbanites, the characters are doubly prone to angst. The action is barely under way before one of them, the Broadway musical-comedy queen Buzz Hauser feels threatened. "If this is going to be Pick On Buzz weekend..." (*ibid.*, 10), he wonders after one of his comments is misconstrued. Then some gay pride demonstrators are seen getting clubbed on television a continent away in Seattle (*ibid.*, 107). Will's words from *Some Men* spring to mind: "Gay is not good. Gay is loneliness, secrecy, and a lifetime of shame" (*Two Plays* 2007, 38).

Manderley hasn't shielded the weekenders from the ravages of the patriarchy. What's worse, it can aggravate them. The rains that wash out tennis games also soak the firecrackers brought to help celebrate July 4th. The electricity goes off. In the human sphere, a guest breaches the privacy of his host's diary, after which an old resentment reignites. It gets worse. Bobby Brahms, the play's, and perhaps the canon's, most angelic figure, has sex with the dancer Ramon Fornos. Bobby, called by Frontain "the most Cordelia-like character in McNally's canon" ("Trafficking" 97), has betrayed, in Gregory Mitchell, both his weekend host and his lover of four years. The goodwill that served Midge Barker in *Deuce* (*Two Plays* 2007, 170) has taken a dark turn.

Has a virus of malevolence hit Manderley? In his odd way, John might have been right to fault Gregory for his "startling unoriginality" in choosing a name for his rural retreat. *Rebecca*, Daphne du Maurier's 1938 novel and the 1940 "kitsch-classic [Alfred Hitchcock] movie" based on it (*Two Plays* 22) referenced by John hails the triumph of unconditional love. So does *LVC*, another work of romantic suspense. But it operates differently. *LVC* stands in regard to the popular Gothic romance of the 1990s (one of whose ace practitioners, Barbara Cartland, it mentions [*ibid.*, 92]) as Jane Austen's *Northanger Abbey*, which a weekender reads (*ibid.*, 80), does to this then thriving subgenre. It's a send-up. Gothic conventions and guidelines in both the late 18th and 20th centuries ignored the way most middle-class people were leading their everyday lives.

Not so, *LVC*; for all of its oddities, it's a mainstream stage comedy. It tries to reconcile us to life as it's really lived rather than inflating it or suggesting that we chuck the whole mess. Instead of putting the truth beyond our reach or peddling it as romantic fantasy, *LVC* finds life rewarding. People will always keep making the same mistakes while they and those around them suffer and die. A story that John is telling in Act Two begins to bore its listener. Ramon tells John to "cut to the chase" (a phrase used by another young man-on-the-make in "Cleopatterer" [*15 Plays* 356]). But his diktat that John get to the good part of the story is snubbed. Ramon is told: "It's all good part" (*Two Plays* 96). The snub might be extended. *LVC* is all good part, too. The weekenders can't ignore the emotional chaos flaring around them, some of it new. Shattered by the news of his sister's death, Bobby tells Gregory near the end of Act Two about his treachery with Ramon. But before the act ends, Arthur Pape and Perry Sellars celebrate their 14th anniversary, exchanging gifts and then dancing.

Goodwill hasn't collapsed. But it faces a hard fight. Forget that Clum called *LVC* "the American theater's most probing satire on homophobia" ("Where We Are Now," Zinman, ed. *Casebook* 96). Regrets pile up in Manderley. Though the play omits any acts of kindness extended to gays by the patriarchy, no blanket catch of straights could damage Gregory's gay visitors more than they do themselves. The victims of the gay bashing in Seattle have a better chance of recovering from their knocks than the play's two AIDS casualties.

LVC shows what happens when sex and death occupy the same bed. Also, as is inferred by the truth that neither Buzz nor James were HIV-infected by women, the play notes in passing that James's brother John and Arthur's spouse of 14 years, Perry, both dated Buzz. As the debauchery of Ramon and Bobby shows, sexual loyalty is rare in gay society. *LVC* uses the scourge of AIDS to reckon the cost of this bed-hopping.

* * *

Clum's 1997 overview of the people in the play strikes home. Gregory and his guests are "all prosperous, relatively apolitical artists or supporters of the arts" who are "either living with AIDS or with the fear and survivor guilt that AIDS inspires" (*ibid.*, 104). The first part of this description fits Buzz, costume maker for Gregory's dance company and a volunteer at an AIDS clinic in Manhattan's Lower West Side (*Two Plays* 16). Buzz has trouble clicking with other men, probably, because like Mendy of *LT* (another Nathan Lane role), he's too avid in his courting, looking for love quickly and leaving nothing to the imagination (McNally favors some mystery, indirection, and holding back in dating; a January 1959 term paper of his cites "the fatal implications of the lovers' impetuosity" in *Romeo and Juliet* ("Shakespeare's Early Development as a Tragedian" 1). Buzz's proclivity to fall in love immediately drives away the men he attracts. Unable to control his heart, he's done in by it. Hard-luck Buzz has AIDS.

He's not crushed, though. This self-proclaimed "gay imp" (*Two Plays* 41) uses his expertise in Broadway musical comedy to voice some of the best gags in the play. In this regard, he's the polar opposite of *LT*'s Stephen; Buzz likes musical comedies because they end happily. His life differs from a pre–Sondheim Broadway musical, too. Happiness proves as elusive to him as it is precious. Pain and grief hem him in. They have also sharpened his response to a picture of a sick Somalian child: "Clearly the kid is dying.... Five feet away a vulture sits and waits. He's not even looking at the kid. He's that confident where his next meal is coming from" (*ibid.*, 51). The picture sits on his desk at the Chelsea clinic; he needs to keep reminding himself that such heartbreaking injustice needs to be fought with laughter. That's why he has learned how to make *us* laugh.

McNally has also built laughter into the play's tempo, having placed many of Buzz's jokes to block dramatic drive. He's avoiding the mistake of rushing to dramatic climaxes. But Buzz's jokes have to be more than funny to stop audiences from feeling manipulated. Here's Buzz's explanation of why a recent dating relationship of his failed: "I got too intense for him. That's my problem with people. I'm too intense. I need someone like Dennis Hopper.... In the meantime, I'm through with love and all it meant to me" (*ibid.*, 23). What is there in these words that take them beyond fun? Does Buzz's reference to a bygone show tune lighten, dismiss, or heighten his pain? McNally knows the difficulty of responding to such concoctions of truth, distortion, and, perhaps irrelevance. He has made Buzz part Pierrot, part stand-up comic, and part Pagliacci. While Buzz accounts for much of the fun in *LVC*, his practice of aiming many of his best jokes at his knocks and aches curbs our laughter.

Tempering his agitation is the relative calm of Perry's bond with Arthur. This "politically and socially conservative couple" occupy a tony lower Fifth Avenue apartment "filled with all the ... appliances and electronics coveted by us members of the American bourgeoisie.... They contribute to charities, work for AIDS groups, and do *pro bono* work for arts organizations" (Clum, "Where We Are Now" 103). They also look unassuming and careful to a fault—which also makes them look misplaced in Manderley. Methodical, organized, and reliable, they both move to a different beat and live within different boundaries than their fellow weekenders. But these two envoys from the professional business class mesh smoothly with their counterparts from the "artsy/fartsy" world of the performing arts (*Two Plays* 29). They chat good-naturedly with Bobby during the drive from the city, and later both of them enjoy the company of "the ultimate Musical Comedy Queen" (Clum, "Where We Are Now" 103), Buzz, Buzz's having been Perry's lover posing no barrier to the fun.

McNally made Perry a lawyer and Arthur an accountant to highlight their conservatism. The rise of global free markets and its effects upon Wall Street mean more to these mainstream urban professionals than the Broadway stage. Late in Act Two, Arthur says, "I can catch a ball. I genuinely like both my parents. I hate opera. I don't know why I bother being gay" (*Two Plays* 100). To celebrate their anniversary, he and Perry exchange a set of towels and a calculator. But they're not flat and dull. If their nine-to-five white-collar jobs call for restraint, caution, and a gift for planning, they haven't stilled the clamor in the men's hearts. Arthur and Perry belong to the human family, which makes them ambiguous, inconstant, and, without being tomcats, prey to the lures of the flesh.

Arthur grew up in Republican Kansas (*ibid.*, 82), where he attended a Catholic boys' school. This careful accountant who always wears slippers in Manderley to stay warm is teased about having too many convictions (*ibid.*, 30). He hews to the rules. "[I]t's never right to hurt another person" (*ibid.*, 31), he believes, and, sensitive to grief, he always tries to defuse his spouse Perry's emotional flare-ups (e.g., *ibid.*). Yet he has tried Perry's temper. He stepped out on him and, in what might be another act of wantonness, told him about it. What should he have done? The question recurs. Rather than living with his guilt after betraying Gregory, Bobby also devastates the man *he* loves by confessing his guilt. Were he and Arthur being selfish? Cruel? Though McNally gives no answer to this question, he asks it with terrific brio. Yes, Gregory put Bobby out of the house after Bobby owned up to his defection. But, as Bobby was leaving to attend his sister's funeral in Texas when he confessed to Gregory, McNally might have let both men off too easily.

Perry speaks of "how badly I'd handled" (*ibid.*, 112) Arthur's cheating. Perhaps his job with the Jewish-run firm of Cohen, Mendelsohn, and Leibowitz (*ibid.*, 55) aggravated in him a flair for retribution that led him to study law in the first place. Yet the soul of this one-time English major at Williams College has survived the rigors of practicing the law. The same impulsiveness that led Arthur to cheat on him is teaching both men how to sympathize with the sexual vagrancy of others. McNally judged well by making Arthur the weekender who finds Bobby reeling in the aftermath of sex with Ramon.

McNally has made us wonder how to handle a lover's confession of disloyalty. Perry is still smarting from Arthur's confession. He accuses Arthur of ogling the hunky Ramon, who has been sunning himself on a raft in the middle distance. When Arthur says he feels like a swim, he's accused of wanting to visit his "boyfriend on the raft" (*ibid.*, 80). The distrust fueling this accusation meshes with Perry's lawyer-like adherence to duty. Arthur picked the wrong man to betray. And it was his betrayal that kindled Perry's distrust. It goes to the heart of McNally's conservative morality that sexual wrongdoing most hurts the innocent. But the innocent don't suffer alone. The grief induced by the love triangles in *LTTA*, *Master Class*, and *Dedication*, as in Chekhov's *Three Sisters*, always spreads.

None of today's playwrights excels McNally in yoking a character's behavior to his/her motives and back story — in Arthur's case those of his spouse, Perry. When Perry hails Arthur as "the best man in the world" for him to be married to and wishes him "long life, much love, and as much happiness as he's brought me," all that Arthur can muster in reply is "Ditto" (108). His Catholic guilt and his accountant's fixation on accountability have scotched his ability to forgive himself.

Perry credits Bobby, Gregory, and, of course, Arthur for having "remarkably loving nature[s]" because he's remarkably loving himself. His frequent repetition of the phrase, "My Arthur" (*ibid.*, e.g., 11, 14) conveys his kindness and warmth. Arthur has been a good influence on him. Along with Gregory and Buzz, he works free for several AIDS groups. Yet his betrayal has weakened Perry's reserves. Double-faulting at tennis shatters Perry's composure as it did that of two net pros in *Deuce*. "Fuck you, Buzz," he growls across the net (*ibid.*, 68). Nor is this his first foray into profanity. Even though she can't hear it, the driver who cut him off en route to Manderley gets blasted with one of the mightiest fusillades of invective in the canon (*ibid.*, 30).

Living with Arthur while being able to forgive him has cut into his humanity. He later tells Gregory, "You've done enough for AIDS. We all have" (*ibid.*, 48). On the topic of Buzz's dying Somali child, he says with the same combativeness, "It would hurt too much to care" (*ibid.*, 52). He's reeling because the law he practices can't shield him from heartbreak. Perhaps he has no goodwill left for casualties of hunger and AIDS. Later, he's on the sidelines watching the others rehearse Tchaikovsky's *Dance of the Little Swans* for a Carnegie Hall AIDS benefit. The denial of the dance in McNally throttles joy. But Perry has also partaken of this joy. He and Arthur did dance "very well together" (*ibid.*, 108) at the close of Act Two to commemorate their anniversary. Perry also apologized immediately if grudgingly for his crack about Buzz's Somalian boy (*ibid.*, 52).

McNally's point? Perry and Arthur are mixed creatures like the rest of us. Their conservative ways haven't immunized them against inconstancy. Nor are they as straight-laced and solid as they seem. Their hearts and nerves can fray as easily as those of their friends. Admittedly, this fraying occurs less often. But it causes the same amount of pain. The two men are vital to the play: they show that the gay community includes conservative, subdued people along with the flamboyant. They also embody one of the main tenets of McNally's ontology — the difference between seem and be; even the most placid-looking relationships between those deemed tidy and conformist seethe with dangerous undercurrents.

His blindness gives Gregory's lover Bobby a totally different take on the appearance-reality dualism from the other players. Sitting in the same car with Arthur and Perry suffices to tell him that they're in love. He identifies a flower he can't see (*ibid.*, 105). His powers have precedents. A connection between blindness and poetry has long since become a classical trope. Blindness in works as different as *Oedipus Rex*, Henry Green's first novel, *Blindness* (1926), and the movie *Scent of a Woman* all confer upon the blind special powers of insight and intuition. Though no poet, Bobby, like Colonel Frank Slade, the 1992 Oscar-winning role played by Al Pacino, has these powers in abundance. He seems older and wiser than the events unfolding around him. Gregory rightly perceives him as angelic. He resembles Dostoevsky's figure of the holy fool who has attained peace beyond understanding. As soon as he arrives at Manderley, he greets the house and the nearby lake (*ibid.*, 40). Then he thanks God for bringing him and the other weekenders together. He's so happy that, like Dostoevsky's Prince Mishkin from *The Idiot* and Frankie's Johnny, he's deemed insane (*Three Plays* 155).

His last name, Brahms, evokes Parsifal, the eponymous fool saint of Richard Wagner's final opera, who sets out to save the world. German music is his leitmotif, a musical trope made famous by Wagner (*Two Plays* 20, 36).

But he's no passive angel. He helps with the cooking and the washing-up. He swims. Refusing the help of others, however well-meaning, he climbs back onto the stage by himself after falling off. He's outward bound. When the others tarry and dawdle, he'll say things like "Well, come on" and "Let's go" (*ibid.*, 134, 141).

But his upbeat nature and inner vision both fail him. Like most of McNally's warmest, most honest figures, he finds — or puts — himself in the middle of an uproar. None of his body parts are safe. A shard of glass that a sighted person might have spotted slides into this foot. He cuts his hand after stumbling on a rake. Crawling around the raft puts a splinter of wood in his hand. His spirit is also at risk. The news of his sister's death sends him into gales of grief. Through Bobby, McNally is using the archetype of the blind seer in order to dismantle or deconstruct it.

He's not finished. Bobby dropped a milk bottle while "*kissing furiously*" (*ibid.*, 10) with Ramon. He was thinking with his dick (cf. *Two Plays* 2007, 35; *D* 45) when he and Ramon were mouthing and groping one another. He had left Gregory's bed to get a glass of milk from the refrigerator downstairs. Suddenly unimportant, the bottle he's holding falls, "shattering milk and shards of glass everywhere" (*Two Plays* 11). Sex has disproved the adage about not crying over spilt milk, the sign of which is the racket the bottle makes when it bursts on the floor. The discharge of sperm, a milk-white fluid, causes tears and regrets. Arthur brings a temporary reprieve. Having come downstairs, he tells Bobby about "the very obvious stain" (*ibid.*, 17) on his pajamas. An anxious Bobby is grateful because he wants to hide his treachery from Gregory, which Gregory will discover anyway. McNally's warm, loving weekend host gets worse than he deserves and suffers more than would most of his coarser-grained guests. The milk of human kindness has soured in this first of the three weekends he and his guests will spend together, tellingly, that of Memorial Day; certain wrongs are easier to remember than to overlook and forgive. An acausal effect of the wrong Bobby inflicted on his host and lover appears swiftly. Later that same night, Gregory dreams that the needle on his recording of Anton Webern's *Engel*, or *Angel*, has stuck in one of its grooves while being played. His Dutchess County Eden has darkened. A passage from Webern's song, "*In der Kindheit, frühen Tagen/ Hört ich oft Engeln sagen*" (*ibid.*, 20), i.e., "In the early days of childhood/ I have often heard angels say, refers to this darkening." What the speaker, or I figure, heard from the angels remains unspoken in McNally's text. Later, Gregory will call Bobby, possibly the play's youngest character, *his* angel (*ibid.*, 36).

He's mistaken. The sin of his fallen angel has blotted both his house and his life. This is a real pity. Gregory and Bobby make a fine match. The love that binds the stutterer and the blind man has razed their handicaps together with a 20-odd-year age difference. They make love so furiously that they put hickeys on each other's necks. They're also so well-tuned both emotionally and temperamentally that the stab of pain Bobby gets when a splinter of wood from the raft drives into his hand coincides with a shout that comes when a leg cramp fells Gregory during a tennis match (*ibid.*, 71–72).

Soon after this painful coincidence, Bobby, bewailing the death of his sister, says, "It's all so fucking fragile. So fucking arbitrary" (*ibid.*, 79). He's dissembling. Chance didn't send him to the raft. He swam there to make a date with Ramon; reaching for something off limits drove the splinter into his hand. Now McNally never says whether gays are hornier than straights. More important is that Bobby and Gregory stand near the top of the list of his noblest characters, not only in *LVC*, but, rather, in the whole canon. The beautiful love that both joined them and elevated their spirits has now caved in to lust.

It won't awaken regardless of how many hickeys they bite into each other's necks — their biting alluding to the play's Eden parallel. It only took one bite, or sin, to pollute the original Eden. Bobby's sexual bout with Ramon has kindled in him a craving for younger flesh. Prurience kept his head turned. His love for Gregory, genuine as it is, can't stop Bobby from doing what he dreaded, playing the archetypical role of the young man forsaking the older one. Something very special has been lost. What was tender and urgent has drowned inside the commonplace; a character in *Some Men* will say of an acquaintance, "I heard he took up with a younger trick. That's what usually happens" (*Two Plays* 2007, 54). Concupiscence will dominate Bobby's decision, after the play's present-tense action, to ditch Gregory for Luke, whose twice-repeated name (*ibid.*, 138) gives Bobby's defection to him the ring of Gospel truth. Keep in mind that sightless Bobby welcomed Ramon's lewd pass without knowing its origin. Carnality has shredded Bobby's belief in the divine virtue of unconditional love (*ibid.*, 87). The damage caused by his breach of faith vibrates beyond the play we are watching. Gays can smash up each other in ways undreamed of by straights.

The man who turned Bobby's head, the Puerto Rican-born dancer Ramon Fornos (McNally's "Hidden Agendas" mentions the avant-garde Cuban-American dramatist Irene Fornos [*15 Plays* 372]), has, in Clum's words, "the self-confidence and independence that comes with youth and beauty" ("Where We Are Now" 107). This creature of "open sensuality" (*ibid.*) reaffirms youth and beauty as coin of the realm in the gay sexual market place. And, a dramatist to his fingertips, McNally will show Ramon dancing to flaunt that youthful beauty. No surprise, he's "terrific" (*Two Plays* 115) singing and undulating, spinning and stepping, to a Diana Ross tune, advisedly sharing the stage with Gregory, who knows about his trysts with Bobby. Ramon's splendid footwork isn't the only act of genius displayed here. His dazzle has roused McNally's moral intelligence. After watching Ramon's brilliant display, Gregory will subjugate the personal to the aesthetic and the communal. Yes, he's so furious with Ramon that, highlighted by his only sortie into profanity into the play, he stuffs Ramon's fingers into the kitchen drain and threatens to cut them off. But he stops himself. It wasn't for nothing that in Act One he spotted a likeness between Ramon and himself when he was Ramon's age (*ibid.*, 28). (Nor was it a casual afterthought that gave Gregory the same last name that one of McNally's most caring people, Katharine Mitchell Brynne of *Ganesh*, was born with).

This recognition has stayed with him. Ramon's brilliance as a dancer has made deep inroads into Gregory's psyche. Instead of severing his fingers, Gregory offers him the lead role in the ballet he has been scoring. He has proved to himself that forgetting the self in favor of a larger good can end his enslavement to raw instinct. It's a breakthrough for both men. Gregory's vivid affirmation is as life-enhancing as it's difficult to achieve. Its persuasiveness also confirms the power of that which repulses even as it attracts. Gregory's moral awakening rises from treachery and violence. Though tempting to dismiss, this aspect of McNally's Hudson River Gothic snags the mind.

Ramon expands upon this offbeat power. Equally amoral, calculating, and power-hungry, he had wasted no time ambushing Bobby, and he declares frankly his ambition to become a great dancer. Yet he also knows to his credit that he's not that great dancer yet. But he's ready to slave countless hours to become one. Like Maria Callas of *Master Class* and *Golden Age*'s Vincento Bellini, he knows, too, that he'll have to fight back any impulse to congratulate himself on whatever progress he makes toward his goal. This self-doubting artist has bought into the hard truth that success for him means, rather than exulting in his feats, using them as steps toward the next level of achievement. McNally judges success in any field of endeavor a never-ending clarion call of self-denial.

For all his Latino fire, Ramon defies moral judgments. He's selfish, arrogant, and nasty; as soon as two of his fellow weekenders visit him on the raft, he asks them to race him back to land, knowing they are too tired to oblige him. Obligations are the order of the day. Any gratitude or admiration he feels toward his host has wilted in the surge of his lust for Gregory's Bobby. But he's no monster. His upside includes the offer to carry the older Arthur's luggage to the house (*ibid.*, 39). Nor does he only get close to people he can use. He displays tenderness and compassion when he tells Bobby, as he's leaving Manderley for his sister's funeral, "I have a sister, too. I love her very much. I'm sorry" (*ibid.*, 104).

He also feels the odd man out in Manderely. One can see why. He's the only guest whose his cradle tongue is not English. He came to Manderely with John Jeckyll, his much-older lover of three short weeks, a man he knows the other guests dislike. He feels slighted himself by John, and we admire his pluck in letting John know it. "Look, I'm sort of out of my element this weekend," he says of his Memorial Day visit to Dutchess County. "You're all old friends. You work together.... I'm just somebody you brought with you. I'd appreciate a little more respect, okay?" (*ibid.*, 33)

He's not alone in his vulnerability. Blind Bobby from Texas considers himself an outsider. AIDS will kill both Buzz and John's brother, James. Even before Bobby's disloyalty with Ramon, Gregory felt stressed by having to host the weekend outing while soldiering on with the ballet he's writing. The bond of the veteran married couple Arthur and Perry has hit a snag. There's something more. Neither of these mainstays of the corporate structure is Nellie or Butch any more than he's active in the arts. Yet both qualify as gay — without either one feeling professionally devalued or adrift. At one point, Buzz asks John to play "gay music written by a gay composer." The answer he gets, "There's no such thing as gay music, Buzz" (*ibid.*, 57), comes from no-nonsense, practical Perry.

McNally endorses both Perry's answer and its offshoots. In his introduction to the volume that includes *LVC*, he recalls having been "recently asked to appear on a panel saluting "The Golden Age of Gay Theatre.'" His reply? "Nonsense. This [i.e., 1995] is the golden age for the theatre, both gay and straight" (x). Yes, gays can feel lonely and unwanted, even among other gays. But *LVC*, with its cast of gays, transcends homosexuality, even though it could never be re-scripted or staged as straight drama. It succeeds so well because of its honesty; it expresses what McNally knew and felt at the time he was writing it. This integrity goes beyond gender preference. The world-class choreographer and ex-ballet star Gregory has excelled in a gay-dominated field. Yet the ferocity of his commitment — he breaks chairs when his writing stalls — is gender free. While his guests are reveling, he labors alone on his ballet-in-progress.

He won't neglect his guests. This gracious host opens his home to his friends. He makes sure they have blankets and towels. Once they're settled in, he enjoys eating, drinking, and socializing with them. He'll organize tennis matches. Perry is wrong to call Gregory stubborn (*ibid.*, 111). Try dedicated, thoughtful, and grounded. Even throw in adaptable. His legs gnarled and aching from decades of dancing, he learned choreography to continue practicing the art he loves. He'll continue in his own way. Like all serious artists, he knows that he's committed to a regimen of downgrading the value of both his work and himself. "I'm not. Um. Very honorable" (*ibid.*, 71), he says early in Act Two, his stammer conveying Freud's classic view of the unfit artist, from Vulcan, or Hephaestus, the hobbled god of fire James Joyce took as his template for his weak-eyed embryonic writer Stephen Dedalus.

Gregory's self-critical bent cuts so deep it might have caused his stammer. But it also meshes with the objectivity he displays when he hears the news of Bobby's cheating. Shattered and shocked, he tells Bobby, "Go to Texas tonight [for the funeral]. I don't want you in *our* house" (*ibid.*, 87; emphasis added). His farewell to Bobby early in Act Three shows the same admirable self-control. Embracing Bobby without kissing him goodbye, he says, "Hurry back to me" (*ibid.*, 105). He's bridling his conflictiveness. Whereas he knows he'll forgive Bobby, he's not ready to do it now. Having distanced himself from his pain, he's nearly treating it as that of another person.

Gregory also maintains grip while teaching his non-dancing friends to step to *Swan Lake* for the upcoming Carnegie Hall AIDS benefit. His efforts will bring him little gratitude, let alone contentment. He's by himself at the end of Act Two. Having just learned about Bobby and Ramon, this world-acclaimed dancer and choreographer is watching Perry and Arthur's anniversary dance. He may have never felt so adrift for years. But he soon sheds his role as a pop idol. He does it by denying whatever vestiges of ego cling to him. Forecasting the scene in *CC* where Joshua heals the cursing, abusive HIV-positive Philip ("I think you can suck my dick now, faggot" [*CC* 44]), Gregory, disregarding the taunts of Ramon, pours him a cup of coffee — preparing it, moreover, in the way his taunter likes it and then presenting it in the taunter's own language: "one café con leche for Ramon" (*Two Plays* 118). It's a triumph of self-overcoming for Gregory. He has confirmed the supremacy of forgiveness. Within moments, he and Ramon will join hands to work together on the ballet scheduled to open the coming fall in New York.

Another of the afflicted who's blessed with the power to forgive is James Jeckyll, a costumer for the National Theatre in London. Stricken with AIDS, he has come to the U.S. to seek comfort from his twin brother, John. But John, dubbed John the Foul as James is James the Fair (*ibid.*, 65), begrudges his presence at Manderley. He has always resented his dying brother and doesn't want him around. As with Maria and her sister in *Master Class*, he always felt second-fiddled while growing up. Whether he helped fuel this disfavor is unclear. Unclear, too, in John's mind is the blowback of his envy. Anyone who hates his twin hates himself, too. Can the sting be drawn? In the play's lone confrontation between the brothers (who are played, miraculously, by the same actor), James parries all of his twin's expressions of hate with words of love and forgiveness.

John feels stymied. He's too bogged down in hate to let in the healing powers of James's tear-laced words. But these same words have opened new vistas for *James*. His bond with his fellow AIDS patient Buzz becomes the purest, least self-regarding one in the play. The sickly have humbled the ablebodied. But how impressed should we be? This bond, though loving, is perforce chaste. Without trying to demean it, McNally is indirectly asking if the absence of sex has preserved and even created its selfless purity. He'll revisit this concern in *Dedication* (2004). For now, the range of his moral sensibility makes it safe to ask if he's questioning the fabled special relationship between the Brits and the Yanks. As his master Shakespeare showed in tragedies like *Hamlet* and *Othello* and the dark comedies *Much Ado* and *Measure for Measure*, sex can spark a firestorm of troubles. Buzz and James attest to the harsh irony that an act performed to join people can kill them; again, love and death occupy the same bed.

Eros claims other victims, both gay and straight. Sam Truman of *LTTA* is scalded by his wife Sally's unfaithfulness. The calamity of being dropped by Aristotle Onassis will keep gnawing at Maria. Stephen stabs his lover Mike to death. Buzz Hauser's plaint about his failure to form a lasting love-tie ends with his quoting some words from the Malnick-Livingston tune, "I'm Through with Love" (*ibid.*, 28). He has it wrong. Love is through with *him* and, having no more use for him, has left him for dead. Like the vulture in his picture of the starving Somalian child, it has claimed him. Nor will Buzz be any happier to recall that vultures eat animal decay.

Much of this harshness reaches us through the repetition of the word "anyway," which we and Buzz hear spoken at least eight times in the play. That it's said regularly by the irascible Perry (e.g., *ibid.*, 15, 53, 92, 130) bespeaks the pain heaped on him by Arthur's treason. He makes the bogus claim that he says it when he's "overcome" (*ibid.*, 62). What has been ringing his bell is his inability to forgive Arthur. Like the phrase "It is what it is," "anyway" signifies the resigned acceptance of the status quo; ugly as things are, nothing can be done.

Appropriately, John says the word even more often than Perry. Spoken by him, it's both the first utterance of Act Two (*ibid.*, 65) and, again coming from him, the play's curtain line (*ibid.*, 142). Like Perry, John is too conflictive to merge with the tide of life. He's writing a musical about Houdini (*ibid.*, 15) because he craves release from his self-imposed bonds. The public has been rough with him, too. A musical he wrote in Britain shut down after 11 performances in he U.S. He has since become an American citizen and taken a job as Gregory's rehearsal pianist (*ibid.*, 14–15), we learn from Perry. Tellingly so; Perry hates John because he resembles him ("anyway").

This resemblance is not to be coveted. The first words John speaks in the play target his malice. He says of the sled that his host Gregory got from Jerome Robbins and displays proudly, "It's not an antique.... It's a piece of junk" (*ibid.*, 10). The next time he appears on stage, with his back to us, he's again flaunting, in a reversal of his arch-critic-cum-mirror image Perry's words, his "fundamentally hateful nature" (*ibid.*, 14). If Buzz plays the role of Lear's fool in *LVC*, Bobby Cordelia (Frontain, "Trafficking" 97), and Gregory, Othello, John invokes Iago, Shakespeare's outstanding figure of vice.

So nasty is he that, in Act One, all the other six characters on stage with him say in unison, "Fuck you, John" (*Two Plays*, 56). There's more in him to object to than they know. Invoking Hawthorne's villains Ethan Brand and Roger Chillingworth of *The Scarlet Letter*, he probes other people's hearts. He reads Gregory's diary illicitly to discover his hidden self: "I am obsessed with who other people really are. They don't tell us, so I must learn their secrets" (*ibid.*, 21), says this foe of life's basic decencies. Instead of loving people, he collects information about them. He's dangerous. Life as McNally describes it (no casual afterthought made Bobby a fellow Texan) is difficult enough. Most of us have enough trouble surviving what Walker Percy called the malaise of everyday without having to worry about having our privacy violated. It's baffling why Gregory invited John to Manderley for the three summer holiday weekends. His snooping threatens everybody's fun.

But, perhaps as Gregory suspects, he has a place — McNally again avoiding blanket moral judgments. That place matters. Yes, his thirst for knowledge about others is fed by heartlessness and cruelty. This malice, though, enriches the play. It makes John the reader's or playgoer's friend, and more. He recounts events we couldn't have witnessed first hand. The information he shares with us from Gregory's diary also imparts knowledge we wouldn't have otherwise had. In this regard, he's also befriending McNally, saving him pages and pages of exposition the inclusion of which would slow the pace of the play.

His information gathering is also dramatic. Somewhere in Graham Greene's *Stamboul Train* or *Orient Express* (1932), a novelist calls himself God's spy. Others have played this role, too. *LVC* is McNally's longest play because it has to delve into eight different lives. This formidable job also makes it his most novelistic. *LVC* profits from the novel's uncertainty about whether it's a story told by a single teller or a play enacted by a number of actors. It adapts from *Ganesh* the conventions of the Greek chorus and the *raisonneur* of the French well-made play. These conventions belong historically to the theater. But McNally's liberality with them also invokes the omniscient Victorian author who moralized about the action of the novel he/she was recounting.

Like Dickens, according to Robert Gates's *The Dickens Theatre* (1965), McNally wears different garb and throws his voice. *LVC* often pauses to allow a Perry (*ibid.*, 12) or a Buzz (*ibid.*, 25) to fill in background data, record both the passage of time and the shifting of scene, and also provide moral slants on what we've been watching. It's nearly safe to argue that the play posits a world in which everybody is a (gay) writer. An intrusion can be funny. Aware that he's a character in a play, Bobby assures us midway into Act Two, "Don't worry. I'm not going to fall off [the stage]" (*ibid.*, 87), as he did in Act One while preoccupied with thoughts of Ramon.

The parallel between Bobby's literal fall and his fall from grace conveys the vitality of the play's many intrusions. Besides supplying important commentary along with some great laughs, the intrusions give insights into both the speakers and those being spoken of. Our curiosity about how such insights will apply to the coming action sustains our attention. Invoking narrative convention again, the McNally of *LVC* resembles Flaubert's ideal novelist. He's present everywhere but nowhere to be seen.

* * *

Superior technique had given the action a flying start. Its first words, spoken by Gregory, voice his love of his rural retreat. He lauds the cabinetry, wallpaper, and roof of his 1915 house, citing its roots in the "golden age" of American domestic architecture (*ibid.*, 9–10). He has voiced the territorial imperative, a bourgeois pride in the ownership of property. If he values Manderley as a place to host his friends, he also basks in the security and belonging it has given him. Manderley confirms his stake in the physical world. He needs this confirmation. He has never been able to cure his stammer. In addition, the kinks and aches tormenting his 43-year-old body have ended his career as a dancer. Age has tightened its grip on him. He tires easily; he can only move with grace for brief periods. To his sorrow, Bobby, the man he loves, never saw him dance. Time will spank him again when Bobby drops him for younger men.

These defeats, though, lift his spirit while bruising it. Forgiving Ramon for stealing Bobby from him opens his eyes and heart to Ramon's dancing genius. And McNally's crafting of the forgiveness motif? As in *The Rink*, little is said about it. It happens on its own. And it changes everything. Forgiveness has so much moral and psychological clout that it needs no commentary. In fact, as Johnny of *F&J* has started to learn, words can only smudge, sidetrack, or diminish it.

McNally's discretion boosts *LVC* elsewhere. The dramatic monologues or soliloquies in the play run much shorter than those found in O'Neill's *Strange Interlude*. Economy and selection have helped turn characters into stars or novelists. Each of them is allowed to express his distinct personality—often at night under the moon. Speaking their minds has made them independent centers of significance. McNally isn't practicing inverse snobbery. The dramatic monologues in *LVC* support David Richards's tribute to him: "His view of humanity has to be as generous as that of anyone working in the American theater today" (1994, 1).

This generosity harks again to the soliloquies. The play's opening moments put us in mind of the near impossibility of dramatizing certain areas of human activity through dialogue. Soon after Gregory rhapsodizes about his house, the action jump-cuts to Bobby and Ramon "*kissing furiously*" (*Two Plays* 10). The power of this clandestine episode stems from the deliberateness and intensity of its presentation. As Henry James enjoyed saying, what counts the most in imaginative writing is the quality of the imagining. Too much would be lost if Bobby and Ramon were shown devouring each other had the scene showing their clinch not followed the quiet, meditative one in which Gregory voices his love of Manderley. If the old saw about *sexual* love, the focus of the next scene, is true, Bobby's literal blindness has made it doubly so.

Bobby's being unable to — or not wanting to — identify his lover of the moment sharpens his joy. Then Arthur appears on stage to fill in the implications of the spilt-milk incident. Note Perry's words: "Bobby had gone downstairs for cookies, Pepperidge Farm Brussels, and a glass of milk. Whether Ramon had followed him or was waiting for him like a cat, his feet cold on the bare wood floors, I don't know. I was upstairs asleep with my Arthur" (*ibid.*, 10–11). The clash between the domestic ("Pepperidge Farm Brussels," "upstairs asleep with my Arthur?") and the anarchic ("Ramon ... waiting ... like a cat") repeats the one that took the action from its quiet opening scene, one that also showed two men on stage. The oscillation of these forces will continue to dictate the play's rhythm.

Sleeping, as he said, at the time of Bobby and Ramon's clinch, Perry didn't eyewitness it. Distance continues to prevail. Though Arthur removes the tell-tale whitish stain from Bobby's pajamas, he talks about this event months, maybe years, after it happened. The stain has only been removed in the physical sense. Buzz's reaction to the incident leading up to its appearance, besides creating a counterpoint of voices and moods, prefigures the time-shifts and leitmotifs the play will use to develop the issues it raises: "I was upstairs, asleep with myself. All this I heard later that summer — when everything changed, for good and bad but forever — but I wouldn't have been surprised" (*ibid.*, 11). *We're* surprised, though; besides covering a great distance, the play's musical structure has also laid tracks for future lines of development, all within a few minutes of opening curtain.

This polyphony has gotten the proper treatment, Buzz and Perry reminding us that time in *LVC* will be fluid rather than straightforward. McNally underscores the point; "I'm not in this conversation," and "I'm upstairs sleeping," Perry will soon say (*ibid.*, 17). Asides like these open up a spread of thematic turf. McNally has benefited from careful planning. He'll demand as much from himself in this 1994 play as he had done heretofore and would some time since. Next, *The Rink*, and *Ganesh* were basically, if not literally as in "Botticelli," "Next" and *F&J*, two-character plays; the snappy tone of *The Ritz* and *IOAP* ruled out character analysis. The building blocks of *Master Class*, *Corpus Christi*, and *Golden Age* came from the public domain.

Robert Brustein flubbed when he said of *LVC*, "The play has no subject other than sexual relationships" (1). It carefully foregrounds and then treats with the same care a wealth of subjects and ideas. Straight readers may feel uneasy or even reluctant to carry on after entering this uncommon world. Soon, though, they feel glad to be there. McNally's artistry has convinced them that watching people who both resemble but also differ stridently from them may not just entertain them but, rather, expand the range of their moral concern.

LVC is vivid, colloquial, funny and hard-hitting, often, as if being gay weren't steep enough on its own. Even the sighted and the non-stammering feel damaged in body and soul. AIDS will soon kill two of them. This news makes us flinch. We have come to feel for them and their survivors alike. The strange animating magic of McNally's prose has made it all resonate, combining surface action and ominous depths. The play's soliloquies and asides add the benefit of making the people their own explainers. As distance shrinks, Shakespeare-like, between the wronged and the guilty, the play in which they appear gains credibility as a mirror of contemporary life.

But it's McNally's commitment to his materials that generates the most force. The men dance, accompanied by John at piano "with surprising grace and dignity," says Frontain, to Tchaikovsky's "Dance of the Little Swans" ("Terrence McNally and the Dance of Death" 25). Their skill defies cognitive discourse. It can nearly be overlooked that the troupe is incomplete. Perry only harms himself by sulking on the sidelines rather than dancing with his friends. James *does* dance but collapses before number's end. Much has been salvaged. The spectacle created by the dancers wearing toe shoes, feathered headdress, and tutus is both ridiculous and heroic. It also reminds us that group effort can improve *most* human undertakings; if the undertaking remains flawed, so do most of our endeavors, including, regrettably, the way we love each other.

The play brims with evidence to support Bobby's view of life as "so fucking fragile, so fucking arbitrary" (*Two Plays* 79). The common cause the dancing men embrace pads the jolt of this outrage; they deserve an audience at Carnegie Hall. Both the coming AIDS benefit and the dancers' preparation have sharpened their awareness of death; they're reminded that none of them will get out of the world alive. Facing this news together, though, sparks the therapeutic insight that *all* ordeals, not just our mortality, are better dealt with in the company of intimates. All the better if we're dancing with them; we've made our "fucking fragile" world a moving hospice. Frontain has said it best: [W]hile the men cannot save each other from the inevitability of death, they can rescue each other from the paralyzing idea of dying" ("Terrence McNally and the Dance of Death" 48).

The play's closing — or dying — moments revive this poignant idea. David Richards's belief that "life has always been out of our hands" (13) is both vindicated and dismissed. Night has fallen. The men haven't only moved stage rear. They're also facing away from us in this moonlit finale. Because music enhances dramatic action, the men sing while preparing to skinny-dip. Their song, "Harvest Moon," calls to mind "Beautiful Dreamer," the one they sang at curtain up. The singers have created a circuit of Americana that includes them; they're part of America, and America belongs to them. The moment is one of "timelessness" (Franklin 129). But it passes. Because the weekenders, like all of us, inhabit linear, as well as cyclical, time, the American national pageant they've blended into has absorbed them. They've been gathered into the continuum they kept alive.

As they fade from view and their voices recede, they're sliding into the lake naked, just as they entered the world. No mawkishness mars their passage. The lake they slide into calls forth the Ganges at Varanasi in *Ganesh* when the tourists' skiff's hitting a dead cow and then the corpse of a baby gives Katharine a sense of rightness and inevitability that includes her and Margaret (*Two Plays* 245–47). Bodies of water in McNally represent, along with life's inevitable flow, a washing away or melting of differences. Others will replace Gregory and his friends at the lake, which will always provide swimmers a source of fellowship and fun — perforce overhung by the threat of drowning. The dialectic, as Nancy Franklin says, is both "hilarious and ... devastating" (130). By siting it under the stars and accompanying it with traditional American music sung by friends, McNally has boosted its value. Fun, like hardship, gains from being shared.

When enhanced by music, the rewards multiply. The moonbeams illuminating the continuity-change dualism, or spectrum, reveal better glimpses of our shared life under God than can be found in the glare of the sun. Included in the picture is the caving-in of Bobby to the hot urgencies of sex. McNally is asking with voluptuous candor if we can repel our physical cravings. He already dramatized the issue in an exchange between Bobby and Perry. When Bobby says, "I'm not strong that way," he's told, "Most people aren't" (*Two Plays* 18). They aren't, McNally isn't, and neither are we. No tears; *Love! Valour! Compassion!* is so immaculately made that it salutes its audiences — and their frailties. The play's closing musical cadences mark an acceptance of the idea that everything ends with a release into process.

CHAPTER SEVEN

The Madness of Art

Like Henry James, McNally has been spending much of his career writing about art and artists of different stripes. Often, he'll rework the life-art dualism central to Jamesian works like *The Aspern Papers*, "The Lesson of the Master," *The Sacred Fount*, and *The Wings of the Dove*. His range of interest in art's resonances is wide and varied. *It's Only a Play* (1985) and *Dedication* (2004) deal with the staging of plays. Opera and operatic production power both *Master Class* and *Golden Age*. Through it all, McNally has been defining art broadly. He has studied opera in the round. His first opera-based play, *The Lisbon Traviata*, reaches us from the perspective of the audience, or fan, whereas in *Master Class* the point of view is that of the performer or interpreter, and in *Golden Age*, the composer or creator. Then *Corpus Christi* evokes the Eucharist, i.e., the elevation of a crust of bread into the body of Christ, to Jean Genet the greatest theatrical transformation in history. A dancer and a choreographer in the cast of *Love! Valour! Compassion!* build both context and momentum for the group dance near the end of the play. The characters in *Whiskey* (1973) all acted as The Lush Thrushes in a television soap opera. The undated "Hidden Agendas" and "Street Talk" (1988) reflect upon stage technique and production.

I

The art form under scrutiny in *Full Frontal Nudity* (2004) is statuary. Three American tourists and their guide have come to Florence's Accademia Gallery to view Michelangelo's *David*. Bimbi, the tour guide, identifies David early on as the "Old Testament hero who defeated the giant, Goliath, and so saved his people from the Philistines" (*SS* 9). There's a lesson here that will apply to the tourists. The heavy odds David overcame to kill Goliath match up with the uphill fight they — and we — must all wage to acquire both humility and reverence, mindsets crucial to the appreciation of great art.

Michelangelo's *David* focuses this lesson as did India in a different way in *Ganesh*. Like the sleeping man whose snores close *PG*, the horn on the minivan blaring at final curtain in *Nudity* suggests the obstacles the physical world intrudes between us and authenticity. As if the self didn't slip in its own barriers; to access our full potential, we have to probe regions of our psyches we've either been ignoring or denying. Again, the freedom-quester must tally the cost of his/her freedom. In one of those passages of interior monologue set between parentheses in *Nudity*, a tourist recognizes that what's blocking his appreciation of beauty is — himself; the mulishness of both Hector Charlotte's flesh and spirit blurs his response to *David*. He has more to fret about. Aggravating the hindrances he must stave off is the self-disgust that overtakes him for backing down to them: "All your life you dream of this moment and then it's here and part of you thinks, So what? There should be two of us standing here" (*ibid.*, 5).

Discoveries in McNally are always self-discoveries. Those kindled by great art keep plaguing the retired professor Hector by their absence as well as their presence. Having sent him deeply within himself to a place he'd prefer to ignore, *David* reminds him of his need, in the later years of his marriage, to look away from his aging wife; Violetta's physical flaws, he feared, would blunt his love for her were he to watch her walking naked from the shower to their bedroom. *David* tries Bimbi, the tour leader, in a different way:

> Come off your high horse, Bimbi [she rebukes herself]. What makes you superior to these people? That you speak four languages? That you know the difference between a Fra Angelico and a Botticelli? That your husband loves you and you love him? So what? How does that make you better? Luckier, that's all. Different, yes, better, no. But I feel superior to them. I can't help myself. It's my delusion [*ibid.*, 31].

Inversion marks the opening of *Nudity*. Like Hector, she both knows and dreads the separating effects of the benefits caused by chance, like having good looks. The play opens with a medley of voices:

> Lights up.
> We are in the Accademia Gallery in Florence.
> At first we hear the sounds of a crowded gallery. French, Italian, German, Japanese — all are being spoken [*ibid.*, 5].

Art speaks across time and nationality as politics can't, lifting us to a nobler place. McNally is alluding to the power of art to raze national, racial, and linguistic differences; Michelangelo's great statue has brought strangers from everywhere to the Accademia. As a tour guide, Bimbi has the expertise in Renaissance art to further this integration. She has chosen the right line of work. In a reflection of her job as both information-giver and guiding spirit, she embodies the linguistic and national variety that greeted us at play's outset: "I'm not an Italian. My father was Albanian, my mother Greek. I was born in the Philippines, but I grew up in Perth. My first husband, Svet, was Swedish. After we got married, we migrated to Norway ... where I met my present husband, Gian Carlo Noni, a well-known and much respected journalist" (*ibid.*, 18). Blending and then communicating this variety to others is hard work. It taxes Bimbi. A couple of minutes into the play, she says to herself, "The worst part of my job is asking people what they think because then I have to listen to what they think" (*ibid.*, 6).

What she hears and sees during the play helps break down this arrogance. Great art, she has learned, never stops teaching, delighting, and mystifying us. After scores of visits to *David*, she joins her tourists, all of whom have returned to the statue at play's end for one last look of indeterminate length. The world of timeless beauty has trumped that of deadlines and quotas.

So what if the group misses the Duomo, the Uffizi, and other spots on their tour? Together, they have concocted the Stendhal Syndrome, defined by Bimbi as "an emotional/physical response to art" that occurs "when art speaks to something deeper in us than perhaps we understand" (*ibid.*, 27). Hearing in person Wagner's *Tristan und Isolde*, which is featured in *Prelude & Liebestod*, the companion piece to *Nudity*, roused intense emotions in 19th-century operatic audiences ("faces flushed, corsets were loosened, smelling salts were necessary" [*ibid.*, 27]).

These transports took these audience members unaware, as they will Bimbi and her tourists. They've already worked their magic on Bimbi, whose last words in the play, addressed to her charges, "May I join you" (*ibid.*, 38), voice the humility conjured in her by artistic perfection. The guide-client relationship has dissolved, leaving the four viewers equal before *David*, as they'd be at the communion rail. All can partake of art's raptures. Chiming with McNally's belief that every life contains a good story is his faith in our equality at the altar of art.

Ben Brantley's review of *Syndrome* nails McNally's imaginative intent: "Like Mr. McNally's 'Lisbon Traviata' and 'Frankie and Johnny,' 'Nudity' explores the chasm between the smallness of ordinary lives and the vastness of timeless art works" along with the "fleeting moments in which that gulf is bridged" (2). An extreme close-up of one of David's eyes after Bimbi's explanation of the Stendhal Syndrome infers that great art takes *our* measure. Reversing the customary subject-object dualism, a great statue, poem, or symphony tests *us*. The test results are also unpredictable. Though *Hamlet* affects us differently at age 30 than it did at 18 because we bring different experiences, inner and outer, to it, we won't know how till we read or see it again. Hector says, "If we really let a work of art in, if we embrace it totally, it would overwhelm us" (*SS* 27). He's right. So what if we faint? We've been touched by the divine. Someone nearby will loosen our corsets or belts and wave smelling salts under our noses.

The McNally of *Nudity* builds upon the idea that late 19th-century English literature, rather than dealing with the poetry of religion, made a religion of poetry, i.e., the English Decadents who touted the supremacy of art, an attitude later voiced by Virginia Woolf and Wallace Stevens. The very title of McNally's 2004 play, *Full Frontal Nudity*, implies the benefits but also the great risks of submitting totally to art. So does the "[e]xtreme close-up of the right eye" (*ibid.*, 27) of *David* that looks at the visitors to the Accademia. Our contingency has been pitted against the absoluteness of artistic masterpieces. The idea isn't new. Examples from religious history abound where the divine can't be named or faced, starting with the ancient Greek matriarchies. The effects may be so awesome that we fail to notice them even as they're revolutionizing our lives.

We have come under scrutiny in spite of ourselves. Great art in *Nudity* induces humility and awe, and less dialogue, chiefly political. Bimbi said at play's outset, "Words would only diminish this experience. I'll just let you take it in" (*ibid.*, 5). She's not stinting her duty She knows that the process of taking it in defies analysis. It also varies with each person. A minute or so from final curtain, one of her charges says to himself, "Don't be a jerk, Leo. Take something away from this. Yeah, but what? How are you supposed to explain this? Maybe you don't have to" (*ibid.*, 37). The other tourists share this attitude while standing with him before *David*. When one of them says, "You may never pass this way again," she's not talking about geography. McNally inserts the following stage direction to extend her idea: "The three of them are looking at *David*. They are becoming more statuelike themselves as they become more rapt in their concentration on the *David*. At the same time the pictures of the *David* are getting smaller and smaller. His image is receding" (*ibid.*).

This is important. The more of ourselves we invest in an endeavor, the more we can take from it. As *David* shrinks in size, more and more of it enters the hearts and souls of its viewers. As with a Henry James novel, it can be said of *Nudity* that, by play's end, nothing has happened, but much has been revealed. Also, like *Corpus Christi*, the McNally play that deals most directly with spirituality, *Nudity* investigates the non-material sources of reality. Joshua (Alfie Byrne of *A Man of No Importance*, too) found these sources within Himself. Great art has this same incomprehensible power, a truth Bimbi prepared us for in her second speech in the play: "Coming here every day, sometimes twice, six days a week, fifty-two weeks a year, and it takes my breath away every time!" (*ibid.*, 5)

The disunity or sprawl prominent at curtain up has gained a focus. As art opens souls, it also joins them. While razing linguistic and national barriers, it also eases the barriers dividing people. The internal responses that have been making the viewers statue-like and perhaps even statuesque have been bringing them closer to the perfection of great art. Though this mystical change defies cognition, the tourists' inner responses to *David* have raised the event of seeing it into something precious.

Sharing it both awes and stumps them. But what has chastened them is the keenness of their response. The excitement roused in them by *David* has confirmed their vitality. Even though the confirmation has distressed them, it has also humanized them in a way they had never previously known. They've moved from apathy to the vulnerability that sensitizes us to stimuli both external and internal.

This process, though, poses obstacles that, as will be seen again in *Master Class* and *Dedication*, can waylay the vulnerable. For the wide-awake, the freedom unleashed by great art must be both embraced and closely monitored. Notice again that the three tourists taking in *David*'s splendor are growing "statuelike themselves as they become more rapt in their concentration" (*ibid.*, 37). Are they being swept into an eternity where they can no longer function as they had been doing? The play grazes this danger. The divinely inspired *David* lives forever, but chilled in stone, it lacks the surge and throb of us living creatures despite our flaws and follies. An animal in a zoo has more brute reality than one in a museum that's frozen in stone or painted on a canvas.

The image of the visitors to the Accademia standing together and facing in the same direction tallies another danger posed by art — the loss of individuality. As *LT* showed in the regret overtaking Stephen while looking at the Polaroids taken of him and Mike eight years earlier, Leo Sampson, one of Bimbi's clients, finds the grandeur of *David* so far above his everyday self that he hates it. It has attained a magnificence beyond his imaging. He'd like to smash this reminder of his frailties and flaws. The statute's perfection makes him feel as if he were made to die. He's frightened and angry.

He already said of the answering chord created in him by seeing and discussing *David*, "That's one of my troubles: I see everybody's point and I end up not having one of my own" (*ibid.*, 26). He's ready for the internal growth that has been realigning his values. He has scuttled the he-man image he had been hiding behind. His new humility and restraint are stripping him of everything he had defined himself by, including his inner demon of destructiveness. But the dross that *David* has pared away from him also includes the inhibitions and restraints that comprise civility. His new freedom is dangerous. If he can't control it, he might pay heavily; Frankie's Johnny, with his love of Shakespeare, has done jail time.

Lending this possibility weight is its consistency with Leo's persona. Bimbi's tour group consists of what looks like a random cross section of America's middle class — a retired widower, a divorcé, and a separated wife, all of whom are middle-aged. This randomness confirms McNally's ability to wrest drama from the commonplace. Like the cast members of a WWII submarine movie, William Inge's *Bus Stop* (1955), or the 1998 Steven Spielberg film, *Saving Private Ryan*, those in *Nudity*, besides being strangers, differ in social and cultural levels, spend their spare time differently, and have different personalities and values. Their shared humanity, though, has made all of them receptive to art; though few of us are artists, most of us value artistic beauty.

Bimbi's three clients all know the loss of love. Troubled by love's absence, they all want to bring to their lives a secure emotional structure. Lana Maxwell, who came to Italy to distract herself from a nasty divorce action, seems too sidetracked by thoughts of food to give *David* its due. In her second speech in the play, she starts worrying about lunch. But her hunger vanishes along with any glossy Hollywood image her parents may have had in mind when they named her after movie star Lana Turner. Her responding to *David* from the heart makes her humble and likable. When told that the statue took four years to carve, she says, "Four years! I couldn't do something like that in four centuries!" (*ibid.*, 11) Her humility perseveres. Michelangelo's dedication to both his genius and his subject has also put her in mind of her wifely shortcomings: "Everything gets harder if you really want to be good at it. Start with marriage" (*ibid.*, 18), she tells Bimbi. Moments later, Leo's calling the husband she's separated from a "bastard" (*ibid.*, 19) makes her cry. Being caught off guard has shattered the mask of cynicism she was wearing. It also shows her the futility of casting blame. Standing in the shadow of *David*, she feels small and smudged.

But not whipped; the same sublimity that has diminished and shaken her has also given her wings. She's more deeply moved than she knows. Minutes after announcing her intent to walk away from the statue, she concocts a story about this "really gorgeous guy [named David] running around Renaissance Italy" who served as Michelangelo's model for a plaster-cast likeness of the Old Testament hero. Forget that she got her facts wrong. The inventiveness of her story's finale shows that her imagination has taken flight: "The real David, the guy in the [plaster] mold, got married, had kids, got fat eating too much pizza and died. But he lives forever in the beauty and joy of youth in this statue" (*ibid.*, 23).

Aloft she stays, but she has drifted into a danger zone. The craving for power and freedom awakened in her by *David* prompts her to want to touch it. Bimbi's complicity here is vital. Not only does she agree to remain passive while Lana climbs the platform holding *David*; she also tells her to act quickly before the guard assigned to watch *David* returns from his lunch. Bimbi seems to be conniving to insult the statue. But, instead, she's schooling Lana. She's helping her use great art as a vehicle to surpass herself, the impulse that brought her to the Accademia in the first place. It's important that Lana's wish to touch *David* is driven by trophyism. Like a hunter posing with his foot on the big-game animal he just killed, she wants her picture taken with her hand on *David* because "what's the point of doing something if there's no proof you did?" (*ibid.*, 33).

Lana regrets her trespass. Only her hand can reach the pedestal on which *David* stands, to begin with, and she recoils quickly after touching *it*. Her first words after rejoining the others, aimed at Bimbi, "You were right not to touch it" (*ibid.*, 34), voice her letdown. But before going to the ladies' room to wash her hands, she adds, "The next person who wants to touch the *David*, Bimbi: Don't let them" (*ibid.*, 35). Dazed and annoyed with herself, she has paid the price of literally overreaching. Art's noblest products, like God Himself, can only be glimpsed briefly from angles and in low indirect light. Faced directly, great art can appear baffling and ugly at first look, as the seminarian narrator of Yukio Mishima's *The Temple of the Golden Pavilion* (1956) discovers in the storied Kyoto-based building of the novel's title.

To transgress the barrier between human contingency and divinely inspired beauty is to risk disaster. This barrier is inviolate. To look at *David* is to be blessed. That should have sufficed Lana, whose wings got scorched flying too close to the sun. Perhaps she wasn't the first of Bimbi's clients who tried to touch *David*. But Bimbi scored a success by not stopping her. Only direct experience could have served Lana the lesson she needed. Less lucky is the Conductor in *Prelude & Liebestod* (1989), who immerses himself in the harmony and radiance of Wagner's "Liebestod" at the cost of his life. The greatness of the great artist in Thomas Mann, Wagner's fellow German, is also his undoing. Defying common sense, he's compelled both to extend and to smash frontiers. Wisely, McNally doesn't make the Conductor German. But his choice of composers whose work appears on the program, Wagner and Bruckner, adds traction to the Nietzschean warning being served.

Leo Sampson, the tourist who agreed to photograph Lana touching *David*, also covers great psychic ground during his stay at the Accademia. Like that of Troy Maxson in August Wilson's *Fences* (1987), his name mirrors the he-man image he affects: "Sampson's the name and mighty is the frame" (*ibid.*, 14) is how he introduces himself to a fellow tourist. A two-fisted bruiser deserves, he feels, privileges. Without asking anyone, he takes the front seat on the minivan that brought him and the others to the Accademia. But, as happened in *Witness*, *Bringing It All Back Home*, and *Lips Together, Teeth Apart*, his hyper-maleness soon proves itself a mask. McNally wastes no time distinguishing between his he-man image and the frailty beneath. Leo's first words in the play, addressing his reactions to *David*, voice the fears that being far from home have sparked in him: "I don't see what the big deal is. I've got a bigger dick. I mean, proportionally bigger" (*ibid.*, 6). (Another chronic self-doubter who affects a macho persona, Sam Truman of *LTTA*, bragged about the size of his "whopper" [11] of a penis.)

Leo's fears have revived. When he sees Bimbi laughing with Hector Charlotte, the other man on the tour, he asks inwardly, "What is it with women and gay men? I don't get it" (*SS* 12). This, soon after Lana's having presumed that Leo is gay (*ibid.*, 11). Leo's penis fixation supports her presumption. The first thing he had noted about David was his "dick," a word he'll repeat later amid references to his "willy," his "wiener," and his "johnson" (*ibid.*, 10, 13, 14). He has become fascinated by David's penis, the sight of which, he had attributed in a flight of fancy rivaling Lana's, sent spellbound motorists to their deaths before the statue was brought indoors — in reality, to shield it from the wear-and-tear of the weather.

Yet Bimbi values Leo's nutty story about the life-threatening mishaps caused by David's "uncircumcised dick" during its years outdoors. "You have a vivid imagination, Mr. Sampson" (*ibid.*, 14), she says. Perhaps she has guessed that *David* will stoke Leo's moral along with his pictorial imagination. She's right. He'll outdo his earlier self when he says later, "Show me someone who hasn't suffered loss and Ill show you someone who hasn't really lived" (*ibid.*, 21). *David* provokes dark truths; few of us understand the burdens of mortality or will voice them as thrillingly as Michelangelo. Leo has responded as vitally to this truth as any of his fellow tourists.

David's rough power has made Leo look at his own frailty as it did Lana, his fellow tall-tale raconteur. In an imaginative leap he'd have been incapable of making prior to viewing the statue, he tells her, "We all suffer. It's when we hide our suffering from one another that we get into trouble" (*ibid.*, 24). He has seen the emptiness behind his super-jock posturing. He has *not* seen that, like Frankie's Johnny, his vulnerability makes him more likable and accessible, having opened in him a gentle, wondering side he never knew about. This side includes his new-found candor, a virtue that helped him overcome his earlier defensiveness. He's confronting his feelings. To Bimbi's words about the power of great art to overwhelm us, he answers, "Wow! This is heavy stuff. This is what I came for. Right on" (*ibid.*, 28). A connection has been made. To Bimbi's statement that touching *David* was "a sacrilege, a profanation," he had said, "I can understand that" (*ibid.*, 25).

McNally admires this openness. Leo is learning that great art, rather than making our decisions for us, helps make us better deciders. He may have already set out on this path, as the last words spoken by him in the play — to himself—suggest: "Maybe you don't have to ['take something away']" from the viewing of *David* (*ibid.*, 37). Viewing it was its own reward. By forsaking the acquisitive, competitive creed of his culture, he has probably traveled a greater psychic distance than his three counterparts. The story is over; the story will start again. A sort of miracle will help him face it with a courage he didn't know he had.

The other man in the tour group, Hector, takes the role of the outlier, or the joker in the pack, a character type that has been interesting McNally since *Bump* (1964). Serious and introverted, this retired English professor is one of McNally's most artfully drawn nonconformists: "I've waited a lifetime for this" (*ibid.*, 18), he says about viewing *David* in person. His earlier worries about feeling deflated by the statue have fallen away. "I could stand here forever and still not see it," he says, and, "It's perfect, it's sublime" (*ibid.*, 20). His joy has shown him that the more of himself he invests in the statue, the more humble he feels. He needs humbling. His aloof and prissy airs have been annoying Leo and Lana, as also may have been his early retirement, which stemmed from a large inheritance from his wife. McNally, though, rises to the artistic challenge he has posed. Repudiating the humor character found in Chaucer, Ben Jonson, and Dickens, i.e., one led by his ruling passion, he takes a close, patient look at Hector.

If Hector is the "pain in the ass" (*ibid.*, 17) Bimbi accuses him of being, he has also brought to Florence a heavier heart than the others. Leo and Lana came to Florence to forget about their bad marriages. By contrast, Hector, had a good one — which ended suddenly just before a drunken driver smashed into the car he was driving with his son at his side. Hector is suffering from survivor's guilt. Though he couldn't have steered his car out of danger, he was nonetheless at the wheel when Andrew died. His inner struggles since that moment of anguish have been epical, even Biblical. His car crashed en route to his wife's funeral.

The motif of the dead son has returned from *PG*, but without any words about Andrew's sexual orientation. Such words would be irrelevant, even distracting. Hector's great sorrow will join him to the others. Leo, who had been at odds with him, apologizes for having insulted him and promises to pray for Andrew and Vi at the next church the group visits. The sorrow of another has taught him true manly dignity. The moment forms a breakthrough for both men. Witnessing *David* had shown Leo that Hector, whose alleged effeminacy he had mocked, is stronger than he.

Hector's strength continues to build after his brief dignified acceptance of Leo's apology. Lana's talk about her name had launched a conversation about Lana Turner, the stabbing death of her lover Johnny Stompanato, and her 14-year-old daughter Cheryl Crane, his killer (*Facts on File Yearbook* 18

[New York: Facts on File, 1959], 115). They're in Florence, not Hollywood, and they should act accordingly, Hector snapped. He learned, though, that the outburst of family violence that ended in Johnny Stomp's stabbing death had reduced the distance between Filmland and the Florence of the wicked Medicis. (A character in *Dedication* complains that violence has cheapened the afternoon soap operas he loves to watch [*D* 49–50].) The real-life Hollywood family murder had also marked canonical plays like Sophocles's *Oedipus* trilogy, *Hamlet*, Webster's *White Devil*, and Eugene O'Neill's updates of classical tragedy, *Desire Under the Elms* (1924) and *Mourning Becomes Electra* (1931), both of which became movies (1958, 1947). Perhaps Hollywood stands closer to Florence than Highbrow Hector thinks.

He posits the link himself by asking about Steve Reeves, who had a foot in both camps, the heroic and the popular. Reeves (1926–2000) portrayed Superman, Hercules and David's victim, Goliath, among many other roles in low-budget Italian-made movies. Echoing developments in McNally's *IOAP* and *F&J*, Hector has joined popular commercial entertainment to art. Why shouldn't he? He has sensed that both genres draw their material from the same source. At the same time, Lana's disavowal of her movie actress namesake ("Not every Lana is a Turner" [*SS* 7]) shows her rejecting Hollywood glitz. Where will her rejection take her? Her touching the pedestal holding *David*, though a foolish misstep, took her in the right direction; an engagement with art wiped out her craving for lunch and, in the process, also sharpened her eye to Michelangelo's genius with detail: "I love the veins in his hands. I had a boyfriend with veins in his hands like that. Right after we broke up, this was in high school, he turned into a junkie. Life is weird" (*ibid.*, 37).

Does her insight foreshadow another development just as weird? During the action, she and Leo had been playing a cat-and-mouse game of flirtation. Perhaps they had been gauging each other as potential dating partners, even lovers. As they might; they both seem to be the same age, belong to the same socio-educational class, and feel the weight of post-marital stress. But internal changes in her and Hector have also been moving *them* closer. Though we never find out if they click, the possibility has come to mind. Lana's new sensitivity to high art matches *his* retreat from or reassessment of it, as is seen both in his references to Steve Reeves (*ibid.*, 36, 37) and his practice, while talking to Lana, of calling his wife Vi, rather than her full name, Violetta, after Verdi's heroine in *La Triaviata*. Lana's disavowal of Lana Turner suggests itself here along with Hector's need of the consolations of sex. Like her, Hector has love to give. His early retirement (*ibid.*, 17) blurs any great age difference that might disqualify him as an inappropriate companion.

The play has rebooted itself after final curtain. Like our unanswered questions about how much of the uplift provided by *David* will shore up the tourists after they return home, any intimacy that may develop between Hector and Lana will occur after final curtain. They're having been touched by an experience both aesthetic and religious marked a deep sharing of great transformative power. This happened before. Artifice had made Titania of *A Midsummer Night's Dream* love an ass. Though neither Lana nor Hector is asinine, plain old dumbstruck sexual love could turn both of them into asses. Bottom, the object of Titania's love, says, "To say the truth, reason and love keep little company together nowadays" (3.1. 127–28). The Old Testament hero, David, who was sculpted just before slaying Goliath, might have added that the clashes that are normal in sexual love make asses of us all, at least briefly. Great art reads us. But its mystery remains as undecipherable to us as its beauty. We're left scratching our heads. As Lana said, life is weird.

II

Dedication Or the Stuff of Dreams recalls Tennessee Williams's *In The Bar of a Tokyo Hotel* (1969) and Caryl Churchill's *Top Girls* (1982). It's a play about stage production with political undertones. McNally's second love letter to the stage after *IOAP* is also a self-inventory. It brims with talk about theater history, actors, and acting. It revels in this milieu that McNally is so smitten by. *Dedication* displays the practical realities behind stage production like paying utility bills, printing programs, auditioning, swapping tickets for the cooperation of local business people, and preparing the stage before opening curtain. A cloudcar appears on stage along with a snow machine, a gallows, a towel Sophie Tucker once used, Oscar Wilde's podium, and a steamer trunk that once belonged to James O'Neill, the playwright's actor-father.

Theater is more than a metaphor or a collection of mementos in *Dedication*. The play's action spills into the house or auditorium. Characters climb on and off the stage, sometimes speaking their lines from the center aisle of the house. Another character is lifted onto the stage. An important exchange of words begins with a line spoken from the top row of the balcony. Nor does McNally, eager to portray the evocative power of live theater, stop here. After the cast members walk behind the curtain they brought down, they return to view to find two strangers on the apron of the stage. They're shocked but not stopped. Actors have always been distracted, astonished, and inspired by non-actors. Chicago's Second City comes to mind together with Pirandello's *Six Characters* (1921). Drama fosters, nay encourages, the free interchange between players and audiences.

This exchange fills *Dedication* with echoes, combinations, and re-combinations. Recalling *F&J*, the play returns to McNally's earlier work both to investigate dramatic art and to judge his own stage artistry. Like *PG*, McNally's 2004 play quotes Shakespeare's *Henry V* (*D* 17). It uses an acronym, "C.L.A.M.J.M.T.F.C.O.A.A.," to label the theatrical company which the play's main figures have formed, Captain Lou And Miss Jessie's Magic Theatre For Children Of All Ages (*ibid.*, 35), reprising Margaret Civil's "Offamof" (*Two Plays* 23), an acronym of the first words of the Prologue of *Henry V*. Reminders of other McNally works appear in *Dedication*. The motif of the dead son returns from *Bringing It*, *PG*, and *Nudity*. A professional singer is advised to end her act with some stagecraft that recalls the ending of *LVC*: "Ida, this would be great for the show. You know, during 'Crying All the Time Now,' you just slowly sink out of view. You're sinking, you're singing ... you're gone" (*D* 28).

From McNally's 1994 play also comes the device of quoting an old song to voice one's own misery. Instead of singing, "I'm Through with Love" (*Two Plays* 23), as Buzz did, though, a character in *Dedication* adapts, with more sting, "There'll Be Some Changes Made." Wrenching the blend of the new and the familiar is the identity of the adapter, a dying hag, who tells us, adding another wrench, "No one wants to fuck you when you're old and gray" (*D* 45).

This brutal shock reminds us that McNally didn't festoon *Dedication* with markers from his earlier work to make it a sentimental journey through his writing career. As is seen in Mrs. Annabelle Willard's takedown of Donaldson and Overstreet's song, the rarely staged *Dedication* is a work of transgressive vitality. It questions the role of goodness in our lives. There's much more bad than good in the lives of the people, and it's felt more keenly. At times, it looks as if goodness will nosedive in a world dominated by indifference, divided aims, and bare-faced cruelty. One character asks, "Why does goodness come so easily to some people and to others not at all?" (*ibid.*, 33) Those people in the first group, we might add, rarely feel good about themselves.

Perhaps God has been either hiding or looking away. Another possibility: He might have revealed Himself in the splendid architecture, detailing, and acoustics of the grand old theater in upstate New York where the action unfolds and then abandoned the people connected with it to fend for themselves. In the 19th century, when it opened, the artifacts made by craftsmen of different kinds — engineers, carpenters, weavers, and interior designers — weren't only beautiful; they were also made to last. Posterity ranks low as stewards of this legacy. The Main Street theatre has become both too big for the town where it stands — and too small to be commercially viable. A substance-abusing rock star who depends on gaudy special effects could never work there. She'll soon sing to 50,000 people at a ballpark.

It's here that the comparison between today's tawdriness and the glories of the past go smash. In the days extending from Charles Dickens (*ibid.*, 13) to Eleanora Duse, who died in 1924 (*ibid.*, 21), people would die of diseases that medical science has either tamed or wiped out — an important issue in a play that has made illness a major trope. The trope includes a recoil action. A man who calls himself a cancer victim is rebuked; "Everyone has cancer, or they will. It's the human condition" (*ibid.*, 21).

Just as vital an issue to McNally, who was being treated for lung cancer while writing the play, is homosexuality. Openly gay people would have felt like exiles in the small town that sites the play. The dead son in *Dedication* could not have been gay like Walter in *PG*. But the warped spinal column, deafness, blindness, and lack of motor skills plaguing Annabelle Willard's baby boy symbolize the depredations of homosexuality to McNally; pre- or early adult males in his work get savaged (e.g., *Door, Bump, Nudity, PG*; a "young, emaciated" Vietcong soldier gets "cut down by a seemingly endless volley of gunfire" in "Botticelli" [*15 Plays* 58–59]). The dead one-year-old's name, Justin (*ibid.*, 60), targets justice, its negating or nullifying, and its astonishing manifestation as an act of divine intervention in a play that includes those heart-rending words from *King Lear*: "As flies to wanton boys, are we to the gods. They kill us for their sport" (4. 1.156–7; *D* 55).

What brings this passage to mind is a rock tune called "Roadkill," which asserts that "we're all gonna get it sooner or later, [and] how we're all just so much roadkill to the gods" (*ibid.*, 55). Nor is this conceit a random spurt of nihilism. Ida Head, the tune's singer and composer, says of her go-fer and lover, "Toby's my soundman. He's the best in the business. Without him I'd sound like shit" (*ibid.*, 21). Yet how does she react to this blessing? Not only does she treat him "like shit" (*ibid.*, 29); she's also thinking of aborting the child she has conceived with him.

Ida, called by Ben Brantley "a self-destructive rock star fresh [i.e., six weeks] out of rehab" (3), admits that she treats her mother like shit in the same conversation where she tells her, "I should be dead" (*D* 46). Ida drips death. Death is closing in on others, too. It's embodied by the play's oldest character, Mrs. Willard, called by Brantley "a terminally ill, rancidly rich misanthrope" who sees life as "a cruel, pain-filled ride to the graveyard" (2005, 1–2). Even the play's subtitle, from Shakespeare's *The Tempest* (iv.1. 156–57), questions the worth of human endeavor. It's no wonder that *Dedication or the Stuff of Dreams* begins in total darkness.

The play follows *The Roller Coaster* and *The Rink* by unfolding in a vast, rundown place that has been forgotten along with the relics and values of its heyday. These reminders of a cherished past have been caught in the same drift as those who have chanced upon them. Following the stage direction that starts the action, "Darkness. Utter. We don't know where we are" (*D* 7), comes the news that Jessie Nuncle is springing her husband Lou a birthday surprise. She has taken him to that magnificent wreck of a playhouse on Main Street that its owner, Mrs. Willard, agreed to open for her and Lou when Jessie told her a lie: that Lou had esophageal cancer.

Her lie worked. Though shut down for decades, the sagging old ruin touches the showman Lou's heart. Lou notes with joy that it has retained signs of its prior splendor, time having spared some of its striking materials and workmanship. Such elegance befits the worthies who performed in this Main Street palace in a town where, today, you can't buy Starbucks coffee or Perrier water.

"It's very humbling" (*ibid.*, 11), Lou says while taking in the faded glory of the old playhouse, a proper response, McNally showed in *Nudity*, to a grand artistic achievement. The stage veteran Lou, who has been toiling together with Jessie in vacant storefronts in strip malls, is the theater's ideal audience. Competition and the prohibitive cost of food, rent, and utilities had driven his and Jessie's Magic Theatre out of New York City. But their love for the not-for-profit children's theater group they founded has survived. The group has continued to do plays like *Old King Cole* and *Little Red Riding Hood*, *The Velveteen Rabbit* and *Peter Pan*, for small, noisy audiences on makeshift stages.

Do these modest productions matter? An approach to the question lies in the breadth and generosity of McNally's view of culture. Lou and Jessie's heroic efforts have a small, but important place in the realm of dramatic art. The couple's devotion to the goal of showing children of all ages the "goodness of hope and love" (*ibid.*, 61) lifts their revels from the ragged fringe of show business. The stage is a fluid, inclusive medium. After denying the existence of gay theater ("Some Thoughts about Myself," *Two Plays* x), McNally said through a character in *LVC*, "There's no such thing as gay music" (*ibid.*, 57).

He dislikes labels because of the limits they pose. At times, such as when Mrs. Willard's chauffeur, Edward, explains his addiction to soap operas (*D* 49), McNally seems to be putting all representative art on a par. The idea resonates. When Ida calls her lucrative branch of show business "dog-eat-dog," Lou tells her that children's theater is "[c]ompletely vicious" (*ibid.*, 25), too. His branch of showbiz also resembles Ida's aesthetically. Good writing, clever sets, and inspired acting don't insure success in either field. But without such pluses, success is unlikely anywhere in stage production.

A performer's greatest gift, though, is his/her devotion. Lou rates it a good night's work if his performance made one child feel loved and wanted, a feat that calls for an actor's total commitment to his materials. Jessie says of the "Theatre Anonymous" she has created with Lou, "It's not the Big Apple.

It's not even a small apple. I feel blessed" (*ibid.*, 28). The mid-fortyish stage veterans Jessie and Lou are more professional than the mega-rock star Ida, who faults the Main Street theater her elders find so impressive. Neither the technical gear needed to mount one of her shows nor the audience needed to earn the show a profit would fit into it. It's too small.

But the former Texan McNally, who never equates size with quality, is friendlier to Ida's rock-and-roll extravaganzas than *she* is to legit theater. Her claim that she's a creative artist whereas her mother merely reproduces lines "written by someone else" (*ibid.*, 45) recalls his decision to make Stephen of *LT* an editor rather than a novelist or a doctor. Painting landscapes takes more skill than photographing them; it's harder to run track than to drive a motorcycle. Also to Ida's credit is her singing her own songs before tens of thousands of shouting, screaming fans, many of whom saved up for weeks to see one of her concerts. The Magic Theatre plays to small, ill-equipped houses.

This contrast bleeds into the mother-daughter rivalry powering it. It's more counter-supportive than oppositional. Ida claims that legit theater is dead. But she based her song, "Roadkill," on *Lear*. In her small way, she has, like McNally, shown performance art to be a mansion with many rooms. Even before her arrival on stage, he had inferred the synergy between house and stage by distributing the action of *Dedication* in the seats, aisles, and balconies of the Main Street theatre, which sometimes staged vaudeville shows along with the plays of Shakespeare and readings by literary giants.

The play has lowered the barrier between highbrow and commercial popular art. At times, it even favors the Children's Theatre; Ida's fine singing voice goes unheard amid the shouts and screams of her audiences. Lou and Jessie have different problems. Harder to please than adults, children are also more resistant to dramatic illusions. Their shorter attention spans make them impatient and restless faster than adults, too. Another contrast: Having already compromised their youthful ideals in order to follow a safer middle course, adults relish the chance to glimpse the road not taken. Children live closer to the world of wonders, which makes them harder to convince or impress. Lacking experience, they have few disbeliefs to suspend.

* * *

The abundance of shams, counterfeits, and lies flooding *Dedication* wards off the suspension of adult disbelief, as well. Lou and Jessie, who live together, claim to be husband and wife. They have created an illusion so intertwined with both their jobs and daily public routine that their neighbors have no reason to question it. Mrs. Willard's reference to "the great theatrical tradition of lying" (*ibid.*, 61), spoken five minutes before final curtain, forces us to reinterpret much of what we had been looking at. Mrs. Willard had been told some big lies. For instance, Lou told her that Jessie was his wife, a designation that, in its falsity, belies the name of their act, "Captain Lou and *Mrs.* Jessie..." (*ibid.*, 35, emphasis mine).

Lies are the order of the day. Jessie, who, says Lou, "tells ... awful lies" (*ibid.*, 25), had already lied to stage-four cancer victim Mrs. Willard — about her supposedly sick husband Lou's having cancer — to coax her into opening the Main Street theater as a birthday gift to him (*ibid.*, 15). Mrs. Willard invites lies. Her chauffeur, Edward, cheated to get elected Mr. Vermont. Even his muscles and 6 percent body fat might not have won him the same prize in his home state of New Jersey, whose greater numbers posed him stiffer competition.

Mrs. Willard rightly calls him a cheat (*ibid.*, 52). More dishonest than she knew, Edward lied on his résumé about having attended Yale. His past deserves more scrutiny than she gave it before hiring him. Invoking the naked wrestling scene in Lawrence's *Women in Love* (1920), Edward's offer to wrestle the older, out-of-shape Lou invites the possibility that he, a gay man, has spotted Lou as a fellow homosexual. But what does his boss's calling him a cheat amount to? Her wig is a false sign intended to deceive others. She seems less genuine than Edward, whose workouts for the Mr. Vermont contest forced him to either maintain or regain the physique he had when he wrestled for SUNY-Binghamton.

All this has registered with her. Before Lou kills her to end her suffering, the two of them discuss *Othello*. She had asked to be smothered by a pillow, which is how Othello killed Desdemona. But Lou stands as far from Othello as this dying crone does from Desdemona. No general, he's a make-believe captain whose homosexuality might have barred him from military service. The younger, stronger, and more violence-prone Edward would have been a much better choice as Mrs. Willard's assassin. His misanthropic pottymouthed boss had reasons of her own to pick Lou for the job.

McNally has revived the idea that the drama, like any other art form, thrives on the synergy generated between audience and artifact. The Stendhal Syndrome, we recall, hails art's power to raze the life-art dualism. The transports flown into by over-stimulated listeners of Wagner's *Tristan* exert greater force than the protocols observed by most stage audiences (*TM, SS* 27) — but not always those on Main Street, where *Dedication* unfolds. Bimbi, who explained the Syndrome in *Nudity*, felt humbled by the majesty of *David*, as does Lou when he first saw the Main Street theatre. She had also discussed the statue's nakedness with her clients.

Humility and nakedness join hands in *Dedication*. The great art that overwhelms us also leaves us defenseless or naked. We feel marooned and weak. The encounter between our contingency and the perfection of *David* or the Taj Mahal is no standoff or mirror meeting. But it signals the perfection within us that lets us be shaken by artistic beauty. Many different art-related things can shake us. Lou was humbled before the present-tense action of *Dedication* when a show he had designed the lights for in Cape Cod continued to play after he caused the power outage that would send him to the hospital (McNally, *D* 11).

He needs more taking-down. Nor will it happen on its own. Mrs. Willard must prepare him for it. She mentions *Othello* minutes before her death (*ibid.*, 60) not merely to facilitate his rite of passage but, mostly, to remind him of the transforming magic of the stage; death can beget life, even if the begetters fail at the job of everyday life. Recording this transformation is the name she makes Lou promise to give the theater she has bequeathed to him in exchange for killing her. Justin Makepeace Willard was the severely damaged son she murdered at age one. *Ars longis, vita brevis*, the play reminds us when, in an act of rough justice, Justin's mercy killer targets herself for a mercy killing. Accounts have been squared. Perhaps more than squared: Its new name will strengthen the old nameless theater's hold on life as Mrs. Willard gives birth to her son a second time.

The peacemaking confirmed by this passage came at the expense of brutal birth pangs, turning Justin's middle name into another of the play's ambiguous signs. Nor is it the play's last. *Dedication* might have been subtitled *The Stuff of Nightmares*. To the inapt strains of Tchaikovsky's *Sleeping Beauty*, the dying old Mrs. Willard puts up "tremendous resistance" in her "violent, ugly struggle" (*ibid.*, 62) with her murderer-deliverer. Invoked in this mortal combat is one like it where a savagely resentful Pip uses excessive force to rescue his false fairy godmother Miss Havisham from a fire in *Great Expectations*.

McNally had prepared for Mrs. Willard's death by murder. Besides mentioning Dickens (*ibid.*, 13), he referred to both *A Christmas Carol* (*ibid.*, 47) and *A Tale of Two Cities* (*ibid.*, 54); too, the justice theme in *Dedication* harks to *Oliver Twist* and *Bleak House*. Germane to these references, both stated and implied, are Dickensian names like Lou Nuncle, Ida Head, and Arnold Chalk together with Mrs. Willard's noting, in great pain, "the great theatrical tradition of lying to the audience" (*ibid.*, 61). The villain in *Great Expectations* is the actor Compeyson, who compounded his villainy — he jilted Miss Havisham at the altar — by taking up a career in forgery (the wicked Peter Quint in James's *Turn of the Screw* also has an actorish air).

Dickens, who might have performed at the old Main Street showplace (*ibid.*, 13), would discover the tie-in between the lies that fuel stage drama and those that hasten death. He died within hours after appearing on a stage (Simon Gray, *Little Nell* [London: Faber, 2006: 48–50, 53]). Dickens called himself "the Inimitable," just as the actor-counterfeit husband Lou will refer to "the inimitable Jessie Nuncle" (McNally, *D* 9) while groping in the dark in Act One (darkness and fog were the governing metaphors of *Bleak House*). And while the celebrated novelist Dickens won added fame for both his acting and his dramatic readings, so does Mrs. Willard, Miss Havisham's reverse alter ego, gain a proxy immortality. The art that mirrors life can also mirror art, even though it may need the ruptures and cacophonies of black comedy to smooth its way. The wicked witch Mrs. Willard will be reborn as a fairy godmother.

This infanticide needs the help of the bogus husband Lou, whose alleged wife Jessie, in another skewed mirror image, disconnected *her* terminally ill mother from life support (*ibid.*, 59). Mrs. Willard wants to die. She also dictates the way she'll die. Unknown to Lou, she had watched him re-enact the defining moment of his childhood: putting on his mother's "beautiful big skirt" (*ibid.*, 40) and then twirling very quickly to flare it around him. The Dickensian coincidence of her eavesdropping on Lou decided both the identity of her killer and the style of her killing. Moments before her death, she asks Lou to twirl for her; an angry Lou is more likely to kill her than a calm one. The play's interdependence theme has reasserted its force. The help he extends Mrs. Willard will recur in reverse; she had predicated her gift to him of the old theater upon his agreement to kill her. What's more, she knows how to enforce the agreement or contract. Lou discovers himself by twirling, his circular movement restoring him to his starting point; performing doesn't build character so much as reveal it. Mrs. Willard has hedged her bets. Before dying, she says to him four times, "If what you told me was the truth" (*ibid.*, 41). She judged well to count on his honesty. His dancing his way to the truth made his words on the subject irrelevant.

If her watching him twirl for the first time is a contrivance, it doesn't hurt *Dedication*. A play in which everything is perfect is a waxwork. A play that's alive is never perfect. Mrs. Willard helped send Lou back to his childhood, where, like ours, most of the important truths of his life lodge. This vital connection will improve both his acting and his understanding of the theater, which is useful; he has room for improvement. For instance, his hatred of Shakespeare (*ibid.*, 17) belies his frequent practice of either quoting or referring to plays like *Henry V*, *Julius Caesar* (*ibid.*), *Romeo and Juliet* (*ibid.*, 31), and *Othello* (*ibid.*, 58). Having connected with his inner child will strengthen his tie with Shakespeare, giving his acting more resources to draw from. The Main Street theatre's owner-to-be has also expanded upon Jessie's words about the place: "If these walls could talk, they would shame us with their eloquence" (*ibid.*, 56).

Some words uttered by Mrs. Willard in anguish before her death, "The pain is coming more and more frequently, rather like labor pains" (*ibid.*, 60), recall the moment that foreshadowed them, itself enhanced by Ida's boyfriend-sound man's practice of calling her "Eye" (e.g., *ibid.*, 54). This handful of motifs conjures up, in McNally's family drama about dead mothers and a murdered son who happened to be blind, Sophocles' *Oedipus Rex*. It also puts us a short step away from Hector Charlotte's saying in *Nudity*, while looking at *David*, "I could stand here forever and still truly not see it" (McNally, *SS* 20). Yes, the more we give of ourselves to a work of art, the more we gain from it. But this outlay of time and imaginative effort also tells us how much we're missing; the greater the artifact, the more it withholds. *Dedication* is an enigma much of whose power lies in the surmised and the deliberately withheld. But we've not been trapped in a zero-sum game. Opening in complete darkness, the play will light the path to this enigmatic power.

Behind every fortune lies a great crime, Balzac pronounced. If his pronouncement also refers to the stage, then Lou must resist caving in to the guilt bound up with his role in fathering the new Justin Makepeace Willard Center of the Performing Arts. He'll struggle. The moral darkness he's implicated in, as evocative in its evil as Shakespeare's later contemporaries John Webster and Thomas Middleton, builds around him. Lou is twirling at play's end, dressed as a rabbit, a symbol of fecundity. But what will his progeny be like? Jessie has just assured him, Her Prince Charming, of her love. She's replaced on stage, though, by Mrs. Willard dressed as the Fairy Godmother, whom Lou addresses, having missed his cue in the script being enacted. Then he starts twirling as the stage goes to black.

Fantasy has overthrown his identity as Jessie's Prince Charming. He talks about a little boy from the past named Louis Nuncle (*D* 63). The infantile fantasy he's acting out could sink him — and the Children's Theatre with it. Occurring at his moment of triumph — the launching of the Willard Center — it reminds us that the suicide of the Conductor in *Prelude and Liebestod* coincided with *his* great breakthrough. Frontain called "Lou's involvement with children's theater ... a sign of his sexual and emotional immaturity" ("Trafficking" 114, n.5). Lou's delirium reverses Oscar Wilde's claim that artistic creation is a means of self-avoidance, not self-expression. The claim also invokes the title of McNally's 2004 play, subtitle and all. Lou has reverted to childhood because he no longer has an adult self to express, if he ever did; the death of Justin's murderer has made childhood safe for him. He had made a career of children's theater to escape the snarls of adulthood. Sounding like a fugitive, he said of the small town where he and Jessie had taken their act, "I thought we were safe, Jess and I, with our little theatre" (*D* 54).

He thought wrong. As in *Oedipus Rex*, the enemy has already settled inside the gates, except that he seems at times more of a savior. Lou was addressing Arnold Chalk, the theater troupe's indispensable tech director, when he bemoaned at another time the shattering of his illusion of safety. Echoing developments in both *F&J* and *Deuce*, Arnold's wife abandoned him and his two sons before the play's present-tense action. His unpaid dogsbody's work with the troupe — some of which is technical — includes replacing dead fuses, picking up programs at the printer's, and prompting the on-stage actors. Without his help, the troupe would fold. He notices everything. "A dirty theatre usually means an indifferent production" (*ibid.*, 25), he says while sweeping the stage of Mrs. Willard's old showplace, even though it hasn't hosted an event for decades. Everything theatrical fascinates him, another trait he shares with McNally, who made him English for the same reason that he's not a stage actor: to lend distance and thus weight to his statements about drama in America. His status as both insider and outsider recalls the setting of "Teachers' Break," a coffee lounge inside of the high school where the play's action occurs. Most of the theater history in the play comes from him, and it's all delightful.

One can see why Jessie has been sleeping with him. Why she won't marry him and be a mother to his sons, whom she loves, is another question. In this regard, Lou's homosexuality has receded from the status of the love that dare not speak its name to that of the love that must be stifled and denied — no great setback for him. As befits a man with a very low sex drive, he tells Jessie late in the play, "I've forgotten what it's like to be held" (*ibid.*, 57). He's a stranger to the healing power of touch. *Dedication* owes as much to Henry James on this score as it does to D. H. Lawrence. Something momentous has been broached but was left hanging fire. The love triangle centering on Jessie will persist even though she's "not very proud" (*ibid.*, 43) of her place in it. It's easy to agree with her. She comes home to Lou most nights reeking of the sex she just enjoyed with Arnold. Yet Lou knows that the sex means so much to her that he tries to ignore it.

His goodwill might be misplaced. Even though the survival of the Children's Theatre depends upon the love triangle, the cost may be too high. McNally makes this point through selection. Instead of revolving around one parody of marriage, the play adds another. Jessie and Arnold have been lovers for three years, leaving them and Lou stalemated. Gerard Raymond of the *Advocate* had it right when he said in 2005, "*Dedication* examines the price people pay for the fulfillment of their dreams" (67).

Has it all been worth it?, we wonder. McNally, whose *Lisbon Traviata*, *Master Class*, and *Nudity* also looked at art as a vehicle of self-avoidance, contrasts dreams, including the ones that appear in the subtitle of *Dedication*, to what Freud called the reality principle. Dreams, said Freud, forswear the objective world because of their unreason, incoherence, and antisocial impulses. The dreamer gets what reality denies him; dreams fulfill his secret wishes (Chapter III of *The Interpretation of Dreams* is called "A Dream Is the Fulfillment of a Wish") heedless of the wreckage he trails behind him.

Goals are reached more easily in dreams than in waking life. But the claims of waking life persist. Dreaming in *Dedication*, which torques on the theater, brings to mind Prospero's last-act monologue in *The Tempest*, the passage that supplies the play's subtitle. Yet a committed stage artist like Jessie, whose heart, says Lou, is "right" (*D* 16) and whom Mrs. Willard calls "a good person" (*ibid.*, 59), will devote her life to the theater. She has drawn the sting from Mrs. Willard's "great theatrical tradition of lying" (*ibid.*, 61). She sews and knits costumes, acts and sings, and swaps free tickets for publicity with local businessmen. The energies that high-caliber people like her direct to *any* endeavor ennoble it. She knows that good drama can turn the lies that stump Mrs. Willard into a great overarching truth.

* * *

And what of Lou's energies? The imaginative effort McNally invested in this stranger to physical passion (*ibid.*, 58) makes the question intriguing. Again echoing Oedipus, Lou stands at a crossroad in both his career and personal life. Called by Brantley "one of McNally's agonizingly conflicted souls" (2005, 2), he feels his future mashed up with his past. Whatever erotic impulses stir inside him he aims at other men, which weakens his hold on both Jessie and his live-in arrangement with her. He's complicit in this travesty of marriage because he cherishes it despite his unfitness as a husband. Lou Nuncle resembles a loon(y) uncle, a role that bans him from fatherhood. He teaches other people's kids, an arrangement with drawbacks as well as rewards. His pupils leave him after acting class to return home. Only briefly does he stand in lieu of their parents.

The words (lune, lunatic, and lunacy) also come to mind in one of *Dedication*'s affinities to *F&J* (Mrs. Willard's statement, "This isn't small talk" [*ibid.*, 60], voiced at a time of physical agony harks to Johnny's insisting to Frankie during a fraught moment, "This isn't small talk. This is enormous talk" [*Three Plays* 112]). Lou has dropped out of the pragmatic materialistic society that dismisses him as a loon or lunatic. A lunatic, or moon-gazer, he is. He depends upon the money-driven society whose strictures he has disavowed. But his total dedication to his not-for-profit children's theater conveys McNally's — and John Fowles's and Dostoevsky's — belief that any society's health depends on nonconformists like him who are ruled by a sense of wonder and awe that clashes with the pragmatism of the marketplace. Perhaps he deserves to be admired rather than dismissed. His faith in life's beauty has made him an arch-individualist in a society built on rugged individualism and self-reliance. His actions support his beliefs. His immaturity, if he is immature, has a big upside. He chose children's theater as a career because he knew the importance of instilling values like love and hope in young audiences. That he's a good teacher as well as a good actor (*D* 28) rates high with McNally, a former student of Mrs. Maurine McElroy, whose memory he cherished enough, 50 years after studying with her, to put her name in the play (*D* 31) and, 9 years after that, to praise her in a commencement address at his alma mater, Columbia College (web).

McNally thinks more of Lou than Lou does of himself. He's ridden with self-doubt, the plight of the kind and the caring in McNally, himself the target in his teens of gibes from crypto Texas he-men he dismissed rationally but, unfortunately, not emotionally. Lou's remark to Jessie, "Sometimes I feel like such a failure" (*ibid.*, 16), shows him both worn down and hurting in a way that McNally could relate to. Lou also feels stressed. The time has come for him, in his mid-forties (McNally was 65 when *Dedication* premiered), to set down roots. He can do this by securing his commitments. It's time for him to act. The action of *Dedication* occurs on his birthday. Coincidentally, his de facto stepdaughter Ida will announce on this day that she's pregnant. Lou has to parlay these signs of renewal with an effort of his own, and it must come from within, even if he can't explain it.

This duty to himself he accepts; he tells Ida that the Children's Theatre has been kept alive by love. To Ida's attempt to define this love ("Of children? The Theatre?" she asks), he replies for her, "Of everything." Arnold sides with him: "Good answer, Lou" (*ibid.*, 26). Ida, who was looking for something more concrete, disagrees. She's misguided. What looks like evasiveness to her is a powerful, all-swathing reality. Lou lives it rather than analyzing it. Like the "little, nameless, unremembered acts of kindness and love" from Wordsworth's childhood noted in "Tintern Abbey," the Children's Theatre is prized for itself. To define it would be to miss — and perhaps smudge — the magic of the Magic Theatre for Children of All Ages. By saying that he wants to stage plays "that make children ... confident about their future" and "that make them want to be better people" (*ibid.*, 61–62), Lou has redefined maleness. He doesn't need Eddie's "rock-hard" (*ibid.*, 52) abs.

Yes, his spirit flags. He needs Jessie's help to keep the project going in "a town that neither appreciates it nor deserves it" (*ibid.*, 16). He faces other constraints, like sickness, which can strike anywhere. Arnold, who's as vital a force to the Theatre as Jessie and Lou, is recovering from a heart attack (*ibid.*, 17–18). The esophageal cancer that killed Jessie's mother, that Lou fakes, and that's ravaging Mrs. Willard darkens the play's action, as do her words, perhaps all the more for being spoken in delirium: "Everyone has cancer, or they will. It's the human condition. We all have cancer and we're all going to die" (*ibid.*, 61).

Cancer has the same corrosive force in *Dedication* that the will has in

Schopenhauer; no sooner is one wish granted than we will another, and the granting of a wish always lacks the might of one that's frustrated. But Schopenhauer added that this corrosiveness could vanish in the joys of great theater, especially Shakespeare. Lou may be close to renouncing his hatred of Shakespeare (*ibid.*, 17). He has made some vital first steps. His twirling at final curtain, a reprise of a similar act he performed as a child, charts a regression he may never snap out of. But it could also show him moving forward by moving backward, a major trope in American novels like Fitzgerald's *Gatsby* (1925), Ellison's *Invisible Man* (1952), and Bellow's *Augie March* (1953). Echoes also sound from McNally's other work. Lou's off-script twirl looks freakish and goofy as do similar gestures toward self-authentication in *Bump*, *LVC*, and *The Full Monty*. Confronting his past could give Lou the self-command he praised as the theme of *Cyrano de Bergerac*: "[U]nless we know who we truly are we can never experience the true love of another" (*ibid.*, 36).

But acting on these words takes self-command. The self he has unearthed is that of a cross-dressing child, a role that sorts ill with the world he's being reborn into. The local bank that shut down after years of operation implies the disregard he can expect from the adult world of getting-and-spending. Other options? The rigors of the stage, now that he has revived a dead theater, will test him deeply. He has the advantage of knowing that cancer doesn't have the final say. Like Ida's song, "Roadkill," the melodrama that culminated in the opening of the Willard Center has shown him the kinship between life and death.

These defining realities share a lot of common ground. Arnold brings a gallows and a snow machine (snow symbolizing death, as in Joyce's "The Dead" and Frost's "Stopping by Snowy Woods") from the pit, where the props of the Main Street Theatre had been stored. Toby tested for safety the guillotine included in Arnold's haul. But had Ida put her head into its groove to demonstrate the hologram effect of her song, she'd have died. The blade on the guillotine severs the head of a broom from its shaft even though Toby had locked the safety. Randomness and absurdity have routed reason again. Nor is anybody standing on the stage alongside the guillotine cheered by the knowledge that a beheading symbolizes sexual murder as in Oscar Wilde's *Salomé*, (*ibid.*, 13) which is staged in *A Man of No Importance*.

Lou's career choice of children's theater has been screening him from the kinship great art has always had with danger and pain (nowhere does the play mention the *Märchen* tradition of goblins and trolls associated with the Brothers Grimm). But he might have been fooling himself. Pain cuts a broad swathe in *Dedication*. A reference to "pearl onions" (*ibid.*, 14) and the phrase "casting pearls before swine" (*ibid.*, 31), both of which come from Jessie, link beauty to pain; a pearl's formation around a grain of sand coincides with the pain afflicting its mollusk host. *Dedication* discloses the link between art and danger much more quickly. While Lou is marveling at the faded elegance of the Main Street Theatre, he and Jessie are standing near an open trap door they could have stepped fatally into. Arnold, who opened the door, is standing beneath them in the pit. He probably overheard Lou and Jessie's conversation, too. But he didn't warn them about the trap door.

The portent holds. Only a lie and an act of murder will revive the theater where Lou and Jessie could have fallen to their deaths. This offspring of Albee's statement from *The Zoo Story* about needing to go a great distance out of one's way to cover a short distance correctly (30) argues that prizes of great value come at a high cost. By contrast, the lovemaking of Jessie and Arnold occurs in the aftermath of Mrs. Willard's cackling to Lou, "Fuck me" and "Fuck me again" (*D* 39). She'll settle, hours later, for a twirling exhibition. "I'm giving you my theatre. You're giving me yourself" (*ibid.*, 41), she says, redeeming her earlier obscenity by re-tuning it as a potential birth scene. She's helping Lou discover himself in a bargain that began as an overture too monstrous to consider.

But not out of context; her ugly words square with the vulgarity surrounding Joshua's birth in *Corpus Christi* ("You have some kid chewing on your tits and see how you like it" [*CC* 20]). Mary, who spoke these words, also pronounces, "I'm a woman who loves to dance" (*ibid.*, 25). Lou Nuncle will discover *him*self by twirling, or dancing. His description of himself twirling as a child in his mother's dress as a drowning into life (*D* 40) foreshadows his readiness for the ordeal of murdering Mrs. Willard — a consummation that began with her lewd proposition; there's only room for one woman, Jessie, in his intimate circle. Exclusiveness remains a prod. That neither his blood mother nor her symbolic stand-in ever twirled makes him unique; twirling belongs to him alone. His equating twirling with his survival (*ibid.*) inscribes his drifting with the one current in the heaving, tossing action of the great sea mother that has kept him alive.

Sex and death had already fused in Ida's thoughts about having an abortion. These thoughts chime at a different level with both Jessie's mercy killing of her blood mother and Lou's, of his surrogate mother Mrs. Willard. Family love faces stiff odds in *Dedication*. Jessie's love for Arnold's sons has the comfort of distance. What would she do about them if Arnold had another, fatal, heart attack after marrying her, as he wants to do? She has been blaming herself for the self-destructiveness of Ida, whose father didn't want Jessie to have her. Does she regret ignoring his advice? Perhaps he foresaw the high cost of Ida's emergence as a singing, or talking head in a musical extravaganza (*ibid.*, 28); his last name was Head.

Speaking of her history of drug abuse, Ida had said, "I should be dead" (*ibid.*, 46). Nor, a scant six weeks out of drug rehab, has she fought clear of death. But death remains a threat. Her CDs have titles like *Lies My Mother Taught Me* and *The Curse of a Broken Heart*. Mike's words in *LT* resonate here: "What a fucked-up time we picked to live in" (*Three Plays* 53). Why shouldn't Ida write and sing songs about curses, lies, and roadkill? Her America is morally depleted, politically torn, and on the brink of a depression. Her father also abandoned her when she was small. Tuning herself to this depredation has tapped into her country's malaise. It has also, logically if also painfully, won her a big following.

Life's horrors have found a home in upstate New York, where they still cloud her psyche; it's appropriate that she has come here, too. Just as she's struggling to stay drug free, she and the people of her past barely make contact. Denial and evasion have replaced the apologies found in McNally's earlier works like *F&J* and *LT*. Replying to obscenities, they say things like, "It hurts my ears" ([Mrs. Willard:] *D* 75), "I hate that word" ([Jessie:] *ibid.*, 42), and "I don't like that word" ([Lou:] 51). They also shrink from hard questions and tough decisions. The play's brightest moment, the re-opening and re-dedication of the old showplace, leaves behind it a trail of misery and lies; the lies Jessie told Mrs. Willard about Lou line up with the ones Ida sings about. What's equally important, the Willard Center is a gift, its donor a *dea ex machina*. So much for Yankee diligence and grit. It's the Englishman Arnold whose unpaid efforts will keep the Center afloat.

McNally's darkest play to date also indicts marriage. Now, McNally hasn't redefined marriage as Simon Gray (who in 1982 adapted into English Molière's *Tartuffe*, the action of which gets resolved by a *deus ex machina*) did in works like *Butley* (1971) and *Close of Play* (1979). Instead *Dedication* holds a mirror to the deformities and anxieties of its age. The mates of Jessie and Arnold have both fled. Ida is thinking of dumping Toby despite knowing that, without him, both her life and her art will nosedive. Along with Lou, Arnold, and her mother, she and Toby are living a parody of marriage they've enacted by default. This young singing sensation treats like shit the two most important people in her life, her mother and her techie-lover, Toby, whose expertise keeps *her* from sounding like shit. Ida needs all of it. As is seen in the subjects of her songs, lies, heartbreak, and roadkill, she's already mired in shit. Professional success for her flies in the face of both peace of mind and happiness. Her success has precluded self-acceptance. It's no wonder she's a junkie.

Taking the coward's way out, she and Toby's elders set no better example. They fear that any change in their collective *raison d'être* could cave in the Children's Theatre. They may be right. Lou's words, "A stage trap represents the bowels of the earth, where evil and depravity lie" (*ibid.*, 18–19), apply to Arnold, who first comes into view rising from the pit beneath him and Jessie.

If the treasure he brings from below, e.g., Sophie Ticker's handkerchief and James O'Neill's steamer trunk, invokes Satan's tempting Christ with earthly treasure (a scene described in *CC* [37–38]), it also channels the truth that the Children's Theatre needs Arnold as much as it does Jessie and Lou. As in Hawthorne's "The Birthmark," good and bad have knit so tightly in the Theatre that any attempts to improve it will topple it, perhaps fatally. The bowels of the earth, indeed; a false step, and theater people of two generations could drown in a tsunami of shit.

Thus Lou and Arnold don't deserve praise for voicing their respect for the legitimacy of each other's claim on Jessie. They're merely shoring up a stand previously taken, having connived to reinstate a status quo that's breaking them down. The working premises of their love triangle are evasion and denial. They're like card players who have tacitly agreed both to cheat and be cheated by each other in their nightly game. Running their life and their art together has stripped them of options.

* * *

Dedication opens like *Nudity*, another dramatized treatise on the life-art dualism. Some people (two, though, not four) are marveling at an art object of great beauty. Standing in for Bimbi, the tour guide in Florence's Accademia Gallery, will be a third party, Arnold Chalk. Arnold reviews the proud history of the ramshackle Main Street Theatre, citing Edwin Booth, Sarah Bernhardt, and Houdini among the luminaries who performed there. Then he adds, "This is your history, America. Why are you so careless with it?" (*D* 13) A ray of hope briefly pierces the gloom caused by his indictment. Ida appears on stage to mend fences with Jessie. But her fence-mending scheme lacks common ground; her roaring success as a rock star and her self-destructiveness clash with Jessie's quiet resignation to professional obscurity.

Other problems loom. Lou had introduced conflict even before Ida's first on-stage appearance. Despite his denials, he *has* been "pissy" (*ibid.*, 19) lately, more than a birthday celebrant should be. He's quick to take offense. When told by Jessie that anything, even the acoustics inside a building, can have "balls," he snaps back, "Was that a dig?" But nearly immediately, any doubts about his manhood dissolve when he says "I thought we were going to have kinky sex on my birthday" (*ibid.*, 9). Did we misread his disquiet about lacking balls? The uncertainty has snagged our attention.

And held it; Arnold's appearance on stage from below revives the issue of sex. After Arnold accuses America of dissing her past, Lou tells him, "If you're so unhappy in this country" (*ibid.*, 13). He needn't finish his thought.

Later, he'll accuse Arnold of saying, "Everything is better in the English theatre" (*ibid.*, 18), a charge Arnold denies with Jessie's support. Lou *is* pissy. But why? Nothing we've seen has made us doubt that he and Jessie are happily married.

Our a-verbal answer to this question explodes at curtain up for Act Two, which finds Jessie and Arnold kissing and clinching prior to debating their future together. Mrs. Willard's appalling mock offer of sex had ended Act One. But its shock was rhetorical. Here, it's physical, and it's backed up by a solid offer. Arnold wants Jessie to marry him and be a mother to his two sons, whom she already loves. He adds that she needs a husband who can give her sex. McNally had clinched this point the way a playwright should — by showing Arnold and Jessie being close; our seeing them locked together impacts us more than being told about their revels.

The play had been moving toward sex. Lou's fiddling with a light board blew out all the circuits in the Cape Cod theater where he was working as technical director. By contrast, Arnold quickly repairs the faulty old fuse box in the Main Street Theatre. Why shouldn't he? The existence of his two sons describes him as a circuit maker. He can give Jessie a fuller life than Lou. Perhaps, though, she's to be admired for staying with Lou, as she had promised. Less praiseworthy, as she admits, is her practice of coming home to Lou carrying in her vaginal vault Arnold Chalk's chalk-white discharge.

Love triangles always prove destructive in the canon. In *Dedication*, the motif evokes the Henry James of *The Wings of the Dove*. By trying to please everybody in her makeshift family, Jessie has brought them and herself to grief. Outwardly entertaining and seemingly effortless in its fluency, *Dedication*'s insights into human behavior are more intricate and deep-driving than they first seem. Mrs. Willard's end-of-act offer to Lou has left a residue. The play sets off a domino effect of visual, political, and psychological associations that lead to a maze of murky emotions, most of them referring to the tidal pull of sex. There are ways to hammer a bloke besides telling him he lacks balls.

III

Balls, sacrifice, and *Mut* (the German word for courage) also galvanize *Master Class*. This one-set play unfurls in a recital hall of New York's Juilliard School of Music in the early 1970s, several years after Maria Callas, the adjunct professor conducting the class, had stopped singing professionally. The petulant, obstructive Callas will emerge as something more than a stock villainess. Even while striking attitudes of magisterial coldness, she retains audience appeal. McNally's 1995 Tony Award-winner puts a complicated larger-than-life firebrand on center stage who does evil and to whom evil has been done. The play captures chinks and gleams of her oddities, her acidic frivolity, professional pride, fear of aging, and fragile psychological intelligence — and, through it all, the honesty and balls that helped make her a superstar. Toby Zinman both saluted this achievement and suggested how the play treats it in *Variety*: "'Master Class' is about *courage* and the discipline it takes to make great art. The play ... celebrates the value of technique and rigor, of intense, self-sacrificial commitment to the work" (Zinman, "Tryout" 6).

Its disruption of ordinary habits of perception and understanding moves *Master Class* toward the modernism of Joyce and Picasso, both of whom shifted their focus from the what to the how of it. McNally's *Prelude and Liebestod* (1989) had already made art the subject of his artistry while discounting any conventional hierarchy of events behind plot-making. Disavowing artistic gradations again, he based *Whiskey* (1973) on a fictional TV soap opera. Much of the fast, allusive *IOAP* (1985) consists of talk about acting by actors, a director, and a playwright . The undated satire "Hidden Agendas" gives insights into post-mid-century theatrical production.

These works primed McNally to portray in later plays like *Nudity*, *Dedication*, and *Master Class* the mysteries of sculpting, the staging of plays, and singing. Addressing the same messianic fervor that drives the artist, *Golden Age* includes in *its* scope the impulses governing opera production. These plays rate people over theory or ideology. While making art the subject of art, all of them probe the effects of an artistic career upon the artist. The process peaks in *MC*, an international saga of hatred, abandonment and sacrifice, cruelty and endurance. Charles Spencer has explained the time setting of the play: "La Divina [comes before us] in her later years, when the singer's voice was shot and Aristotle Onassis had dumped her for Jackie Kennedy" (2). She has been trying to forget these heartbreaking losses. Above all, she wants others either to forget or deny them, too. Her misguided persuader? Although her halcyon days have passed, she expects all the perks and privileges of a diva in full prime.

The action of *MC* outpaces the constraints of both the physical world and the rational one that try to hold it in check. With the travel, the politics, and the drudgery of rehearsals behind her, Maria indulges thoughts and feelings about intensely personal matters. Introspection is the play's staple. With expert control over her inner world, McNally gives her self-communion the depth and privacy of an Ingmar Bergman movie. His main strategy, harvested from *F&J*, *P&L*, and *LT*, shows him playing the prosaic against the highly sensitized. It works. By framing Maria dramatically in a psychological space that swings between cognition and the unconscious, McNally also respects her inner mystery, i.e., that region of variables and imponderables that keeps her, finally, unknowable, even to herself.

This enigma leaves McNally unfazed. His portrayal of the daily needs in the routine of his prima donna shows no signs of strains and hits no false notes. It renders both the woman and the diva, depicting those sharp, desperate edges of loss and fear that have taken her to where she can't tell her two selves apart; it's not for nothing that her initials also supply the first letter in both words of the play's two-word title. This mirroring effect includes risks. With an instinct for music that is nearly frightening, she tells a soprano who's singing a passage from Verdi's *Macbetto*, "This isn't just an opera. It's your life" (*MC* 50). Later she recalls singing years before the same "letter scene" aria her student is practicing. Is her life wheeling in tired circles? "Ambizioso spirito/ Tu sei, Macbetto." Within moments, having remembered singing the same phrase she's now listening to, she exclaims, "Ah, Verdi! Ah, Shakespeare! Ah, my own ambition!" (*ibid.*, 56)

Memory and desire have collided. She's soon telling her elderly husband, Battista Meneghini, a tireless champion of her career whom she'll later drop to take up with Onassis, "We have made as unholy a pact as Macbeth and his lady" (*ibid.*, 58). She has walked that fabled crossroad where blues master Robert Johnson said he gave his soul to the devil. Her next words, "I've become thin" (*ibid.*), refer to the weight she shed to become La Divina, an ordeal that included both the loss of humanity ("Love can wait" [*ibid.*], she told Meneghini) and the setting down the of demonic roots of great art. The evening she crowned herself the Queen of La Scala (*ibid.*, 57), starry-eyed from her 37 curtain calls, also marked her bolt from Battista. Such cruelty comes easily to someone whose success has twisted her values.

Hilton Als has summarized this fraught drama and its effects on her:

> Callas met the Greek shipping tycoon Aristotle Onassis in 1957, while she was married to an Italian industrialist ... Meneghini, whose money and management skills had propelled her career forward. Two years later, she had left her husband, and she spent the rest of her life in love with Onassis, who eventually dumped her for Jacqueline Kennedy (whom he married in 1968). Callas's sadness over this lost love distanced her more and more from the world in which she had made her name [72].

Like *Dedication*, another study of stage art and artists, *MC* is one of those plays in which not much happens but which brims with characters and incident all the same. It's a life study, as its initials imply, but one portrayed with dazzling brio. We share Maria's triumphs and troubles alike. Her inner awakening is also handled so gracefully that it doesn't feel clichéd or stilted. Its pacing is so unhurried, i.e., slow but smooth, that it never makes us want to press the fast-forward button.

Buttons be damned. Maria's delusional mind goes into overdrive as she dwells on the loss of love. We don't enter her memory, though. We stay outside it, watching it unfurl and back up on itself. This back-and-forth creates huge shifts in tone, like switching from third to first person. The dramatic torque shifts midway into the play's first act. Maria has been coaching the young soprano Sophie de Palma through Amina's sleepwalking scene in Bellini's *La Sonnambula* (1831):

SOPRANO: This is hard.
MARIA: Of course it's hard. That's why it's so important we do it right. What's hard is listening to you make a mockery of this work of art.... I'm not getting any juice from you, Sophie. I want juice. I want passion. I want you [*ibid.*, 16].

She has stumbled into the danger zone where art and life meet — or collide. The subject of Sophie's aria rekindles in her heart her own tragedy — and, with it, her professionalism. Writing in February 2012, Michael Billington of the *Guardian* noted Maria's "rapt attention to technical detail" (1). He was right. Maria not only knows every singer's part in the operas she discusses with her students; she has also studied their sources, i.e, Shakespeare's *Macbeth* and what Verdi made of it. "The melody broadens here. Let it flow through you" (*MC* 49), she tells the soprano Sharon Graham at the point in the letter scene when Lady Macbeth discovers the Scottish throne within the grasp of her husband.

Maria isn't boasting. Knowing the operatic tradition that began with Claudio Monteverdi (1567–1643) and that produced the composer Verdi always helps steer a singer's attention to matters of cadence and transition, modulation and articulation. "Bite into those words. Spit them out" (*ibid.*), Maria will tell Sharon. Her knowledge that power and definition both stem from the particular, not the general or the abstract, stokes the following exchange:

SOPRANO: Someone comes in and.
MARIA: Not someone. No one is someone.
SOPRANO: A servant.
MARIA: Now you're talking! [*ibid.*, 51].

"We're talking turkey" (*ibid.*, 38), Maria had said earlier while discussing how a singer's physical presence can impact her audience before she sings a note. Her metaphor needs noting. Her idiom, based on straightforward conversational American English, will shift to Italian and German to clarify a point. Her mentoring bespeaks the play's economy of means. Sometimes, she'll translate a passage (*ibid.*, 49) or, along with a student, summarize the action of an opera to help us, yes, but also at a professional level to make sure that the aria being auditioned supports both the action and the consistency of its source.

"Always the music. You are its servant," she had said in the play's opening speech, adding, "Attention must be paid to every detail.... A career in the theatre demands total concentration. One hundred percent detail " (*ibid.*, 2). She rides her students hard because, she believes, a singer must commandeer the song she's singing. This act of sovereignty comes as a byproduct. Only the proper homework, self-confidence, and artistry will bring out a song's beauty and power. Conversely, lack of emotional discipline will mutilate the composer's imaginative intent. Artistic excellence is built on the mastery of technique. Master the technical details. "The rest is kaka-peepee-doo doo" (*ibid.*, 54), Maria insists after delivering a volley of charged, elevated language. One of the great pleasures of *MC* is its unforced, effortless, supple voice.

John Ardoin's *Callas at Juilliard: The Master Classes* honors both this vocal range and the humanity that powers it. Maria says that a singer must bring an indifferent or adversarial audience to its knees (*ibid.*, 37). But she must first learn how to breathe properly. This advice is typical of her. The following passage from Ardoin's 1987 book notes Maria's respect for basics. She's helping a student fit her voice to the "Jewel Song" from Gounod's *Faust* by resolving the technical problems the music poses: "Do not lose time with 'c'est la fille d'un roi.' This is tempo. Breathe after 'salve' and try to sing through the high B in one breath. You can do it if you don't slow the tempo down on the trill. If you have to breathe, take a very quick one before the turn, and attack the B on 'ah'" (222). Premised on the belief that trusting a musical score will show a singer how a passage should be sung, the Maria of McNally's 1995 play alludes to the wealth of solid practical advice she offered her Juilliard students. Her words to Sophie in Act One, "Vowels are the inarticulate sounds our hearts make.... Consonants give them specific meaning" (*MC* 15), carry the clout of a top-quality singing career.

"A performance is a struggle. You have to win. The audience is the enemy" (*ibid.*, 37), Maria will tell Sharon. But judging from some of her other comments, she has extended this enmity to her students — whom, tellingly, she refers to twice as "victim(s)" (*ibid.*, 4, 33). She fuels the inequality behind her words. She exceeded her charter as singing coach by criticizing the clothes worn by both Sophie (*ibid.*, 23) and Sharon (*ibid.*, 35).

Sharon is so upset by her rebukes that she vomits. Nor does La Divina care. Perhaps she's gloating. At times, she seems to be using whatever ploy has come to mind to wreck her students' poise. Instead of helping Sophie relax in Act Two, giving her the confidence to sing well, Maria tells her that she *should* feel "terrified" (*ibid.*, 7), makes her repeat herself, and claims to have forgotten her name (*ibid.*, 10). She also accuses her of being frivolous.

She has had the knife out from the start. Before hearing Sophie sing a note, she tells her that her career will consist of minor supporting roles (*ibid.*, 7). The knife stays out. Sharon she *will* hear sing, but, citing her "limitations," says that roles like Lady Macbeth or Bellini's Norma make demands beyond her skill set (*ibid.*, 60–61). The two young sopranos would stop singing now if she had her way. And what a way that is. She keeps interrupting them either to correct them or, rarely, cheer them on. Sophie, as the tenor Anthony Candolino says, never got past the first word of her aria from *La Sonnambula*. Was this Maria's aim? "Interruptions every moment" (*ibid.*, 13), she had grumped, presumably unaware that they all came from *her*.

Tony she treats differently, even though, as with the two sopranos, she offers him no useful advice. No sooner does she see him walk on stage than she asks for a glass of water (*ibid.*, 37). She's smitten even before this "young tenor ... infuriates [her] ... with his arrogance" (Canby 1). Infuriates but also charms; her first words to him include the statement that he's "a good-looking man" (*MC* 38). Then she calls him "Mr. Tony Tight Pants" (*ibid.*, 42), invoking the praise heaped on trousers worn by men in "Noon" (1965) and *LT* (1989) by would-be lovers (*15 Plays* 28; *Three Plays* 60).

Tony's "*bella figura*" (*MC* 42) has rattled her. She's moved, too, by his standing his ground after being dismissed, allegedly for coming to his lesson unprepared. Defying her, he sings the painter Cavaradossi's aria from the first act of Puccini's *Tosca*. And she does listen, coaching him en route. But she soon runs out of patience and goodwill. He too is rushed off the stage, like Sophie and Sharon, without being told how to improve his singing. Maria claims to feel faint, just as she asked for water when she first saw him. Is she too full of herself to help an aspiring singer? Though retired from the stage and the concert hall, she keeps stonewalling her students. Her obstructiveness is both high-handed and ill-judged. Sophie, Sharon, and Tony, with his MFA in voice from UCLA, aren't just ordinary singers. To qualify for a master's class with Maria, all three outpaced classmates who, like them, had studied for years with gifted, committed teachers.

But how committed is Maria to teaching them? Her sitting down just as soon as Tony leaves the stage belies her earlier statement, "It's our work that matters. Only our work" (*ibid.*, 5). She has little flair for the work she acclaims. She'll glance at her wristwatch (*ibid.*, 17, 52) and inspect her purse (*ibid.*, 14). After distracting Sophie from singing, she accuses her of wanting to end the lesson (*ibid.*, 16). Then she tells her, "no one is keeping you" (*ibid.*, 18). Sophie stands her ground. But at the end of her aria, Maria calls for a break and leaves the stage (*ibid.*, 29). She'll also ask Tony, "Are we scheduled of a break?" (*ibid.*, 44) instead of honoring his request to hear him sing again.

Sharon's parting shot to her makes her the frightened demon of envy who resents any junior who might supplant her. "You're old and you're scared and you don't know what to do about it" (*Two Plays* 118), Ramon of *LVC* had told Gregory. His thunder could have erupted from Sharon. Maria is even more preoccupied with her age than Gregory, as were other figures from this early autumnal phase of McNally's career in *LT*, "Cleopatterer," and *LTTA*. She had remarked inwardly, "Reckless. You bet I'm reckless" (*MC* 28). She might have been awaiting Sharon's assault: "You can't sing anymore and you're envious of anyone younger who can. You just want us to sing like you, recklessly, and lose our voices in ten years like you did (*ibid.*, 61).

Billington would commend these accusations. Addressing the loss of Maria's moral compass, he said, "Callas's casual cruelty is somehow a product of a damaged soul" (2). Maria is damaged, down *to* her soul. The "wrecked and broken" sound coaxed out of a "voice in ruins" when she tries to sing, a "terrible moment" (*MC* 47) on its own, charts the sad comedown from her former greatness. Greatness it was from the start. Life has always been a struggle for her — from the Nazi occupation of Greece, which meant walking miles to her singing lessons armed with a pencil rather than the orange she craved but gave up for it; with other singers, whom she mocks while pretending not to (*ibid.*, 9); and with the "pretty, slim blonde" sister (*ibid.*, 27–28) who outshone her in the eyes of both their mother and the music teacher who gave her the choice role that should have gone to a then overweight Maria.

Vexing her most is the breakup with Onassis, who, indifferent towards opera, dismissively called her his "canary" (*ibid.*, e.g., 26). Sharon's choice of a song belonging to the same role in *La Sonnambula* that Maria lost to her less talented sister — whom she won't deign to name — sharpens her pain. She must continue struggling with demons real and imagined, past and present, even though her spirit, like her shattered voice, falls short of the job. She has been worn down by the clash of wills, and, outside of the recital hall, she lacks "victims" to bully. This flagging ex-mega-star who never had a childhood needs to rest.

Does she try to bully music, as well? Another question, from Maria herself, offers an approach to the question she asks Sharon, "Do you think Verdi composed it [*Macbetto*] without knowing his Shakespeare?" (*ibid.*, 46) The question is rhetorical; she had said earlier that singers serve the music they sing (*ibid.*, 2). "The composer tells you. It's all in the music" (*ibid.*, 49), she insists, but, moments later, she claims in one of her many self-contradictions, of the phrase Sharon is singing, "the music here is ridiculous. Ignore it" (*ibid.*, 52). She had already denied that Amina was sleepwalking during her famous aria, calling it "[s]omething some writer made up" (*ibid.*, 11). Obviously, Bellini wasn't godlike when he wrote *La Sonnambula*, which clashes with her earlier statement that "the composer is God" (*ibid.*, 2).

She's not deliberately trying to confuse Sharon. Intimate knowledge like hers of a celebrated piece of music like Amina's sleepwalking aria only follows many years of singing it. And since she had been studying, practicing, and singing it since her Athens girlhood, she knows the difficult spots in it. A similar moment, treated at greater length in Ardoin's *Callas at Juilliard*, shows her trying to shape a phrase, from the duet, "*E'il sol dell' anima*," from Verdi's *Rigoletto*, to a singer's voice and airways:

> This phrase is badly written, I'm sorry to say. I do not understand why Verdi gave more stress to the second syllable of "sento." In speaking it would be SEN'-TO, and in singing it you must accent it that way. However, the long note is on the second syllable, so you will have to work around this by making the note more piano [135].

This blend of humanity, common sense, and professional savvy infers a gap between the real-life Maria and the one Cary H. Mazer called "a cruel and egotistical and magnificent monster" ("*Master Class* and the Paradox of the Diva," Zinman, ed. *Casebook* 175). Mazer didn't overstate by much. Maria may not set out to foil or mislead the students she badgers. But she'll give contradictory advice, and she's hard to please. When she's not stopping a student to grouse about the way she looks, his or her supposed lack of preparation, or failure to walk on stage properly, she'll whine about the temperature in the room, demand a cushion and a foot rest, stop a lesson until she gets a glass of water, or fume over a bouquet of flowers put on the piano to honor her between the play's two acts.

Her fragile outsize ego keeps intruding on the job at hand despite her denials. "Someone somewhere is always behind you plotting your downfall" (*MC* 9), she recalls of her career. Later she'll say, "I know they're all out there in the dark. Enemies. My mother. My sister. The other singers. Smiling. Waiting for me to fail" (*ibid.*, 28). She's paranoid. Though she has stopped singing, she still feels pain wreaked by supposed enemies. The wounds burned into her psyche still smart.

This nightmare tells in part why McNally called *MC* both his "most autobiographical work" (Rizzo 2) and "a very autobiographical play of my feelings" (Savran 129). His smashing professional success had trivialized the gibes of his bullyboy schoolmates. But his a-causal, a-historical self, where the real meanings lie, was stinging just as much in 1995 as when he dramatized them in *Roller Coaster* (1960). Perhaps they'll always sting. Maria wonders if she's the butt of a "dig" (*MC* 4) early in *MC* as Lou Nuncle will, too, early in McNally's 2004 play, *D* (9). Old wounds have long memories. Maria-like, McNally ramps up the pain to better serve his art, despite knowing that the misery will top the satisfaction gleaned from his Tonys, Guggenheims, and Rockefeller.

He chose opera as a vehicle to bare himself symbolically to theater audiences because, like Stephen of *LT*, he equates opera with loss and loneliness (*Three Plays* 20). Later in the play's first act, Stephen and Mendy hear Franco Zeffirelli on PBS-TV call Maria's loneliness "the price for being God's instrument" (*ibid.*, 48). Infinity stands alone in a world of finite creatures. In this vein Mazer called Maria's loneliness "sublime" and "too horrifying to be emulated" (Zinman, ed. *Casebook* 175). How much horror can she take? McNally had already sought peace by featuring in both *LTTA* (1991) and *LVC* (1994) bodies of therapeutic water, i.e., what Conrad called the destructive element in *Lord Jim* (1900). In neither work was he making an existential leap in the dark. Such acts only occur when all is lost, and he knew he was writing at the top of his form.

He and the American-born Maria both direct the American frontier values of boldness, diligence, attentiveness, and *Mut* to their respective arts. Both do it with open eyes. Maria, who sang to the Nazi troops during her hungry years in Greece, had always sacrificed herself to her art — and thus deepened her commitment to it. In her early 50s, she is drowning in it. Nor is this development new. She says of her years with Onassis, "Like Amina, I'd been sleepwalking" (*MC* 27). Outside of opera, what awaits her is the loneliness that frets gay men in *LT*, "Cleopatterer," and *Some Men*.

Can she avoid it? She hasn't connected with her students. A bewildered Sophie tells her, "I don't know what you're talking about" (*ibid.*, 16). Like her, Tony leaves the recital hall feeling puzzled. Sharon tells Maria flat out that she dislikes her (*ibid.*, 61). Opera had brought these three hopefuls together with Maria, and opera, Frontain said, depicts longing, to McNally "the fundamental state of human existence" ("Supper, Song, and Salvation" 7). Maria's sad little world hasn't just cut her off from people. At times she even feels disconnected from herself.

Despite her needs for a cushion, a foot rest, a glass of water, and more heat in the recital hall, this high-maintenance diva keeps touting her unimportance. "This isn't about me" (*ibid.*, 4, 5) and "Forget about me. Poof! I'm invisible" (*ibid.*, 4, 10), she insists, despite her constant maneuvers to hog the spotlight. Her statement to Tony, "Great music always takes so much out of me. I feel quite faint" (*ibid.*, 44), voices a vital truth. The blaze of genius *can* overwhelm us; anyone who touched the rough stone platform holding *David* felt sorry afterward.

Her encounters with the divine fire have ransacked Maria's powers of concentration. Her nonstop talk amounts to a silence. Having made opera her life, she talks relentlessly to keep her scorched, brittle world whole. Her lessons *are* about her. But she can't organize or control this protracted silence. "I'll speak more about that later" (*ibid.*, 3), she says along with, "Well, that's a whole other story" (*ibid.*, 9), "But [or 'but'] that's another story" (*ibid.*, 5, 9, 11, 17), and "That's another story" (*ibid.*, 9). So eager is she to keep talking, lest reality intrude, that she keeps piling words upon words regardless of how they fit or where they're taking her.

Something else: Rudyard Kipling would sometimes end a story by saying, "That's another story." These tales often took place in India during the time of the British Raj, a conceit that applies to Maria. Though charismatic enough to focus a full-length play, she has fallen so far from the grandiose image she projects that she has dwindled into a ragged outpost of her former imperial self (Kipling was mentioned in *PG* [*Two Plays* 232]).

She conflated her everyday self with opera and then regretted it. "It's a terrible career" (*MC* 45), she blurts out in an unguarded moment. Other big issues come before her mind's eye. "Ho dato tutta a te" (*MC* 32), she recalls Medea telling Jason. She might well recall it. I gave everything to you, the play's main proposition, holds fast. But its context has changed. This "Queen of La Scala" (*ibid.*, 57) performed an act of lyrical surrender. She gave up singing for love and "end[ed] up empty" (*ibid.*, 32). Her impulsiveness recoiled on her. "Know how much suffering there can be in store for a woman" (*ibid.*, 53), she'll tell Sharon. Love has withered her soul. The balls or *Mut* that drove her fabulous career failed her in the sphere of love. Frontain's statement, "For McNally, art is the space where the real and the ideal are reconciled" ("Supper, Song, and Salvation" 1), wisely omits the artist.

Maria blundered by putting herself in the equation. She saw herself and Onassis as "the richest-man-in-the-world Greek and the most famous singer-in-the-world Greek" (*MC* 25), just as Giovanni Rubini will call himself and his beloved Giulia Grisi the "world's greatest tenor and the world's finest soprano" in *Golden Age* (*GA* 63). These auguries both run afoul of messy, stubborn everyday life. Grisi marries a lesser talent, and Onassis never prized Maria as anything more than the pet canary he had bought in a seedy world in which everything has a price tag and a use-by date. Himself and Maria, he saw as freaks. The vocal thunderbolts she hurled at rapt audiences he dismissed as "boring shit music" (*MC* 25)—an affront that might have boosted him in her esteem. As was shown in her master class, compliant people bore her, whereas the defiant (viz., Tony) stir her up.

Not only did she acquiesce in Ari's refusal to marry her. In a bomb that only erupts at the play's end, she also agreed to abort their child even though, "not a young woman" (*ibid.*, 59), she'd probably never get another try at motherhood, and her career was in decline. There might have been another reason why she'd have gladly swapped singing for a family. Though unconfirmed at the time, McNally included the abortion theory in *MC* not so much because of the currency it enjoyed among New York's opera buffs, but, instead, for its emotional truth. Headlong and impetuous on the one hand but controlled to the point of self-denial on the other, Maria knew the wild and the rash. She had enslaved herself to Ari. Having ousted her much older overweight husband Meneghini, she tumbled into the embrace of Stephen's operatic paradigm from *LT* that fused love with sorrow and death. She was still in the grip of the devil's pact she made with Meneghini (*ibid.*, 58). Ho dato tutti a te: the attempt to join ranks with her neighbors and followers always dooms the light-bringer or savior figure.

Nicholas Gage, whose *Greek Fire: The Story of Maris Callas and Aristotle Onassis* (New York: Knopf, 2000) came out five years after *MC* debuted reworks the emotional truth of McNally's abortion theory. Gage bases his book on a different set of facts. He says that Maria didn't abort her child with Onassis at his bidding in 1966, as was rumored. She had the baby, but in 1959, when she and Onassis were both married to other people. It was named Omero, after Homer, the greatest of Greek writers, and not Odysseus, as Maria talked about doing in the play (*ibid.*, 59), a choice that put her on the right track. Omero had terrible luck. He died on the same day he was born, 30 March 1960. Gage, who claims to be the first person to go public with his heartbreaking story, reproduces photographs of both Omero's birth and death certificates (206). He adds that Maria would have never have aborted the child that formed her main hold on Onassis. The 1966 abortion, Gage's argument runs, was a lie she used to punish him for dropping her to court Jackie Kennedy.

* * *

Did she blunder again? Lacking a voice and a career, a man and a baby, Maria "looms eternally" in Alvin Klein's words as "a symbol of singular triumph and unconscionable waste" (2003, 2) — which is also to say that McNally wrote about this guttering comet, as Ibsen did Hedda Gabler, at a time when she was most intriguing, like the spy who's lured into the cold for a last dangerous job. The willpower and the nerve that extended her career after her reckless singing overtaxed her voice had both gone dry. Nor, as McNally told Savran, can she teach the artistry and commitment that won her world-wide celebrity: "She's as fucked-up as anybody who ever lived. She's a terrible teacher in trying to communicate what she has that made her great. It's her secret, and she can't give it away because she doesn't know what it is. So she gets very angry" (139).

Mostly with herself; "Maybe this whole business of teaching is a mistake" (*MC* 61), she says a minute or two before final curtain. Nothing would change had she married Onassis and had her voice kept its thrilling beauty. She'd still feel angry and confused. She knows that her students deserve better. What she has been giving them only makes them cry, vomit, and/or walk away feeling cheated and cross. Her brusqueness makes the solid advice she does provide ("Bite into those consonants. I want to hear them" [*ibid.*, 14]) shake their composure and self-confidence. They're not getting their money's worth; besides her interruptions, her mind wanders when she finally lets them sing. But motifs operate on more than one level in *MC*. Her musings convey more vitality than the fitful bravado she offers her students. Recording her regrets and resentments, they enrich the play. McNally couldn't have included them in any other way without forfeiting dramatic economy.

That said, she has also found herself getting paid to lead her charges toward careers that might end, like hers, in grief. Tony can't know the ironic effect of his words on her: "I want to be a great singer. Like you. I want to be rich and famous. Like you. I want it all. Like you" (*ibid.*, 39). Suddenly her mouth goes dry. There's nothing she can do besides end the lesson or speed him to his doom; he's the only student of the three she auditions whose talents she doesn't disparage (*ibid.*, 22, 60). With Sharon she emboldens herself. "I'm not an actress. I'm just a singer" (*ibid.*, 46), Sharon says after being scolded for believing she could sing Lady Macbeth's role without having first mastered Shakespeare's original. Such demands Sharon finds unfair and extreme. By making them, Maria is trying to make the world "dangerous" (*ibid.*, 61). Sharon doesn't know the half of it. As Wayne Kostenbaum said in *The Queen's Throat*, Maria "seems to value expressivity over loveliness." His argument ramps up: "I worship her because she makes mistakes.... Callas put forth the effect of nature as opposed to the appearance of order, and offered an acceptable, digestible anarchy, a set of sounds on the verge of chaos — but enjoyably so" (136).

Onassis was right to call her "freakish" (*MC* 25) without knowing why. Maria wasn't trying for a smooth, melodious embroidery of sound, the aim of more classically correct but less daring singers. Her harshness and her wobbles formed part of the emotive singing style she spent years developing. Planned and rehearsed many times, the discords she'd shock her audiences with conveyed hidden truths and mysteries embedded in the piece she was singing.

Resembling her in this regard was Vincente Bellini. The cruel demands made on him by his art in *Golden Age* (2010) drove him to keep searching for new ways to improve it. His lonely, punishing career offered neither satisfaction nor relief. "Here I am alone backstage at the premiere of my latest opera [*I Puritani*] at arguably the greatest opera house in Europe [Paris's Théâtre Italien] ... and all I feel and fear for its reception is loathing for myself that it's not better. I want to start a new one [based on *King Lear*] at once" (*GA* 37). That opera won't be written. Bellini died within months. Maria Malibran, the day's greatest soprano, viz., 1835, whom Maria mentions (*MC* 57) and for whom Bellini planned to write his new opera, died the following year. Conversely, the retired composer, 43-year-old Gioacchino Rossini, who limps on stage near play's end, would live another 33 years without writing any new music.

Devotion to artistic creation doesn't guarantee longevity, a point that Maria's death at 54, Malibran's at 28, and Bellini's at 33 all show. Many different causes can bring down a golden age. Bellini boasts that the cast of *I Puritani* includes Europe's four greatest opera singers. He won't boast for long. Here's how two of them respond when Bellini asks them if, rather than working with him on his next opera, they'll be singing in Donizetti's *Don Pasquale* after *I Puritani* ends its run:

> GIULIA: I'm a singer, I sing — different operas by different composers.
> LABLACHE: We also have to eat. I have a wife and thirteen kids at home [*GA* 36].

Singers are merchants who sell their services, usually to the highest bidder; their voices, they know, won't last forever. None of them in *GA* has dug so deeply into his psyche or exposed it to so much as the desperately honest Bellini. None will leave the triumphant premiere of *I Puritani* feeling more shaken — even though, ironically, like Shakespeare's Lear, Bellini is spared from knowing the worst, his death in seven month's time.

Sharon calls Maria dangerous because the demands she makes on her students interfere with normal everyday living. Sharon is right. Maria is mad to expect them to sacrifice as much as *she* did to her singing. But Sharon miscued by blaming Maria for plotting the impositions and exigencies that have shredded both her voice and her life. The artist in McNally is a subversive who pays heavily for the risks she takes. Although she'll accept these risks, she didn't invent them. They were long in place when she bought into them. Had she backed away from them, she'd have been forgotten.

After Maria corrects one of Sophie's mistakes, she tells her, "It's life and death, like everything we do here" (*MC* 19). She's not voicing an anomaly. The demands of artistic self-expression outweigh all else. It's a cruel lesson. In the end, the artist may find, like Maria, that she has no soul left to express and no voice to express it with. To make the point, McNally has Bellini say, "Great art is capable of killing us. That's why there's so little of it" (*GA* 33). After twisting the artist's sanity and soul, great art teaches bad habits. Singers are particularly at risk. Maria's belief that the human voice is "the most expressive instrument there is to reveal human emotion" (*MC* 18) puts singers on the edge to begin with. She has described voices upon which rigorous, often excessive, demands both have and will have been made.

Art is always a stern, brazen taskmaster. Included on its casualty list are Jessie and Lou in *D*. Even though their Children's Theatre would be snubbed by others as low-grade art, McNally was speaking of *all* actors, singers, composers, and painters when he said, "the artist must be prepared to sacrifice everything" (Savran 120). He was certainly speaking of himself. In 1997, he told Toby Silverman Zinman, "I think the play [viz. *MC*] is about playwriting — about the need for art, about what we can do with our enormous feelings, how we can keep some sanity — I don't think the play is about Maria Callas and opera" ("Terrence McNally on *Master Class*," Zinman, ed. *Casebook* 149). *MC* is so memorable, penetrating, and funny because McNally kept mining his psyche to make it so.

This ruthless self-excavation explains in part why the artist in his work is a cold-hearted beast as in Patrick White's *Vivisector* (1970) and Ian McEwan's *Atonement* (2002). She can never atone for the missteps she takes with others. And these others? As Maria's pupil Sharon learned, an artist's calling is a public menace. But it also benefits the same public it menaces and, with it, posterity. Civilizations are honored more for their artistic achievements than for their scientific advances or their conquests in business and industry. Maria broke rules to extend guidelines and boundaries. She, Janis Joplin, and Jimi Hendrix all burned out their voice boxes because they overcame formal restraints in their pursuit of new musical vistas.

John Ardoin joined the conversation when he called *MC* "an investigation of what it means to be an artist" ("Callas and the Juilliard Master Class," Zinman, ed. *Casebook* 158). This rich, resonant play implies that without people like Maria, willing to die for their art, their art dies. Though doomed to loneliness, a Maria will rarely doubt the value of her sacrifice. Why should she? She has shown the Sophies, the Sharons, and the Tonys of music the creative difference between being warmed by the holy fires of creation and being scorched by them.

The lesson she serves herself? This chatterbox and self-promoter nailed it when she said, "This isn't about me" (*MC* 4, 5) and "Poof! I'm invisible" (*ibid.*, 10). She'll vanish inside her body of work, an absorbed, rather than an applied, presence that will both fuel and reshape existing ideas about opera. If this feat fails to cheer her, it won't make her fret, either. Having foregone the sensual joys of childhood amid the rocks and gales of Greece, she never expected much.

IV

The opening scenes of *Lips Together, Teeth Apart* hark to D.H. Lawrence, who claimed that, following the example of George Eliot, he'd substitute in his novels two relationships for a conventional plot. Once more in the Lawrencean vein, personal bonds crisscross and entwine in *LTTA*, sometimes invoking events and issues from the past as far back as the cradle. Recalling *Women in Love* (1920) in McNally's inquiry into the dynamics of two marriages, a member of each couple are brother and sister.

His decision to base his 1991 play on mood and tempo rather than a plot served him well. His people's inner dramas connect their choices to the moral dilemmas of the traumatized society they belong to. Besides trying to keep their homes together, the people also face the more basic ordeals posed by selfhood, i.e., keeping their heads above water in a play that unfolds at land's end, in a seaside community.

The excesses of the early 1990s — the promiscuous sex, rampant drug use, trendy local restaurants, and high-tech gadgetry — have impacted the people together with the decline of American capitalism. *LTTA* shows some of the effects of the de-industrialization of America, a process that began when Fortune 500 companies began trading factories for finance. As William Gaddis's *JR* (1975) showed, the czars of American industry were shutting down what had been for a century the engines that drove their nation's economy.

The past invoked in *LTTA* includes but goes beyond family history. One character, the owner of "a construction company that has a funny way of almost going under every three months" (*LTTA* 11), has been fretting during America's transformation from industry to finance-driven capitalism. This change has also been troubling the play's other three characters. The 1970s, during which time they were high-schoolers, was the only decade since the 1930s in which Americans grew poorer. Productivity kept slowing in the 1980s and nearly stopped. Some sectors of American industry could no longer compete with foreign manufacturers.

The malaise plaguing McNally's people in *LTTA* has been plaguing others. As our country's share of the world market shrunk, so did the American middle class. What emerged from this slump was the figure of the Reagan Democrat. Fed by patriarchal, racist, and other revanchist emotions, these often blue-collar discards of the new economic order, including *LTTA*'s Sam Truman, embraced populist politics. Thus Sam's discovery that the same brother-in-law who serves as admissions officer at an elite New England prep school has also cuckolded him has been driving both his bile and blood pressure to new, heretofore unknown, heights.

McNally's "comedy that hurts" (Rich 1991, 11) goes at its American theme sideways, with cunning and craft. Stephen Watt has discussed the importance of its physical setting: The "play is set in an affluent gay community on Fire Island called The Pines, which forms a kind of Arcadia or 'place where its safe to be gay' located between the 'formal civilized' border of New York City and the sea" (9). Before long, though, the good-natured comedy rips off its mask to reveal a surreal darkness. Sam's wife Chloe says, while looking out from the sundeck of the beach house where the foursome is spending the 4th of July weekend, "This is paradise" (*LTTA* 3). Her memory is short. Her brother Sam, it has come out, fell off the nearby boardwalk carrying groceries. And in another reminder of falls from paradise, Sam will discover — and kill — a live snake in the house's basement.

Sam keeps struggling in Chloe's paradise. In the play's second act, he hears a vocal recording of "O Paradiso," from Giacomo Meyerbeer's *L'Africaine* playing from the house next door. His wife Sally had just tried to quiet his anger by telling him to listen to the waves. But his response to her, "I hate waves. I hate the beach. I hate nature" (*ibid.*, 54), shows that he's not easily humored or soothed. Nor would his grouchiness lift if he knew that Meyerbeer's 1865 grand opera featured a mighty sea storm together with acts of murder and suicide on the same picturesque island being enthused over in "O Paradiso."

Like Meyerbeer's rich island priests and Lisbon magistrates, the people in *LTTA* face anxieties that no amount of cash or political guile can relieve. *LTTA* unfolds in a mood of fatigue and nervous tension. Its people have come to Fire Island to process the estate of David, Sally Truman's newly dead brother, whose assets include the $800,000 beach house where they're weekending. It's through David that McNally revives the practice from *Bringing It All Back Home* of exploring difference between presence, absence, and nonexistence. He notes early on that the wildly different reactions to the AIDS casualty David show that absentees, including the dead, can feel more real than the persons standing in front of you.

David calls forth the suppressed turmoil of his 40-something survivors, all of whom have been sagging under the tyranny of things known but not spelled out — things that may be thought but not said, and things that shouldn't even be thought. John Haddock, who flies a kite and does a crossword puzzle on stage to calm his anxieties, will confess late in the action, "I love avoidance." His wife Chloe's answer, "You invented it" (*ibid.*, 94), though on target, has an edge.

Earlier, he had noted inwardly, "I talk too much, probably because it's too horrible to think about what's really going on" (*ibid.*, 48). Sally, tacking in the opposite direction, rightly wondered, "Why do people have to speak to one another? Why can't we just be? (40) As in a Pinter play, talk is a form of silence in *LTTA*, a dodge to cover the poverty of our nakedness. The play's rich, terrifying subject matter makes it a private distress call. It shows what happens when the self's internal support systems have been shaken past the point where they can be relied on. The bourgeois Sam Truman, for instance, is both thrilled and appalled by sexual feelings he didn't know he had.

A lesser playwright would have satirized him as a shallow, materialist racist who gets the comeuppance he has long deserved. McNally told Steven Drukman that all four of the play's characters, though not gay bashers, are homophobes (340). Using homosexuality as a litmus test, he draws attention to the way Sam and the others process time and give it meaning. This vital issue doesn't need to be spelled out. McNally is too wily and inventive to invite stereotypes, or straw men, in order to topple them. The weekenders challenge us with our *own* fears about where we truly belong, where our loyalties lie, and where to place our trust.

As tensions build and dovetail, the dread wearing down the people grows lethal. *LTTA* resembles *LVC* (another three-act play from McNally's most fertile period) in its belief that we're most fully ourselves at leisure, a time when there's no work routine to screen us from our demons. Tellingly, the play mentions Chekhov (*LTTA* 24), who used setting the same way. Its turning our minds specifically to *The Sea Gull*, some lines from which formed the prologue to *CC* and which *LTTA* alludes to (*ibid.*, 37, 41), sends out an alarm; the two youngest characters in *The Seagull* both die, events that could recur in the deaths of David and an and anonymous young swimmer whom Sally has fixated on.

Here is realism so sharp and vivid that it borders upon the surreal. But only borders; McNally knows when to stop. He's an unmagical realist who finds enough pathos and fun in the everyday without needing to debunk objective truth or tart it up with surrealistic flights. Like Conrad and O'Neill, he finds character unreadable and dangerous. After hearing John say, "I respect the distance between people," Sally, his sister-in-law and ex-lover, following suit, tells him, "Right now I feel much closer to you than I ever did when we were making love. You're not even pretending to let me in" (*ibid.*, 83). McNally is trying to capture, through this exchange, as he did in the tooth-brushing finale of *F&J*, the mysteries of the inner self. Sally and John are granting the unknown and the unshared more potency than the familiar. Characters who hold each other at bay or who brush their teeth together without speaking invite insights into their hearts too private to be voiced.

McNally will use the device of the dramatic monologue to disclose this danger. He uses it to greater effect in *LTTA* than in *Prelude & Liebestod*, *LT* (both 1989), and even the wonderful *LVC* (1994), works in which the complexities of family life matter less. A hearty blend of the distanced and the familiar, *LTTA* pulls us to and fro with a fierce and spacious energy. The people in this cramped domestic drama tell themselves things they don't want others to hear. Sometimes they say nothing, but even these silences have meaning; they refer to the things the people shrink from hearing. There's more. Tender and passionate, funny and raw, the monologues help make *LTTA* a great creation.

* * *

Sam Truman's name evokes that of *Nudity*'s Leo Sampson. Its immediate association with manhood, Uncle Sam, and America's thirty-third president also calls to mind Protestantism's hallowed preference for simplicity, common sense, and direct observation over elaborateness and high reflection. Sam is literal minded; he's happiest with what's in front of him. But he learns that, as life follows art, science follows delusion; technological advances haven't improved the quality of his life. The nature, depth, and quality of our lives will never translate to physical terms, this inveterate dabbler in gadgets discovers. His gadget-dabbling might have even made him paranoid. "I know they talk about me. I've never left a room without knowing people talk about me" (*ibid.*, 16), he says before seeking comfort in a toolbox.

He has always enjoyed the prosaic, the visible, and the tangible. Late in Act One, he tells Sally, "I grew up ... picking locks. I could hot-wire any car in thirty seconds flat. I seriously considered a life of crime, but then I met you and went straight. I like that" (*ibid.*, 29). He's glad, too, that he has channeled his tinkering toward socially approved goals. Feeling useful and solid rates high with him. His neo–Benjamin Franklin's embrace, after meeting Sally, of stamina, discipline, and honesty has given him the zeal of a religious convert.

It follows that his straight-edged attitude toward work has made him both anti-elitist and scornful of the elite's non-material values, a stance that has also set him against minorities. This gadget junkie stands in a direct line of the post-confederate rubes of McNally's high-school years seen in *Bringing It* (where he's also called Sam), *Witness*, *Whiskey*, and *Corpus Christi*. But less rearguard and dull-witted than these testosterone-happy precursors, because he's more brutally tested, Sam is McNally's most sympathetic portrait of an industrial worker whose energies and foibles have helped form the character of today's America. It's easy to grasp why the workaholic Sam feels displaced relaxing for a long weekend, on Fire Island. Equally clear is the upshot of his displacement. "My brain has become a collision course of random thoughts.... Sometimes I think I'm losing my mind. I'm not sure of anything anymore," says this man who has trouble swallowing his food (*ibid.*, 30). His troubles grow. Since he doesn't know his mind, he can't trust his words when he speaks it.

This trauma he's forced to deal with. The prospect upsets him. His kind of American heavy lifter has rarely won acclaim for being in touch with his heart. It's no wonder that he has a hernia, that he likes his steak "very rare" (*ibid.*, 38), and that his idea of gourmet cooking consists of "a baked potato and sour cream" (*ibid.*, 5). It also follows that he used to prefer freedom and adventure, viz., crime, over roots and connection. We know why. He was trained, as a guy, to be self-contained, smart, and rational, and to avoid sentimentality. In making him a childless cuckold who fears he may be sterile, McNally tested himself. All of us tend to deny the violent and contradictory feelings powered by either devastating loss or its prospect. Sam's great fear, that Sally will leave him, is tearing at his guts.

McNally uses a free, unobtrusive conversational style to convey Sam's distress. But the puritan notions of virtue and rectitude that underlie Sam's conformist moral code can't help him deal with Sally's betrayal. He calls himself a "goddamn maniac" (*ibid.*, 53) because the concrete practical terms that frame his inner world have grown irrelevant. His preference for the simple and the straightforward has led him to reduce life into a series of measurable physical acts amenable to — tools and instruments. First seen lifting a chlorine gauge from the pool on David's sundeck, he'll later handle a hammer, a telescope, and a shovel — the one he'll use to kill the snake he finds under the beach house. So much for his sister Chloe's paradise.

The chlorine gauge that tells him that the water in the pool is "perfect" for swimming (*ibid.*, 3) will be his last encounter with the clean and the pristine. He'll soon face *im*perfection in its most primeval form. What he finds will magnify his anxieties. First, his wife Sally's response to his killing of the snake unnerves him: "I don't know why you have to kill everything" (*ibid.*, 27). Billie Holiday's recording of "You've Changed " that he'll soon hear applies to him more strictly than it does to any of the others. More's the pity that this portent has come to him from a dead black woman. Like *LT*'s Stephen, this racial bigot hates change. But he can't hide behind a he-man image that includes an "old-fashioned" preference for "a woman [who] toil[s] on his behalf" (*ibid.*, 5). Life has stopped conforming to familiar precepts, leading him to say late in Act One, "I'm too sensitive, that's my problem" (*ibid.*, 37). His outlook darkens. His saying to himself earlier, "I'm talking to myself. No one wants to listen to who we really are" (*ibid.*, 30), voices his panic over having to face his anxieties alone.

He wishes he could ask for help. The defenses of this owner of a construction company are being ripped away. Aware of his frailties, John calls him a "little jerk" and a "miserable little asshole" (*ibid.*, 50) before beating him in a ferocious bare-knuckle fight. It's a shameful moment for Sam. After caving in quickly to the Williams College-educated John, he has to be helped to his feet by Chloe and Sally. His macho act has bombed. Violence has won him nothing, and he doesn't know what to do next. John is right to call him "the least defended of all of us" (*ibid.*, 97).

There's more to say about Sam, who, while being trounced by John, refused to admit he was "a stupid piece of shit" (*ibid.*, 52) even if it meant having his arm broken. This show of courage in the teeth of great physical pain wins our esteem — and, more notably, McNally's. The crypto he-man Sam deserved punishment for his arrogant narrow-mindedness (like Leo of *Nudity*, he brags about the size of his dick, and he denounces gays and blacks). But McNally has looked beyond his biases. By showing him struggling with huge marital angst, McNally not only extends patience and understanding to him, but also love. To set things right with Sally, Sam knows that he'll have to put his gadgets away and scrap the narrow-minded values he has been relying upon. He does just that. Crisis brings out his coping power. This new strength shows McNally tapping into the sense of purpose and new-world energy that helped make America great. *LTTA* contains as many acclamations and cheers as it does growls and reproaches.

Sam (like Buzz in *LVC* and Lou in *D*, a Nathan Lane role) is much more fragile than he lets on. One brother-in-law David has died of AIDS following a long heartfelt bond with his black lover, Aaron. His other brother-in-law, John, Sam believes, has been sleeping with Sally. He and Sally have just driven hours from New Jersey to Fire Island, a grind that unleashes his forebodings. He's on alien turf. There's no escaping from the bugbears of John, the gay neighbors, and interracial gay sex. What's more, Sally wants to sell the beach house and give the money to Aaron, to whom David willed it. But she, John and Chloe — Sam more dimly — see that they can't sell the house until they work out its meaning in both their and their country's evolution.

No easy task, this. According to Sally, "The truth is too formless to grasp" (*ibid.*, 15). The others would agree with her. Formlessness has been badgering all four of them. First, death invaded their circle. Not only did David die literally blind, as if his being sighted might have helped him lead his survivors to clarity. The word, fecund from the crossword puzzle John is doing (*ibid.*, e.g., 8, 11, 15), takes on alarming weight, like the AIDS virus that blinded David before it killed him. The cancer in John's esophagus, he believes, will soon "ripen and flower" (*ibid.*, 17) and then kill *him*. Fecundity of a different sort has been vexing Sally, John's former lover and David's sister in their tight little homophobic circle. Though Sam is able to impregnate her, she keeps losing the new life he helps create. She feels haunted and helpless. And she doubts that Sam can help her in view of his evasiveness and lack of inner strength. This is only the half of it. She has failed to see that her adultery has been hammering this simple working-class Joe with a problem bigger than any he has ever faced.

This development — or non-development — is another example of McNally's preference for the ambiguities of literature over the false certainties of ideology. Soon after opening curtain, Sam discloses his grouchiness when he bridles at Sally's habit of misnaming movie titles (*A Star Was Born* for *A Star Is Born* [*ibid.*, 10]). John's reading the *New York Times* had already upset him so much that he tore the paper out of his hands (*ibid.*). Everything is making him pissy, like hearing about a naked man walking across the beach for an ocean swim. "It's against the law," he fumes, adding, "Suppose I wanted to whip my dick out?" a question that prompts John's terrific laugh line, "This is Fire Island, Sam. I would strenuously argue against it" (*ibid.*). Sam feels too de-manned to whip out anything. In frustration, he'll soon smirch Ben Franklin's tradition of the American tinker, to which he belongs, by smashing open the lock on David's lock box.

His inner wounds have leaked blood. His spousal woes had already been inflaming his resentment of the ethnic and racial cacophonies of our madding cities. He begrudges Sally's giving the expensive beach house to Aaron, despite his being David's legal heir. Sam's bigotry has deep roots. In a term paper called "Shakespeare's Early Development as a Tragedian," written in January 1959 at Columbia, McNally called Aaron of *Titus Andronicus* "the incarnation of evil, for his skin is black and blackness is the mark of the devil" (6). Sam applies this bigotry to David's Aaron. A member of a tainted underclass, Aaron, he says, probably gutted the house of valuables already and then bolted the island.

Sam's prejudice against gays, a more conspicuous minority in the play, has a surprising kick. At first, he dismisses them, turning the sculpted physiques of some of them into a collective moral flaw: "It's one of their requirements. If I had nothing to do all day but work out, I would [have a chiseled body], too" (*LTTA* 11). Benilde Montgomery has shrewdly noted Sam's "boyish simplicity" soon morphing into an "intense curiosity about his gay neighbors" (1993, 50). Even John, whose stint in Chad with the Peace Corps has softened his prejudice against blacks, mutters, "Goddamn fairies" (*LTTA* 28). Sam is miffed that gays have acquired the savvy and clout to buy choice seafront property. David belonged to this elite with his Fire Island beach house and condo in Manhattan (*ibid.*, 46). Sam reacts more emotionally to gays than John. "I didn't know about ... AIDS and homosexuals," he says in Act Two. "I don't want to. It frightens me" (*ibid.*, 82). He has spoken home. He's gripped by the sight of his gay neighbors dancing together to loud music on both sides of David's beach house. His fixation will soon reach striking new depths. Clapping eyes on a gay couple having sex in a poison ivy patch sparks in him a malign fascination beyond his powers to handle.

* * *

LTTA stands light years away from the neoclassical comedy of Molière (1662–73), a dramatic form reflecting his age's preference for balance, order, and regularity in both human behavior and the arts. Rather than mocking eccentricity and irregularity, though, the three-act *LTTA* tallies their rewards. Its model could be the finale of Wagner's *Götterdammerung*. The immolation scene, which ends with Brünnhilde singing and then riding her horse into Sigfried's funeral pyre, confirms love as life's most compelling force. Wagner's lovers in *Tristan and Isolde* had also surrendered to love's supremacy despite its fatal cost. And now against all odds, the sight of two men on Fire Island necking and groping each other in a poison ivy patch has made McNally's Sam Truman facing head on Wagner's vision of love as a higher reality, perhaps the ultimate reality.

Sam's epiphany has another side. The passion he beholds is a welcome relief from the caution urban gays had to practice in 1991. The city casts long shadows. David's centricity in the play suggests that his former neighbors on Fire Island share a common fear and loathing of AIDS. The drowned, disfigured gay corpse who riveted Sally hours earlier while setting out for his fatal swim tells us again that gays won't inherit the Earth. Homosexuality goes with death. Should we fret? As Montgomery shows, David's ex-neighbors, their carnival of percussive sex and all, have curbed their fears to opt for fun and frolic. They know how to enjoy a vacation. Montgomery's sharp 1993 article on *LTTA* in *Modern Drama* describes the happy outcome of their revels: "The gay community is open and welcoming ... they dance ... they make love ... they are attractive and wealthy ... they are comfortable with their bodies" (1993, 550).

More high-spirited than their straight counterparts, the gays next door have thrown themselves into the 4th of July merriment. It's the straights, squeezed into the shorter building between them, who hold back. *LTTA* treats this contrast with great comic invention. Rage and tragedy both pulsate beneath the fireworks. Terror has established itself in both the panic radiating from John and the guilt vexing him and Sally. But its intensity drops when John rebukes Sally for exchanging greetings with the neighbors. What has lowered it is neighborly civility. Both John's request that they turn down the volume of their music (*LTTA* 28) and Sally's rejection of their invitation to join them for the fireworks (*ibid.*, 61) leave the neighbors unfazed. Instead of taking umbrage, they throw a bundle of small flags to their straight neighbors.

Only Sam holds back. "I feel like an idiot" (*ibid.*, 88), he carps when asked to wave his flag. But the appearance on the deck of confetti and red, white, and blue streamers drifting down from above had already brightened his mood. Within moments, he joins John in singing "lustily" "America the Beautiful." Then, after wishing the neighbors a "Happy Fourth" (*ibid.*, 89), he thanks them for their generosity.

He's not alone extending cheer. Under a full moon and within hearing distance of the sea, Chloe, his sister and John's wife, calls out, "Makes you proud to be an American" (*ibid.*, 87). Frank Rich judged well to say that McNally's 1991 play deals with "what the hetero- and homosexual communities have in common" (1991, 2). He hit upon a vital issue. Shared qualities have always interested McNally more than divisive ones. *LTTA* connects with both gays and straights. As Montgomery notes, members of both groups have prospered while surviving the violence their country was built on (1993, 554).

The finale of *LTTA* evokes both the celebration of Krishna in the last part of Forster's *A Passage to India* and the music dramas of Wagner. Blasts of auditory and visual stimuli have produced total sensory immersion. We're engrossed. McNally's tornados of sound and visual theatrics fuse national themes with family tensions. There's more. Actuated by the gay lovers next door "huffing and puffing and biting and licking and kissing" (*LTTA* 85), the straight characters feel the lure of sensuality. Nietzsche's distinction between the Apollonian virtues of clarity and harmony and Dionysian frenzy has collapsed.

Self-consciousness and dread, though rampant, have been denied the last word, but only briefly; the imperatives of a society that's frayed, smudged, and unraveling slide noiselessly but inevitably into place. They have formidable allies. Not only does what Rich calls "an infected diminished civilization" (1991, 2) reassert its claims; The people also find themselves squaring off against the sublime, as formulated some 200 years earlier by Ann Radcliffe and Wordsworth. Building from danger and malign beauty, nature in *LTTA* is both other and otherizing. During a pause in the din of the fireworks, the bug lamp next door grows *"very loud"* (*LTTA* 89).

This loudness charts a killing spree. Night has fallen in Act Three, bringing with it the heavy moist air beloved by mosquitoes and other insects. Stillness already felled the kite John was flying (*ibid.*, 72), and, as if nature were hostile to human purposes, a rainstorm in Connecticut has canceled the hayride his and Chloe's kids had counted on taking (*ibid.*, 73). Perhaps Sam had his reasons to hate nature (*ibid.*, 54). The humidity throttling Fire Island recalls John's earlier preoccupation with the words, fecund and fecundity (*ibid.*, 11, 15, 17) from the *Times* crossword puzzle in Act One.

As without, so within; no outside force, the cancer growing inside John's esophagus occupies a "fertile bed of malignancy" (*ibid.*, 17) that's shaping his behavior. He's angry at himself. He berates himself not so much for beating up Sam but, rather, for wanting to shame him in front of his wife and sister. This cruelty defied decency; moreover, it failed to produce anything good, as violence never does in McNally's work. He's right to say, "There's no apology deep enough to undo what I did to Sam" (*ibid.*, 56). Yes, Sam started the brawl, but with reason, which isn't to excuse him. John's sinned more darkly. By tupping Sam's wife, John also betrayed his sister.

This betrayal cuts deep. Both Sam and John have legitimate claims on Chloe. Even though John's are more complex and demanding, with their mutual obligations of homemaking, money management, and parenting, Sam's reach to the cradle and include a huge storehouse of memories. This bond John respects. Contritely, he'll later fetch Sam a towel, a polo shirt, and a pair of slacks after his shower (*ibid.*, 63–64). Then he sterilizes the tweezers he uses to remove a splinter from Sam's foot.

Things affect other things in McNally's interactive world. Both the swimming pool on the deck of the beach house and the ocean near which John's acts of kindness occur augment their potency. Conjuring up both the Dutchess County lake of *LVC* and the Ganges of *PG*, both the nearby sea and David's pool remind us that life flows on. Say what? The pool's former owner is dead, and the ocean killed the handsome swimmer Sally had cast in the role of his substitute. There's more devastation. The amniotic fluid in which the embryos inside Sally have been dying and the lethal Portuguese man-of-wars her husband reads about, in *Life* Magazine no less, imply that the waters covering two-thirds of the Earth's surface and, in the same ratio, our bodies, both share this fearsome trait. We're party to their malevolence.

Tellingly, John had mentioned a new biography of Herman Melville (*ibid.*, 8), who saw seas, lakes, and rivers as hostile; Pip the cabin boy in *Moby-Dick* loses his mind after falling into the ocean. But Melville, and Conrad after him, deny this evil the last laugh. The seafaring ships in both writers stand for community, a source of joint effort and goodwill that, though unable to tame the sea's malevolence, can withstand it and even put it to good use as both a storehouse of saleable goods and a channel that can take them to market. What's more, the ship in both writers promotes solidarity and teamwork together with a source of adventure and cash. Finally, it provides refuge. Surviving the ravages of a gale at sea lifts comradeship over differences of race, language, and, in Melville, sexual orientation.

Melville's doctrine of linked analogies grazes *LTTA*. The grief overtaking Sally is both cruel and commonplace. David Richards's review of the play says on this subject: "Sally can't shake her grief for her dead sibling or the terrible thought that he got what he deserved" (1991, 5). She has been wearing two hearts on her sleeve — one that beats with sympathy for a gay world she can't know and the other for a heterosexual whiteness she can't disown. "I wish I had a better opinion of all this," she says of her dancing neighbors. "I was glad I never saw my brother dancing with another man, and now I never will" (*LTTA* 90), she adds. That man might have been Aaron, who suddenly ousted her as David's best friend and whose blackness deepened her resentment of him. But there's more to say on the subject. Her saying that she'll never see David dance with a man, no casual afterthought, conveys regret along with relief. As John Updike showed in *Couples* (1968), getting what we want can hit us harder than being denied.

Gay death has muddled Sally. But even if she can't disclaim its finality, she believes that it can be redeemed. She's desperate. AIDS has killed David, and John's cancer is destroying his esophagus; some perversity, she believes, keeps killing the babies Sam has been planting inside her. She rivets on the naked young man who waved at her while walking to the surf. She has connected him with youthful strength and self-confidence. Soon, though, she senses the pitfalls of this connection. The youth's "steady, powerful strokes" (*ibid.*, 9), she sees, have taken him too far from shore.

To support Sally's emotional stake in this striking, energetic youth, McNally ends the play's first act with Sally's desperate wish that the small object she sees in the distance is the same swimmer whose safety she has been praying for. Consequently, the finale of Act Two shows the counterpart of a four-way conversation yielding to a crescendo. Standing in a *"strong special"* (*ibid.*, 70), Sally reveals, in a dark tonic chord, that her swimmer, now lying flat on the beach, has drowned.

Her walking there alone to see the corpse resembles Katharine's impulse to kiss a leper in *PG*. She has asked too much of herself. Death's implacability frightens and sickens her. While not only disfiguring this once "very handsome man" (*ibid.*, 74), the sea has also scrubbed out his identity. Nobody knows who he is or where he came from. He personifies death, its rawness and its injustice. This news jolts Sally more than it would the others with her on the beach. First seen at her easel, Sally is trying to paint the same ocean that will later smash her hopes to make peace with David's death. In fact, the farewell trio from Mozart's *Così fan tutti* playing at curtain rise foreshadowed her frustrated goodbyes to both David and his nameless foil.

Her hopes for the future are now in free fall. Barely keeping them aloft is the baby inside her. She's praying, here in her late 30s or early 40s, to deliver it safely. It's noteworthy that the only person she has told of her pregnancy is John (*ibid.*, 98). This neat turn re-sites the action in a new key. John's last name, Haddock, is also that of a fish native to the same North Atlantic waters near which he and the others are weekending. It's also John who dives into the pool in Act Three to retrieve a ring, supposedly the one Aaron gave David (*ibid.*, 36, 85).

His rescue of the ring, conspicuously after Sally views the mutilated corpse on the beach, stands as an act that only the fish-named John could have performed. In a Wagnerian echo, the ring conflates love and death. The pool where it lies, which is lit during the third act to show its escalating import to the people, could share the malignancy of the ocean nearby. Toxic particles of piss and sperm that may be floating in it have created this danger. The pool evokes both Forster's Marabar Caves and its offspring in *PG*, the long, dark train ride through the Chitaurgarh Pass, India's longest tunnel (*Two Plays* 223).

McNally wanted the lights in the pool to act like a mirror, showing the people to themselves. As the pool's reflections suggest, this mirroring relationship must be dealt with. The straight visitors to Fire Island face a more daunting task than that posed by the business that brought them there, David's last will and testament. They must splash around in this watery symbol of David's death, even gargle and swallow its contents, before discovering its meaning to them, a joint failure to bring a secure emotional structure to their marriages.

Sally, the artist and thus the guest with the keenest sense of the possible, takes the lead in this regard. She's the first to dangle her feet in the pool. Having been hit the hardest by death, she speaks the bald truth on the telephone with John and Chloe's children — who recoil from her words about the pain and ugliness awaiting them (*ibid.*, 74). John may complain about the difficulty of the *Times* crossword (*ibid.*, 25). But Sally's painting the sea to access its mysteries gives her a greater headache than that afflicting Mr. Haddock (a name she'll address him by [*ibid.*, 81]). In this sense, she's waging war on Wilde's belief that all art is perfectly useless, Joyce's preference for static over kinetic art, and Auden's denial that art is a handmaid to society. The impact in the play made by art's imperatives spans a wide range while sounding great depths.

Sally splashes both Sam and John with pool water after telling them, "One drop of water in your mouth or on an open sore and we'll all be infected." Then she drinks some of the forbidden water, saying, "Let's all get AIDS and die." Nor does Sam fight her off when she kisses him "long and hard on the mouth" (*ibid.*, 80). He has understood that love drove her mad act (though he does run inside to gargle afterward). The two couples are enacting Denis de Rougement's belief, in *Love in the Western World* (1922, trans. 1939), that sexual love, to deserve its name, must risk death, as it did in the medieval Troubadour poets and Wagner's *Tristan*.

McNally's Wagnerian compulsions hold. Within minutes, everybody in the play has been drenched. Water can cleanse as well as spread infection; the ring of the *Niebelungen* returns to the Rhine. Sharing the risk of AIDS soon sparks a sudden rush of marital love. In another analogy to German culture, Sally, the engine of this awakening, has acted in keeping with that paragon of extremism, the title figure of Thomas Mann's *Doctor Faustus* (1948). Accused of having said "the most inappropriate thing [she] could think of" (*ibid.*, 81), she has been violating reason, common sense, and the laws of self-preservation to expand personal and conjugal frontiers. Whether her brazenness helps her grow as a painter is unclear. But the sudden bursts of love she kindles in those around her restore the urgency missing from their marriages, both of which suddenly enjoy fresh blasts of oxygen. If we must love each other conditionally, let the conditions come from (shared) danger, not the dead hands of apathy and miscommunication.

Sally's attempt to paint the heaving, rolling Atlantic had already displayed in her the archetypal artist's curiosity and *Mut*. She stands up to the power of the primitive. She won't flinch when Sam dangles a dead snake in front of her; this adulteress has faced up to her personal symbol of betrayal. Not least of all, she refuses to back down to Chloe, who less than a minute earlier, praised John's ability to do the *Times* crossword "*without cheating*" (*ibid.*, 15; emphasis mine). She needs this resolve. Having already lost her father and her only sib to death, she has been adrift in a world where the truth is "just too formless to grasp" (*ibid.*, 15).

She listens quietly to Chloe's digs about her being childless, certain that her failure to conceive has damaged Sam more than herself (*ibid.*, 14). Yet when she tries to talk to Sam about having a baby, he pulls back. Both in her life and her art, the tough questions she asks go unanswered. Her brushes have brought her little self-respect or relief. In keeping with the humility of the artist, she frets about lacking the skill to transfer "the play of light, the volume, the space" (*ibid.*, 19) of the sea to canvas. She feels blocked everywhere. Sam can seem like such a stranger to her (*ibid.*, 55) that she has to confide in John, her accomplice in deceit, or fellow snake. It gets worse. Her artistic sensibility might have made her McNally's leading self-blamer, a category where she has a lot of company. She feels guilty over the death of the young swimmer whose eyes had met hers in a kind of recognition before he swam to his death, as did Norman Main, the James Mason (and that of Frederic March and Kris Kristofferson in an earlier and later version) character in the 1954 remake of *A Star Is Born* (*ibid.*, 10).

Yet it's Sally who fuels whatever hope brightens the play's closing moments. And this hope stems from her flaws, not her strengths; God is a potter who works with mud. Let's take our cue from Michael T[errence]. McNally's conclusion to his term paper, "Spiritual Movement in *King Lear*," submitted 8 June 1959. Linking suffering to spiritual awareness, McNally concludes, "There is justice in the canon." Perhaps more convincing is Professor Alan F. Chiappe's marginal comment, "or at least love" (24). McNally will be less sanguine some 32 years later in *LTTA*, whose people are both blamed mostly by themselves and trapped in a past they can never escape. But they can hope, anyway. They've earned the right to fall from grace without being killed as they stand together as Americans at both nation's and land's end. They sing "America the Beautiful" together, as they should. The play has been as beautiful, noisy, and complicated as real life. There's comedy here, tragedy, and no small amount of poetry.

To qualify this optimism, the four characters pair off at the end — but not with their spouses. We soon see why. While they're dancing, Sam voices his fear of fatherhood to Chloe, which he'd never admit to Sally — who, meanwhile, is discussing her pregnancy with John, a topic she wants to keep from Sam, lest she fail him again. Then a great change occurs. All four are swept into the rhythm of the dance — the same one that started with their gay neighbors. Our foursome have learned that, if they can't ground their hopes in love, they can still muster the collective goodwill to refresh themselves with Sally's oddball practice of mangling the titles of movies, e.g., *Zorro the Greek* and *Catching a Thief* (*ibid.*, 84). When Sally, switching genres, refers to the song, "There's No Business Like the Show Business" (e.g., 95), none of the others fault her. The desolation marring their marriages has taught them that factual truth counts less than the outgoings of the heart.

Sally has been no great friend of objective truth. Earlier, a frustrated Sam had been following an impulse to prod and force issues. He tore a newspaper out of John's hands, brawled with him, and discovered more than he could handle in the snake he ran to the ground and killed before waving it in front of Chloe and Sally. He also wanted to inspect David's lock box. Sally, despite her more legitimate claim to look inside the box, balked: "I don't want to know any more of my brother's secrets" (*ibid.*, 16).

Objective knowledge won't move her either when she drinks the water in David's pool (*ibid.*, 84), which could have the same rectangular shape as his strong box, seedbed of the personal data she recoiled from. Her fearlessness moves the others. "There's No Business Like the Show Business"; why must deliverance stem only from facts or the throes of sexual love? The benevolence Midge Barker relied on to see her through life's distress in *Deuce* (2007) provides an unswerving path to redemption in our flawed world in the 1991 play *LTTA*. Sally's failure at charades signals her attachment to more vital truths than those found in make-believe, e.g., the lightweight community theater that Chloe, the game's instigator, acts in.

"Zorro the Greek"; not only tolerating but rather delighting in human error can fend off the threat symbolized by the nearby ultraviolet bug lamp. The threat is real, the lamp's insect-zapping invoking Gloucester's baleful words from *Lear*, "As flies to wanton boys, are we to the gods./ They kill us for their sport" (IV.i.156–57). Sally takes the zapping in stride because, as an artist, she's more in step with life than the others — which also explains why she suffers more. Sam's dentist advised him that sleeping with his lips together and his teeth apart will stop him from grinding his teeth. The advice is worthless. No sleeper can control his facial movements. Sam has worn down his teeth because he's bracing for a crisis that may never happen. In Sally's words, "He sets himself against the tide and won't go with it" (*LTTA* 96). He complains too much. And fault-finding breeds anger. It's also self-replicating. The goodwill Sam and the others later extend to Sally works better as a survival mechanism. We have to take the world on its own grim terms. So what if the tide that Sam fights kills an innocent swimmer? He, Chloe, and John have found nothing better to help them avoid getting zapped like insects in a world that's at best indifferent to them.

LTTA adds to McNally's inquiry into expectations and self-entitlements. How much can we reasonably ask from life?, he has always wondered. The conductor's search for perfection in *Prelude and Liebestod* caused his suicide. In different ways, Gaetano Proclo of *The Ritz* (1975) and the persons comprising the bizarre *ménage à trois* in *Dedication* all have to gallop to preserve a status quo that rankles all of them. In an irony worthy of Dickens, the direst threat to the threesome comes from the fulfillment of Lou Nuncle's great expectation; Lou could stay trapped in the childhood he had to enter to bring it about. The status quo in *LTTA*, a better play than *Dedication*, includes the immensity of nature—the great sea mother who devours life and then spits it out in a form so ugly that it's unrecognizable; the clammy night that helps breed insects it will soon zap; the same-sex preference that made well-to-do Fire Island a gay enclave where the HIV virus can spread and cause more death.

Love redeems such fatalities on their own bleak terms. When John hawks a funnel of pool water in Chloe's face and tells her, "Now we're both infected," she doesn't panic, as she did earlier when she saw Sam's dead snake. Nor does she run into the house to gargle like Sam (*ibid.*, 82) after swallowing a mouthful of pool water. Instead, the risk of dying together with her husband sparks a burst of love. John has *shared* the threat of death with her just as Eve did with Adam in the Garden of Eden: "Just so long as you're all right," Chloe tells John. "You're my life" (*ibid.*, 84). Moments later, she'll tell him again, "You are my life" (*ibid.*, 86). Her love for John, she sees, is one with his for her. The danger of becoming HIV-positive has shown her that life means nothing without John at her side to share or help her fight it.

McNally outdid himself in *LTTA* in his delivery of sharp insights into the complicated motives of complex, ambiguous people. Chloe, for instance, is both John's wife and the concerned mother of their three kids. But she's also Sam's elder sister. Nearly all of her actions with Sam display McNally's awareness of the dark side of American family life and of human nature itself. Sam tells her early in the play, "[I]f you weren't my sister I'd jump all over you" (*ibid.*, 5). And how does his statement affect her—this woman who dances expertly with him, looks into his mouth to see his ground-down teeth, and asks to see his penis—a request she knows he'll grant, as he can't deny her anything? He has cast her in the role of elder sister-*qua*-seductive mother (he calls her "Mother" [*ibid.*, 43]). His edginess with John, who also calls her "Mother" (*ibid.*, 34), supports this eroticism. Defending Chloe's honor, Sam bristles when John refers to his having had with her "New England's longest-running ... shotgun marriage" (*ibid.*, 7). Later, this woman who'll call Sam an "*homme fatal*" (*ibid.*, 45) tells John that, unless he makes wild love to her soon, her "own brother isn't safe" (*ibid.*, 32).

Behind these words lurks her knowledge about John's rut with Sally. The unspoken carries great weight in *LTTA*. Lying under each spurt of discord in the play prowls a dangerous truth involving the betrayal of trust and the need for atonement and forgiveness. John, the school admissions officer who awaits his admission into the ranks of the dead, is very frightened (*ibid.*, 21). He needs forgiveness to calm his suspicion that the cancer destroying his esophagus is his punishment for having slept with Sally. As in *Bringing It* and *Deuce*, infidelity in *LTTA* signifies weakness. John tells Chloe, "I have no willpower. You married a weak man." Chloe's angry retort signals her agreement with him (*ibid.*, 20).

It takes the threat of death to open up this paragon of avoidance (*ibid.*, 94). Convinced that he'll soon die of cancer, he risks little by diving in the pool for David's ring. Any comparison McNally might have invited between John and the evil dwarf, Alberich, who stole the Rhine gold in the first part of Wagner's Ring cycle, breaks down here. The morbid, destructive behavior John is accused of (*ibid.*, 84) will both tear down his inhibitions and refresh his marriage, in a way he and Chloe cherish all the more for not understanding it and not wanting to try.

He's wise to take on trust this resurgence of love rather than trying to analyze or improve it like Frankie's Johnny. As in works dating as early as *The Roller Coaster* (1960), *This Side of the Door* (1962), and *Things That Go Bump in the Night* (1964) (and arguably all of Edward Albee), John, like Sam, is weaker than his female foil. He and Sam fight because they lack the inner strength and sense of purpose of their wives; female harmony trumps male justice in *LTTA*. Chloe (who sings in musicals), for instance, kept the news of John's past affair with Sally a secret from Sam because she doubts Sam's ability to handle it. She was right. Hearing that she believed John's confession of guilt rattles him. He stays rattled. His sister wanted to believe John because she had to. Disbelieving him would have cost her her home and family.

It's a troubled home and family she's trying to save. She calls John "Daddy" (*ibid.*, 29) after getting rebuked by him. John calls her "Mother" (*ibid.*, 34), just as Sam addresses Sally as "Mama" (*ibid.*, 69), echoing Mike's "Yes, Mother" in *LT* (*Three Plays* 55), said in response to a reprimand from Steven, who'll murder him within an hour. Being babied by Sally is nearly a principle of survival to Sam. Though he lets John fetch and sterilize the needle he'll use to take a splinter out of his foot, he insists that Sally remove the slivers that John missed.

Domination and control express themselves differently in John and Chloe's marriage. She's a handful, so much so that he'd not have married her had he not gotten her pregnant. This thin-skinned woman (*LTTA* 62) claims that she can "stand anything but being misunderstood" (*ibid.*, (53). She's likely to remain "a walking nerve end" (*ibid.*, 59); she lacks self-knowledge and self-control. Though she claims that the weekend she's celebrating with the others has "[n]o agenda" (*ibid.*, 4), she keeps moving between kitchen and deck with food and drinks; she puts out a first call for alcoholic drinks at about ten A.M.; she calls for a game of charades. Another of McNally's nonstop talkers, she has been dodging self-confrontation. Though she loves to swim (*ibid.*, 39), her chlorine allergy will keep her out of David's pool (*ibid.*, 4), that bog of sickness and dread where the true affirmations lie. Nor, unlike Sally, does she use art, in her case, acting in light Broadway musicals, to seek the truth.

Her offering Sally a "teeninetsy suggestion" (*ibid.*, 45) and then "one [more] teeny, teeny ... tiny suggestion" (*ibid.*, 59) about self-management implies that she can unriddle everyone's life but her own. The implication holds. She buries herself in the brand names of the foods and drinks she brought to the island. Pursuing salvation in high-end consumerism, she believes, can stop her from flying out of control. Her pursuit is failing her. She keeps annoying John by kissing him on the top of his head (*ibid.*, e.g., 29), as if he were her little boy. But she's nobody's idea of mature and protective. Her own idea of "grown-up time" consists of saying, "Fuck, fuck, fuck.... Cunt, cunt, cunt" (*ibid.*, 29).

Typically, she announced a mid-morning "[f]irst call for alcohol" (*ibid.*, 22), this busybody who opened the play by asking, "Is anyone still hungry... I've got eggs, bacon, bagels" (*ibid.*, 1). She's always moving things along. Needing a change, mostly from herself, she keeps changing her clothes, pouring rounds of drinks, and speaking French before she orders a game of charades (*ibid.*, 91). Maybe this frenzy of activity will disclose a self she likes better than the one dividing her from the one she wants to be. Sam, who's slow to fault her, calls her "hyper," adding, "She hasn't shut up since we got here" (*ibid.*, 13). Chloe's problems run deeper than he knows. When Sally identifies a piece of music by Schubert, she's told by Chloe that she knows everything (*ibid.*, 21).

Perhaps she's accusing Sally of being a disembodied head or half-lifer. Sally's having no children is a misfortune she enjoys reminding her of (*ibid.*, 12, 78). Loss of control also shows in her being shaken because the July 4th reunion on Fire Island marks the first meeting of the two couples since John and Sally stopped having sex. This mother of three is buckling under the pressure of living with a secret that could destroy two families. Despite her frequent wardrobe changes, enacted to make her feel like a character in a play rather than a wife on a slippery slope, she has remain trapped in a real-life role that has been grinding her down. The likeness between her name, Chloe, and the word, chameleon, proves misleading. She's more like the leopard that doesn't change its spots. Another feature of her carefully chosen name: the resemblance between *it* and the chlorine she's allergic to (*ibid.*, 39) signposts a person at war with herself.

The inability to change of this woman of many stage roles has made her dangerous. Though she needs the distraction, she's bedeviled by the coming ordeal of having to lose a lot of weight to play the role of Miss Adelaide in *Guys and Dolls*, a night-club singer whose 14-year engagement to gambler Nathan Detroit matches the length of time she has been married to John. Her playing Adelaide won't take her as far from herself as she'd like. The others have been watching her carefully. They often try to ignore her; so fragile is their hold on themselves that they're afraid that her hyperactivity might cut them from reality altogether. Sam does open the sliding glass door for her early in Act One as she's carrying a breakfast tray to the sun deck (*ibid.*, 11).

Later in Act One, though, she has a long wait before Sally opens the same door for her. She feels slighted in her motherly role of food preparer and bringer. The act ends with a tray full of food sliding and shattering on the floor after she had failed to get any help with the door. Another fall comes immediately. The decreasing speed with which Chloe cleans the mess until she stops altogether, "*isolated*" (*ibid.*, 37) in her own spotlight, marks her nadir in the action up to now. She's unheard and unseen, an actress without a script or an audience.

* * *

Showing his usual appreciation of the value of contrast in stage drama, McNally puts her near the others — and on her feet — to open Act Two. Defying the augury caused by the scattered food was the music pealing just before intermission, "*Che puro ciel*," from Gluck's *Orfeo*, in Sally's words "a description of paradise" (*ibid.*, 36). Such grandeur can rectify any problem. Sam is relaxing as Act Two opens, while hands-on, proactive Chloe, who's grilling hamburgers, has reassumed her role as food giver. No longer feeling isolated or depressed, she'll later take pride in being an American (*ibid.*, 87), call the others' attention to a shooting star at play's end (*ibid.*, 100), and find the wit to credit Sally's mangled title of the song "There's No Business Like Show Business" as the correct one (*ibid.*, 95). Perhaps providence can redress hardship.

The tie between providence and music says a lot about both *LTTA* and its author. A playwright's work mirrors his character. Set in an opera house during a performance, *Golden Age* will unravel some of the tricky snarls created by the junction of music, business, and human nature. Like it, *LTTA* confirms the truth that the proper subject of social history is social change; the one both embodies and reflects the other. McNally's confirmations link the whole to the part, i.e., the public to the private.

His 1991 play notes from the start the misapprehensions any group may have about any other, e.g., blacks and whites. The motif in *LTTA* falls into line with the contrapuntal style of baroque music rather than the harmonic inventions of Wagner; the play's action folds in different viewpoints on topics like gays and straights in a stop-start tempo that advances the action. The interplay of speech and music reaches its apotheosis in the fugue, a form in which melodic lines chase each other in changing patterns. The patterns unfold according to an internal logic governed by the people's inner lives.

Organizing them into an artistic whole is a precision of language carefully tuned to the psyches of the people. The tuning is crucial. It allows the riffs to generate moment after moment of strong emotion lightened with inventive humor that rarely falls flat because of the terrible clarity joining them. Prominent in this regard is McNally's skill in character deployment. By sending Chloe inside the house for food or Sam either to the utility shed or the outdoor shower, he creates a counterpoint of on-stage voices different from that rising from the four-way conversation that occurs over lunch. Sometimes two speakers appear on stage, sometimes three, shaping both the type and the tone of the subject matter under discussion. Speakers aren't always in view. Some off-stage words spoken by a character signal the impropriety of what she has overheard (*ibid.*, 25).

At other times, the script demands that all of the people be on stage together. Act Two ends with a counterpoint building to a dark crescendo; Sally, standing in a "*strong special*" (*ibid.*, 70), announces the drowning death of the young swimmer. This dark tonic chord both collects and reshapes those passages of monody or plainsong that have been alternating with the dialogue, or polyphony. As Montgomery says, the play's internal monologues are "heard only by the audience, [which] allows ... [the monologists] to confide in strangers what they fear to say to one another" (1993, 552).

Gritty, mordant, and often deeply sad, these passages take on a luster by coming from different voices, varying in length and both differences and similarities in subject matter. The similarities create a telling irony of discrepant awareness. Sometimes the people seem to be reading each others' minds. Two monologues can address the same tense topic in sequence, as they'd do in conversation, except that the issue they're broaching is too fiery, even frantic, for direct speech. Framing family intricacies in a bold new scale, the play's monologues blast open a new path for the dramatic imagination.

Music heightens it all, as McNally inferred when he called *LTTA* his "most operatic play" (Zinman, "Interview," Zinman, ed. *Casebook* 4). Produced within three or four years of *F&J*, *LVC*, and *LT*, it's like them, an AIDS play. But to call it a work of antiphonal voices and other sounds is to pay due diligence to its visceral honesty and beauty. To locate a work in a genre isn't to diminish it but, rather, to embed it where its vitality is richest. This energy declares itself immediately. Foreshadowing the life-art dichotomy that will pulsate throughout, the play begins with the farewell trio from Mozart's *Così fan tutti*. The music will play for several minutes before releasing the four on-stage characters into "*real time*" (McNally, *LTTA* 1). The elegance and the beauty of the trio will clash with the confusion and clutter of the human realm. McNally's attitude toward this clash recalls Pirandello. Despite its poise and refinement, the trio comes from a story that has been told; an artifact, it lacks the brawling vigor of everyday sensual life. But, as is implied by the passage from Gluck's *Orfeo* near the end of Act One, by the Taj Mahal in *PG*, and by Michelangelo's *David* in *Nudity*, divinely inspired works, having human origins, connect with people. The ending of *LTTA* slides those works into the human camp, if only just; sometimes, if only briefly, we're graced with the wit to take in their transcendent beauty.

At play's end, after Sally, John, and Sam say "Zap" (*ibid.*, 100), the newly awakened Chloe shows them the shooting star. "Oh" (*ibid.*, 100–101), they'll all say, too. She has distracted them from the mosquitoes who've been dying in the swampy night air. Mozart's farewell trio from *Così* starts blaring as both stage and house lights blaze, catching cast and audience in the same extravaganza. The beauty, solemnity, and joy provided by Mozart's music has capsized the life-art dualism, bathing everybody in the same flow of light and sound. We have the same chance to transcend ourselves as the characters. Like us, they can't be reduced to their problems or traits; they remain a riddle to themselves. As we do to *our*selves; the English translation of Mozart's 1790 opera, "They're All Like That," a script that turns on the swapping of sexual partners, conveys the same frailties dealt with in McNally's. *LTTA* follows *Così* in being both light and serious, cynical and beautiful.

There are other resemblances. The opera ends with an act of forgiveness; the women are absolved of their mistakes. Accordingly, the stunning composite image ending McNally's play revives in us those intuitive flashes that disclose within us, for just an instant, a hint of a reality beyond both our control and our imagining. This hint, or intimation, a recognition of our visionary selves, sparks a theophany that almost always occurs in McNally alongside others rather than alone. Stephen Dedalus's epiphany during his mystical, wordless encounter with the bird girl, his muse, at the end of Chapter 4 of *A Portrait* showed the alone communing with the alone. The same moment of sufficiency, as Virginia Woolf calls it, occurs while Mrs. Ramsay is by herself in Part One of *To the Lighthouse*.

Such serendipities or touches of grace called the Stendhal Syndrome in McNally gain meaning and power from being shared with others in *PG*, *Nudity*, *Dedication*, and *LTTA*. They include the knowledge that, having bypassed material gain, they imply that God has been with us on life's journey and that our acts matter to Him. We've been armed to return to the world of betrayal, death, and small joys comprising the "real time" (*ibid.*, 1) beyond the stage.

LTTA has both the ache and inevitability of real time. Like other great plays, it's not merely lifelike, as if the job of making a play lifelike weren't hard enough work. Most of all, it transforms life, granting its people and the events they enact a preeminence that's usually lost inside the clutter of everyday routine. But the play neither competes with nor tries to change this clutter. Because it takes its building blocks from it, *LTTA* helps us both see more clearly and feel more deeply. It thus furthers a finer appreciation of conduct, feelings, and thought. This appreciation marks its triumph. It extends and deepens our understanding of our humanity. Perhaps we should add that it's also very enjoyable.

At the end, after the betrayals and the deaths, the people make peace with each other, if not wholly with themselves, which always poses a tougher test in McNally. They've stopped thinking that the world is up for grabs. Wickedly intelligent, beautiful and jaggedly keen to American rigor and raciness, the play pivots on an inscrutability that propels it into the future. All of it makes for a thrilling, inimitable ride. If the people keep living beyond final curtain, so do we. We've brought about this ultimate payoff together. Refreshed by wonder and awe, we take our first steps on the same spiritual path as they do. But our feet remain on earth, too. We dwellers of a world elsewhere will keep a foot in two realms. The sense of what's coming won't stop us from being emotionally outflanked by it. But our having known *LTTA* improves our chances of righting ourselves soon.

Conclusion

Few of today's playwrights evoke as many mixed feelings as Terrence McNally, largely because he works on the edges of social and ethical conventions. Nor does he always stick to the edge. As in the singing of Edith Piaf, Billie Holiday, and Maria Callas, many of his most powerful effects flout the boundaries of the official culture, which, in his case, includes mainstream theater. The very materials he uses can be beautiful or repellent, making us reel. Instead of turning reflexively to irony, McNally, intense and utterly honest, voices universal anxieties. He wrings poetry out of both Frankie's canned peaches in *F&J* (*Three Plays* 145) and the "English muffins, French muffins, Dutch muffins, German muffins" Chloe serves for breakfast in *LTTA* (1). The polish and clarity of his work vie for our attention with the ugly, the menacing, and the blasphemous. This is deliberate. As is seen in the closing moments of *LVC*, McNally takes us into a realm of ordinary and prosaic objects and feelings that's fading from view.

This adventure evokes lonely, bewildering places where, shocked out of our inhibitions, we laugh our heads off. Sometimes, we can't believe what we're watching or reading. The dazzling immediacy of his dark, quirky jokes keeps splitting our sides. But should we be laughing?, we wonder. Much of his wildest comedy comes at moments that are usually treated with high seriousness, like the birth of Jesus, or Joshua, in *Corpus Christi*, which he settles quickly, having Mary snaffle a doll from under her skirts (*CC* 17). Such directness has a strong, even a staggering, impact. Humor and morality are inextricable in McNally; his great moments occur when a moral point is being made as the audience laughs.

Like Mark Twain, McNally speaks openly about the hallowed, the embarrassing, and the obvious. This frankness affirms art's capacity to transform and release. Again, like Twain — and Hawthorne, too — he finds political correctness as intolerant a system of thought as the Salem witch trials. He downplays his scorn, though his deceptive tropes and conceits hiding considerable craftsmanship. Nor does he cave in to a weakness that often dogs comic writers—flattening his minor characters by exaggerating their flaws so he can play them for laughs. Emma, the cabdriver enters *It's Only a Play* at the end of the play's first act. Having brought copies of the *New York Times* containing Frank Rich's review of the play that premiered just hours earlier, she speeds the action of McNally's 1985 play. She sees what's in clear view, unlike Jane Austen's Emma Woodhouse, which explains why she's given some of the play's most important lines, e.g., "If I had a best friend, I'd cherish him" (*Three Plays* 226) and "New York without a theater district might as well be Newark" (*ibid.*, 228). In this regard, it should be noted that Angel, the Liza Minnelli role in *The Rink*, is "30 years old.... She looks like hundreds, no thousands of young women" (9). (Later in his career, like the later Osborne, Pinter, and Albee, McNally will write more often about the well heeled.)

Roles like Angel and Emma join McNally's democratic values to his emotional insight, a boon in a playwright who ranks character over both plot and structure. The primacy of character in his work pays big dividends. Some of his people, like Mendy of *The Lisbon Traviata*, Buzz of *Love! Valour! Compassion!*, and all four of the characters in *Lips Together, Teeth Apart* conjure up Chekhov. Their lives seem an insoluble mess of sorrows, baffled hopes, and missed chances. But to view them simply as a collection of traits is to belittle them—and to cheat ourselves. On this score, we should heed the words of Mrs. Willard in *Dedication*, who often knows more than she lets on: "Shakespeare put real people on the stage," she says in Act One, adding that "he trafficked in mere humanity" (*D* 34). She's using the word, mere, in the way Shakespeare and the W. B. Yeats of "Leda and the Swan" did; it means total, not trite. Shakespeare has remained McNally's model and inspiration. Like him, he transmits the individuality of individual experience. There's something both simple and complex in the transmission. Which he captures; looking into the baroque business of human existence, he shows what it feels like here. For him, as with Chekhov, this everydayness is crucial.

He tells his stories in human rather than ideological terms, underscoring Yeats's claim that people can embody the truth without ever knowing it. Thus there's always the sense in McNally that everything must vanish at the end. But along with it, there's the impression that even though everything changes or goes away, nothing is lost. Poignancy looms over his beautifully written, precisely detailed comedy, but not sentimentality, i.e., unearned feeling. A foe of emotion that overshoots what provokes it, McNally fends off easy answers. He has read his audience carefully. As works in progress, we value questions over answers, a preference that shapes both *our* beauty and the beauty of McNally's plays.

The plays are about people living normal lives, if normal means mingling with others like them instead of shrinking into a corner or joining those who've already arrived at moral conclusions. The upshot of this mingling is also normal. Things don't turn out the way they were supposed to, but what can you do? You have to take life as it comes and make the best of it, being careful not to wreck your best chances. Good ideas rarely play out in expected ways.

McNally's gives this shopworn idea wings. Because every commitment poses restrictions, the conclusions his people reach can cause regret, like the anger burned into Buzz of *LVC* by his picture of a starving Somalian child "so weak from hunger he can barely lift his head." The child is under a death sentence. "Five feet away a vulture sits. Sits and waits. He's not even looking at the kid. He's that confident where his next meal is coming from" (*Two Plays* 51). Yet rather than backing down from this horror, Buzz pushes back. He works at a clinic that's looking to cure AIDS. An AIDS victim himself, he knows he's fighting an uphill fight. His sense of purpose typifies McNally's flair for hard-won insights into complex issues and people. Hard-won because life is hard; McNally has made both his people and their problems believable. Like the rest of us, his characters are both clever and defensive, sweet and loyal, generous and venal. There are a lot of them, too.

And their kind has always been around. What they're like shouldn't surprise us. Thinkers as different as William James and Freud agreed that civilized man harbors a monster inside. McNally would add that all human traits carry within them their opposites. Our strengths can easily become our weaknesses. Nor should we be frightened by evil. That of John Jeckyll of *LVC*, perhaps the canon's foulest character, has relatively little impact; even his twin brother, to whom much of it is aimed, defuses it. It's the gentle, loving characters who do most of the harm, both to others (Bobby to Gregory in *LVC*) and to themselves (Jessie Nuncle of *D*). Good motives often cause bad decisions and worse conduct. Sally of *LTTA* and Katharine of *Ganesh*, both of whom make excessive demands on themselves, often feel like failures. If he had his way, Vincente Bellini would cancel the premiere of his opera, *I Puritani*, into which he has "poured ... [his] life and soul into these past 16 months" (*GA* 8) so he can hurry home and start a better one. Composers aren't the only musicians who suffer inside, either. The setbacks of world-class singer Maria Callas of *Master Class* impact her more than her triumphs.

There's more to say on the topic. Defying augury, she and her kind in the 1995 play are adrift in the half-tones of moral and emotional ambivalence. They're both good and bad. In McNally, self-acceptance and self-castigation co-exist. What also intrigues him is how easily one attitude can rout the other. The self-images of his people are always changing, forcing us to keep pace with them. Should we bother? The wicked John Jeckyll rightly says, "I'm good for something. I'm not entirely bad!" He could be referencing his skill as a pianist. Perhaps, though, he's being profound. He follows up his remark with another that comes as close as any other in the canon to the heart of McNally's ethics. After apologizing to his lover Ramon for disrespecting him, he says, "Forgiveness is good. We all need it from time to time" (*ibid.*, 61).

Or much of the time? McNally's belief that lust governs much of our conduct has given adultery or sexual betrayal, both gay and straight, great force in his plays. *LTTA* includes, in addition to illicit sex between in-laws, a cuckold who's both excited and appalled by his confused sexual feelings.

McNally takes Sam Truman's emotional quandary in stride. Following Shakespeare, he excels in building emotional sympathy for his people. Hamlet's insistence on treating people better than they deserve ("Use every man after his desert, and who should escape whipping?" [2. 2. 469–73]) comes to mind; the vicious "mole of Nature" (1.4.15) he finds in men is redeemable. McNally told Steven Drukman in 1993, "I do believe there is a divinity in all of us, but we run into problems" (Drukman, "You Got to Have Friends," Zinman, ed., *Casebook* 17, 132). And they're inescapable. McNally uses empathy to convey the texture of life without moralizing or pontificating. Our transgressions, he believes, denote a turning away from our better selves. Part of us, maybe the divine part, always knows the right thing to do.

The wrongs we've done clog our minds. When McNally's endearing cheats and defectors speak their minds, it's rarely to defend themselves. Nor are their words evasive or nasty. Their painful honesty in fact makes the people's insights into their misdeeds some of the plays' most affecting moments. These moments display in McNally an imagination of frightening intensity, baring his soul while making common cause with his people's private yearnings.

The dark undertow of the text keeps pulling against the laughs. A huge gap has opened between the elegant polish of the dialogue and the dread that lurks below. Works like *And Things That Go Bump in the Night* (1964), *LTTA* (1991), and *D* (2004) don't only deal with trauma; they're traumatized plays. As is suggested by the years between their production dates, they're not unusual. Characters like John of *LVC* and Maria of *MC* are condemned to keep returning to the primal wound of being the lesser favored child in their families of origin.

Over-doers like Katharine and Margaret of *PG*, on the other hand, have run afoul of the great imperative in McNally — to embrace the hurt and the mess that love entails. No easy job, this. Muddying it is the self-doubt that haunts all his people. He wrote about this haunting so well because he both knew it and lived it. A closeted artistic gay teenager growing up in Texas doesn't need much teasing and bullying by hyper-macho cowboy types to feel deeply wounded. McNally's wounds and anxieties have survived his several incarnations, e.g., the prodigy, misfit, *Wunderkind,* and admired genius; a MacArthur Foundation Genius Award would be a fitting prize even if it wouldn't halt the pain.

This most recent phase has found him reeling between what Wallace Stevens in "The Snowman" called the "nothing that is not there and the nothing that is." Let's look at another account of this plight. Success has made him struggle with having become what Lydia Davis calls a "positive nothing" after having slogged for decades to fight past the shame of being a "negative nothing." "It's so confusing," Davis says in "New Year's Resolution": "You spend the first half of your life learning that you are something after all, now you have to spend the second half learning to see yourself as nothing" (Lydia Davis, *The Collected Stories of Lydia Davis* [New York; Farrar, Straus, and Giroux 2009: 315]).

Davis has hit the bulls eye. No creative artist can revel in his success. First, self-acclaim chokes incentive. The complacent artist works from the middle of his creativity rather than exploring the prickly edges, where the hard-to-find but more vital truths lie. Next, the success that came too early to rock singer Ida Head of *Dedication* turned her to alcohol, drugs, and a preoccupation with death. Death and damnation remain issues. Maria Callas's thirty-seven curtain calls followed hard after the pact she made with the devil. Satan exacted his due by bloating her self-esteem and then snatching from her both the voice that thrilled audiences worldwide and, in Aristotle Onassis, the man she loved.

But McNally casts his net beyond the struggles of artists, as the best creative writers should; the Everyman figure in *Ulysses,* Leopold Bloom, spends more time on the page than the fledgling writer and Joyce's younger alter ego Stephen Dedalus. Others have caught this drift. The non-artistic character type McNally set both his sights and sensibility on inspired David Kuhn's *The Neglected Voter: White Men and the Democratic Dilemma* (2007). Between 1970 and 2003, an age of vastly increased productivity, Kuhn says, the working class lost real wages, more than 60 percent of the gains going to the top 1 percent of the workforce. This outcome threatened the status of men like the Window Washer in *Witness,* Johnny in *F&J,* and Sam Truman of *LTTA.* Many of the laid-off factory hands in *The Full Monty* lost their traditional roles as providers. So much for McNally's elitism. Though he adapted the play, his sympathies for these blue-collar workers made it natural for him to move the setting of 1996 movie version of *Monty* from the English Midlands to Buffalo, New York.

The workers' trusted code of masculinity kept thinning out. One wife and mother in the play moves in with an employed man. Others seek jobs to bring money into the house and, perhaps, to gain an upward mobility for their kids their out-of-work men could no longer supply. Other signs of masculine domination outside the home pressured the men. The unions' rejection of right-wing populism moved many unskilled white workers and the self-employed to the political right; the race issue loomed; gun ownership rose. So did the divorce rate. Frankie's Johnny was divorced by his wife while doing jail time for forgery, a crime that tempts the non-violent unemployed.

Johnny might have lost his family because of the lengths he went to to keep it together. Marion Cheever divorced twice before we meet him in "Next" (1967); Sam Truman's greatest fear is that his wife Sally will divorce *him*. Again alluding to *LTTA*, many white professionals during the years Kuhn writes about, 1970–2003, took their graduate degrees and taste for fine wines and foreign films to the political left. John Haddock angers, terrifies, and vexes his blue-collar foil Sam without trying to. Sam discovers, too, that this member of the brie-and-Chablis set has been sleeping with Sally. Is there another discovery McNally is hinting at? Very little in his best work has one simple meaning. Still smarting from an early ache, John might have indeed wanted to do Sam dirty. His reference early in the play to his "fecund shotgun marriage" to Sam's sister Chloe (*LTTA* 7) exudes reverse social protest. Just as Sam married up, John may have married down in an act forced on him by Chloe's unplanned pregnancy.

The proper response to such betrayals, regardless of their provocation, comes in the author's "Note" that prologues *The Rink*. In it, McNally calls his 1985 play "a story of forgiveness," adding that its main figures, a mother and her prodigal daughter, "learn to let go of the past in order to be free to move into the future" (8). Note that McNally is discussing two women. His plays identify more with the cultural values of femininity than with the hard rational qualities of the male mind. But supporting this imperative differs from applying it. Shedding the baggage of years marred by rancor and spite is hard work. The mutual acceptance gained by Anna and Angel, though real, is fragile. McNally returned to the mother-daughter clash in *D* (2004) — but without resolving it. Happy resolutions are very rare in McNally. The off-stage characters, the son in *PG* and the brother in *LTTA*, were both gay. They're also dead, which hinders the unfinished work of their female survivors. But it doesn't stop them. Forgiveness in both plays entails a full, steady look at the homosexuality that caused the deaths of the son and brother, in one case by AIDS and the other by a gang of armed gay bashers.

McNally has always rated forgiveness over spite, not least of all because, as in *The Rink*, forgiveness not only opens the future but, mostly, disables wrath and its poisonous offspring, vengeance. His term paper, "Spiritual Development in *King Lear*," makes this case. This twenty-four-page effort was submitted to Professor Andrew W. Chiappe, concluding for McNally a year-long course in Shakespeare, in which all the plays were studied chronologically. The challenge it posed might have crowned McNally's college education. It treats both the impotence and the soul-devouring recoil action of malice. The kind-hearted Kent believes in the "benevolence of the gods." He and Cordelia, McNally said, "share an unwavering faith in the gods as supporters of moral order" (5). By contrast, those foes of divine justice, Edmund, Goneril, and Regan, "flourish ... and then die ... rapidly" because the evil that drives them can't "regenerate itself," having petered out "in a turmoil of lechery, intrigue, and vice" (8).

McNally's focus is steady. It's more important, he believed, to understand and forgive than to punish. But his plays will also depict, to his credit, the obstacles that must be hurdled to achieve this goal. The theater, all imaginative literature, really, renders the felt experience of things rather than serving moral lessons. In an untitled essay written on A. C. Bradley's *Shakespearean Tragedy*, he noted a tragic irony he'd later adapt to Katharine and Margaret of *PG*: "What is true of Kent and Fool is true of Cordelia. They help Lear's soul but they harm his cause" (5). Hegel's definition of tragedy as a collision in which both opponents are right comes to mind. Yet energies can also line up in our favor. Sometimes, for instance, divine and natural justice merge. What looks like God's providence will clear a path to the future. Mrs. Willard, the murderer of her infant son decades before curtain up in *D*, becomes a murder victim. Like Tolstoy, McNally believes that life, though raw and messy, contains moments of awkward grace. The long, crazy struggle of Anna of *The Rink* to win the love of her daughter Angel makes fleeting sense. McNally uses such efforts to say, with Tolstoy, that the world is mostly rational and orderly—and, if you look carefully, what happens in it makes sense, if not perfect sense. Angel, to begin with, returned home voluntarily, and Anna dawdled selling the rink she came home to claim.

McNally's people are more tuned to each other than they know. The Conductor in *Prelude and Liebestod* thinks of having sex with a young stranger in the audience at the same time his wife muses, "There's a man over there who has Ralph's mouth. Those full sensual lips I adore." Her next inwardly directed words, "I wonder what my husband would do if he ever knew about us [viz., her and Ralph]," recoil on her. As her husband's next words show, he already knows about his wife's affair (*SS* 54). Each tiny overlap in this one-acter from 1989 is calculated, though all of it sounds spontaneous. This is to say that everything is complex yet fresh. The monologues in *P&L* suggest that the speakers have electronic scanners that give them access to each others' minds. Thoughts run in tandem. Endorsing Mann's belief that music is the most seductively erotic of all art forms, both the Conductor and his wife in *P&L* fantasize about having sex with other people while listening to Wagner.

The play also suggests that people are mostly good, want to be good, and welcome the presence of goodness and beauty in their lives. The cranky Concertmaster says of the Conductor, whom his wife calls, "My poor darling" (*ibid.*, 62), "This is more like it. I gotta hand it to him, when he's at his best, there's no one like him" (*ibid.*, 66). That their own failure to meet this high standard hurts the characters more than the knocks heaped on them by others both confirms their honesty and suggests their basic goodness. That goodness may be more accessible than the characters think. As we saw in *LVC* and *D*, not to mention *CC*, wrongdoing in McNally always hurts the wrongdoer most. This idea ramifies. Wrongdoers, by refusing to justify themselves or blame their misdeeds on others, are hinting obliquely at their perfectibility. The non-judgmental McNally's illuminations have become our recognitions.

Such signs of organicism in McNally's work tally with his rejection of coherence and closure. They appear most prominently in the arts, viewed by McNally as an ever-growing storehouse of integrated perceptions. Frontain's 2007 statement that "*A Man of No Importance* may be viewed as McNally's meditation on the power of theater to create community and to transform how people think" ("After the Gay Jesus Play" 22) both carries forward and re-sites Shelley's belief that poets are the unacknowledged legislators of the world. The community Frontain is speaking of reappears when *Golden Age*'s Vincenzo Bellini improvises on the piano Harold Arlen's "Stormy Weather," the Gershwins' "A Foggy Day," and Stephen Sondheim's "Send in the Clowns" (16–17). At least he thinks he's improvising. Both the storm raging outside the theater and the aimlessness, as opposed to the sense of purpose, with which Bellini picks out tunes that wouldn't be written for 175 or, in Sondheim's case more than 200 years, confirms the importance of what he's doing. Life's most startling affirmations often come when we're looking elsewhere.

What's being affirmed too is Duke Ellington's answer, when he was asked to classify different musical genres, that there are only two kinds of music, good and bad. Members of the same family, musical geniuses of different centuries might well tap into the same community of sounds that unites them. All good songs, operas, and symphonies are connected. Music isn't mere entertainment; it swathes a conversation spanning eras, nations, art forms, and language. Nor does this grand synthesis gainsay McNally's counter-intuitiveness. Plato's cave analogy, Kant's distinction between the phenomenon and the noumenon, and Tolstoy's belief that history is slowly acquiring consciousness all buttress the idea that we live in a world of appearances, signs, and accidents. But we're not groping in the shadows. The dovetailing of art and spirit in *Nudity* and *Dedication* has taught us to rely on the madness of art both to pierce everyday reality's drabness and sludge to winnow the extraordinary from the commonplace.

* * *

From the start, McNally brought many skills to the art of playwriting. He had a keen eye for urban landscapes, defined his characters, and understood the tensions between our private lives and the larger shape of society. His first Broadway play, *And Things That Go Bump in the Night* (1964), made audiences wonder how its 25-year-old author could have gained such a mature grasp of human foibles. When its overwriting isn't trying our patience, the play is alternately hilarious and heartbreaking. It also sends out shock waves emanating from the 1960s obsession with drugs, sex, rock-and-roll music, and Hindu-flavored spirituality. Just as remarkably, it foreshadows McNally's later concern with the weakening of interpersonal bonds and the thinness of domestic life in our cities, usually because of mechanical sex or, as in *Bringing It* and *The Lisbon Traviata*, the lack of sex between partners. *Bump* also includes false indicators. Traces in it of fusing homoeroticism with the muscular militarism found in Walter Pater's *The Renaissance* would depart the canon along with casual references in the play to social wrongs like poverty, hunger, and income inequality.

McNally's next full-length play, *Where Has Tommy Flowers Gone?* (1971) nods towards American novels whose characters must first get lost to find themselves, e.g., Ishmael's sea, Huck's river, Dean Moriarty's open road, and the coal hole of Ralph Ellison's Invisible Man. Following these men, Margaret Civil and Katharine Brynne have to go to India in *PG* to gain self-knowledge. In a different vein, the stage veterans Lou and Jessie Nuncle flee Broadway, the flaming quick of the American stage, before finding a theatrical home hundreds of miles away.

Returning to McNally's early work, we see in "Next" (1967) a simple, exquisite one-acter whose writing is so transparent and guileless that it makes us wonder how it keeps us so involved and attached. This triumph isn't unique. What McNally found in Tennessee Williams's early work also applies to his own: "Almost every one of the plays from this period has a moment that is gloriously prescient of the artist to come" (Foreword, *An Invisible Cat* xi). Like "Next," some of McNally's other early plays add to something considerable, forming a secure foundation to both the canon and his ongoing search for himself. At the same time, to discuss them all would overexpose the subtlety of his approach and make it look mechanical. Another thing: like his fellow Columbia Lion, J. D. Salinger, another celebrant of childhood and youthful turmoil, McNally may have simply found that growing up had snuffed out the urgency of subjects vital to him as a young adult, in his case, the protests spawned by the Vietnam war in "Botticelli" (1968), "Witness" (1968), "¡Cuba Si!" (1968), and *Bringing It* (1969). He had nothing left to say.

The growth of his comic energy also stemmed from a ripening of judgment. Starting with *F&J* (1987), his characters become both better developed and more carefully differentiated. His politics tone down. And the homosexuality that used to be a major concern now acts like a prism through which he treats the larger themes of urban America; even the AIDS plays *PG* and *LVC* urge their casualties to work at knowing each other or die of hatred or indifference. Cosmopolitan in both setting and attitude, the later *Some Men* (2007) aims a strong but nuanced voice at the same idea. This accomplished gathering of layered stories touches down in various Manhattan settings from 1922 to 2007. This variety labels McNally a writer willing to take new risks with plot and character. An early scene in Sur la Mer in Long Island (*Two Plays*, 2007, 19–25) foreshadows one that that takes place there 83 years later in 2005.

This issues in the play (*ibid.*, 80–91) justifies its length. The first scene at Sur la Mer showed David Goldman enjoying the afterglow of sex with the family chauffeur, Padraic. McNally's joke is clear. Goldman Sachs was the Wall Street giant that was charged in 2007, the same year *Some Men* debuted, with misleading investors, a felony that would rack up debts, take away jobs, and foreclose homes all over America. More thematic is David and Padraic's shattering of class boundaries on the beach. McNally, though, doesn't rejoice in this breakthrough. The gay rights movement that followed it decades later, he prefers to note, would launch problems stemming from gains made by gay, lesbian, and transgendered people in matters of security, liberty, and self-governance. But besides staging some of them, he'll also touch in during the second scene at Sur la Mer several references to the Goldmans, their mansion, and their lavish life style. The scene ends with a joke, as it should — but one consistent with the mood of the place in its 1922 heyday.

The character called Perry says in 2005, "The Goldmans had something better than money." He's talking to Marcus, who retorts with the remark, "Don't look at me when you say that." Perry's references to Padraic in his next two speeches (*ibid.*, 80–81) carry the authority of the blood; Perry is Padraic's great-grandson (*ibid.*, 88). His knowledge of the ex-chauffeur's love-making with David Goodman isn't the scene's only example of upward social mobility. The African-American Marcus is Perry's long-time lover, not his servant. He and Perry, in fact, are so secure in their mutual love that they want to adopt a child, a step that enrages Perry's father, Bernie, who visited Sur la Mer as a child — and who, more tellingly, is gay.

This occasion marks Bernie's fifth appearance in the play, each of them charting shifts in his identity as a gay man (*ibid.*, 5–8; 8–15 34–39; 60–63) dating from 1968, the time of his first homosexual rut, with a hustler who keeps forgetting his name. He's next seen in 1971, when the confusion and guilt engulfing him as a gay husband spoil his lunch at the exclusive New York Athletic Club. His next appearance shows him during his first visit to a bathhouse four years later, after having left Susan and the children. He meets, at the baths, the librarian Carl, who'll become his partner. He's still partnered with Carl in Sur la Mer in 2005, where he's fuming. This one-time frightened closet gay who feared that his kids would cut him dead if he came out is giving his son Perry a reason to stop talking to him.

He has grown crusty and rearguard. He objects to Perry and Marcus's adopting a child because, as gay men, they can't provide the kind of healthy, stable home a child needs. His attitude, called elsewhere in the play "internalized homophobia" (*ibid.*, 71), would never have arisen had Bernie gotten the same news from a straight couple. He has gone faux-traditional. McNally has made the most of the brilliant conceit of putting a gay father and his gay son on stage together. Restoring the motif of the enemy within from *LTTA*, *LVC*, and *D*, he has shown that the direst constraints facing gays may not only come from fellow gays but, rather, from one of them whose support ranks foremost with any son, his father.

The play sprouts more fresh data from our shared millennial lives by siding with the inconclusive and the irrational. Though its circular time scheme (its last scene, a wedding, carries forward in time from the first) and the telescoped reminiscences along the way put out tantalizing echoes, they yield no resolutions. The randiness of Michael, one of the grooms, is threatening his marriage before it begins. A month earlier, this avid Internet trawler (*ibid.*, 26–33), having just had sex with a stranger, confessed his inability to be faithful to his future spouse (*ibid.*, 96). Yet his reference to "God's love" (*ibid.*, 32) and his recognition of passages from both Forster and the Bible (*ibid.*, 29, 31) (even though there's no Ecclesiastes 4: 23 in the King James Version) suggests that he's more finely grained than he credits.

The passage he might have been thinking of, one that has McNally's full approval, from Ecclesiastes 4, comes in verses 9–11: "Two are better than one, because they have a good reward for their toil. If they fall, one will lift up his fellow; but woe to him who is alone when he falls and has not another to lift him up. Again, if two lie together, they are warm: but how can one be warm alone?" Like everybody else in the play, Michael has a chance at self-transcendence through love. This ambiguity is typical. Shifting focus, viz., characters and settings, *SM* fends off predictability. Another black man called Aaron appears in it, but, besides being an overworked M.D., he's also the astute, devoted lover of Scoop, whom he had met years before during their undergraduate days at Tufts (*ibid.*, 70). (David's black lover, Aaron, never showed his face in *LTTA*. Another Aaron, an AIDS victim and the lover of Greylines guide Chick Hogan, committed suicide in *Unusual Acts of Devotion* [53].)

SM both challenged McNally artistically and denied its audiences the pleasure of judging him. S. A. Kuftinec and F. J. Ruff discuss a reversal of expectations featured in it in their review of the play. They're talking about the scene called "*A LONG-TERM RELATIONSHIP*" (70–80), which unfolds in Washington Park in 1998. Two gay gender studies majors are interviewing Aaron and Scoop. The reviewers said of the Vassar students, "The two queer undergrads, despite perceiving themselves as cutting edge, appear far more narrow minded and doctrinaire than the content older men ... clear to the older couple and the audience but not to the two college boys" (310). Pushing back against constraints often reaps gains in McNally. Those that faced the younger Scoop and Aaron in an age more hostile to gays than the one the Vassar students know sweetened the intimacies they shared.

This scene follows one that also takes place in Greenwich Village, but in a hospital late at night. The people, the dialogue, and rhythm created by the action's moving between indoors and out, daytime and night, match up so well that transitions seems effortless and seamless. The episode called *Internet* (*ibid.*, 25–33) shows the seamlessness with which the computer is woven into our lives in our Information Age. Also depicted are the uses to which it can be put—but not all of them. The on-line supervisor in the chat room will disconnect any computer where the raunchy talk has overheated. But there's more to say about *Internet*. The scene forecasts our dizzying age of computer imagery, digital animation, and video games. This software, even in 2007, had been moving inward from the edges. The men keyboarding in the chat room at two A.M. on a Saturday night keep returning to problems stemming from both rejection and acceptance, an issue first broached by McNally in *F&J*. Tracing "patterns of commitment and loneliness, like *At the N.Y.A.C*," *Internet*, describes, said Ben Brantley, "the instinct that makes gay men both want and not want to be married" (2007, 2).

McNally's placing the 2004 chat room episode between ones that take place at Sur la Mer in 1922 and the N.Y.A.C. in 1971 discloses a cosmopolitanism he builds upon in *Golden Age*. This 2010 gem uses a supple, mid-register conversational voice that avoids calling attention to itself. Though some of them enjoy iconic stature, the people in the play have both known and worked with each other too long to strike attitudes. Their addressing each other informally helps promote an important development. This relaxed, conversational idiom allows McNally to write about places outside today's America, viz., 1835 Paris, not as a playground for American visitors, but, rather, as central to itself.

This issue never surfaces in the play, as most of the characters are, if not French, then Italian. A center of artistic activity, Paris has always attracted foreigners. The play even puts a sophisticated spin on this truth. Art is most useful when it deals with timeless problems and questions in a manner relevant to the present. This process of remembering what we have learned shows the present constantly becoming history. Shakespeare's *Julius Caesar* and *Lear* and, more recently, Arthur Miller's *The Crucible* (1952), John Osborne's *A Patriot for Me* (1965) and Terence Rattigan's play about Lord Nelson, *A Bequest to the Nation* (1970), show that engaging with the past hones a playwright's art. McNally's engagement with history has been public, complicated, and prolonged, as is seen in the settings of *RC* (1960), *The Rink* (1985), *CC* (1998), and *Deuce* (2007). Throughout his career, he has never tired of matching his talent with that of his favorite writer, Shakespeare, even as he continues to devise his own forms of self-expression.

Adam Hetrick called *Golden Age*, which was included in a five-week-long tribute to McNally in 2010 at Washington's Kennedy Center, "a kind of *Noises Off* at the opera" (1). Hetrick spoke home. McNally selects in *GA tableaux vivants* from the historical record — which he hand-works with great care — to depict in the lives of musical stars of the 1830s parallel events we thought we knew. The play works as both alternative history and opera criticism. The quips traded by fast-track, status-obsessed people keep matters zipping along. But, as the play's title suggests, there's a darker big picture. A persistent subject in *GA* is the post–Romantic idea of the author as a tortured big-name genius. More trouble looms: the author, or composer, Bellini, calls his favorite tenor, Giovanni Rubini, "a Romantic, a true Romantic" (21).

McNally makes this point as he should, with a vibrant image. The play's first act ends with two of its leading figures lying down on the stage, calling to mind that moment in Part Two of Beckett's *Waiting for Godot* when all of the play's characters sprawl out on the stage. Celebrity, power, and wealth stand closer to desolation than we had imagined, an idea that will recur in the second act of *GA*. The distance between success and bare subsistence, even between life and death, can be leaped in a heartbeat. This issue is familiar in McNally. As was seen in *LTTA* and *LVC*, falls in the canon carry thematic weight. Advisedly, a workplace fall by the Window Washer in *Witness* would kill him instantly.

The falls and the references to paradise in these earlier plays target the Garden of Eden. As he made clear in *PG* and *CC*, McNally enjoys looking for spirituality where it has always belonged — wherever life is happening. Powering religious themes in the plays is his ongoing fascination with the mundane and those instances where the known becomes foreign or the everyday discloses its sinister roots. What often drives these revelations are wrenching social and cultural displacements. These stem from the tense intricacies of ethnicity, culture, and language in "Tour" (1967), *PG* (1993), and *Nudity* (2004). We see ourselves in the displaced and the alienated. They're all threatened by loneliness. The shadows darken. Engulfment often looms over likeable, sometimes adventurous people throughout the canon — whom we identify with. An unfaithful but otherwise likeable husband in *Unusual Acts* (2008) says, "We try to do the right thing and end up doing absolutely the opposite" (82). Like us, he and his kind can be imagined groping for words, forgetting a colleague's name or face, and reading a sentence three times without getting it.

McNally told David Savran, "The theme of *The Lisbon Traviata* is people trying to connect and failing. I think there's some real connection. It's between people in *Love! Valour! Compassion!*" (1999, 34). Connection and its failure drive much of what goes on in McNally's work. An Internet surfer in *SM* pronounces moments after saying that connections "are all we have," "Only connect." His converser recognizes the quotation. "E.M. Forster, right?" (*Two Plays* 2007, 29) But connecting presumes honesty, an essential because many of McNally's people have identity problems. They're in hiding. Whether they're fragile or aggressive (which amounts to a pumped-up machismo built on insecurity), they forfeit a measure of their humanity by denying feelings of sadness, confusion, and hurt.

Denial comes easily to them. People pay a heavy price to connect in *F&J*, *LVC* and *LTTA*. But because their connections are often sparked by unforeseen events, like the burn Johnny gets from backing into a skillet, the ring that falls into the pool in *LTTA*, and the death of Bobby's sister in *LVC*, they fall outside the normal routine of those who are changed by them. This is to say that they come close to violating Aristotle's law of probability. Mrs. Willard's chance meeting with Jessie Nuncle, for instance, make us ask if a benevolent God has intervened on their and Lou's behalf. Related motifs in *D*, like the art-religion bond and that fixture of Christian myth, betrayal, make the question reasonable. McNally hasn't been treading a slippery slope, after all.

* * *

Lending his footing purchase are his colorful characters, the delicious insider details, and the smart, evocative dialogue that help shape a scene. And the direction a scene will take? Though reputations in the theater are often based on predictability, McNally's plays dodge audience expectations, as they well might; they're dramas of both detailed observation and sympathetic insight into motives framed to intensify our experience of people, manners, and morals. Fantastic, grotesque, violent, tender, and confrontational, they rank among the most profound and entertaining theater of today. Nor has their range and bite gone unnoticed. The number of awards he has won may be unrivaled (McNally, *SS* 68). Playgoers, too, have been marveling at the beauty and brilliance of his work, its raw emotional exposure, and the consistency that stokes it.

Models of compression and clarity, McNally's heartfelt plays, though often conventionally shaped, have in them passages of crazy exhilaration and shocking invention. These passages take us by surprise. The comedy doesn't always temper freedom with tact. Jokes may be slathered over a previous layer of ones that haven't had a chance to dry. McNally planned it that way. Not only is he so smart, creative, and intellectually alive that it's an honor to spend time within his head. This master of dramatic tempo also handles his materials with a sure touch and a commendable sense of purpose.

His having wanted to be a journalist as a high-schooler accounts in part for his sharp eye for the idiosyncratic detail (e.g., Maria's saying of herself during her overweight 20s, "I ... looked like an American flag singing *Madama Butterfly*" [*MC* 36]). Key here is his gift for the riveting turnabout (the revelation that the Conductor in *P&L* knows about his wife's presumably secret love affair [*SS* 54]) that keeps theater audiences as off balance as the characters. Much of this freshness and surprise leaps from small particulars that pop out and make us take note, a function of McNally's intense physical awareness of his surroundings. He's a fierce notice, undauntingly curious, and he's blessed with a tenacious memory.

His keen powers of observation may be unrivaled on today's stage. May he set a good example to his peers. A playwright should both notice things missed by others and use seemingly random details to fashion solid work. What comes to mind in this regard is the scene in *CC* where Mary and Joseph check into the motel where Joshua will be born while a football game blares from a nearby television. The components of the scene argue its point. The Nativity takes place in Texas, many of whose nominal Christians would be more shaken by breaking news about the Dallas Cowboys than by the Savior's birth.

This episode conveys the quality of McNally's scene-building skills. They appear elsewhere. It makes sense that Gregory Mitchell, who has worked in ballet as both a dancer and a choreographer for more than 20 years should spot straightaway a work as central to the repertoire as Arnold Schoenberg's *Verklärte Nacht* (*Two Plays* 27). It's just as fitting that a movie fan named after Lana Turner like Lana Maxwell of *Nudity* should know that the actress's boyfriend was killed by her daughter (14-year-old Cheryl Crane knifed blackmailer-extortionist Johnny Stompanato [1925–58] to death some 49 years before the premiere of *Nudity* [*Facts on File Yearbook*, 18 (New York: *Facts on File*, 1958: 115)]. McNally's Lana came just short of the mark by calling her "Cherry" [*SS* 7])— but that she should flub the daughter's name (McNally, *SS* 7). This may sound like nitpicking. But creative writers, no less than scientists and teachers, must get their facts right. A few wrong details, and readers begin to lose faith in the big picture.

And the big picture in McNally features a striking economy of words that moves the action without giving any signs of haste. His blends of hilarity, gravitas, and mystery have made audiences think about the theater in new ways. Dramatists are called playwrights, like shipwrights and wheelwrights. They deserve to be. Besides providing more satisfaction, "making" sounds more worthwhile than saying. In her feature story about *SS*, Alex Witchel may have had this in mind when she called McNally "one of the theater's most acclaimed, and durable, playwrights" (1). His work is made to last.

McNally has risen to the ranks of the leading playwrights of the past 50 years because he says things of importance in vital, intriguing ways. It's not enough to cite his instinct for the outrageous or to call him the most extravagantly fearless voice on Broadway. Fueling his funny, brilliantly inventive plays are richly nuanced, slow-burning character studies. Like Shakespeare, what interests him most are characters who want to invest their lives with substance and joy. Their efforts, even the ill-considered ones, give off light and warmth. McNally's sympathy with these attempts to banish cold and darkness draws you in. The no-nonsense energy and abrasion with which he depicts them are exhilarating.

An astonishing medley of beauty and vulgarity, his character portraits, which recall the Russian soul-speak of Pushkin and Dostoevsky, have made fearsome demands on his stamina. It has all been worthwhile. His brand of black comedy comes from his people's lack of self-awareness, their bad judgments, and the honesty of their struggles toward the light. This honesty is contagious — and liberating. Playgoers may conclude that they're not so different from the "little, insignificant, magnificent lives" (*Two Plays* 160) unfurling on stage before them. McNally takes us a step further. When the feeling of superiority it creates wears off, his satire gives rise to sympathy. You've discovered that the creative glow he emits has been inside you all the time. He has restored you to yourself newly armed and refreshed. And that's the miracle, just that.

Bibliography

Works by Terrence McNally

Plays
(IN ORDER OF PRODUCTION)

The Roller Coaster, Columbia Review 40.3 (Spring 1960):42–60.

This Side of the Door, 1962 (typescript). Harry Ransom Humanities Research Center at the University of Texas-Austin (HRC), Terrence McNally Archive (Box 49, Folder 5).

And Things That Go Bump in the Night, in *Collected Plays: Volume II*. Lyme, NH: Smith and Kraus, 1996: 1–78.

"Tour," in *Apple Pie: Three One-Act Plays*. New York: Dramatists Play Service, 1969: 5–11.

"Next," in *15 Short Plays*. Introduction by John Guare. Lyme, NH: Smith and Kraus, 1994: 61–82.

Noon, in *15 Short Plays*: 23–50.

"Botticelli," in *15 Short Plays*: 51–60.

"¡Cuba Si!," in *15 Short Plays*: 83–96.

"Sweet Eros," in *15 Short Plays*: 97–113.

"Last Gasps," in *¡Cuba Si!, Bringing It All Back Home, Last Gasps*. New York: Dramatists Play Service, 1970: 45–53.

Where Has Tommy Flowers Gone?, in *Collected Plays: Volume II* Lyme, NH: Smith and Kraus, 1994: 79–165.

Whiskey, in *15 Short Plays*: 139–94.

Bad Habits, including "Ravenswood" and "Dunelawn," in *15 Short Plays*: 195–268.

The Ritz, in *15 Short Plays*: 269–332; (Garden City, NY: Nelson Doubleday, 1976).

It's Only a Play, in *Three Plays by Terrence McNally*: (New York: Plume, 1976): 157–241.

Frankie and Johnny in the Clair de Lune, in *Three Plays by Terrence McNally*: 89–156.

"Andre's Mother," in *15 Short Plays*, 347–51.

"Street Talk," in *15 Short Plays*: 363–7.

The Lisbon Traviata, in *Three Plays by Terrence McNally*, rev. ed. New York: Dramatists Plays Service, 1992: 3–88.

Prelude & Liebestod, in *15 Short Plays*: 331–46, rev. ed. Terrence McNally, *The Stendhal Syndrome*. New York: Grove Press, 2004: 38–67.

Lips Together, Teeth Apart. New York: Plume, 1991.

"The Wibbly, Wobbly, Wiggly Dance That Cleopatterer Did," in *15 Short Plays*: 353–61.

"Hidden Agendas," in *15 Short Plays*: 369–73.

A Perfect Ganesh, in *Love! Valour! Compassion! and A Perfect Ganesh: Two Plays*. New York: Plume, 1995: 143–256.

Love! Valour! Compassion!, in *Love! Valour! Compassion! and A Perfect Ganesh: Two Plays*: 1–142.

Master Class. New York: Plume, 1995.

"Dusk," in Joe Pintauro, Lanford Wilson, and Terrence McNally. *By the Sea, By the Sea, by the Beautiful Sea*. New York: Dramatists Play Service, 1997: 47–68.

Corpus Christi. New York: Dramatists Play Service, 1998.

The Stendhal Syndrome. New York: Grove Press, 2004.

Dedication or the Stuff of Dreams. New York: Dramatists Play Service, 2006.

Some Men and *Deuce*, in *Two Plays by Terrence McNally*. New York: Grove, 2007.

"Teachers' Break" (13-page typescript, produced 2008).
Unusual Acts of Devotion (93-page typescript, produced 2008).
"The Sunday Times." *24 by 24: the 24-Hour Play Anthology* Mark Armstrong and Sarah Bisman, ed. New York: Playscripts, 2009: 129–38.
Golden Age (89-page typescript, produced 2010).
Mothers and Sons (98-page typescript, produced 2013).
And Away We Go (127-page typescript, produced 2013).

PLAY COLLECTIONS

15 Short Plays. Lyme, NH: Smith and Kraus Contemporary Playwrights Series, 1994.
Collected Plays: Volume II. Lyme, NH: Smith and Kraus Contemporary Playwright Series, 1996.

OPERA LIBRETTOS AND BOOKS FOR MUSICALS
(IN ORDER OF PRODUCTION)

Here's Where I Belong. Music by Robert Waldman. Based on John Steinbeck's *East of Eden*, 1969.
The Rink. Music by John Kander, lyrics by Fred Ebb. New York: Samuel French's Musical Library, 1985.
Kiss of the Spider Woman. Adapted from the novel by Manuel Puig; music by John Kander, lyrics by Fred Ebb. New York: Samuel French, 1992.
Ragtime. Adapted from the novel by E. L. Doctorow; music by Stephen Flaherty, lyrics by Lynne Ahrens.
The Full Monty. Adapted from the 1996 movie directed by Simon Beaufoy, music and lyrics by David Yazbeck. New York: Applause, 2002.
Dead Man Walking. Adapted from the memoir by Sister Helen Prejean and the 1995 movie by Tim Robbins; music by Jake Heggie.
A Man of No Importance. Adapted from the 1994 movie directed by Suri Krishnamma; music by Stephen Flaherty, lyrics by Lynn Ahrens. New York: Stage and Screen, 2003.
Catch Me If You Can. Based on the book by Frank Abagnale, Jr. and Stan Redding and the 2002 movie by Jeff Nathanson. Produced 2010.

MOVIE REVIEWS

Published in *The Seventh Art*, for which McNally was the film critic from 1963 to 1965.
"The Antonioni Trilogy." Review of Michelangelo Antonioni's *Eclipse*.
"Long Day's Journey into Night." Review of Sidney Lumet's *Long Day's Journey into Night*.
"The New Films": "The Leopard." Review of Luchino Visconti's *The Leopard*.
"Review of Joan Littlewood's *Sparrows Can't Sing*.
Review of Abby Mann's *The Condemned of Altona*.

UNDERGRADUATE TERM PAPERS
(COLUMBIA COLLEGE)

"Shakespeare's Early Development as a Tragedian," submitted 9 January 1959, 1–12 (HRC Box 57, Folder 6).
Untitled paper on A. C. Bradley's *Shakespearean Tragedy*, submitted 1 May 1959, 1–6 (HRC Box 57, Folder 6).
"The Family as a Dramatic Theme in *King Lear* and *The Winter' Tale*," c. May 1959, 1–12 (HRC Box 57, Folder 6).
"Spiritual Movement in *King Lear*," submitted 8 June 1959, 1–26 (HRC Box 57, Folder 6).

ASSORTED PROSE

"Theatre Isn't All Broadway." *New York Times*, 28 April 1974: 2: 1.
"A Few Words about the Plays." *The Ritz and Other Plays*. New York: Dodd, Mead: 1976, vii–viii.
"Introduction." *Broadway Song and Story*, Edited by Otis L. Guernsey, Jr. New York: Dodd, Mead, 1985, xi–xii.
"Stage Struck." *Broadway Song and Story*, 286–94.

"A Few Words of Introduction." *Three Plays by Terrence McNally*, ix–xii.
"Preface." *15 Short Plays*, v–vi.
"Some Thoughts." *Love! Valour! Compassion! Two Plays*, ix–xi.
"Introduction." *A Man of No Importance: A New Musical*. New York: Stage and Screen, 2003, n.p.
"Letters to the Editor," *Sondheim Review* 17 (Spring 2011), 3:3.
"Foreword: An Invisible Cat Enters Mewing." Tennessee Williams. *The Magic Tower and Other One-Act Plays*." Thomas Keith, ed. New York: New Directions, 2011, ix–xiii.

Works by Others

INTERVIEWS

Albee, Edward. "In Conversation with Terrence McNally." *Broadway Song and Story*. Edited by Otis L. Guernsey, Jr. New York: Dodd, Mead, 1985, 251–65.
Bryer, Jackson R., ed. *The Playwright's Art: Conversations with Contemporary American Playwrights*. New Brunswick, NJ: 1995, 182–204.
DiGaetani, John L. "Terrence McNally." *A Search for a Postmodern Theater: Interviews with Contemporary Playwrights*. Westport, CT: Greenwood, 1991, 219–228.
Drukman, Steven. "Terrence McNally." *Speaking on Stage: Interviews with Contemporary American Playwrights*. Edited by Philip C. Kolin and Colby H. Kullman. Tuscaloosa, AL: University of Alabama Press, 1996, 332–45.
Rich, Frank. "In Conversation with Terrence McNally." *Dramatists Guild Quarterly*, 24 (Autumn 1987), 11–29.
Rosen, Carol. "Terrence McNally: The Theaterweek Interview." *Theaterweek*, 27 Feb 1995, 12–24.
Savran, David. "Terrence McNally." *The Playwright's Voice: American Dramatists on Memory, Writing, and the Politics of Culture*. New York: Theatre Communications Group, 1999, 119–38.
Simon, Neil. "In Conversation with Terrence McNally." In Guernsey, ed., 172–83.
Simonson, Robert. "Playbill.com's Brief Encounter with Terrence McNally." *Playbill.com*, 10 March 2010, 1–3; web.
Zinman, Toby Silverman. "Interview with Terrence McNally." *Terrence McNally: A Casebook*. Edited by Toby Silverman Zinman. New York: Garland, 1997.
_____."Terrence McNally on *Master Class*." In Zinman, ed., 147–50.

PANEL DISCUSSIONS

(All from *Broadway Song and Story: Playwrights/Lyricists/Composers Discuss Their Hits*. Edited by Otis L. Guernsey, Jr. New York: Dodd, Mead, 1985.)

Eve Merriam (moderator), Terrence McNally, David Mamet, Albert Innaurato, "Short Plays, Small Musicals," 405–20.
Russell Baker, Jules Feiffer, Herb Gardner, et al., 371–83 (McNally: "I love low humor," 371.)
Terrence McNally (moderator), Arthur Laurents, Stephen Sondheim, and Jule Styne, "Gypsy," 55–74.
Terrence McNally (moderator), Leonard Bernstein, Arthur Laurents, et al., "West Side Story," 40–54.
Terrence McNally (moderator), Mildred Natwick, Mike Nichols, and Neil Simon, "Barefoot in the Park," 102–14.
Terrence McNally (moderator), Richard Barr and George Grizzard, et al. "Who's Afraid of Virginia Woolf," 87–101.
Terrence McNally (moderator), Robert Anderson, Elia Kazan, "Tea and Sympathy," 24–39.

CRITICISM AND OTHER COMMENTARY

Abel, Sam. "Uneasy Transitions: Reassessing *The Lisbon Traviata* and Its Critics." In Zinman, ed., 37–54.
Als, Hilton. "Swan Song: Maria Callas Haunts the Stage in 'Master Class.'" *New Yorker*, 25 July 2011, 72–4.
Ardoin, John. *Callas at Julliard: The Master Classes*. New York: Knopf, 1987.
_____. "Callas and the Juilliard Master Classes." In Zinman, ed., 157–63.
Barnes, Clive. "Making the Most of 'Ritz'

Steam Bath." *New York Times*, 21 Jan 1975, 40; review of *The Ritz*.

Billington, Michael. "Master Class-review," *Guardian*, 7 Feb 2012, 1–4; web.

Blankenship, Mark. "Moments in History, Converging Anew." *New York Times*, 15 Oct 2008, 1–4.

Brantley, Ben. "Theater Review; A Maestro Hears Music as Echoes of His Ego." *New York Times*, 17 Feb 2004, 1–3.

_____. "She Hates the Theater, but She Steals the Show." *New York Times*, 19 Aug 2005, 1–4.

_____."8 Decades of Gay Men, at the Altar with History." *New York Times*, 27 March 2007, 1–3.

Brustein, Robert. "Aspects of Love and Compassion." *New Republic*, 3 April 1995, 30–1.

Buttel, Helen T. "McNally's Films of His Broadway Plays." In Zinman, ed., 71–87.

Canby, Vincent. "McNally, True, but Vaguely Neo-Chekhovian." *New York Times*, 6 Nov 1994, C5, 32.

_____. "Theater Review; Patti LuPone's Arrival Changes the Effect of McNally's Script," *New York Times*, 26 July 1996, 1–3.

Clum, John M. *Acting Gay: Male Homosexuality in Modern Drama*, rev. ed. New York: Columbia University Press, 1994.

_____. "Where Are We Now: *Love! Valour! Compassion!* and Contemporary Gay Drama." In Zinman, ed., 95–116.

Collins, Glenn. "A Comic Triumph as a Tragic Callas Worshipper." *New York Times*, 4 June 1989, C19.

Crutchfield, Will. "Dishing about Divas and Other Opera Chat." *New York Times*, 4 June 1989, 15, 20.

Davis, Lydia. *The Collected Stories of Lydia Davis*. New York: Farrar, Straus, 2009.

Drukman, Steven. "You Got to Have Friends: Gay Reception of *Love! Valour! Compassion!*" In Zinman, ed., 117–33.

Franklin, Nancy. "McNally Men, Wasserman Women." *New Yorker*, 14 Nov 1991, 129–31.

Frontain, Raymond-Jean. "'All Men Are Divine': Religious Mystery and Homosexual Identity in Terrence McNally's *Corpus Christi*." *Reclaiming the Sacred: The Bible in Gay and Lesbian Culture*, 2d. ed. Edited by Raymond-Jean Frontain. New York: Harrington Park Press, 2003, 231–57.

_____."'I Don't Believe This Whole Night': Transgressive Festivity in Terrence McNally's *The Ritz*." *Philological Review* 29 (Fall 2003), 2: 79–126.

_____. "'There is someone out there': The Failed struggle against Immolation in Terrence McNally's *And Things That Go Bump*." *Literature and Criticism: The Journal of the Literary Society of India*, 4 (August 2004), 11–31.

_____. "McNally after the 'Gay Jesus' Play." *The Gay & Lesbian Review* (March–April 2007), 21–4.

_____. "That Obscure Object of Fulfillment." *The Gay & Lesbian Review* (September–October 2007), 47, 50.

_____. "McNally and Steinbeck." *ANQ: A Quarterly Journal of Short Articles, Notes and Reviews* 21:4 (Fall 2008) 43–51.

_____. "What Matters to McNally, After All." (January–February 2009). *The Gay & Lesbian Review* (January 2009); rev. of *Unusual Acts of Devotion*.

_____. "Terrence McNally and the Dance of Death." *The CEA Critic* 71:2 (Winter 2009): 25–56.

_____. "James Coco, AIDS, and the Genesis of *A Perfect Ganesh*." *ANQ*. 23:4 (Winter 2010): 1–9.

_____. "Trafficking in Mere Humanity: Shakespeare, McNally and the Reach of 'this wooden O.'" *Explorations in Renaissance Culture* 36:1 (Summer 2010): 93–118.

_____. "'Mutual Admiration,' Sondheim and playwright Terrence McNally began a collaboration in 1991." *Sondheim Review* 17:3 (Spring 2011): 29–33.

_____. "A Preliminary Calendar of the Works of Terrence McNally." *ANQ* 23:2 (2010): 105–23.

_____. "Supper, Song, and Salvation: Terrence McNally's Nights at the Opera." *The CEA Critic* 73:3 (Spring–Summer 2011): 1–31.

_____. "'Allow, Accept, Be': Terrence McNally's Engagement with Hindu Spirituality in *A Perfect Ganesh*." *Comparative Drama* 45:3 (Fall 2011): 213–44.

_____. "Salamon, Julie, 'Wendy and the

Lost Boys: The Uncommon Life of Wendy Wasserstein'," *ANQ* 25:2 (Spring 2012): 123–6.

———. "McNally, Cheever, and the Secret of Unconditional Love," 40-page unpublished typescript.

Gage, Nicholas. *Greek Fire: The Story of Maria Callas and Aristotle Onassis*. New York: Knopf, 2000.

Gardner, Lyn. "Unholy Racket." *Guardian*, 11 Aug 1999, 1; review of *Corpus Christi*.

Gates, Anita. "Theater Reviews: Was It Too dismal For you, too?" *New York Times*, 11 June 2006, 1–2; review of *Frankie and Johnny*.

Guare, John. "Introduction," Terrence McNally, *15 Short Plays*, ix.

Guernsey, Otis L., Jr. *Broadway Song and Story: Playwrights/Lyricists/Composers Discuss Their Hits*. New York: Dodd, Mead, 1985.

Gussow, Mel. "Stage: 'Lisbon Traviata,' Tale of Two Opera Fans." *New York Times*, 19 June 1985, C14.

———. "Agony and Ecstasy of an Opera Addiction." *New York Times*, 7 June 1989, C21; review of *Lisbon Traviata*.

———. "A New, Non-Violent Ending for 'Lisbon Traviata,'" *New York Times*, 1 Nov 1989, 22.

Hetrick, Adam. "All That Glitters: Bobbie Talks about McNally's *Golden Age* at the Kennedy Center." *Playbill.com*, 5 May 2010, 1–3; web.

Kaufman, David. "Frankie and Johnny Are Modern Lovers." *New York Times*, 11 October 1987, sec. 2: 13–14.

Kernan, Joseph. *Opera as Drama*. New York: Vintage, 1959.

Klein, Alvin. "Theater; A Transcendent Journey for McNally's Women." *New York Times*, 7 May 1995, 1–2; review of *A Perfect Ganesh*.

———. "Theater Review; On stage, a diva's Diva Dazzle in 'Master Class.'" *New York Times*, 3 March 2003, 1–2.

Kostenbaum, Wayne. *The Queen's Throat: Opera, Homosexuality, and the Mystery of Desire*. New York: De Capo, 2001.

Kramer, Mimi. "The Chocolate Soldier." *New Yorker*, 19 June 1989, 74–6; review of *Lisbon Traviata*.

Kuftinec, Arsham, and Felice J. Ruff. "Review of *Some Men*, by Terrence McNally." *Theatre Journal* 2 (13 May 2007), 31–2.

Marowitz, Charles. "The Lisbon Traviata." *Theater Week*, 31 Dec 1990, 38–9.

Mazer, Cary M. "*Master Class* and the Paradox of the Diva." In Zinman, ed., 165–79.

Montgomery, Benilde. "*Lips Together, Teeth Apart*: Another Version of Pastoral." *Modern Drama* 36 (1993), 546–55.

———. "*A Perfect Ganesh*: McNally's Carnival in India." In Zinman, ed., 135–45.

Nuechterlein, James. "The Gayest Story Ever Told." *First Things* 88 (Dec 1998), 9–10.

Raymond, Gerard. "Catch Him If You Can." *Advocate* 946 (13 Sept 2005), 66–7.

Rich, Frank. "'True to Form.' The Theater Was Full of Surprises." *New York Times*, 28 Dec 1986, C1.

———. "Struggling to Love, But Aware of the Odds." *New York Times*, 26 June 1991, C11, 13.

Richards, David. "Two Shapes of Comedy — Tragic and Spoof." *New York Times*, 14 July 1991, 5, 8.

———. "In the Hearts and Minds of Men Who Love Men." *New York Times*, 2 Nov 1994, 1–3.

Rizzo, Frank. "In a Master Class: Terrence McNally Still Writing Important, Provocative Plays." *Hartford Courant*, 21 May 2006, 1–4; review of *Master Class*.

Simon, John. "All Wet." *New York*, 15 July 1985, 67–9, review of *Lisbon Traviata*.

———. "The Plot Thins." *New York*, 20 Jan 1986, 56–7, review of *It's Only a Play*.

———. "Anti-Romances." *New York*, 19 June 1989, 71–3; review of *Lisbon Traviata*.

———. "Something Borrowed, Something Blah. *New York*, 13 Nov 1989, 130–1; review of *Lisbon Traviata*.

———. "Saucy! Schmaltzy! Slow Moving." *New York*, 14 Nov 1994, 79–80; review of *Love! Valour! Compassion!*.

Spencer, Charles. "Master Class, Vaudeville Theatre, review," *[London] Telegraph*, 8 Feb 2012, 1–3.

Stein, Howard. "The Early Plays of Terrence McNally," In Zinman, ed., 17–35.

Tanner, Michael. "Role Reversal." *Spectator*, 21 April 2012, 44.

Taylor, Paul. "Master Class, Vaudeville Theatre, review, [London]." *Independent*, 11 Feb 2012, 1–3.

Torrens, James. "'A Perfect Ganesh.'" *America*, 14 Aug 1991, 22.

Watt, Stephen. "*Lips Together, Teeth Apart*: Bodies in search of a Dramatic Form." In Zinman, ed., 55–69.

Wertheim, L. Jon. "Game, Set, Matchless." *Sports Illustrated*, 6 Feb 2012, 54–8.

Witchel, Alex. "Theater: Love! Valour! Survival!, High Drama." *New York Times*, 15 Feb 2004, 1–2.

Zinman, Toby. "Tryout: Master Class." *Variety*, 6–12 March 1995, 72.

Zinman, Toby Silverman, ed. *Terrence McNally: A Casebook*. New York: Garland, 1997.

Zinoman, Jason. "Theater Review 1 'Corpus Christi': A Modern Gay You-Know-Who-Superstar." *New York Times*, 22 Oct 2008, 1–2.

Index

Abraham, F. Murray 53
Adler, Alfred 46
AIDS *see* HIV-AIDS
Albee, Edward 2, 50, 58, 69, 72, 124, 228, 235; *The American Dream* 53, 55; *The Death of Bessie Smith* 61; *A Delicate Balance* 76; influence on McNally 53, 77, 116; *The Sandbox* 53, 55; *Who's Afraid of Virginia Woolf* 53, 77, 113, 116; *The Zoo Story* 14, 53, 77, 99, 116, 124, 196
Allen, Woody 47
Almodovar, Pedro: *Johnny Guitar* 113; *Women on the Edge of a Nervous Breakdown* 111, 113
Als, Hilton 25, 72
"America the Beautiful" 226
Antonioni, Michelangelo: *Eclipse* 8, 32
Ardoin, John: *Callas at Juilliard: The Master Classes* 203, 206
Arlen, Harold: "Stormy Weather" 89
Armstrong, Mark: *24 by 24: The 24-Hour Play Anthology* 2
Auden, W.H. 11–12
Austen, Jane: *Emma* 235; *Northanger Abbey* 157
Azarenka, Victoria 150

Babes in Arms (Mickey Rooney and Judy Garland) 17
Bach, Johann Sebastian: *The Goldberg Variations* 94, 95
Ball, Lucille 135
Balzac, Honoré de 191
Baraka, Amiri: *Preface to a Twenty-Volume Suicide Note* 72
Bates, Katharine Lee 1
Bates, Kathy 34, 53
The Beatles 82
Beaufoy, Simon: *The Full Monty* 16
"Beautiful Dreamer" (Stephen Foster) 17
Beckett, Samuel: *Waiting for Godot* 77, 82, 124, 246
Bellini, Vincenzo: *I Puritani* 10, 24, 210, 211, 236; *La Sonnambula* 108, 202, 204, 205, 206

Bellow, Saul: *The Adventures of Augie March* 195; *Henderson the Rain King* 67
Bergman, Ingmar 200
Berne, Eric: *Games People Play* 113
Billington, Michael 202, 205
Bizet, Georges: *Carmen* 112
Bradley, A.C.: *Shakespearean Tragedy* 240
Brantley, Ben 23, 175, 185, 193, 245
Brecht, Bertolt 39, 40, 130, 135
Brigadoon (Alan Jay Lerner and Frederick Loewe) 95
Brisman, Sarah: *24 by 24: The 24-Hour Play Anthology* 2
Brokaw, Tom 57
Browning, Robert: "Two in the Campagna" 32
Bruckner, Anton 179
Brustein, Robert 171
Bryer, Jackson R. 17
Buttel, Helen T. 9, 23, 93

Cage, John 38
Caldwell, Zoe 34
Callas, Maria 24, 25, 108, 207, 210, 234, 236, 238
Cartland, Barbara 157
Chandler, Raymond 14; *The Big Sleep* 2
Chaucer, Geoffrey 181
Chekhov, Anton 39, 42, 43, 46, 58, 81, 102, 152, 235; *The Cherry Orchard* 58; *The Seagull* 135, 215; *The Three Sisters* 121, 160; *Uncle Vanya* 155
Chiappe, Alan F. 225, 239–240
Churchill, Caryl: *Top Girls* 183
Clum, John 2, 93, 97, 157, 159, 163
Coco, James 14, 93
Columbia University 2, 6, 23, 55, 72, 74, 194
Conrad, Joseph 112, 215, 222; *Lord Jim* 207
Coward, Noël 154
Crane, Cheryl 181, 248
Cyrano de Bergerac (Edmond Rostand) 195

Daly, Tyne 25

257

258　　　　　　　　　　　　　　Index

Dante 80
Davies, Robertson 16
Davis, Lydia: "New Year's Resolution" 238
Debussy, Claude: *Clair de Lune* 100, 101
Delaney, Shelagh: *A Taste of Honey* 77
De Rougemont, Denis: *Love in the Western World* 224
Dickens, Charles 64, 92, 168, 181, 185, 227; *Bleak House* 189, 190; A *Christmas Carol* 189; *Great Expectations* 119, 189, 190; *Little Dorritt* 119; *Oliver Twist* 189; *A Tale of Two Cities* 189
DiGaetani, John 38, 104
Donne, John 120
Dostoevsky, Feodor 65, 66, 69, 75, 161, 193, 249; *The Brothers Karamazov* 66, 79, 138, 147; *Crime and Punishment* 80; "The Double" 66; "The Gambler" 66; *The Idiot* 161; "Notes from Underground" 66, 83
Dreiser, Theodore: *An American Tragedy* 33
Drivas, Robert 14, 93
Drukman, Steven 7, 93, 215, 237
Duchamp, Marcel 38
Du Maurier, Daphne: *Rebecca* 157
Durant, Ariel: *The Story of Civilization* 113
Durant, Will: *The Story of Civilization* 113
Dürrenmatt, Friedrich: *The Visit* 58
Duse, Eleanora 185

Eliot, George 212
Eliot, T.S. 120; "Gerontion" 31; *Murder in the Cathedral* 135
Ellington, Duke 241
Ellison, Ralph: *Invisible Man* 195
Ellroy, James 15
Emerson, Ralph Waldo 11, 17, 31, 40, 155

Feydeau, Georges: *A Flea in Her Ear* 34
Fitzgerald, Scott: *The Great Gatsby* 2, 117, 195; "The Rich Boy" 98
Flaubert, Gustave 169
Fornos, Irene 163
Forster, E.M. 31, 244, 247; *Howards End* 12; *A Passage to India* 31, 117, 121, 123–124, 131, 221, 223
Fowles, John 193
Franklin, Benjamin 216, 219
Franklin, Nancy 172
Franzen, Jonathan 97; *Freedom* 117
Freud, Sigmund 64, 80, 165–166, 192, 236; *Civilization and Its Discontents* 43; *The Interpretation of Dreams* 193
Frontain, Jean-Raymond: "After the Gay Jesus Play" 241; "All Men Are Divine" 139; "Allow, Accept, Be" 123; "I Don't Believe This Whole Night" 13, 15, 84, 85; "Mutual Admiration: Sondheim and Playwright Terrence McNally" 98; "A Preliminary Calendar of the Works of Terrence Mc-

Nally" 1; "Supper, Song, and Salvation 207–208; "There Is Someone Out There" 11, 79; "Trafficking in Mere Humanity" 3, 156–157, 168, 191
Frost, Robert: "Stopping by Woods on a Snowy Evening" 67, 195

Gaddis, William: *Carpenter's Gothic* 156; *JR* 213
Gage, Nicholas: *Greek Fire: The Story of Maria Callas and Aristotle Onassis* 209
Gandhi, Mohandas 117, 140
Gardner, Lyn 142
Garland, Judy 17, 24
Gates, Anita 97
Gates, Robert: *The Dickens Theatre* 168
Gershwin, George 4; *Concerto in F* 47; "A Foggy Day" 241; "How About You" 3; *Rhapsody in Blue* 47; "'S Wonderful" 4; "They All Laughed" 3
Ginsberg, Alan 55
Gladwell, Malcolm 9
Gluck, Christoph Willibald: *Orfeo* 230, 232
"The Good Old Summertime" 70
Gorky, Maxim 9
Gray, Simon: *Butley* 49–50, 65, 197; *Close of Play* 197; *Little Nell* 189; *Quartermaine's Terms* 65
Green, Henry: *Blindness* 161
Greene, Graham 31, 32, 122; *Stamboul Train* (*Orient Express*) 168
Grimm, Brothers 195
Guernsey, Otis: *Broadway Song and Story* 2
Gussow, Mel 115
Guys and Dolls (Frank Loesser) 230

Hammett, Dashiell: *The Maltese Falcon* 33; "[Shine On] Harvest Moon" 172
Hawthorne, Nathaniel 11, 149, 234; "The Birthmark" 198; "Ethan Brand" 168; *The Scarlet Letter* 168
Hegel, G.W.F. 17–18, 154, 240
Hegge, Jake 3
Hemingway, Ernest 14
Hendrix, Jimi 212
Hetrick, Adam 246
Hitchcock, Alfred 157
HIV-AIDS 14, 92–93, 103–104, 121–122, 126, 155, 158, 218, 236
Holiday, Billie 24, 25, 60, 67, 68, 217, 234
Hopkins, Gerard Manley 118
Hopper, Dennis 158

Ibsen, Henrik: *Hedda Gabler* 209; *Peer Gynt* 29; *The Wild Duck* 57, 76, 114
"I'm Through with Love" (Malnick-Livingston) 167, 184
Inge, William 42; *Bus Stop* 178
Ionesco, Eugene 52

James, Henry 170, 176, 192; "The Aspern Papers" 173; "The Lesson of the Master" 173; *The Sacred Fount* 173; *The Turn of the Screw* 189; *The Wings of the Dove* 173, 199
James, William 236
Johnson, Robert 201
Jonson, Ben 181
Joplin, Janis 212
Joyce, James 3, 4, 63, 64, 200; "The Dead" 195; *A Portrait of the Artist as a Young Man* 68, 84, 121, 166, 233; *Ulysses* 64, 82, 238
Juilliard School of Music 2, 199
Jung, Carl Gustav 36

Kafka, Franz 65; *The Trial* 57, 76
Kant, Emmanuel 241
Kaufman, Andy 38
Kaufman, David 32
Kazan, Molly 70
Keats, John 26, 100; "La Belle Dame Sans Merci" 67, 100
Kennedy, Jackie 209
Kerouac, Jack 55; *On the Road* 242
Kierkegaard, Søren 29, 65
King, Martin Luther 140
Kipling, Rudyard 127, 208
Kirdahy, Tom 3
Klein, Alvin 130, 131, 209
Knowles, John: *A Separate Peace* 147
Kostenbaum, Wayne: *The Queen's Throat* 105–107, 210
Kramer, Mimi 107
Kristofferson, Kris 225
Kuftinec, S.A. 245
Kuhn, David: *The Neglected Voter: White Men and the Democratic Dilemma* 238

La Bute, Neil 90
Lane, Nathan 34–35, 49, 53, 158
Lansbury, Angela 34
Laurents, Arthur: *Gypsy* 48
Lawrence, D.H. 13, 28, 101, 192, 212; *The Plumed Serpent* 142; *The Rainbow* 105; *Sons and Lovers* 44; *Studies in Classic American Literature* 67; *Women in Love* 188, 213
Lee, Harper: *To Kill a Mockingbird* 59
Lewis, Sinclair: *Babbitt* 117
Littlewood, Joan: *Sparrows Can't Sing* 36

Malibran, Maria 211
The Mamas and the Papas 82
Mann, Thomas 64, 179, 240; *Doctor Faustus* 66, 224
Marowitz, Charles 112
Marx, Harpo 82
Mason, James 225
Maugham, Somerset 127
Mazer, Cary H. 206, 207

McCullers, Carson: *The Member of the Wedding* 59
McElroy, Maurine 3, 64, 194
McEwan, Ian: *Atonement* 212
McNally, Terrence: *And Things That Go Bump in the Night* 6, 7, 10, 27, 38, 46, 48, 53, 57–61, 66, 70, 74, 76–82, 83, 84, 95, 115, 195, 228, 237, 242; "Andre's Mother" 14, 19, 29; "Apple Pie" 3; *Bad Habits* 8, 11; "Botticelli" 1, 19, 52, 53, 55, 171, 185, 242; *Bringing It All Back Home* 8, 14, 19, 29, 38, 55–57, 59, 62, 74, 76, 83, 84, 214, 216, 228, 242; Calvinism in 5–6; *Catch Him If You Can* (Mark Shaiman and Mark Wittman) 2–3; *Corpus Christi* 3, 6, 19, 21, 29, 30, 31–32, 40, 47, 132–142, 154, 155, 166, 171, 173, 176, 196, 198, 216, 234, 241, 246, 248; "¡Cuba Si!" 22, 38, 39, 242; dancing 15–18, 94, 131–132; *Dead Man Walking* (Jake Hegge) 3, 123; *Dedication* 2, 3, 6, 9, 12, 13, 14, 29, 35, 39, 40, 53, 54, 67, 68, 72, 89, 99, 115, 116, 162, 167, 173, 177, 182, 183–199, 200, 201, 212, 218, 227, 233, 235, 237, 238, 239, 240, 241, 242, 244, 246, 247; *Deuce* 1, 2, 11, 13, 15, 37, 47, 49, 51, 66–67, 92, 122, 125, 132, 133, 143–155, 157, 160, 192, 226, 228, 246; dramatic technique 6–8, 34–54, 152–153, 168–172, 243, 247–249; "Dusk" 39; "Eros" 23; "The Family as Dramatic Theme in *King Lear* and *The Winter's Tale* 6; feminism 92, 119, 132–133; forgiveness 146, 237, 240–241; *Frankie and Johnny in the Clair de Lune* 2, 3, 12, 13, 14, 21, 22, 27, 32, 35, 39, 44, 49, 63, 92–102, 109, 110, 115, 116, 121, 132, 139, 154, 156, 161, 169, 171, 173, 177, 180, 182, 183, 192, 193, 197, 200, 215, 232, 234, 238, 243, 245, 247; *Full Frontal Nudity* 10, 14, 29, 40, 139, 173–183, 184, 185, 186, 188, 190, 192, 198, 200, 216, 228, 232, 233, 241, 246, 248; *The Full Monty* 2, 3, 9, 14, 16, 17, 26, 40, 45, 195, 238; *Golden Age* 1, 10, 25, 30, 41, 63, 134–135, 143, 164, 171, 173, 200, 208, 210, 231, 241, 245–246; "Hidden Agendas" 39, 40, 52, 173, 200; highlights of his theatrical career 2; homosexuality 19, 21–22, 33, 69–70, 103–107, 133–134, 141–142, 161, 163, 165; *It's Only a Play* 3, 5, 18, 37, 41, 46, 47, 51, 54, 86–91, 95, 106, 115, 154, 171, 182, 183, 200, 234; *The Kiss of the Spider Woman* (Manuel Puig) 2, 14; "Last Gasps" 22, 38, 39; *Lips Together, Teeth Apart* 5, 12, 15, 18, 19, 21, 22, 29, 30, 31, 32, 35–36, 39, 42, 47–48, 50, 57, 60, 66, 70, 97, 115, 139, 149, 160, 166, 167, 179, 180, 205, 207, 212–233, 234, 235, 236, 237, 238, 240, 244, 246, 247; *The Lisbon Traviata* 2, 7, 8, 11, 15, 18, 21, 22, 25, 27,

30, 33, 36, 37, 43, 44, 49–52, 64, 72, 79, 102–116, 133, 145, 156, 158, 173, 192, 197, 200, 204, 207, 209, 215, 217, 229, 232, 235, 239, 242, 247; *Love! Valour! Compassion!* 2, 5, 9–10, 12, 18, 19, 21, 26, 27, 30, 32, 33, 35, 37, 63, 70, 79, 92, 116, 155–172, 173, 184, 186, 195, 205, 207, 215, 218, 222, 232, 234, 235, 236, 237, 241, 243, 244, 246, 247, 248; *A Man of No Importance* 1, 3, 8, 13, 19, 21, 32, 36, 40, 62, 69, 72, 133, 137, 176, 195; *Master Class* 6, 8, 10, 14, 25, 29, 37, 46–48, 52, 53, 70, 86, 89, 108, 132, 133, 145, 160, 164, 167, 171, 173, 177, 192, 199–212, 238, 241, 248; music 24–27, 126, 231, 243–244; "Next" 22, 43, 46, 53, 60, 83, 171, 242; "Noon" 22–23, 38, 110, 204, 237; *A Perfect Ganesh* 1, 9, 10, 13, 14, 15, 21, 24, 29, 33, 35, 62, 72, 92, 97, 116–132, 133, 137, 139, 145, 147, 155, 168, 171, 172, 174, 181, 184, 185, 222, 223, 224, 232, 233, 236, 237, 239, 242, 243, 246; *Prelude and Liebestod* 23, 25, 38, 48, 175, 179, 191, 200, 215, 227, 240, 247; prose style 46–50, 59; psychology 6–7, 65–70, 75; *Ragtime* (E.L. Doctorow) 2, 8; religion 6, 30–32, 126–127, 155–156, 240–241, 246–247; *The Rink* 2, 3, 15, 17, 28, 30, 51–52, 54, 55, 58, 59, 92, 146, 169, 171, 185, 235, 239, 240, 246; *The Ritz* 2, 3, 6, 9, 18, 24, 34, 35, 40, 41, 47, 52, 79, 84–86, 103, 106, 132, 171, 227; *The Roller Coaster* 38, 53, 55, 60, 66, 70–75, 76, 83, 146, 185, 206, 228, 242, 246; sex 8–9, 12–14, 18–19, 28–29, 31–34, 166–167; "Shakespeare's Early Development as a Tragedian" 103, 219; social criticism 19–21, 55–57, 213, 231, 238–239; *Some Men* 2, 3, 7, 12, 14, 16, 18–19, 21, 26, 28, 35, 36, 44, 51, 52, 55, 63, 69, 74, 133, 138, 156, 162, 163, 207, 219, 243–245, 247; "Some Thoughts About Myself" 186; "Spiritual Movement in *King Lear*" 6, 225, 239; The Stendhal Syndrome 249; "Street Talk" 38, 173; "The Sunday Times" 2, 12; "Sweet Eros" 19, 26–27, 53; "Teachers" Break" 62–65, 141, 192; Texas background 3–4, 36, 69–71, 88, 187, 237–238; *This Side of the Door* 3, 6, 7, 30, 58, 60–63, 67–68, 73, 116, 139, 185, 228; "Tour" 22, 43, 59, 67, 116, 246; *Unusual Acts of Devotion* 2, 14, 49, 52, 58, 60, 63, 67, 244, 247; *Where Has Tommy Flowers Gone?* 21, 22, 38–39, 47, 58, 70, 79, 82; *Whiskey* 3, 22, 40, 46, 53–54, 76–84, 173, 200, 216, 242; "The Wibbly, Wobbly Wiggly Dance That Cleopatterer Did" 12, 19, 28–29, 35, 44–45, 157, 205, 207; *Witness* 19, 20, 21, 22, 26, 30, 42, 55, 57, 179, 216, 238, 242, 246; work ethic 5, 8–11, 40, 48, 163–164, 210–212, 235–238

Melville, Herman: *Moby-Dick* 67, 222
Meneghini, Battista 201, 209
Meyerbeer, Giacomo: *L'Africane* 214
Michael, George 37
Middleton, Thomas 191
Miller, Arthur: *All My Sons* 57; *The Crucible* 246
Minnelli, Liza 15, 235
Mishima, Yukio 71; *The Temple of the Golden Pavilion* 179
Molière 219; *Tartuffe* 90, 197
Monroe, Marilyn 70, 135
Monteverdi, Claudio 202
Montgomery, Benilde 123, 128, 219, 220, 221, 231
Mother Teresa 123
Mozart, Wolfgang Amadeus: *Così Fan Tutti* 39, 223, 232; *Idomeneo* 86; *The Magic Flute* 61, 86

Neuchterlein, James 136
Nietzsche, Friedrich 66, 75, 80, 179, 221; *Thus Spoke Zarathustra* 67
Noises Off (Michael Frayn) 246

Oates, Joyce Carol 97
Odets, Clifford: *Awake and Sing* 6, 52
Olivier, Laurence 70
Onassis, Aristotle 27, 209, 238
O'Neill, Eugene 149, 215; *Desire Under the Elms* 182; *Long Day's Journey Into Night* 6; *Mourning Becomes Elektra* 182; *Strange Interlude* 34, 50, 169
Orton, Joe 71
Osborne, John 235; *A Patriot for Me* 246

Pacino, Al 161
Pater, Walter: *The Renaissance* 242
Percy, Walker 168
Piaf, Edith 24, 183, 234
Picasso, Pablo 200
Pinter, Harold 7, 48, 84, 111, 214, 235; *The Birthday Party* 77; *The Caretaker* 91; *The Dumbwaiter* 114
Pirandello, Luigi 232; *It Is So If You Think So* 76; *Six Characters in Search of an Author* 183
Plato 241
Poe, Edgar Allan: "The Fall of the House of Usher" 25
Pope John XXIII 126
Porter, Cole: "Begin the Beguine" 131
Prizzi's Honor 97
Proulx, Annie: "Brokeback Mountain" 69; *Wyoming* 69
Puccini, Giacomo: *Turandot* 77
Pushkin, Alexander 249

Radcliffe, Ann 221

Index

Rattigan, Terence: *A Bequest to the Nation* 246
Raymond, Gerald 192
Reeves, Steve 182
Rice, Elmer: *Street Scene* 52
Rich, Frank 2, 87, 88, 89, 213, 221, 234
Richards, David 222
Riefenstahl: *The Triumph of the Will* 81
Rimbaud, Arthur 66
Robinson, Edwin Arlington: "Luke Havergall" 60
Ross, Diana 163
Rossini, Gioachino 211
Ruff, F.J. 245

Salinger, J.D. 242
Satie, Erik 38
Savran, David 8, 34, 67, 247
Scent of a Woman 161
Schopenhauer, Arthur 195
Schubert, Franz 229
Second City (Chicago) 183
Seldes, Marian 34
Seles, Monica 150
Shakespeare, William 3, 7, 42, 77–79, 103, 191, 195, 235, 246, 249; *Hamlet* 73, 94, 95, 111, 120, 122, 136, 167, 175, 182, 237; *Julius Caesar* 246; *King Henry V* 118, 122, 127, 184; *King Lear* 6, 12, 185, 187, 210, 211, 226, 240, 246; *King Richard III* 6; *Macbeth* 42, 202; *Measure for Measure* 90, 167; *The Merry Wives of Windsor* 95 *A Midsummer Night's Dream* 183; *Much Ado About Nothing* 167; *Othello* 42, 81, 101, 168, 188, 189, 190; *Romeo and Juliet* 72, 158; *The Tempest* 185, 193; *Titus Andronicus* 219; *Twelfth Night* 13
Shaw, George Bernard 53, 154
Shelley, Percy 241
Shepard, Matthew 137
Shepard, Sam: *True West* 114
Simon, John 115
Simon, Neil 2
Slumdog Millionaire 117
Sondheim, Stephen: "Send in the Clowns" 2, 89, 241
Sophocles 90; *Oedipus Rex* 27, 120, 136, 161, 182, 191, 193
Spencer, Charles 200
Spielberg, Steven: *Saving Private Ryan* 178
A Star Is Born 224
Stein, Howard 53, 66, 79
The Stendhal Syndrome 175, 233
Stevens, Wallace 176; "The Snowman" 238
Stompanato, Johnny 181–182, 248
"Stormy Weather" 241
Strindberg, August 77
Sutton, May 151

Tanner, Michael 108

Tea and Sympathy (Robert Anderson) 2
"There'll Be Some Changes Made" (Donaldson and Overstreet) 184
Tolstoy, Leo 155, 240, 241; *The Kreutzer Sonata* 33
Tom of Finland 69
Trilling, Lionel: *E.M. Forster* 31
Troy, Mary: *Beauties* 97
Turgenev, Ivan 83
Turner, Lana 178, 181, 248
Twain, Mark 234; *Huckleberry Finn* 242

Updike, John: *Couples* 223

Verdi, Giuseppe: *Macbetto* 108, 201; *Nabucco* 84; *Rigoletto* 206; *La Traviata* 105, 107, 111, 182

Wagner, Richard 221, 223, 231, 240; *Götterdammerung* 220; "Liebestod" 179; *Der Meistersinger* 115; *Parsifal* 161; The *Ring* cycle 81; *Tristan and Isolde* 175, 188, 220, 224; *Die Walküre* 81
Wallace, David Foster: *Infinite Jest* 149; "Octet #6" 44
Watt, Stephen 213–214
Weber, Max: *The Protestant Ethic and the Spirit of Capitalism* 5
Webern, Anton: *Engel* 162
Webster, John 191; *The White Devil* 182
Welles, Orson: *Citizen Kane* 81
Wertheim, L. John 150
West Side Story (Leonard Bernstein, Arthur Laurents, Jerome Robbins, Stephen Sondheim) 2
White, Patrick: *The Solid Mandala* 97; *The Vivisector* 66, 212
Whitman, Walt 31; *Song of Myself* 130, 140
Wilde, Oscar 5, 19; *Salomé* 8, 195
Williams, Tennessee 21, 42, 71; *In the Bar of a Tokyo Hotel* 183; *An Invisible Cat* 242; *A Streetcar Named Desire* 41, 53
Wilson, August: *Fences* 179
Wilson, Lanford 88
Witchel, Alex 249
Wolfe, Tom 52
Wood, Grant: "American Gothic" 131
Woolf, Virginia 176; *To the Lighthouse* 233
Wordsworth, William 26, 221; "Tintern Abbey" 194

Yeats, W.B.: "Among School Children" 17–18; "Byzantium" 119; "Leda and the Swan" 14, 235

Zeffirelli, Franco 207
Zinman, Toby Silverman 9, 11, 17, 40, 42, 49, 66, 200, 212
Zinoman, Jason 138

www.ingramcontent.com/pod-product-compliance
Lightning Source LLC
Chambersburg PA
CBHW051214300426
44116CB00006B/575